THE COMPLETE
ENCYCLOPEDIA OF
TERRARIUM

THE COMPLETE
ENCYCLOPEDIA OF
TERRARIUM

**Reptiles, amphibians,
spiders, and insects–clearly
surveyed per specie**

**Everything about nutrition, accomodation,
treatment, disease, and breeding**

EUGÈNE BRUINS

REBO
PUBLISHERS

© 1999 Rebo International b.v., Lisse, The Netherlands

Text and photographs: Eugène Bruins
Redaction and production: TextCase, Groningen
Cover design: Minkowsky Graphics, Enkhuizen
Layout: Signia, Winschoten

ISBN 90 366 1593 3

Contents

Foreword

Increasing numbers of people are discovering the fascination of a terrarium. It is possible to see things at home that are rarely seen in a zoo, such as eating, drinking, and shedding of the skin. There is also the tremendous challenge of successfully breeding the creatures kept in a terrarium. Zoos and seriously-minded enthusiasts extend the knowledge about the animals kept in terrariums and they increase the love of nature. In some cases the breeding and keeping of species can help to prevent them from becoming extinct.

Some would-be enthusiasts and animal dealers get involved with terrarium animals with little or no knowledge but this is strongly inadvisable because it is essential to understand all the factors bearing on the creatures and their environment before becoming involved and hence reliable information is a pre-requisite.

It is my wish to provide a readable book that all can understand which will put would-be enthusiasts on the right track but also provide fresh impetus for those already engaged in the hobby. Information such as this can not only give the terrarium owner greater pleasure but also reduce mortality, increase reproduction, and create less pressure for replacement animals.

A substantial portion of this book is devoted to arthropods because the many species of this phylum or group is neglected by most other books. Fewer reptiles and amphibians are dealt with but the ones that are get comprehensive coverage, including their breeding.

The methods outlined in this book are not the only ones for keeping and breeding these creatures but they have proven successful.

Finally I wish you much enjoyment with this book and your hobby.

Eugène Bruins

Introduction

How to use this book

This book starts with a number of general sections which everyone should read containing information of value across the subject range. The information about vitamins, minerals, and the law are essential reading.

The subsequent parts of the book that deal with the animals themselves are hierarchically structured so that if you wish to know what a green iguana eats, you should read not only the paragraph on this species but also the sections about iguanas, lizards, and reptiles because iguanas are lizards, which are reptiles. The information contained is written from a point of practical use in keeping a terrarium.

If the care of a particular tarantula for instance does not differ from the information contained in the general section about these creatures then the information is not repeated.

To keep the book accessible to all I have chosen to keep matters reasonably general. There are so many different species of arthropods, reptiles, and amphibians that for every generalized rule there will be exceptions. The methods described have proven successful but countless enthusiasts and professionals alike will have had similar results with other methods.

Difficult words are explained at the back of the book in a glossary. The dimensions given for terrariums follow the format length x breadth x height.

This book is not written for the purpose of recognising individual species of animal. Make sure you always get the correct scientific name and origin of animals when buying them. The physical descriptions of the creatures have been kept brief because almost every type of animal dealt with in this book is featured in photographs.

Where possible the use of proprietary names for lighting, vitamins, and mineral preparations has been avoided, with the reader being recommended to consult a specialist dealer or vet who will often be able to suggest a specific make from their own experience.

The book also tells you how to create your own terrarium but there are of course many products available that are useful (and a few of little or no value). It is worthwhile becoming acquainted with these before you buy.

Preparation

Reasonable preparation is required before acquiring an animal to be kept in a terrarium. Think about matters such as:
- Is the family happy about having such a creature?
- What do you want from the hobby? Bear in mind that most terrarium animals will become ill and/or stressed by constant handling. Handling is the main interest for children and for some adults. Many terrarium animals move little and

A dyeing poison dart frog (Dendrobates tinctorius).

Leopard gecko.

Left: Zonocera elegans.

Is everyone happy with the newcomer?

Animals bred in captivity can often be bought at shows.

can quickly become boring. This is not a hobby for just a few weeks. Many tarantulas, large lizards, and snakes can live for 15 years and tortoises much longer.

The hobby is best for those who are interested in a terrarium as a source of learning about the creatures and who wish to breed them but here too it is essential to be well informed before commencing. Certainly you should decide which type of creature you wish to buy before visiting a shop of dealer.
– Is the food easily obtained? Chirping crickets escape and mice can smell. Most lizards of 50 cm (approx. 20 in) such as the bearded dragon eat a great deal, consuming at least 20 adult crickets per week with the occasional mouse or baby rat.
– What does the terrarium hobby cost? The cost of acquiring the animals and the terrarium may be a one-off cost but the price of electricity and food continues to have to be met. More than the one terrarium may be needed. Cutting corners to save money on accommodation or food leads to problems.
– How much time is needed to keep a terrarium? Compared with keeping a dog, a terrarium is less demanding in terms of time but as interest deepens much more time may be required.
– How much space is needed? Small animals can grow to be quite large. It is necessary to separate the males and females of certain lizards and for breeding both space for an incubator and special breeding terrarium will be needed.

Information

Get as much information as possible: read books, association newsletters etc. but do not necessarily believe everything written down.
Seek out other enthusiasts (through a club or association) and visit them and listen to what they say of their experiences. Fortunately there are also some professional dealers who have a higher regard for the welfare of animals than mere profit. Much of the published material is in English but it

is useful to be able to convert both dimensions and temperatures.

1 inch = approx. 25 mm or 2.5 cm
1 foot = approx. 300 mm or 30 cm
1 yard = approx. 915 mm or 91.5 cm
1 US gallon = 3.8 litres
1 UK gallon = 4.5 litres
A 100 x 40 x 40 cm terrarium of 160 litres would equate to 40 UK gallons.

To convert Fahrenheit to Celsius the formula is $(t°F-32) \times 5/9$ in which t represents the value to be converted. For quick reference refer to the following table:

32°F	= 0°C	80°F	= 27°C
40°F	= 4°C	90°F	= 32°C
50°F	= 10°C	100°F	= 38°C
60°F	= 15°C	110°F	= 43°C
70°F	= 21°C	120°F	= 49°C

Acquisition

You need to be properly prepared in terms of knowledge and in possession of your terrarium before you acquire an animal for it.
Beginners should never buy an animal captured in the wild because these adapt less readily, remain

The insecticide strip in this shop terrarium is a sign that animals caught in the wild often carry parasites such as mites.

shy, and are more demanding in terms of both accommodation and diet. These animals also often carry many internal and external parasites and have been weakened by their capture, storage, and transport. The results of this may not be immediately apparent but it is difficult for a beginner to get such a specimen back into good condition.

Animals which have been commercially reared in the tropics may also suffer from parasites and be weakened through the stress of transportation.

Beginners should buy specimens of medium size that have been bred in captivity and avoid both expensive specimens and those which have costly appetites. Finally it is best to choose a species that is easy to breed. Examples of such are:

- Tarantulas — *Brachypelma albopilosa*
- Praying mantis — *Sphodromantis* species
- Stick and leaf instruments — *Extatosoma tiaratum*
- Scorpions — *Pandinus imperator*
- Salamanders — axolotl
- Frogs and toads — fire belly toad
- Lizards — leopard gecko
- Snakes — Corn snake *(Elaphe guttata)* or garter snake *(Thamnophis sirtalis)*
- Terrapins — red-eared slider terrapin
- Tortoises — Hermann's tortoise

Very young animals are inexpensive by have a greater risk of Dying. Semi-mature animals are more expensive but have greater chances of survival. Never buy specimens from a crowded or dirty terrarium or from one in which any of the animals appear sickly. Never ever buy an ill or neglected animal out of pity.

Be prepared to admit defeat

If you find that the hobby is costing more in terms of money and time than you can afford or that it really is not the hobby for you then be prepared to admit defeat and either reduce the number of animals to a level you can manage or give the hobby up altogether. Do not neglect or abuse the animals

A cross-bred male: Brachypelma smithi *x* B. emilia.

A 'missing black' corn snake: one of the commonest varieties of Elaphe guttata guttata.

for they did not choose a life with you. It is not a sin to admit failure and early recognition will ensure the animals can find a new home while they remain in good condition.

Breeding

If the animals in your terrarium thrive and you enjoy the hobby then it is likely that the animals will breed. Because of the stress it causes young offspring do not take your new arrivals repeatedly in small containers to shows in order to sell them. Once may be acceptable but it is far better to sell them from your home by means of advertising and far better to give them away to a good home than sell them to a suspect one. Give ample information about the animals care with them by means of copies of articles. Each section in this book contains advice on care for the different creatures. Read the information also on page 15 of this book.

Cross-breeding

Breeding of terrarium animals will become more essential as the laws governing import and export of endangered species are further tightened. Certain species are already at the stage where their survival rests entirely in the hands of breeding by enthusiasts and zoos. With species such as these, it is essential to prevent them from cross-breeding.

Cross-breeds do not contribute to the survival of a species and rarely, if ever, contribute to the knowledge about the relationships between species. The only thing achieved through cross-breeding is uncertainty. It is not always apparent whether a specimen is cross-bred or not.

Colour varieties

Mutations resulting from genetic variations and temperature changes during incubation can both give rise to colours other than the normal for a given species. Some terrarium owners are intrigued by these possibilities and actively seek to introduce new colour varieties. There is nothing against this in principle provided that the original colour of the wild species does not disappear and that the variations do not result in suffering for the animals thus reared.

Scientific names

Anyone becoming involved with a terrarium even at hobbyist level will be quickly confronted with Latin scientific names. These are widely used because:
- not every animal (or plant) has an English common name
- some species have a number or even many common names in English
- ieach species in principle has one scientific name (with a few synonyms)
- the scientific names are international, giving access to a wider range of information.

For these reasons the scientific names are widely used throughout this book. Where a standard common name is well accepted it is also used.

It is therefore important to have an understanding of the international system of taxonomy (or naming) of living things on our planet. The names of species, genera (singular is genus), families, and other groupings have a hierarchical relationship with each other.

There are general conventions for writing these scientific names which give clues. For example *Brachypelma smithi* is the scientific or Latin name of the Mexican red knee tarantula but this

Parasphendale affinis *is one of many praying mantids.*

A *young* Phelsuma madagascariensis.

common name is not universal. The scientific name is written in italic script, except when the general text is in italics, which gives a first clue.

This species, together with *Brachypelma albopilosa* and numerous other species all form part of the genus *Brachypelma*. The genus is written with an initial capital letter while the species has a lower case letter. Genera can be abbreviated (e.g. *B. smithi*) provided the name has already been used in full and there is no likely confusion. When the species is unknown the convention is to write *Brachypelma* sp. to represent 'a species' of that genus or spp. for more species of that genus.

Sometimes a third italic name is used, e.g. *Iguana iguana rhinolopha*. This additional name indicates a subspecies, which may be a geographical variant. Although it is not customary to abbreviate species names, it has been done in this book (e.g. *I. i. rhinoplasta*). Where the species has arisen through man's intervention, the third name is not written in italic script and usually appears between quotation marks, e.g. *Elaphe guttata* 'missing black'.

There is no great mystique behind scientific names which all have a meaning. For instance, the gecko *Phelsuma madagascariensis* originates in Madagascar and the lizard *Takydromus sexlineatus* has six *(sex)* stripes *(lineata)*. The stick insect *Parahyrtacus gorkomi* was discovered by the

Dutch stick insect specialist Van Gorkom. A clue to these attributions, such as gorkomi and smithi is given by the -i at the end of the species name. When the name itself ends in an -i or -e then the species name ends in -ii. These rules apply to male discoverers. Where the name is of a woman then the species attribution will end in -ae instead of -i. Where an additional name and year is given after the species name, this indicates the person who described the species and year in which it was done. When this is in brackets it indicates that the species was subsequently renamed within a different genus. The species name itself has remained the same, although the gender of its ending may have been modified between -a and -us.

The genus *Brachypelma* together with *Grammostola* forms part of the Grammostolinae subfamily which is written with a capital letter but in normal non italic letters. Subfamily names always end in -inae. This subfamily forms part of the family of tarantulas known as Theraphosidae, also written with a capital letter in normal type but ending in -idae.

Where no subfamily is required, the family is immediately divided into genera (the singular is genus) but where it is necessary to sub-divide a subfamily this is done by introducing a further name which is indicated by the ending -ini. The family Theraphosidae forms part of the suborder Mygalomorphae (tarantulas), which in turn are part of the order Araneae (spiders), which form a part of the class Arachnida (spider-like creatures). This class belongs to the sub-phylum or group Chelicerata (indicating the pincer like jaw appendages), and this group forms part of the phylum or group Arthropoda or arthropods (creatures with articulated legs).

Zoologist are constantly more precisely defining the relationships between different animals, resulting in changes from time to time in the taxonomy or naming of certain creatures. This can be tedious for the enthusiast who has got to know a species of tree python for years as *Chondropython viridis* to find that it is now correctly known as *Python*

Python viridis *is still better known as* Chondropython viridis.

There are also arthropods such as Brachypelma smithi *on the list of endangered species.*

viridis, having also been called *Morelia viridis* for a time. This can cause widespread confusion, especially as some incorrectly regard the older names as synonyms.

The law

The information outlined here is intended for those for whom a terrarium is a hobby rather than traders and importers, for whom different legal requirements apply. Professional traders can advise their customers on the current legal status of a particular species and about the law relating to dangerous species. Clubs, societies, and associations are also a good source of information. Your local authority will advise you if the animal(s) you intend to keep have any restrictions or special requirements, and whether you and they need to be licensed.

All member countries of the European Community have legislation to give force of law in their country to the CITES (International Convention on the Trade in Endangered Species) listed species, with European legislation incorporating the various lists and appendices of CITES into domestic legislation. Some species may not be held without specific authority, others require you to be able to prove that the animal was acquired from a legitimate source (captively bred) and not a wild captured illegal import. The domestic legislation in a number of European countries, including the United Kingdom, is stronger than the CITES convention norms. Information about CITES lists and appendices are available on the World Wide Web at www.wcmc.org.uk or from the Department of the Environment, Transport, and the Regions, Room 8/22, Tollgate House, Houlton Street, Bristol, BS2 9DJ.

The CITES related legislation not only deals with trade in live animals but in dead 'trophies'.

Appendix A (or 1) are the species most threatened with extinction. Trade in these species is forbidden. Wild captured specimens are rarely encountered as special authority is required and the animals may not be sold. The progeny of these animals, bred in captivity, is treated as though in Appendix B, where it can be proved that the animal results from breeding of animals already in captivity. This applies to the tortoises *Testudo hermanni, T. graeca, T. marginata* and all Lacertidae lizard species.

Appendix B (or 2) comprise animals whose future is not severely threatened provided the trade in them observes strict criteria. Species that are in themselves not threatened but closely resemble species which are also find their way also to this list. Appendix C (or 3) comprises species that are threatened only in certain countries so that all the participating countries co-operate to control trade in them. Import of these animals requires special notification to Customs.

Appendix D (or 4) are species not covered by CITES but which the EC wishes to control the import of. No CITES documentation is required for these animals but special notification is needed to customs.

The long and the short of it is that everyone needs to be able to prove that animals in Appendices, B, C, and D were legally acquired, or in other words that they were not illegally imported. This might be by having a copy of the Customs documentation or being able to prove that your were in possession of the animal before the legislation came into force. The other legal option requires you to be able to prove that the animal has been bred in captivity. It is therefore very important to both get and to give paperwork when buying, selling, or exchanging animals. The category for CITES protection is given by each species of animal dealt with in this book.

What you must do when buying protected animals

You must be convinced when buying an animal that one of the previously mentioned proofs will be available if any checks are made on you.

You are responsible for ensuring you get a copy of the CITES document from the trader if you buy an animal in categories B or C. If you buy from a private individual make sure you get a signed transfer document declaring the original CITES number. It is also necessary to get permission to transport the animal e.g. to be lent to another person for breeding purposes. Although captively bred animals are not directly covered you still need to give and receive transfer documents for any transactions to demonstrate the legal origins of the animal. Import of Appendix C animals requires the necessary Customs formalities. If you fail to keep proper paperwork and are unable to show the legitimate origins of a CITES covered animal you risk severe penalties.

Changes

It will be clear from the previous paragraphs that it is essential to keep proper records of terrarium animals. This applies to purchase, loans, swapping, sales, deaths, and births.

Although there is no legal requirement to send this information to the CITES organization in your country, doing so makes it much easier to prove the legitimacy of your animals.

Green iguanas in a shop. Ask to see the CITES documentation or number of it.

A professional shopkeeper can provide information about the necessary paperwork for this python.

In addition to the CITES legislation of the EC countries it must be remembered that many countries have their own local laws to protect wildlife. This means that an animal you see while abroad that is not protected by CITES may still be illegal to capture.

Other legislation

In addition to CITES there are differing laws to protect the natural environment which may mean that the escape of a non-native species, which can pose a threat to the ecology, may put you on the wrong side of the law. Certain types of animal are considered to be dangerous and are covered by separate legislation. In the United Kingdom some of these animals may only be kept under licence and then only when the local authority is satisfied that the animals will be kept under safe and secure conditions.

Dealing with animals

Handling

All terrarium animals should be handled as little as possible. Only a small number of them, such as green iguanas, bearded dragons, and Burmese pythons can be tamed but this requires regular handling from a young age. The best way to handle the animals is dealt with under the relevant group sections. Since reptiles and amphibians usually excrete when they are being handled it is essential to keep the cloaca or excretory cavity away from you. Nervous or other than gentle handling can cause aggression but try not to panic if this happens. Do not suddenly wrench your fingers away if you are bitten for this will make the bite more severe, and never drop the animal.

Wash your hands with soap after handling terrarium animals or any other pets to prevent salmo-

It is best to handle some animals from a young age, such as these newts.

Place large snakes and lizards in a linen bag. This is the grey ratsnake, Elaphe obsoleta spiloides.

nella infections although these are fairly rare. Children, elderly persons, and those with reduced resistance are the most at risk. Such infections cause vomiting, diarrhoea, fever, and stomach cramps.

Maintain a hygienic routine in all other matters too. Keep the terrarium and living areas as separate as possible and do not clean the terrarium in the kitchen. Do not work with the animals with open wounds on your hands or wear rubber gloves. Keep an eye on children in the proximity of the terrarium and if possible prevent them from touching the animals.

Packing for carrying

When an animal is changing owners it will need to be packed for transport. Each animal should be packed separately but see the individual rules for each group of animals. This separate packing should be in a stout, well-insulated box. It must not be possible for the animal to be crushed or squeezed nor to rattle around inside the box. The box should therefore be filled with old newspapers, foam plastic chips, or cotton wool but nothing heavy. Moisture absorbent paper is ideal for dealing with urine. Ensure there is adequate ventilation but avoid openings placed opposite each other which can cause a draught.

Transport

Temperatures must not fall below or exceed those appropriate for the animal during its transport to a new home. A foam box provides a fair degree of insulation but sometimes insufficient. A stationary car gets cold fairly rapidly during cold weather but heats up rapidly in the sun. Specimens can be kept warm with a bottle of hot water wrapped in a cloth or by means of a heat pack. Since heat packs can reach temperatures of 50°C (123°F) they must never come into contact with the animal. Check carefully to ensure this cannot happen. Animals can

A box turtle (Cuora genus) prepared for transport with a heat pack on a damp cloth in a 'cool box'.

also be kept warm by carrying them under clothing, next to the body. The least stress is caused to animals when they are transported in the dark.

Posting

Posting specimens is a risky business and not universally permitted. The Royal Mail in the United Kingdom bans the posting of most live specimens covered by this book and the exceptions are mainly restricted to agreed arrangements between recognized scientific institutions. Where posting is permitted, check if it is not possible for the animal to be transported by someone, before doing so. If this is not possible then use an Express service and avoid sending the package when it will be delayed by the week-end, public holidays, or during times such as Christmas. Ensure the recipient is expecting the package and never send specimens in small envelopes. Use plastic foam or wooden boxes or postal tubes. Take the package to the post office for posting.

Do not feed reptiles and amphibians for several days before they are to be sent. Most of them can survive for two weeks without food. Do not send any arthropods which are about to shed their skins. Plant food for creatures such as stick insects can be wrapped in moist kitchen roll and then protected by aluminium foil to form a moist ball that must be securely fastened.

Mark the outside of the package 'Fragile, No Commercial Value' and add also 'Entomological/herpetological material for science study'.

The terrarium room

If the terrarium hobby develops it may be necessary to set aside an entire room for the hobby. It is best to equip this well from the start and this requires careful planning. This can be done by drawing the terrariums to scale and then arranging them on a similar scale plan of the room. Make sure that each terrarium has a secure solid base

and do not attempt to economize in this matter. Make sure there are power points at a sufficiently high level and in the right positions. Avoid any hanging wires which could cause a fire or mains voltage shock. The installation must of course conform to regulations and if in doubt consult an electrician.

Time switches are invaluable for terrariums and sliding doors are more useful than lids since this permits terrariums to placed one on top of another. The location must be free from bustle and noise, not in the direct sun, or near the heating, nor in a draught. Maintain cleanliness, using either small rubbish bags or empty milk cartons but ensure they are disposed of regularly. Hang a calendar or place a notebook by the terrariums to maintain records for each animal. This is more important than many at first think. It is valuable in times of illness but also aids breeding and your own education. Try to incorporate a wash basin, incubator, breeding terrariums, and facilities for breeding food animals. Try to ensure there are no places where an escaped animal can hide away. Equip the room with adequate supplies of tissues, spare lamp bulbs, containers, dishes, thermometers, tweezers, a trap, torch, multi-vitamins, minerals, and a five litre pressure sprayer with a spray lance. If required, purchase a snake-handling crook, and magnifying glass (for deter-

Part of the author's own terrarium room.

mining sex), or a microscope (for assessing diseases).

A terrarium medicine cabinet can include treatment for worms, flagellates, and amoeba, plus iodine, disinfectant, bandages, tweezers, and cotton buds.

Rats and mice bred for feeding the terrarium animals should ideally be reared in a separate area such as the garden shed. If not they will need to be cleaned thoroughly at frequent intervals. If the temperature in the room where your terrarium is located is 23-25°C (73-77°F) then most arthropods will not need any additional heating. This temperature is too high though for many amphibians.

CARING FOR ANIMALS

The care of the different animals is mainly dealt with in the sections about their housing, feeding, and by the descriptions of the species. Keep the entire terrarium as clean as possible, including the lamps, and filters if these are required. Everything will need thorough rinsing with water after using any cleaning substances.

During holidays arrange for a good friend, preferably a fellow terrarium keeper, to maintain the terrarium. Change as little as possible before the holiday or carry them out early enough to see any

A large pressure sprayer is invaluable.

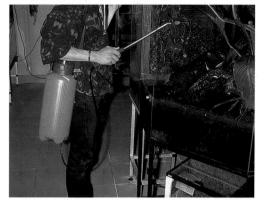

reactions. Make the bottom of each terrarium slightly moister than usual. Write clear instructions and guidance and leave everything needed where it can be found, including spare lamps. Let the person know where additional food can be acquired and give them an address of an experienced terrarium keeper to whom they can turn to for help. Make sure this person is aware of the arrangement.

This power point was under a leaking terrarium. Ensure safety in the terrarium room.

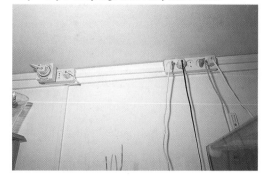

Fix power points up high where they can be seen.

A marsh or swamp terrarium.

Accommodation

Cold-blooded animals

Warm-blooded animals (mammals and birds) can separate oxygen-saturated blood from blood which is depleted of oxygen by means of their four chamber hearts. The metabolism occurs rapidly, producing a great deal of warmth. Cold-blooded animals in contrast have more primitive hearts in which the oxygen-saturated and depleted blood mix together. Most reptiles have a three chamber heart and are unable to heat or cool themselves so that they are dependent on the ambient temperature.

This makes them dependent upon external sources of heat and on their behaviour to enable them to achieve their preferred body temperature, which is 25-35°C (77-95F°) for most reptiles. The ideal body temperature at which the metabolism functions most effectively varies from species to species, and is also dependent on age, the time of day, and the season. Cold-blooded animals warm themselves by means of:

– heat currents in the air and water (e.g. lamps and heaters);

A pressed-glass reflector spot lamp provides the necessary warmth for these lizards.

There are many micro-climates in a natural environment, e.g. a bank, the tree tops, or forest floor.

– direct body contact with a warm surface (e.g. floor heating);
– radiated heat which can produce a higher temperature than the air temperature, which is often required by an animal. This is achieved in nature by sunning themselves and can be replicated by spot lamps in a terrarium.

Temperatures above 47°C (117°F) can be fatal for many reptiles because they have no sweat glands. They therefore need to find cooler temperatures in the form of shade, a burrow, or water, or assume a lighter colour to reflect more heat.

Bear in mind the cold-blooded nature of these animals. A lizard that jumps into icy cold water will become cold, inactive, and drown. A red-eared slider terrapin will eat when the temperature is 20°C (68°F) but is virtually unable to digest its food.

BIOTOPE

A biotope is an environmental area within which a certain animal can best sustain life. For a specific poisonous frog this is just one plant of the Bromeliacae family in which is makes its home. Meanwhile the bearded dragon lizard requires several hectares of semi-desert.

Reptiles, amphibians, and arthropods are often

Chameleo dilepsis in Chad. This animal can choose between 20% humidity in the sun or 70% within the foliage of trees.

precisely adapted to their biotope so that if certain requirements of this environment are missing in a terrarium problems will occur. They will pine away or suffer stress, leading to reduced resistance to parasites. Try to mimic the biotope as closely as possible. This starts with the building or purchase of a terrarium. Be aware of the creation of possible micro-climates in a terrarium. A chameleon finds the relatively high humidity it requires in semi-arid regions between the leaves of clusters of trees.

With an animal that has a widespread distribution across a varied biotope, it can be a matter of guess-work to determine the right conditions for such specimens. It is possible via the World Wide Web to check on the climate of many different parts of the world. Although computerisation of the terrarium hobby is slow to develop, the future offers computer controlled climate control for terrariums which will mimic the conditions in the country of origin.

POSITIONING OF TERRARIUMS

Do not site terrariums in the direct sun, nor in draughts, or anywhere where there is a busy passing flow of people with lots of noise or near a doorway. The terrarium should ideally be close to a power point and based on a levelled platform or plinth of plywood or flooring. Fix the terrarium always at least 10mm (³/₈in) away from the wall to prevent fungus forming.

Creating a terrarium

There are many possible types and size of terrarium available to buy but it is also possible to build your own. The majority are constructed of glass. This does not easily scratch but is heavy. A square metre of glass weighs 2.5 kg (5 lb 8 oz) per millimetre of thickness.

GLASS

Those who want to cut glass themselves will either need to use new glass or thoroughly clean old glass. Old paint and putty can be scraped off with a craft knife blade. Other dirt and grease can

Cutting glass.

Breaking glass along the cut line.

Applying the adhesive.

be removed with a cloth or fine steel wool soaked in turpentine.

The bottom sheet of glass always fits within the sides which must never be mounted on top of the bottom plate. Position the front pane against the side panels. Make allowance for an adhesive layer of about 1mm thickness. Use 6mm thickness glass for terrariums of 50-100cm (20-40in) wide or tall and 8mm (⁵/₁₆in) glass for constructions of 150-200cm (59-79in). Thicker glass is required for an aquarium. If in doubt use thicker rather than thinner glass.

Place the clean, degreased sheet of glass on a clean and flat table with the edge of the glass at the edge of the table so that the glass cutter will not mark the table. Measure carefully where the cut has to be, making allowances for the thickness of the glass cutter itself (usually 2.5mm). Dip the glass cutter briefly in turpentine and place it upright on the glass. Apply a constant firm pressure as the glass cutter is drawn towards you alongside a straight edge. A thin, almost invisible cut results from the glass cutter. Place the cut line precisely along the edge of the table and break the pane along the mark. If a thin strip will be left after cutting, place this on the table and hold the piece of glass to be used over the edge of the table to break along the cut. Alternatively the strip can be removed using the 'teeth' of the cutter or with pliers but this does not result in a clean cut. Grind all sides with waterproof wet and dry paper or with a lava. Glass can be glued using a transparent silicon adhesive/sealant based on a vinegar solvent but this has a limited shelf life and must not be used after that date. Black silicon adhesive/sealant is only suitable for small terrariums. Ample ventilation is required when applying these adhesives.

Degrease all the surfaces to be glued with thinners then stick masking tape parallel with the edge to be glued, leaving the required space for the glue. Cut the tip of the silicon adhesive applicator at an angle and apply the silicon adhesive. Glue one pane at a time, finishing with the front pane. A helper is needed to hold the two side panels in position while the rear panel is glued and fixed in position. Hold the panes in place with adhesive tape while the glue sets. The inside joints can be given a second coating of silicon if required.

Smooth the silicon joints with water to which washing-up liquid has been added and remove the masking tape immediately. Further work on the terrarium can begin in 24 hours after the sealant has set. The silicon adhesive can also be used to fix ventilation grills and u-shape channels for sliding panels. Wait a few days before adding water to the terrarium.

Do not expect your first four or five terrariums to be works of art but you should improve with expe-rience. It is possible to make pentagonal, hexago-nal, and even octagonal terrariums. Old aquaria can also be converted for use as a terrarium.

OTHER MATERIALS

Small terrariums are sometimes made of PVC and can be self-made using PVC sheet and the appro-priate adhesive but the material scratches very easily. Desert terrariums in particular can be con-structed of wood which is easy to work with and relatively cheap. The bottom and sides can be made of 15-20mm marine ply which should be coated with yacht varnish, polyurethane lacquer, or a polyester-based paint to make it virtually wa-terproof. The varnish needs to air for six weeks be-fore the terrarium can be used.

Wood can be used in conjunction with glass, transparent PVC, and/or mesh, and the same is true of aluminium. Aluminium is easy to work with and profiles can be bought with glazing strips and also provision for ventilators. Aluminium does not rust and is ideal for creating racking for holding terrariums.

SIZE

Establish the size a terrarium needs to be before building it or placing it in position. Bear in mind

Fix the deepest double channel profile at the top.

The top of a water's edge terrarium with lids. The hand of the person who cares for them can seem like a bird of prey to the occupants and cause them stress.

the size of the full-grown animals and their type of behaviour. The new owner of a red-eared slider or young green iguana often has no idea where to begin. On the other hand do not put young animals in a terrarium that is so large they cannot find their food.

Ground-living and burrowing animals need a large ground surface while tree dwellers need a tall terrarium. Lively animals need more space than those that are by nature more docile. The sizes suggested in this book are always given as length x breadth x height.

ACCESS

Think about the means of access before constructing a terrarium. With lids, the hand lifting them off can seem to the occupants like a bird of prey: an enemy for many animals. A lid is an essential safety measure though with scorpions.
If the front panel is slid vertically between two plastic U-form channels it will naturally close itself by dropping and reduce the chances of escape. A terrarium lock can be fixed to secure two horizontally sliding panels in runners of twin U-form channels. The deepest channel is mounted at the top so that the glass can be lifted up into the channel in order to drop them into position. Measure the sizes of the sliding panels after the runners have been glued in place. Snakes in particular can easily escape through sliding doors that are not tightly closed.
Vertical hinges for self-closing doors can be made with silicon adhesive reinforced with glass fibres. Piano hinges are also used for wooden terrariums.

VENTILATION

Every terrarium needs ventilation to freshen the air and prevent a build up of carbon dioxide. Good ventilation also prevents condensation and fungal growth. Parts of glass walls need to be replaced by metal grilles, diamond mesh, or very fine mesh of the type used to filter petrol.
The ventilation will be greater if an aluminium reflector with a spot lamp is attached to the grille.

Terrarium with cork bark.

An old computer fan with transformer.

The spot lamp fastened behind a reflector to the metal grille helps to ensure good ventilation.

The hot air from the lamp rises and exits via the grille, drawing fresh air into the terrarium. This ventilation can be observed by blowing a spoonful of chalk into the terrarium. With a 40 Watt spot lamp, the air at the bottom of a 40 cm (16in) high terrarium exits within 5 seconds. Small fans can also be used. Silent running 12 or 24 volt computer fans powered via a transformer are very effective. They are available from as small as 28 x 28 x 8mm. The problem of salt residues on the glass panels can be solved by using distilled or demineralized water provided the occupants can cope with this.
Moist terrariums in particular are ventilated by means of grilles at the top and also at the bottom of the front panel. This allows good ventilation provided no animals are directly exposed to the draught which can cause pneumonia.
Wires and tubes for equipment and filters can be accommodated by cutting a small gap for them in the corner of the top or a side panel. The gap must be filled afterwards with silicon.

Types of terrariums

In general terms it is best to keep just one type of animal in one terrarium and to prevent competition for food, sun basking spots, shelter, egg-laying places, and females. In the cases where animals can be combined this book indicates it by the species descriptions.

Terrariums are so-called because they are containers with 'terra' or earth but there are various forms of them. Specific terrariums for snakes or arthropods are discussed in the sections about these animals. The specialist terrariu ms providing a natural habitat for the occupants such as those seen housing reptiles in zoos are also known as vivaria (singular is vivarium).

QUARANTINE

Quarantine terrariums are intended for animals that are sick or infested with parasites or where this possibility exists. This includes newcomers of which the state of health is unknown. Since many shops do not have quarantine terrariums, terrarium keepers need to keep and observe newcomers in quarantine for four to six weeks. Note the specimen's behaviour, its appearance, and always carefully check its faeces. It is not uncommon for an animal that appears healthy to seriously infect others when added to them. Had the faeces of the animal been checked it would have revealed that it carried an infection for which it had developed a resistance. Maintain a strict hygiene regime to prevent any possibility of cross-infection from one terrarium to others.

Quarantine terrariums should be simply equipped to make them easy to clean. Provide a simple rear wall, basic hiding place, and easily removed terrarium bottom. Allow the new arrivals several days rest before treating them for parasites, whether or not these are apparent.

AQUARIUM

An aquarium is of course a container with water and hence suitable for amphibians. To prevent escapes the top should be protected with either a 5cm (2in) wide strip of glass overhanging the rim or a mesh lid made by fixing mesh between strips of glass or aluminium.

A rear wall, side walls, and hiding place in an aquarium give the animals the chance to rest and helps reduce the risk of stress.

A sick pearl lizard in a quarantine terrarium.

Set plants in a layer of 2-3mm gravel that is at least 4cm (1½in) thick. Provide adequate lighting for the plants, e.g. with light from fluorescent lamps of 2 Watt per 10cm² (1.55 sq in) for aquaria 40cm (16in) deep. Filter the water properly (see p26) and regularly refresh one third of it. Stir the bottom with a finger during siphoning off of the water.

Suitable aquarium heating (½ Watt per litre) must not be switched on when out of the water. Do not add animals to the aquarium until two weeks after the filling, planting, and equipping has been completed.

WATER TERRARIUMS

These are containers, which some call aqua-terrariums, with both water and land areas. There are numerous types and in between variants but the most important are the paludarium and riparium (Latin for specimen containers with respectively swamp and bank environments).

The swamp or marsh terrarium consists of a shallow water area and many plants. If the rear and side walls are kept humid with a spray pump all manner of mosses and ferns will grow. Species of the Bromeliacae family and orchids are also widely used. The top needs to be filled with tubular or point source fluorescent lamps so that ample ventilation is necessary.

Constant water level can be maintained by a sup-

Paludarium or swamp terrarium.

ply tank which acts as a biological filter without the need for a mechanical filter. If water that is low in salts such as reverse osmosis water is used then no chalk deposits will occur on the glass.

The soil or land area must not decompose and should consist of fern roots, peat, or orchid compost. The humidity will be kept high by regular spraying, a waterfall, or misting equipment. A small fan is often used for ventilation.

Poison dart frogs make ideal inhabitants for a swamp terrarium. Bear in mind that many amphibians can quickly find temperatures too warm for them.

Small lizards such as *Anolis* or *Phelsuma* species and some snakes *(Thamnophis* and *Opheodrys)* are often placed in swamp terrariums where they pine away. These specimens have an absolute need of a warm, dry place under the heat of the lamps.

A riparium or bank terrarium seeks to mimic the environment of the water's edge. The water area is larger than in the swamp terrarium so that there is room for fish to swim. The banks should be so constructed that the amphibians and land animals can crawl out of the water. Make smooth banks less slippery by scattering sand on yacht varnish before it dries or by sticking pebbles with silicon adhesive.

A waterfall in a bank terrarium.

A tropical rain forest terrarium of 225 x 200 x 250cm (88¹/₂ x 78³/₄ x 98¹/₂in) with fan heater, pressed-glass reflector lamps and a 120cm (47¹/₂in) long aquarium area and waterfall. It is inhabited by species of Basiliscus, water geckos, and giant toads.

Treat large areas of water as aquaria. The plants are usually larger and more robust than in a swamp terrarium.

An automatic sprinkler can be incorporated to create rain that stimulates certain species of tree-dwelling frogs to reproduce. Water is pumped to perforated tubes so that it falls back to the surface. Excess water can be removed by means of a drainage system. Many water-loving amphibians and reptiles are suitable for a bank terrarium.

TROPICAL RAIN FOREST TERRARIUM

The water area in this type of terrarium is relatively small. Cover the base with woodland soil, peat, or orchid compost and then furnish with many of the desired plants, tree trunks and branches. Provide ample lighting for the plants with tubular fluorescent lamps for instance.

The temperature of the tropical rain forest is fairly constant with a minimum of 23-26°C (73.4-78.8°F) and maximum of 27-30°C (80.6-86°F) by day and about 5°C lower (71.6-86°F) at night. The animals derive about three-quarters of their warmth from air convection and directly from contact with their surroundings and only a quarter from radiation. To imitate this there should be a few spot lamps (animals can always find the sunny places) and gentle bottom or water heating. Take care not to overheat. Lighting should be on for 12 hours and the humidity held as high as 80 to 100 per cent.

DESERT TERRARIUM

This type of terrarium is equipped with a thick layer of sand or sandy soil. Create hollows and climbing opportunities with stones and chunks of natural timber. The hollows provide hiding places from 'enemies,' a place to escape from the heat, and somewhere to lay eggs. The air temperature by day is a minimum 30°C (86°F) and averages 40-45°C°(104-113°F). In the beams of the heat radiators (reflector and pressed-glass spot lamps) the temperature reaches 45-55°C(113-131°F). Further heating is unnecessary since desert creatures are adapted to extremes of temperature. Provide as least one heat lamp per animal. Since such a terrarium requires ample ventilation it can often be difficult to maintain the temperature. In a desert it is often very cold at night to around freezing but cooling is not required since in the burrows of desert creatures (which can often be metres deep) it remains 15-25°C (59-77°F). Imitate this with bottom heating. Switch all the other heat sources off at night so that heat rises from the soil, which is beneficial for nocturnal animals or those that become active at dusk.

Plenty of light is beneficial for the health, activity, and breeding readiness of many reptiles. Use ultraviolet lamps in addition to other sources if possible. These conditions can also be created in open terrariums and containers with acrylic sheet roofs. Prevent creating a chill or overheating with the aid of thermostats, fan heaters and fans.

Imitate the dew by spraying every evening or morning. Sometimes this water is drunk and helps with the shedding of skin. Vitamins and minerals can be dissolved in the spray water. A desert terrarium must never be allowed to remain moist for any time and water should evaporate completely within a couple of hours. Always provide a low container with clean water.

Desert terrarium with slate rear wall.

Desert and steppe terrariums also need a supply of water.

This 200 x 250cm (78³/₄ x 98¹/₂in) steppe terrarium includes three hollows and a 100cm (39¹/₂in) terrarium.

STEPPE TERRARIUM

The level plains of the steppe landscape provide a transition from desert to grassy savannah. A steppe terrarium is fitted out rather like a desert terrarium but with more wood or stone and sometimes with larger plants. Provide a lower day-time temperature of 35-45C° (95-113°F). The night-time temperature is 15-20°C° (59-68°F). A savannah terrarium can be similarly created, except that savannahs have dry and rainy seasons.

Animals from the Mediterranean region are often housed in steppe terrariums with hot, dry summers and cool moist winters during which many hibernate.

MIXED TERRARIUM

A number of different animals are housed in mixed terrariums. This frequently leads to disaster because competition and stress are aroused. Fellow inhabitants must not be too much of a disturbance and must not be enemies or regarded as such. A small lizard cannot differentiate between an insectivorous snake and one that is genuinely dangerous for it so that is becomes highly stressed. It is always best not to combine animals.

ROOM TERRARIUM

Some enthusiasts of chameleons, green iguanas, large day geckos, or monitor lizards fit out an entire room for their animals. Allowing such animals the free run of a room for long periods of time is irresponsible. The animals often are too cold, get too little to eat, and run greater risk of accidents (getting trapped, caught by a cat, falling downstairs, or being caught under an opening door). Tokays and chikchaks are often used to catch and eat escape food animals in the terrarium area but they will need additional food.

A room terrarium needs to have a separate door and partition so that no animals are harmed when the room door is opened. This should be high enough to prevent the animals getting over it. Consider a wall for tortoises or a shower cubicle door for animals that can climb.

Treat the walls with a waterproof exterior wall paint to make them waterproof and insulate cellar and shed walls. Make sure there is adequate ventilation and in summer replace a south-facing window with strong zinc mesh. Ensure ample radiated warmth (see lighting) and if required add heat with fan heaters, central heating, or under-floor heating.

Create sufficient warm spots, hiding places, climbing opportunities, and feeding and drinking facilities. Crickets can be offered in a smooth-sided container from which they cannot escape but if there is a risk of reptiles falling in and not being able to get out then hang a branch part way into the container as an escape route. Crickets will in any case eventually escape.

OUTDOOR TERRARIUM

Tortoises and lizards can be kept in an outdoor terrarium when the temperature permits. Since these are mainly constructed from mesh or transparent plastic sheet the necessary UVA and UVB radiation is provided. Such an outdoor terrarium needs to prevent its occupants from escaping and other animals such as mice, harmful birds, and cats from getting in. Cover the entire terrarium

If animals are left free to roam in a room something is bound to go wrong.

European tortoises are ideal for outdoor terrariums.

with mesh to keep birds and cats at bay. An electric fence (2,900 Volt, 3 Watt) will also keep cats away. Provide a concrete floor to prevent rats, mice, and moles from getting in and make sure that overhanging branches do not provide an escape route for lizards or other occupants.

Ventilate the outdoor terrarium well to prevent overheating. Position the terrarium so that for as long as possible (but at least half the day) sun shines on part of the terrarium. Prevent flooding by providing drainage or by creating the terrarium partially on a slope. Make sure the animals are not in a draught and that they can always find their preferred temperature with for instance pressed glass spot lamps and a covered area. Arrange matters so there is always some shade and position exits from hiding places facing south-east so that the morning sun will warm the animals. Take care that the animals cannot hurt their mouths against the mesh.

Good sub-tropical plants for an outdoor terrarium include yuccas, evergreen oak, species of the genus *Opuntia,* banana *(Musa basjoo* or *M. japonica),* bamboo, cypress, fig, and the hemp palm *(Trachycarpus fortunei).* Protect these plants from persistent frost. All manner of herbs are good ground cover and often excellent food. The animals must all have a frost-free winter quarters. Many European lizards can survive winter in barrels set into the ground that are filled with stones and sandy soil. Terrapins and other freshwater turtles need a pond that is deep enough, while tortoises require a warmed hiding place filled with straw (see p261). Make sure that tropical and sub-tropical animals are brought inside in plenty of time. There are also portable outdoor terrariums that can be put out of doors on sunny days.

CONSERVATORY OR GREENHOUSE

Much the same rules as with a room terrarium apply to the equipping of a conservatory or green-

Always place a portable outdoor terrarium partially in shade.

house for use as a terrarium. Use double or triple-glazed acrylic panels and if necessary add insulation in the form of bubble plastic, additional heating controlled by a thermostat (to prevent temperatures dropping too low), ventilation (to prevent overheating) by means, for instance, thermostatically operated roof vents that are protected by a mesh guard beneath. It is sensible to provide a misting system operated by time switch, to have a concrete floor (to prevent rodents). A sliding patio door can be used as an entrance.

Equipping a terrarium

The following matters are of practical importance in the equipping of a terrarium.

HYGIENE

The materials used should all be easy to keep clean and not likely to rot quickly, become affected by mould, or fall apart in a moist terrarium. They must also be neither toxic or sharp-edged.
Keep the terrarium clean: moulds and bacteria in the excreta of prey can be readily transmitted. Only use peroxide or alcohol-based disinfectants and never any containing phenol. Rinse thoroughly with warm water after using disinfectant. The use of ionising air filters in terrariums is becoming more widespread.

Maintain hygiene by removing droppings regularly.

WATER

Every animal should have access to fresh water. Here too hygiene is important since many infections (bacterial and amoebic) can be spread via water containers. Replace water as often as possible and certainly whenever soiled with excreta or fouled with other material. Clean the container with a scourer and cleaning agent, and rinse thoroughly before drying to put in use again. A water tray or trough with a slimy surface contains some eight million bacteria for every litre of water. By comparison, drinking water is only permitted one bacterium per litre. The water tray or trough must be heavy enough not to be tipped over, when it would soak the terrarium. Do not place the water tray in direct routes used by the animals or it will quickly become dirty. Always give a shallow dish of water to animals, specially after they have laid eggs, and spray them regularly with water. For reptiles, use water that is just warm to the touch (20-25°C/68-77°F) because they will become sluggish and drown if they bath in cold water. Many amphibians though prefer really cold water.
If necessary, place a stone in the water tray so that any prey that fall in can get out.
Larger scale areas of water will need to be filtered and can be regularly refreshed by means of a siphon. Water in an aquarium can also be siphoned by sucking it into a tube. Water will continue running out into a bucket at a lower level until the water drops below the level of the tube in the aquarium. One third to a half of the water in an aquarium should be replaced each week.
A filter not only cleans the water but also causes a current, and oxygenates the water. There is a wide assortment of filters and pumps to choose from but a good aquarium specialist shop should be able to give advice. The capacity in litres per hour and height the pump can lift water should not be too low.
Certain bacteria break faeces down into nitrates (biological filtering). These bacteria need to feed on faeces, have somewhere to remain (in the filter)

Many animals will excrete in their water tray. Replace the water at least every day.

and sufficient oxygen. To achieve this final requirement the water needs to pass the filter at least twice per hour.

Good internal filters are available for aquaria up to 250 litres. Thoroughly wash the foam inserts every two weeks to remove the waste remains (mechanical filtering).

There are also air-powered filters to buy or make yourself (see photograph) for up to maximum of 50 litres.

From 100 litres upwards external filters are often used. These should be cleaned every four to six weeks. A biological filter is very suitable for use with heavy demands. A pump in the filter raises water to cascade as a waterfall down the back wall of the terrarium. From there it flows through an overflow back to the filter. The water passes through a large surface area of the filter medium filled with bacteria and then back to the pump. An additional overflow ensures that the terrarium will not become overfilled should the first overflow become blocked. It is also possible to use pumps with float valves.

All manner of fish, such as cichlids, guppies, and algae eaters break down waste matter. With terrapins these need to be able to swim fast. A rain

A simple internal filter can be made with an air lift. An air pump blows air to the bottom of a thick tube held in place at the bottom of a jam jar filled with cotton wool.

A biological filter: a pump raises water to a cascade and/or the other side of the filter (ideal for replenishing water).

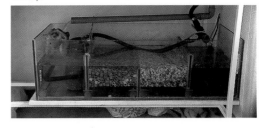

Fish break up excreta and eat food remnants. These are guppies and an Ancistris *species algae eater.*

installation can be created with a pump and spray heads (or holes formed in a network of PVC pipes). Yellow plastic electrical conduit though is not suitable because it gives off toxic substances. With very wet terrariums a drain is needed back to the pump in order to mimic long-term rain. With desert and steppe terrariums the water must be able to evaporate within a few hours.

TEMPERATURE

In nature the temperature does not remain constant. Imitate natural fluctuations in temperature between night and day and the seasons so far as possible. The desirable temperatures are given for the different types of terrarium and the species descriptions. Many animals can withstand cold for a short time but draughts can cause pneumonia.

Temperature can be controlled by means of thermostats. If tungsten filament lamps are used then proportional dimmers can be used which do not just switch on and off but which cause the lamps to gradually burn less brightly. Time clocks can set a lower night-time temperature.

Whichever type of heating you install make sure you check the temperatures for the first few days in the places where the animals will rest before acquiring them. Use a digital thermometer which records maximum and minimum temperatures. Measure in a number of places to work out what temperature choices an animal will have and what the differences are in temperatures between locations.

The activity of terrarium animals is often dependent on the day-night rhythm. Some types start to hibernate or rest up as day length shortens, regardless of the temperature. Animals bred in captivity are less dependent on natural biorhythms. The colour of many reptiles can only be fully appreciated with sufficient light. Lighting enables plants to grow and also provides animals with a source of radiant heat.

Try to mimic the length of day in the land of origin of the specimen as closely as possible. Switch off all white and yellow lamps at night to prevent stress. Animals from close to the equator are accustomed to consistent day length of 12 hours. The length of day in Northern Europe around 50 degrees North varies from about 16 hours in summer to about 8½ hours in winter.

Ensure safety at all times: make sure that hot lamps and electrical components cannot touch the animals or glass.

Tungsten filament lamps produce a lot of heat and relatively little light (35 Lux at 40 Watt). This compares to light in the full sun of the tropics of 100,000 Lux. The floor of a rain forest receives 200 to 500 Lux. The light spectrum of these lamps is also not close to that of daylight and the heat is widely diffused so that nowhere is heated to 35°C (95°F).

Reflector lamps (spot lamps) direct all their warmth and light to one place so that a temperature gradient is created. In a terrarium of at least 40cm (16in) high use 40 Watt reflector lamps. These create temperatures up to 45°C (113°F) at 35cm (13³/₄in) below the lamp. Lamps of 60 Watt can often cause burns at a distance of less than 50cm (19³/₄in).

Pressed-glass spot lamps have the same effect as ordinary reflector lamps but more pronounced, making them suitable for larger terrariums. An 80 Watt lamp produces temperatures of 45 to 50°C (113-122°F) at a distance of 50cm (19³/₄in). Use porcelain fittings with these lamps because normal lamp-holders become brittle, perish, and can even burn.

Ceramic heat lamps do not radiate any light, only heat. Because of this unnatural property they can be dangerous if used wrongly because many animals can become overheated as they do not retreat from the invisible heat rays. They can be used in large terrariums for additional heating and should be used with ceramic fittings.

Tubular fluorescent lamps (and new-type low energy compact fluorescent lamps) produce more light than heat. They are therefore ideal of swamp terrariums in which lots of plants grow and where the temperature should not be too high. Specialist shops and other terrarium experts will be able to advise on the correct daylight light colour to produce ample light for plant growth. Use splash-proof lamp fittings.

The heat generated by the lamp ballast necessary for these lamps can be used as part of the heating for a terrarium. Do not fix the ballast gear directly to wood (fire risk) but fix to metal such as aluminium. Fluorescent lamps flicker in time with the cycles of alternating current (50 or 60 times per second). This is not apparent to humans but many animals are aware of this, so use high-frequency gear which not only has a higher frequency flicker that does not trouble animals and also prevents flickering when switched on.

ULTRA-VIOLET LIGHT

The previous lamps with the exception of some fluorescent lamps produce no ultra-violet light but this is an essential for the development of the important vitamin D3 (from pro-vitamin D). This light is invisible to humans. Ultra-violet light is divided into UV-A (wavelength of 315-400 nanometers), UV-B (280-315nm), and UV-C (100-280nm). The wavelength of ultra-violet lamps is usually denoted on the packing.

UV-A acts upon the skin and helps to maintain an attractive colour. UV-B is used to create vitamin D₃ from pro-vitamin D and thereby helps to prevent rachitis (better known as rickets). Too much

A standard terrarium with half panel ventilation mesh, lamp, and reflector.

of any wavelength of ultra-violet light is harmful but particularly of UV-C which causes skin cancer and eye problems. Natural UV-C is largely absorbed in the ozone layer and is also used to purify water for aquaria. Read the instructions with each type of lamp carefully.

The extent to which ultra-violet lamps need to be used is dependent on the type of animal (sun-worshipper or not), its origins (the open plain or floor of the rain forest), pigmentation, and diet.

The useable spectrum of ultra-violet light does not penetrate ordinary glass so that UV lamps have special 'glass' that allows some of the light through. Ultra-violet will also pass through transparent plastic sheet but will in the course of time degenerate the plastic.

There is much disagreement about the use of ultra-violet light. Scientists have shown that vitamin D_3 is not absorbed through the stomach yet terrarium keepers have shown that if the vitamin is present in sufficient quantity in food that ultra-violet light is unnecessary. It is always beneficial though to responsibly use ultra-violet light. Many reptiles seek out ultra-violet light. Allow them to get accustomed to it gradually by increasing levels slowly.

Most UV lamps radiate virtually no more ultra-violet after six to nine months and need to be replaced. Consequently UV lamps can produce either a lot of ultra-violet light or a lot of infra-red (heat) that in incorrect use can lead to burns, eye, or bone problems. Find out the correct height for the lamp above the animal and also the maximum exposure time. For instance a widely-used 300 Watt lamp may be used for 15 to 60 minutes per day in terrariums of at least 2 cubic metres (70.6 cu ft) provided it is at least 75cm (29^1/$_2$in) above the animals.

Plants in swamp terrariums such as orchids need lots of light. This is Masdevallia militaris.

Pressed-glass spot and tubular UV lamp.

Time switches can turn lighting on an off. This digital switch can work to the minute.

Halogen lamps without filter have a high light intensity, radiate a wide light spectrum including some UV and also a great deal of warmth. The small lamps are suitable for smaller terrariums but they should never be sited too close to combustible materials.

Gas-discharge lamps such as high-pressure mercury vapour, high-pressure sodium, and metal-halide lamps are increasingly successfully used in larger terrariums. The metal-halide lamps are the best artificial imitation of sunlight and comprise relatively high levels of UV. All these types of lamps need control-gear. Use them in large terrariums and replace the lamps once per year.

Miniature low energy fluorescent lamps (such as **PL**) are compact, use little energy and relatively high levels of light. A swamp terrarium of 60 x 60 x 80cm (23^1/$_2$ x 23^1/$_2$ x 31^1/$_2$in) needs three 36 Watt PL lamps and one of 120 x 60 x 100cm (47^1/$_4$ x 23^1/$_2$ x 39^1/$_2$in) needs six of them.

The special UV-B tubular fluorescent lamps for terrariums may be left on all day. Other broad spectrum lamps also radiate UV light and with all UV sources the instructions must be carefully followed.

Get animals that are not used to UV lighting accustomed to it gradually and when an old lamp is replaced by a new one increase the dosing by degrees. Animals must always have somewhere to withdraw away from the UV radiation.

LIGHT BOX COVER

Lamps are often fitted in a cover for the terrarium. Because of their warmth, it is best if control-gear is not fitted inside the cover but preferably under the terrarium on metal that will help to disperse heat, which extends its life, but do not position not more than 15mm (⁵/₈in) away.

The light box becomes fairly hot at 40-50°C (104-122°F) and therefore needs ventilation. Paint the inside of the light box with mat white paint for best reflection of the light and position a light refract-

Swamp terrarium lighting with refractor.

Leopard geckos on a warm stone.

ing grid between the lamps and the terrarium to prevent the animals from suffering from glare (see photograph).

OTHER HEATING

In addition to lamps, **bottom heating** is also used in terrariums, with heating wires, heat mats, and heat stones. Use this form of heating only for specimens that are accustomed to being heated from below, by warmth rising from the soil, such as lizards, those that live in insulated hollows, animals that live on the floor of the rain forest, and nocturnally active snakes and geckos.

Bottom heating alone is unnatural so use it in combination with lamps. Animals that are active during the day need radiant warmth (of spot lamps).

Place cables only under half of the terrarium, never under the entire bottom and insulate the underside. Be careful with the heat rocks and heat cables because many animals have no sense of heat through their bellies and will burn easily. The temperature can be controlled by thermostats, time switches, and transformers. Check the temperature carefully before placing animals in the terrarium.

Position heat mats outside the terrarium. Heat cables must be fixed (stuck between strips of glass) so that they do not cross over each other which would cause overheating.

Fan heaters and small radiators can heat terrariums with a volume exceeding 5m³ (176.6 cu ft). Position these heaters out of reach of the animals and always combine them with reflector lamps or pressed-glass spot lamps to provide radiant warmth.

Thermostatically controlled **aquarium heaters** can be used to maintain night-time temperature for both the water and land areas of moist terrariums. Provide ¹/₂ Watt per litre of water, ensure the water can flow around the heater, and ensure that the heater is never on when out of water. Try to find a heater with as long a lead as possible.

Ensure heat cables never cross over each other. These are glued between glass strips.

HUMIDITY

The moisture content of the soil, amount of rain, and humidity of the air (or relative humidity) are all important to the well-being of terrariums. The relative humidity, expresses the percentage water in the air. Most living rooms are around 50 per cent and the maximum is 100 per cent, which is absolute saturation. Animals have difficulty shedding their skins in terrariums that are too dry while moist ones create problems with mould and fungal growth, and the animals can get pustules and scabs. The relative humidity can vary from one microclimate to another and is at its highest at night in the desert. The preferred relative humidity (RH) values for the various types of terrarium and different animals are given in these sections.

Never increase the humidity by reducing ventilation but by spraying luke-warm water, placing an air pump in the water tray, by means of a cascade, or a humidifier. Air humidifiers intended for domestic use create cold water vapour by means of ultrasonic vibrations. This vapour can be piped by plastic tube to a number of terrariums. Allow the pipes to run slightly downhill so that no water becomes trapped. The slits through which the vapour escapes can be sealed with silicon adhesive. Make sure the temperature does not drop too sharply. If possible buy a unit that can work with tap water

A humidifier spreads vapour to 4 terrariums via plastic tubes.

Cold vapour 'mist' from the humidifier.

A dark box filled with moist sphagnum moss is an ideal hiding and egg-laying spot.

Cork is the most widely used material for rear walls.

and does not require demineralized water.

The humidity of the soil is also important in a terrarium. Many animals of dry biotopes like to rest in a moist hiding place and choose such a spot to lay their eggs. Place a small box or container with an opening and fill it with moist sphagnum moss or sand.

BACK WALLS

Back and side walls give an animal a protected feeling and help to prevent stress. They are also decorative and provide climbing opportunities. A rear wall that is stepped with platforms increases the living space and provides for a greater temperature differential since warm air rises. Most materials are fixed to the wall with silicon adhesive.

Cork sheet is the most widely used material and is to be found in a layer 2-6cm ($^3/_4$-$2^3/_8$in) thick in most shop-bought terrariums. Cork is easy to apply and not expensive. Use cork that has been pressed together without glue because the glue used to bind cork is toxic. Eventually the occupant/s will gnaw holes in the cork and it will in any event gradually crumble, especially in terrariums of high humidity with large lizards. Cork floor tiles of 2mm are also suitable to use.

Cork bark provides a natural-looking rear wall that neither rots or suffers mould. The material is

31

Grey slate and red flagstone.

not flat and therefore more difficult to fix. Crickets can creep behind it and small amphibians can even become stuck behind it. The hollow areas can be filled with a polystyrene foam. However, it is entirely possible to press cork flat if it is first immersed in hot water. Naturally bent cork is of course ideal decoration and provides places for animals to hide.

Thin sheets from **peat blocks** are not at all robust but they are sometimes used in swamp terrariums. Plants grow well on moist peat. Peat blocks themselves are also little used as rear wall material but can be held in place with fishing line glued to plastic sheet which can then be glued to glass. Always maintain a small air gap of a few centimetres (about an inch) because peat swells when it is moist.

A **timber board** rear wall is attractive for animals that live in the company of humans. The wood must be free from splinters. Wood warps readily in the damp conditions of many terrariums.

Fern root is quite often used in swamp terrariums. The material originates from slow-growing tropical tree ferns which are becoming increasingly rare. The removal of the root is harmful to the tropical rain forest and hence increasing numbers of countries restrict the export of fern roots. This material can be fixed with silicon adhesive. When fern root is moist mosses and ferns sprout from it and other plants quickly take root on it. Sprinkle

A mortared rear wall of lava.

fern root with water for a few minutes each day or throughout the day, depending on the level of humidity required, using long plastic tubing. In common with peat and cork, fern root makes the biotope acidic.

Slates are only about 5mm ($^3/_{16}$in) thick and they can be fixed to the rear wall with silicon adhesive. Cover the joints with further pieces of slate. Before fixing slates the terrarium needs to be laid on its rear panel. Gaps can be avoided by embedding the slate in mortar. Thicker pieces of slate of 1-2 cm ($^3/_8$-$^3/_4$in) need first to be fixed to polystyrene foam. The slate wall must not be able to fall against the panes or onto the animals and the same is true of flagstone, which has fewer striations than slate. Lava fixed with mortar provides an attractive

Once fern root is moistened mosses and ferns sprout from it.

heavy and grey-brown rear wall. Lay it one row at a time.

Large lumps of **rock** can be imitated by covering a material such as urethane foam with various finishes. Polystyrene blocks or sheet can be carved or shaped with hot wires, hot air, or a sharp knife. Take care to ventilate well because of the poisonous fumes given off when polystyrene burns. The foam can then be covered with papier mâché, polyester fibres (for polyester resin), or mesh to provide a key for mortar or plaster. Insulating foam canisters produce a foam rather like shaving

Burning off pieces of polystyrene foam for a terrarium.

This is how it looks after applying plaster and scattering with sand.

Polyester fibre coated with polyester resin on chicken wire.

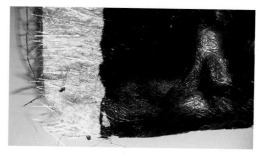

A rear wall of urethane foam.

foam that hardens. This pale yellow or light green foam can be sprayed with car touch-up paint in aerosols. If this is done when the foam has set then the result is smooth but if done while immediately after squirting the foam then the surface becomes pitted and looks a lot like lava. Ten minutes after spraying the foam other materials can be pressed into it such as gravel or small stones. This spray foam is toxic and must be washed thoroughly with about twenty rinses of warm water. This spray foam will not remain fixed to an aquarium wall because of its buoyancy.

Cover the base material several times with a stiff mixture of mortar, quick-drying mortar, tile cement. or plaster. The substrate can also be coated with polyester resin or latex emulsion. While the surface is still moist it can be strewn with sand, grit, vermiculite, sawdust, or sand, or alternatively grit can be stirred into the initial mixture. Paint on polystyrene foam can easily be scratched off and should only be used in terrariums for amphibians, and then provided no gnawing prey will be added.

Polyester resin requires a hardener. After applying to polyester fibre press with a roller to remove air bubbles and repeat the process when the resin has dried. Polyester can be painted if preferred and does not have to look like natural rock.

Powder paint can also be mixed with water to which 3 tablespoons of wood glue is added. This produces a tough layer of paint. Wipe over the paint with a duster for a fine effect. This is best done with the terrarium lighting on so that the effect can be seen immediately.

Urethane foam is like a harder and fine polystyrene foam. It has the same colour all the way through and is easy to apply and creates a natural look. Plants attach themselves to this material, but lizards can scratch it to destruction and crickets and mealworms eat their way through it. Dark-painted glass or a poster varnished to the outside provide an hygienic rear panel. This doesn't provide any climbing opportunities but is ideal for a quarantine terrarium.

DECORATION

With whichever decorative material is used create hiding places, somewhere to lay eggs, and opportunities for climbing. Hollows to which an animal can flee should have at least two entrances. Make sure that they can be readily cleaned and do not position them in either the hottest or coldest parts of the terrarium. In terrariums in which breeding animals are housed there should be no stones of such size that if they are burrowed under they could fall and crush the animals.

Decorative materials can also be used to make a terrarium look more attractive and for instance to hide equipment. Naturally the materials must not be toxic and sufficiently robust. It is possible to use the various materials described for finishing rear walls in a number of ways. Urethane foam can be sprayed into roll-up chicken wire to make an imitation tree trunk.

Living plants are not merely decoration but also provide somewhere for animals to hide and something for them to climb. Plants play no role in provision of oxygen in the terrarium atmosphere and they are often eaten by both the terrarium animals and their prey. They must not have dangerous thorns or spikes such as some cacti and must not be toxic. Poison can also be ingested via prey that feed on the leaves.

Plants struggle in fairly dry terrariums because of a deficiency of light and water, or the wrong type of soil. The moist plants also often provide a source of infections. If the plant remains in a pot the problem is reduced and the plant can be easily removed when necessary. Bearing in mind the disadvantages, succulents (agaves, cacti, and *Eu-*phorbia species), or *Crypthantus* and sansevieria species can be planted in arid terrariums.

The following plants (or plants within these genera) are used for moist terrariums: *Arthurium, Aphelandra,* bamboo, begonias, *Caladium, Calathea, Codiaeum, Columnea, Cordyline, Ctenanthe, Dieffenbachia* (toxic), *Dracaena, Epipremnum, Ficus, Fittonia, Maranta, Monstera, Peperomia, Philodendron, Spathiphyllum, Stromanthe,* plus many ferns, *Bromelia* and orchids (consult a house plant encyclopedia). Other house plants can be tried.

A word of caution: *Ficus repens* (syn. *F. pumilio*) grows quickly in warm, humid terrariums and will quickly push other plants aside. Plants such as *Maranta leuconeura* and species of *Syngonium* need high humidity, moist soil, and plenty of light. *Scindapsus* species need a high relative humidity, a semi-moist soil, and ample light. *Philodendron scandens* (Heart leaf or Sweetheart plant) will grow with moderate humidity, a moist soil, and little light. Give *Hoya* species dry air, a slightly moist soil, and lots of light. Ivy (the *Hedera* species) and honesty (or moneywort) are tough plants that require little light. Ground cover bladderworts *(Utricularia species)* are excellent to grow in moss in a swamp terrarium. The leaves are 2-6mm in size and the pearly-white florets are born on 6cm high stems. Many **Bromeliaceae** *(Bromelia* and *Tillandsia* species) are ideal for well-ventilated terrariums. These are almost all epiphytes of American origin, that is plants that are not parasites yet root in the branches of other plants instead of the soil. These plants can be cultivated in sphagnum moss and then tied to a branch with fishing line. Most species will have formed roots after about six months. They can also be held in place by non acidic glue.

Many Bromeliaceae have very short stems, forming rosettes of foliage with a funnel that often fills with water. This is an ideal environment for poison dart frogs. Moisture is mainly absorbed via the leaves. After flowering, most of these species die but a few new young plants are then formed. Smooth green foliage of the type produced by Bromeliaceae such as *Vriesea, Guzmania, Aech-*

A species of Scinapsus.

Ficus repens *with small leaves, and species of* Philodendron.

One of the bromelias: species of Guzmania.

A Masdevallia ionea orchid.

Most species of Tillandsia are epiphytes.

Air roots.

mea, Neoregelia (syn. Aregelia), and Nidularium are suitable for moist terrariums. Grey and silver and or hairy plants are adapted to drier climates. The colourful Cryptanthus species are mainly small with spiky leaf margins that provide ground cover in a variety of conditions.

Orchids require a great deal of light. For warm terrariums (daytime temperature 18-27°C/64.4-80.6°F) that are very humid (60-80%) seek out small orchids which do not require a period of either cold or dry 'rest'. Orchids that need a rest period can often be recognized by the bulb-like swellings at the base of the leaves. Use orchids from genera such as Brassavola, Dendrobium, Dryadella, Encyclia, Epidendrum, Ionopsis, Leptotis, Masdevallia, Maxillaria, Notylia, Odontoglossum, Oncidium, Phalaenopsis, Pleurothallus, and Stellis. Orchids need the fresh air of ventilation, should be kept free from excreta, and care should be taken not to pass aphids and red spider mites on to them from other plants. Insecticides cannot be used in terrariums. Provide soft water or spray the plants with such. Some orchids live epiphytically (see Bromeliaceae).

Tropical **ferns** grow readily in moist terrariums and many can exist with modest lighting levels. Do not allow them to take over by thinning out regularly. Mosses too are very decorative and require little light. Tropical mosses sprout from planks of tree ferns once these are moistened. Native mosses are unable to withstand high temperatures and quickly die. Java moss (Vesicularia dubyana) that

will grow on very wet banks and on water cascades is sold by aquarium specialists.

All manner of aquatic plants can be grown in the water sections of terrariums. Those with dark leaves have less need of light than those with lighter foliage. Suitable candidates include species of Cryptocoryne, Ceratophyllum, Phymatosorus (syn. Microsorum), and Vesicularia. Swamp plants (which often have robust stems) also grow above the water. Suitable floating plants can be found from the genera Pistia, Eichhornia, and Salvinia.

Artificial plants demand little upkeep and the equipping of the terrarium can be done entirely with the animals in mind. Imitation plants also damage less easily, although green iguanas (herbivores) will scratch and nibble them until they are destroyed. However the false foliage can be dangerous if swallowed and small lizards can become trapped by the waist in a leaf axil of a fixed artificial plant.

Wood is attractive and can be used in a variety of ways. Branches can be set erect in a block of concrete. Wild timber gathered from a wood with its many splits, holes, and rough bark is less hygienic and prone to causing parasitic infections. Disinfect such timber with bleach and/or impregnate it. Undesirable inhabitants such as small slugs can be removed by freezing or drying. Most types of timber will eventually rot and can only be used in reasonably dry terrariums. Air roots or roots of tropical hardwood do not rot when moist but boil them first in a pan of salted water. Cork bark can be

Tropical root wood.

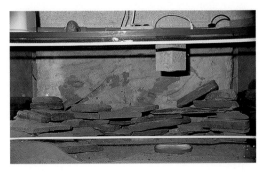

Terrarium for leopard geckos with sand-pit sand.

used in all manner of ways and is resistant to moisture. Timber from grape vines is very decorative thanks to its many contortions and rough surface. Epiphytes can easily get a footing on such timber but grapevines will also rot when in a humid environment. Skeleton cacti are very decorative in desert terrariums but provide no hiding place for crickets. Bamboo shoots can provide fine upright hiding places for creatures such as geckos.

Stone and rock are heavy but can be used in many ways although they must not be too sharp. Animals that spend a lot of time in water are often unable to tolerate limestone of other chalky rock in their water. Chalk causes hard water. Ensure that the stones are firmly placed and not in areas where they can fall on burrowing animals. Read the earlier section also about 'Rear Walls,' where advice is given on how to create artificial rock.

Ready-made hiding places can be bought from specialist shops that can be used in numerous ways.

GROUND

The type of ground material to be used depends on the type of terrarium and its inhabitants. Many appropriate materials can be sterilized by placing in thin layers in an oven for half an hour at 200-250°C (400-475°F). With materials such as wood shavings they will have to replaced by paper if the terrarium becomes infected by ticks.

Coarse-grained sand used for sand pits does not collapse so easily as fine-grained sand when burrowed through and excreta can easily be sieved out of sand to remove it. Because urine and moisture from fruit also finds its way into sand it provides a ready breeding ground for bacteria and should be changed at least once each year. Take care with bottom heating because sand absorbs a great deal of heat and sheds it slowly leading to a risk of overheating. Blockages of sand in reptile stomachs can be prevented by keeping the animals in good condition and providing their food on a dish. Do not use sand with a grain size less than 1mm (such as fine silver sand) since it can get into all manner of bodily apertures. Certain quarried yellow-orange sand becomes hard when moistened slightly and is ideal for desert and steppe terrariums. True desert sand is red-orange and becomes harder than the

Aquarium gravel is not suitable for terrariums because of risk of blockages. The back wall is of flagstone.

sandstone derived sands of Europe but this is expensive.

Aquarium gravel (2-3mm diameter) is fairly sharp, hard, and dangerous if ingested (causing a blockage). Furthermore prey animals and waste matter ends up between the gravel stones. Use this material only for aquarium sections and wash gravel thoroughly with tap water.

Water retention granules used in hydro-culture absorb a great deal of moisture making them hygienic and ideal for use in quarantine and shop terrariums provided there is no danger with the occupants swallowing the grains. This material also becomes a resting place for prey animals and waste matter so wash the grains regularly.

Compost decomposes and smells if it remains sodden with water and fresh compost also often contains pesticides and or fertilizer which might be poisonous for terrarium animals. Old compost can provide for good plant growth in fairly dry terrariums but do not use any compost containing perlite.

Shredded peat does not rot when wet although it creates an acidic soil and water, but this is usually not a problem. This acidity actually slows the development of bacteria and mould. Thin layers of peat dry out very quickly and many plant do not flourish fully in peat.

Peat blocks can be used to create an island in water sections of terrariums and things grow fairly well on them, especially moss. You need to bear in mind that peat can expand considerably as it absorbs water and could force the glass panes apart.

Leaf mould/composted bark chips/ and natural woodland soil are very natural but not very hygienic. Sterilize them in a microwave oven or for 30 minutes at 200-250°C (400-475°F) in a conventional oven. Plants thrive on these materials and reptiles can create burrows and nests. There is a risk of these materials decomposing and causing moulds so replace such soil regularly (depending on the demands made by conditions and animals). In the event of disease or parasites the soil should be removed immediately. It is also possible to add earthworms to the soil since they clean up waste matter and provide additional food.

Orchid compost can be sieved for use in moist terrariums where it decomposes hardly at all and suffers little from mould.

Moss can be used in moist terrariums with amphibians. It retains water well but needs constant replenishment of bare patches. Sphagnum moss also retains moisture well and although it dies quickly does not leave a bare patch behind. Decorative burrows can be made using this material (see Decoration).

Beech wood chips are widely used but cedar chips are toxic and several other types cause lung complaints. Wood chips have a natural appearance and make it easy to remove soiling. This material rots and causes mould in damp terrariums. Make sure the chips cannot become stuck to moist food so that the chips are swallowed. Replace when required or about four times each year.

Wood shavings are easy to replace and perfectly hygienic on their own but the material look unnatural. Snakes like to hide away beneath wood shavings but many lizards and tortoises will sometimes eat them causing internal blockages.

Pressed maize and trout pellets are digestible and therefore not dangerous if swallowed. These materials are ideal for dry terrariums in which no burrowing will occur.

Urethane islands and banks in bank terrariums are hygienic. Use the material as described earlier for back walls. The material is full of air bubbles and therefore needs to well anchored with stones.

A terrarium with timber back wall and woodland soil.

Wood shavings provide the ground material for this terrarium with cork shelters. There are ventilators in the front and top.

An hygienic floor and shelter of linoleum.

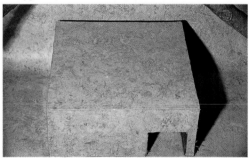

Outdoor matting and artificial turf are easy to wash and therefore hygienic.

Linoleum/vinyl floor covering on the floor and back wall is easy to keep clean and provides little opportunity for parasites, making it very hygienic. Cover with some bark or wood chips for animals that have a problem with smooth surfaces. Make sure there is somewhere to hide and other forms of decoration. This material is ideal for snakes.

Newspaper and kitchen roll can be replaced easily each day making this an hygienic option. Use this material in quarantine terrariums and in the event of illness or parasite infestation.

FEEDING

Although there is an increasing assortment of ready-to-use feeds for terrarium animals available to buy, it is cheaper (and sometimes better) to make up your own. Problems arising out of malnutrition or incorrect feeding frequently only become apparent when it is already too late. Bear the following guidelines in mind when feeding.

Feed adult reptiles and amphibians about three times each week. Give young animals a little food several times each day. Feed snakes once every one to four weeks (see Snakes). With many carnivorous arthropods the amount of food depends on what stage in the skin-shedding cycle they are at. Make sure that herbivorous arthropods have a constant supply of fresh food.

Uneaten prey animals can disturb or even harm resting animals (by night). When it is cold with the lamps out warm-blooded rodents pose a threat to inactive cold-blooded terrarium creatures. Provide fresh food and remove old remnants which might be mouldy. Provide a varied diet and continually try to provide something new. The food should also change across the seasons. Provide herbivorous lizards that have hibernated with fresh green vegetable matter in spring, supplemented with flowers in summer, and fruits and seeds in autumn.

Always sprinkle multi-vitamin and mineral mixtures over the green fodder, insects, or meat for reptiles, amphibians, and arthropods (See Vitamins and minerals). Keep these powdered preparations protected from moisture in a refrigerator (cool, dry, and dark). If they remain dry, the powder adheres to food better.

Too much fat is just as harmful for terrarium animals as it is for humans. Animals that are given too much food prove to be less fertile.

Do not collect prey animals or natural vegetable matter from anywhere where there is a risk of pollution from traffic, agriculture, or industry.

Weak animals can become weaker still and distressed if they remain in a group with others. This reduces their resistance to parasites with all the consequences this brings. Feed such animals separately from the others, trying to remove the inequality and if necessary separate the animals.

It is best to feed terrarium animals that are active by day once they have warmed up under the lamps, around 11 o'clock. This gives them the rest of the day to digest the food. Feed nocturnal animals such as many geckos and tree frogs after the lights have been switched off.

Maintain a regime of hygiene, washing both water and feeding bowls and never move the receptacles directly from one terrarium to another.

Do not thaw frozen food in a microwave or with hot water. Instead place it in the refrigerator the day before.

Vitamins and minerals

The natural diet of wild animals is far more varied and richer in nutrients than the prey animals, meat, and cooked vegetables and fruit provided for their counterparts in terrariums. For this reason food must always be supplemented with vitamins and minerals.

For many arthropods that have lives of under one year it is not usual to add vitamins and minerals to their food. These creatures have a simplified digestive system and their life span is so short that there is not sufficient time for them to suffer from nutritional deficiency.

Mix fruit, endive, and insects with a preparation of vitamins and minerals.

Newly born rats make excellent food for many lizards and small snakes but also for large tarantulas.

Left: Calumma parsonii *eating a cricket.*

CALCIUM AND PHOSPHORUS

Reptiles and amphibian are vertebrate animals with an internal skeleton which requires calcium (Ca) and phosphorus (P) in the right proportions for correct development. Most of these animals require one and a half times more calcium than phosphorus. Scorpions and arthropods are invertebrates requiring calcium for their external hard shell that acts as a skeleton.

In the wild a varied diet, dew and rain water, and soil taken in with the food provides the necessary calcium. On average the food comprises one per cent calcium.

In chalk free terrariums in which the food is also low in calcium, the absence of this mineral can cause rachitis (rickets), evidenced by spongy, weak, and misshapen bones or shells (crooked legs, thickened elbows, broken jaws, and bent teeth), defective eggs, and deformed or dead offspring. A reptile suffering from rachitis extracts calcium from its bones to keep up the level in the blood. In order to continue to have sturdy legs greater amounts of connective tissue are formed. Instead of a thick layer of muscle at the thighs there is a strong and hard mass surrounded by a thin layer of connective tissue. Vertebrate animals, pieces of cuttlefish bone, poultry grit, and egg shells are good sources of calcium for carnivorous animals. Arthropods, meat without bones, and fruit and vegetables generally contain too little calcium, and certainly in too low a proportion to the phosphorus content. This sort of food needs an additive incorporating calcium such as dusting it with a multivitamin and mineral preparation. The different brands all have different proportions but for food with a high level of phosphorus choose a supplement that has a high proportion of calcium.

Additional calcium can be provided by mixing 1 tablespoon of calcium lactate per litre of water and adding this to the food.

OTHER MINERALS

In addition to calcium and phosphorus, sodium (Na) and potassium (K) are important for regulating fluids in the body and magnesium (Mg) needs to be present in reasonable proportions to absorb proteins and for enzymes to function.

What are known as trace elements are required in very small amounts yet their absence can have serious repercussions. Iodine (I) is needed for proper functioning of the thyroid, copper (Cu) for the metabolism and blood supply, manganese (Mn) and zinc (Zn) for the production of enzymes, selenium (Se) to enable vitamin E to work, and iron (Fe) for the haemoglobin in the blood and for the metabolism.

VITAMINS

Depending on the type of animal and its diet, it is also necessary to supplement vitamins in the diet. A deficiency of certain vitamins can cause problems and resistance to illness and parasites will often be reduced. For this reason always sprinkle the food with a multivitamin and mineral supplement. Vitamins A, D, E, and K are soluble in fat and are stored in the liver. This can lead to illness through an excess of these vitamins. Vitamins B and C are soluble in water and a surplus is excreted with urine.

Vitamin A is found as a pro-vitamin in animal fat such as liver and in carotene, a colouring found in carrots. A deficiency of this vitamin causes skin and eye complaints, leading to inflammation of the eyes with poorly nourished terrapins and other freshwater turtles. Problems with shedding the skin or shell can be caused either by a terrarium that is too dry or a deficiency of vitamin A. Serious problems can be dealt with by vitamin A. The dose is 2,000-10,000 IU (international units) per kilogram mixed with the food or 15,000-20,000 IU subcutaneously injected by a specialist vet. The animals will shed the skin or shell several times after the injection.

Deformed offspring resulting from rachitis.

Always sprinkle prey animals with vitamin and mineral supplement powder.

An overdose of vitamin A suppresses vitamin D3. Tortoises which eat carotene-rich vegetable food never suffer from a vitamin A deficiency and therefore should have as little supplementary vitamins as possible.

Vitamin B complex is widely found in yeast, meet, and pulses. There are several sorts of vitamin B, each with a different number. A deficiency of B complex vitamins causes skin and digestive problems. In addition to vitamin B1 (thiamine) below, biotin which does not have a designated vitamin number is important because it is required for the metabolism. A deficiency of biotin causes flaky skin, weakening of the muscles, and slows growth. Infertile raw eggs contain ovidin which depletes the body of biotin, albeit if present in large quantity. For this reason only feed fertilized or cooked eggs to reptiles that need eggs in their diet.

Vitamin B1 (thiamine) is important for the functioning of the nervous system. Many types of fish contain a substance that breaks down vitamin B1.

Vitamin C aids the resistance to disease of an animal. It is present in much fruit and a deficiency is uncommon.

Vitamin D3, is the most important for those keeping animals in a terrarium. The vitamin is necessary for the absorption of calcium and a deficiency causes similar symptoms to lack of calcium.

Overdoses of this vitamin can cause a build-up of calcium in the organs and can eventually cause poisoning and problems with development of bones.

Vitamin D3 can be made in the skin with the help of ultra-violet light. This light is naturally present in sunlight but does not penetrate glass, although it passes through clear plastic sheet. Animals kept in glass terrariums therefore need radiation of UV-B light or a supplement of vitamin D3.

Either hang a UV-emitting lamp in the terrarium or place the animals in an outdoor terrarium. Vitamin D3 can be given as drops or powder by adding it to the drinking water or feed. Various recommended doses are indicated but it is difficult to be certain of these since not every animal drinks or eats the same amount. Provide 500-1,000 IU per kilogram each week for young animals and give adults 100-500 IU per week or add 10,000 IU per litre of drinking water. It's all a bit like waggling a wet finger in the air to find the wind but give some each week.

Vitamin E Among the functions of vitamin E are fertility for reproduction and the working of other vitamins. The vitamin is found abundantly in pulses and germinated shoots such as bean shoots. A deficiency of this vitamin can cause birth problems for reptiles.

Prey animals

Many animals kept in terrariums need to eat living creatures or prey animals. Those bought from shops such as crickets, grasshoppers, and fruit flies (and rodents) are often rather thin and of low nutritional value. This can be improved by feeding them first for a few days e.g. banana for fruit flies, and fish food and fruit for crickets. Self-bred prey animals are often of better quality and much cheaper. The manner of breeding these prey animals is dealt with in this section of the book.

Escaped small prey animals can be captured with a vacuum cleaner with the foot from a pair of tights or stockings fastened in place of the filter or inner end of the hose with a rubber band so that they can be returned to be fed to the terrarium animals. Mites are attracted to the moist or dirty breeding conditions for prey animals but they can be kept at bay by placing a little dried wormwood (*Artemisia absinthium*), available from chemists or herbalists, in the facility.

Insects have a proportion of calcium to phosphorus in a ratio of between 1:3 and 1:15. This needs to be 'corrected' for many terrarium animals to a ratio of about 2:1 (see Vitamins and minerals).

CRICKETS

Of the approximately 2,000 species of crickets

Ribbon snakes like the young Thamnophis proximus *of suffer a deficiency of vitamin B1.*

Increasing numbers of shops sell crickets and other prey.

(class Grylloidea), four are regularly used as prey animals for terrariums creatures. Never attempt to raise more than one species together in one container because one will always dominate the other.

ACHETA DOMESTICA, GREY CRICKET

Appearance
This most commonly reared cricket is 25mm (1in) long, has well-developed jumping legs, and antennae about 30mm (1¹/₄in) long. They are light and dark brown with a black stripe between the eyes. Both male and female have fairly long wings but they rarely fly.

Area of distribution
This cricket originates in North Africa but can be found in warm places in Western Europe such as bakeries.

Accommodation
Use a container at least 40cm (16in) high so that the crickets cannot jump out when the lid is removed and ensure the container seals properly so that even the smallest cricket cannot escape.

The rearing container in the illustration is 80 x 50 x 50cm (31¹/₂ x 19³/₄ x 19³/₄in) and has very fine gauge nylon mesh on the top (fine metal mesh as used to filter petrol would also do). The mesh is glued between strips of glass. The crickets cannot easily reach the mesh and it offers no food to them. Even fine gauge wire mesh is too coarse for this purpose.

The cricket-proof lid is on the right. This rests on the front and rear glass panels and between the left and right-hand strips of glass. Squeeze out a line of silicon along each of the edges and cover this with a polythene bag such as a sandwich bag before placing the lid on top. The silicon will conform to the shape of the lid and set within twenty-four hours. Glue strips of glass around the lid so that it always sits in precisely the same position on the silicon seal.

Warm the breeding container with lamps, heat mats, or heating wires to about 30°C (86°F). If the temperature is cold growth of the crickets is inhibited, limiting production. At room temperature the

Self-reared prey animals are cheaper and better quality.

The cricket rearing container described.

Making a terrarium escape-proof for crickets.

eggs hatch after two to three months and the development into a cricket lasts five to eight months through thirteen stages. At 30°C (86°F) the eggs hatch in eight to ten days and the crickets are fully grown inside a month and seven larval stages.

Keep the humidity at 50-70 per cent. In moist containers mites can become a plague so that ventilation is extremely important. Provide a large surface area with toilet roll centres or egg boxes to reduce cannibalism of the smaller crickets by the larger ones.

An alternative type of breeding container has no lid and therefore good ventilation. Cover the rim with smooth plastic or smear with petroleum jelly which prevents the crickets gaining a foothold but it is impossible to ensure that none escape.

Sex determination
Only male crickets chirrup in order to attract a mate and to drive other males from their territory. The sound is created by rubbing the edges of their wings over each other while the wings are held erect.

Female crickets of all types can be recognized by the ovipositor or egg-laying tube that projects between the cerci or feelers at the posterior of the abdomen. The ovipositor is already discernible with semi-mature females. With the house cricket this ovipositor is 10mm (³/₈in) long and black.

Egg laying

Female crickets start to lay 3mm long white eggs two weeks after their final moult. A well nourished female will lay 150 to 200 of them every day in slightly compressed old compost (in which toxins have been naturally eradicated). Cover the trays of compost with fine metal mesh to prevent the crickets from eating the eggs. The eggs will suffocate in wet compost and dry out in dry compost so keep a careful watch on the moisture level. Provide a minimum of 60mm (2³/₈in) compost, which should be just as moist as a newly-opened bag of compost.

Feeding

Feed poultry pellets without insecticide, dried cat or dog feed, bread, or fish food. Provide moisture by means of fruit and green foliage (grass, dandelion leaves, or endive). Some cooked vegetables contain toxins. Gather a handful of grass with a rubber band so that after a few days the crickets can be shaken off any remnants so it can be removed and replaced with fresh supplies without making a mess.

Spray with a little water twice each week. Too much moisture causes mites and mould. Place cotton wool or sponge in any drinking containers to prevent the crickets from drowning.

Reared in this way, crickets have a higher nutritional value than mealworms, 'super mealworms', maggots, or grasshoppers. This can be increased further by sprinkling the crickets with a vitamin and mineral supplement. Crickets that are not eaten immediately still pass on the dietary supplement by 'washing' themselves to clean off the powder so that it is ingested and hence passed on when they are eaten.

Infections

If the larvae of buffalo gnats invade the cricket rearing container they will damage the cricket larvae and the buried eggs. These larvae reproduce rapidly so that the rearing container needs to be thoroughly disinfected and a start made with entirely fresh materials and supplies. Because of the

Cricket eggs in old compost.

A glimpse of the hatching container without mesh.

A well-run hatchery provides many crickets.

risk of mites and viruses clean the cricket hatchery every three months. Replace the egg boxes and clean the bottom with a stripping knife. Freeze the compost to kill off any undesirable organisms.

Rearing

The example of a cricket hatchery described has a 35 x 40cm (13³/₄-15³/₄in) lid making access easy. For feeding place a beaker or small pot with a smooth rim in the container and shake a few egg cartons or toilet roll centres into the pot. Feed mainly males, older females (that do not have well-filled abdomens and dark rear end), and young adults. Select large well-filled crickets for breeding, bearing in mind that only a few males are needed for each hatchery. It is the number of females that determines the volume of production.

Terrariums in which adult crickets move around also need to be cricket-proof. Alternatively remove the ovipositor to prevent the eggs being inserted into the soil where they may become mouldy or dry out.

Crickets that are not eaten can disturb the terrarium occupants at night or even harm them and will damage cork-lined rear walls by eating them. Offer the crickets with tweezers or place them for several hours in a refrigerator to slow them down.

Do not feed too many crickets to amphibians which struggle with the spiky projections of the legs and fairly thick body shell. Crickets which have been kept in conditions that are too moist often carry mould which is dangerous for chameleons and some other animals.

No-one can prevent some crickets from escaping. They will congregate indoors somewhere warm, such as the back of the refrigerator. Place tall jars with smooth interiors with fruit combined with yeast or beer to attract them. If necessary, catch them with a vacuum cleaner with the foot of tights or stockings on the bag end of the hose. Crickets can also be captured with double-sided adhesive tape.

If necessary mix equal parts of borax, sodium fluoride and grape sugar and place in small trays where neither children or pets can reach it. Crickets which eat the mixture die quickly but these must not be fed to the terrarium animals.

System breeding

By using one container for egg laying and another for hatching the offspring, an even greater number of crickets can be produced.

Equip the hatchery as previously described. Regularly replace the container of compost and move the old on to the hatchery. The eggs hatch in two weeks and the crickets will be fully-grown in six weeks. Place the largest specimens in the egg-laying container and feed the remainder to the terrarium animals. Clean the now empty hatchery before placing a new batch of eggs in it.

This system reduces cannibalism and eating of eggs due the even size of the crickets. Furthermore the crickets are now sorted by size. Professional breeders heat a central area of the cricket hatchery and remove the eggs each day. Some of them feed a fairly high level of bran but others mix a nutritious paste for feed.

OTHER CRICKETS

The following three species of cricket are commonly bred for use as prey animals. Breeding and rearing these crickets is similar to the house cricket, although these species have a greater need of moisture for their eggs to hatch.

Rack with cricket egg-laying unit (100 x 40 x 40cm/39¹/₂ x 15³/₄ x 15³/₄in) in centre and 6 hatcheries (50 x 40 x 40cm/19³/₄ x 15³/₄ x 15³/₄in).

Field crickets at the egg-laying tray (with mesh) and a drinking tray with sponge.

Gryllus bimaculatus, species of field cricket with two patches which chirrups much louder than the house cricket, has a harder shell, and is more aggressive towards sleeping terrarium animals. On the other hand escaped specimens do not survive long out of their protected environment.

Appearance

This sort can be up to 35mm (1³/₈in) long and is predominantly black with two yellow patches on the wings.

Distribution

The range of this cricket is along the coast of the Mediterranean and to the east of this region in Western Asia.

Gryllus assimilis species of field cricket that lives mainly on savannah. This cricket hardly chirrups at all and will not survive long after escape.

Appearance

This species resembles the yellow-spotted field cricket in terms of size but they are tan coloured with brown markings.

Distribution

Africa.

Gryllodes sigillatus or decorated cricket chirrups extensively for long periods. They do not survive after escape.

Appearance

Savannah-dwelling species of field cricket.

The decorated cricket resembles the house cricket but has two diagonal black bands on its chest and abdomen. This species is very productive. The wings of the male of this species cover half of the rear of the body while those of the female are rudimentary. Newly emerging decorated crickets take a long time to mature but leave orchids and bromelias virtually untouched, making them a suitable choice for swamp terrariums.

Distribution

Africa.

LOCUSTA MIGRATORIA AND SCHISTOCERCA GREGARIA: MIGRATORY AND DESERT LOCUSTS

These locusts are of the species that regularly plague Africa. The largest swarms can be greater than 1,000 square kilometres containing a billion locusts.

Appearance

There are two forms of the species *Locusta migratoria:* solitary and gregarious. The solitary form has a green body and brown wings and these locusts form groups of less than 2,000 adults per hectare. Those involved with terrariums only know the gregarious form which migrates and can cause plagues. The females are 60mm (2³/₈in) and the males 40mm (1¹/₂in). Both sexes are light brown with dark brown markings. The wings are flecked with dark brown but with adult males these become increasingly more yellow. Both male

and female have long wings and can fly well. The nymphs are black-orange.

With *Schistocerca gregaria* populations can grow to 500 adult locusts or 5,000 large nymphs or 50,000 immature nymphs per hectare. This species is pinkish-brown with dark brown markings on the body and wings but adult males are more yellow. Females are up to 80mm (3¹/₈in) long and males 60mm (2³/₈in) long. The eyes have vertical stripes and both sexes can fly well. The nymphs are an attractive yellow, green, and black (see illustration).

Distribution

Both these species of locusts are ground and shrub-living creatures of warm, dry climates with *L. migratoria* being found around the Sahara, Asia, and occasionally in Southern Europe, while *S. gregaria* is found in the Sahara, North Africa, and Central Asia.

Accommodation

Ensure a temperature for 16 hours during the day of 32-40°C (89.6-104°F) by using lamps and maintain 25-30°C (77-86°F) at night. The lengthened day causes high egg production. Keep the humidity in the unit low by using a mesh-cage instead of glass. Excreta can fall through a mesh or perforated bottom (diameter 0.8mm perforations) so that it can be removed every day. Increased surface area protected by mesh reduces disturbance of emerg-

Mature female Locusta migratoria.

Breeding cages for locusts.

ing nymphs and crickets. Use a slightly moist compost such as a sand-compost mixture of at least 120mm (4³/₄in) in a pot.

Feeding

These locusts eat all manner of green leaves, hay, and fruit but the main feed in captivity is fresh dry grass, wheat, rye, or barley. Additionally, wheat flour, oatmeal, or bread mixed with milk can be fed. In any event, provide *S. gregaria* with foliage in the form of bramble leaves, cabbage, or lettuce. In the winter fee germinated wheat shoots, reed, or floating sweet-grass. Do not spray the cages for these species and they do not need a tray of water.

Sex determination

The female is larger than the male and the ovipositor is already visible as a flap beneath the rear of the body in semi-mature specimens while the males have a single genital plate. The males make a muted sound by rubbing their legs against their bodies.

Egg laying

Mating lasts several hours and the females press the entire rear end of their bodies up to 120mm (4³/₄in) into the ground where they lay a pink-white frothy collection of some 40 to 140 eggs. The most productive egg layer is *L. migratoria*. Depending on the temperature, the eggs hatch in from ten days to three months.

Rearing

Move the egg-laying tray to the rearing on cage without a mesh bottom and clean thoroughly after each generation. The nymphs are about 6mm when hatched and black. They mature in about three to four weeks and are able to reproduce about two weeks later and live for a further two months.

Feeding as prey

Migratory locusts are eagerly consumed, make little noise, and are neither dangerous or a problem if they escape.

TENEBRIO MOLITOR, MEALWORM

Mealworms are not very nutritious, containing a high proportion of fat and about fifteen times more phosphorus than calcium. Their hard, indigestible shell can cause blockages in reptiles and amphibians. Furthermore these animals often swallow

mealworms alive which can lead to damage to the stomach and intestine walls. Only feed mealworms to tarantulas, scorpions, and praying mantids. Peeled (white) mealworms can be sparingly fed to reptiles and amphibians and the nutritional value can be enhanced by placing the worms for several hours in vitamin and mineral supplements.

Appearance

Mealworms are the larvae of the meal beetle. The 8mm (⁵/₁₆in) long black beetle's eggs produce golden brown larvae. The pupa has no covering and they lie openly on their feeding medium. The beetles rarely fly but must not be fed to terrarium animals because of their hard shells.

Breeding

Use a plastic container with smooth sides of at least 30mm (1¹/₄in) above the meal mixture to prevent escape. Place 20-30mm (³/₄-1¹/₄in) of maize or wheat meal (or similar grain products) in the container and regularly feed a little fruit or vegetable. Dried dog food can also be fed.

Spray a cloth twice each week on which the beetles will lay their eggs. The worms can also be collected on the cloth. The breeding cycle takes about 16 weeks at 25-30°C (77-86°F).

Feeding as pray

Provide the worms as feed in tray with smooth sides at least 30mm (1¹/₄in) high, complete with a slice of apple. Worms that escape can disturb or even harm terrarium animals and they will also chew their way through rear walls of cork.

Mealworms and meal beetles.

Locusta migratoria nymph.

Rearing container for mealworms.

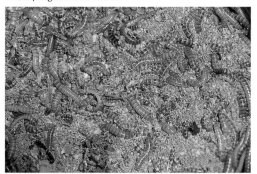
Black fungus beetle larvae.

Pair of 'super' mealworms.

ALPHITOBUIS LAEVIGATUS, BLACK FUNGUS BEETLE LARVA

The larva of the black fungus beetle is also of low nutritional value but does not have the same disadvantages as mealworms.

Appearance

These larvae from the black fungus beetle are a maximum of 15mm (⁵/₈in) long and They are golden brown.

Breeding

Ensure a temperature of 28-30°C (82.4-86°F). Place the beetles in a closed container with a layer of finely-ground chicken feed, flour, and cornflour in the proportions 15:4:1. Place half an apple or other fruit here each week. Sift the mixture each week and remove the beetles, placing them in a new container. Three weeks later the larvae will be maximum size. If necessary, supplement feeding with dried dog or cat food or rodent food.

Feeding as prey

Separate the larvae from their food by placing the mixture in a dish and then place this in a washing-up bowl. The larvae that escape from the food can be fed to the terrarium animals and the remainder will pupate between egg boxes and can be used for further breeding. Place the larvae as food in trays of at least 20mm (2³/₄in) high smooth sides. Place a piece of apple in the tray. Larvae that escape can disturb or harm terrarium animals.

ZOPHOBAS MORIO, 'SUPER' MEALWORM

These much larger mealworms are the larvae of the *Zophobas morio* ground-living beetle of Central and South America.

Appearance

The 'Super' worm is a much larger mealworm of 50mm (2in). The adult black beetles are 3-3.4cm (1³/₁₆-1⁵/₁₆in) long.

Breeding

Because of cannibalistic behaviour containers of at least 10 litres volume of glass or tough plastic are required. Place a 100mm (4in) layer on the bottom of moderately moistened leaf mould or peat mixed with sand. Put several pieces of rotten timber and cork bark on the soil. Egg boxes can also be used as shelters and places to pupate. Ensure the temperature is 25-30°C (77-86°F) and humidity a high 70% relative humidity. Do not provide too much light for the cage and clean it regularly to prevent mites. These omnivores can be fed dried dog food, meat, fruit, and fresh green leaves.

The eggs are laid in fissures in the bark and emerge after eight to twelve days. Spray the cage once each day. The larvae are also omnivorous and will eat other larvae, including their own kind. The larvae seek a suitable place to pupate after two to eight weeks and bore holes in the rotten woods or hide themselves within the egg boxes. The beetle emerges after three to four weeks and lives for about five months.

Feeding as prey

Only feed the larvae and these should be given soon after shedding their skin when they are white.

COCKROACHES

Cockroaches are mainly kept as specimens rather than as prey, because many animals have difficulty eating the wingless types. The green *Panchlora nivea*, which can fly, is quite suitable for feeding to chameleons for example. Given the right temperature, humidity, and food, cockroaches will reproduce profusely.

DROSOPHILA SPP., FRUIT FLIES

These small flies do not have hard body shells, making them ideal for small insectivorous terrarium animals such as frogs, toads, and young arthropods.

Appearance

The various species of fruit flies of this genus are about 5mm (³/₁₆in) long. Hundreds of different species are bred but the following species which do not fly are the main ones used for terrariums:
- *Drosophila melanogaster*, a small species with vestigial wings
- *Drosophila hydei*, a large black species with red eyes and fully sized but inoperative wings
- Species that walk a little then remain still to provide interest.

47

Jars with fruit flies.

The two most commonly used fruit flies can be kept in the terrarium with a piece of banana.

Breeding

A medium on which the flies and larvae can feed is needed in order to breed them. There are countless recipes using yeast, fruit, and grain products as the core ingredients. Here is one example recipe.

Heat enough water and milk to cover the bottom of a pan but do not allow to boil. Stir in oatmeal (porridge oats) until a thick porridge is formed, then stir in 2 sheets of pre-soaked gelatine, half a sachet of yeast, 1 mashed banana, sugar, several drops of vitamin supplement, and the tip of a knife of nipagin (to prevent mould).

The consistency of the mixture should be thick enough to drop naturally from the spoon into a jar or beer glass. Thicken if necessary with more oatmeal or thin with milk.

Close the jar with some kitchen roll and rubber band or a suitable piece of foam rubber. Nylon stocking does not prevent wild fruit flies from mating with the captive ones which will create flies that can fly. Foam rubber is easy to remove and replace and can be readily washed clean. Leave the mixture for 24 hours until the yeast has finished fermenting and no more alcoholic fumes are being released. Place a crumpled ball of kitchen roll in the jar so that the flies can find somewhere dry. Once this is done, shake 200-300 fruit flies onto the medium. The initial breeding stock will need to be purchased or 'borrowed'. From now on the breeding flies will come from your own production. The flies lay eggs from which maggots emerge which eat the medium provided. These maggots pupate, depending on temperature, two to three weeks later into flies. Start a new batch each week. The medium can be kept for several weeks in a refrigerator or freezer. Before using chilled or frozen medium mix a little fruit and yeast with it. If the jar becomes too humid because of the numbers of maggots place another ball of crumpled kitchen roll. If there are too many larvae for the medium supplied, place a piece of banana in the bottom of the jar. If the medium becomes too dry it can be moistened with a slice of ripe pear. The flies, when they emerge can also be kept alive longer by providing them with a piece of fruit.

Such breeding set ups can begin to smell somewhat. There are commercially available instant media available which can be reconstituted with water and that give off no unpleasant odour but these are expensive.

Feeding as prey

Feed the lean, newly emerged fruit flies for several days with the medium or some fruit before offering them to the terrarium animals. The flies can be kept in specific places in the terrarium by placing some pieces of fruit in these spots. The jar containing the remnants of the flies can also be placed in the terrarium.

Wild flying fruit flies can be attracted to a jam jar with some overripe fruit. Cover the jar quickly when there are sufficient flies in the pot and provide them as food to the terrarium animals.

MUSCA DOMESTICA, HOUSE FLY

Appearance

This active prey keeps the terrarium animals occupied and exercised.

Breeding

Cover the top of a bucket with a nylon stocking or tights. Cut an opening in the side of the bucket of about 150mm (6in) diameter and glue a 100mm (4in) length of plastic pipe to the hole with 800mm (31^1/$_2$in) of nylon stocking or tights attached. Cut off the foot of the stockings and tie the stocking to close the gap. Access to the hatchery is via the stocking which prevents flies from escaping.

Bucket as hatchery for house flies.

Put a jar containing one of the following three media in the hatchery.
1) Boil 1,300 cc water after 54 grams of agar has been added. Mix 1,300 cc water with 265 grams yeast and the same quantity of milk power. Mix the second mixture with the first before it has had time to cool. Sprinkle wood shavings or sawdust to the medium. If preferred, smaller quantities can be made.
2) Fill the jars with about 20-30mm ($^3/_4$–$1^1/_4$in) mash of water, dried dog biscuit, and bran and add some wood shavings.
3) Fill the jars with soil mixed with some wheat bran and soaked dog biscuits, together with some milk powder. The flies are attracted by the milk powder and lay their eggs in the medium.

Remove the egg-laying jar (with maggots) at least once per week. Give the flies with a bird bath with a mixture of water, milk powder, and rose-hip syrup. Place a wad of cotton wool in the bottom.

Feeding as prey
When the maggots have pupated place the jar with the pupae in the terrarium. Do not forget to supplement the breeding colony in the bucket with new stock. Increase the nutritional value and life expectancy of the flies by feeding them in the terrarium with fruit syrup and milk powder.

Flies, maggots, and pupae can be kept for two weeks in a refrigerator. After several hours they are sufficiently chilled that it takes them about two minutes before they fly once restored to room temperature.

CALLIPHORIDAE, BLOW FLIES/BOTTLE FLIES

Blow flies can be bought from angling shops as maggots. They are inexpensive but of low nutritional value. Leave the maggots to freely crawl around in soil enriched with bran and milk powder where they pupate which increases their nutritional value. This species can be stored in the refrigerator but never choose the red-coloured maggots.

The maggots or larvae of all flies are eaten by terrarium animals but the resilience of some of them

Feed flies in a terrarium with overripe fruit and milk powder.

Maggots, pupae, and blow fly.

Breeding containers for great wax moths.

make them difficult to chew sufficiently. Because of this the maggot is often swallowed alive which can cause damage to the stomach and intestines of a reptile or amphibian. The larvae pupate after six days at 25°C (77°F). Feed the flies when they emerge with a mixture of powdered milk, sugar, and yeast plus overripe fruit. Both maggots and flies can be kept in a refrigerator for several weeks.

GALLERIA MELLONELLA, GREATER WAX MOTH

These 10mm ($^3/_8$in) moths live in old honeycombs and beehives. Both the moth and its 20mm ($^3/_4$in) caterpillar are eaten readily by terrarium animals. The moths do not eat and are therefore of lower nutritional value than their caterpillars. Since the moths are active at night, they make ideal prey for nocturnal terrarium animals such as geckos and tree frogs.

Breeding
Caterpillars of the great wax moth eat their way through almost anything but they cannot escape from tin cans, hard plastic or glass. Heating to a temperature of 25-28°C (77-82.4°F) is only needed in the initial stage. A productive hatchery will keep itself warm. Use fine metal gauze of the kind used to filter petrol to provide ventilation. Each cycle takes five to eight weeks.

Fill the breeding container with a medium based on honey such as the examples which follow.

Heat 900g (1lb 15$^3/_4$oz) of honey, 880g (1lb 15oz)

Caterpillar of Galleria melonella.

Springtails.

The greater wax moth on old honeycomb.

glycerine, and 200g (7oz) honeycomb until the wax melts. Mix this with 400g (14oz) yeast and 1,360g (3lb) wholemeal flour. The bottom and sides of the breeding container can be covered with layers of corrugated cardboard on which the medium can then be applied. Cover this with further cardboard, then medium and so on.

Alternatively, mix 500g (1lb 1¹/₂oz) oatmeal, 250ml (8¹/₂ fl oz) yeast flakes, 250ml (8¹/₂ fl oz) glycerine, 150ml (5 fl oz) luke-warm water, and 100ml (3¹/₄ fl oz) rose-hip syrup.

The breeding containers can also be filled with old honeycombs from beekeepers. This option produces a greater spread in maturity of offspring. Roll corrugated cardboard up and hold together with a rubber band before placing the rolls in the breeding container. The caterpillars can then be collected easily. Terrarium enthusiasts prefer to rear the great wax moth but old honeycomb is often infected with the lesser wax moth *(Achroea grisella)* which out-competes the larger species. For this reason heat the honeycomb first or freeze it.

COLLEMBOLA, SPRINGTAILS

These small white creatures of 0.5 to 4mm are ideal for the smallest terrarium dwellers such as poison dart frogs.

Breeding

Breed springtails in small pots or jars about 150mm (6in) high with lids that close properly. Provide the pots with pieces of peat block, soil, or moisture-retaining granules and keep this continually moist. Feed with fish food (given in a small lid), slices of cucumber, carrot, or potato. Site the breeding container in a dark, moist and cool place (10-20°C/ 50-68°F). Establish sufficient jars to provide a continuous supply. The initial springtails can be found in moist soil in gardens and woodland.

ENCHYTRAEA SPECIES

The small white worms *Enchytraea albidus* and *E. bucholzi* are useful for amphibians as they live for up to two days in water, although they are rather high in fat. *E. albidus* is 20-25mm (³/₄-1in) long and *E. bucholzi* about 10mm (³/₈in).

Breeding *E. bucholzi*

Use a clean one litre plastic container and place about 2cm of moist broken peat in it. Place specimens of *E. bucholzi* on this base and cover them with a sheet of glass. Cover the container with a ventilated lid and keep at about 20°C (68°F). Feed with small chunks of fruit fly mix (see page 48) but without fruit or sugar.

To feed the worms to an aquarium, flush them off the glass plate with water.

Breeding *E. albidus*

Place a mixture of at least 100mm (4in) of moist sand, peat, and garden soil in a box. Cover the box with nylon stocking, tights, or 'petrol gauze' so that no flies can get in. Place a medium of cooked porridge adding sufficient nipagin to cover the tip of a knife and some vitamin supplement. Alternatively use a slice of white bread soaked in water. Give additional feed of vegetable matter. The food must be eaten every three days to prevent mites being attracted to remains of surplus food. Place a sheet of glass on the medium and keep the box in the dark at 10-20°C (50-68°F). Sprinkle with water to keep the soil moist from time to time. Renew the culture after eight weeks. The worms can easily be collected by the feed or in a moist place.

EARTHWORMS

Earthworms are very suitable for most amphibians, many lizards, tortoises and terrapins, and some snakes. They are also highly nutritious with a calcium-phosphorus proportion of 1:1.

Capture

Capture earthworms by sticking a fork into a moist lawn or grass pasture and move it to and fro. After a short time worms will come to the surface but do not try to catch them too quickly as they will disappear back into the soil. It is best to catch them when it is dark, after a shower of rain.

Keep any surplus in buckets of the soil from which they were captured and store this in a cool place. A lid on the bucket or lamp above it will keep the worms in the bucket.

Breeding

Worms can be bred in a box of polystyrene about 60 x 40 x 40cm (24 x 16 x 16in) with ventilation in the lid. A small light on the lid will prevent worms from escaping. Fill the box with loose clay soil. Feed twice each week at one set place with a little finely-chopped green vegetable but no leek or onion and ground dried dog biscuit. Keep the temperature in the range 15-20°C (59-68°F). The soil should not dry out but it is also essential to have adequate ventilation. Acidic soil is disastrous for earthworms. Digging can damage the small glassy eggs. The entire cycle can take about three months.

VERTEBRATE PREY

Vertebrate prey animals in principle form a complete food which does not need supplementing with vitamins and minerals.

Almost all amphibians are mad about worms.

Capturing earthworms.

Mice are ideal prey for many terrarium animals.

Rats are most nutritious when just removed from mother.

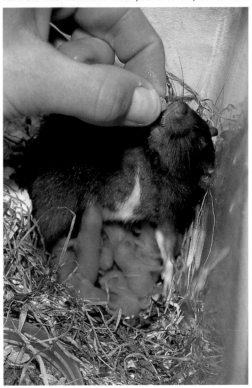

RODENTS

Mice, rats, hamsters, and gerbils are suitable to feed as prey animals. Rabbits too (though not rodents) can be fed to large snakes.

MICE

Most mice grow to 45-60 grams (1½–2oz) and live for one to three years. Mice are able to reproduce at six weeks but it is best to leave the females until three months old before breeding them. Up to ten blind pink offspring are born after 19-21 days. With a little experience it is possible after 1½-2 weeks to discern the nipples on the females. With mature specimens the distance between anus and vulva is about 5mm ($^3/_{16}$in) but 15mm ($^5/_8$in) between anus and genitals with males. The males can also be aggressive towards each other.

Breeding

Breed mice in a laboratory cage or old aquarium covered with mesh. Take care to prevent escape. About five adult mice and their young can be cared for in a cage of 43 x 17 x 15cm (17 x 6$^3/_4$ x 6in). Cover the bottom with hemp fibres or wood shavings. Peat absorbs urine vapour better than sawdust but is more dusty. Offer a cloth or shredded paper as nesting material, not hay, which contains unwanted inhabitants. Clean full cages at least once each week. Mice and rats are omnivorous. Feed mice with dried dog food or rodent food and some vegetable matter. Provide a bottle of drinking water.

Handle mice by holding them at the base of the tail and cup young mice in the hand.

RATS

Rats have much in common with mice. A fully-grown rat is 20-25cm (8-10in) and males weighs 700 gram (1lb 8$^1/_2$oz) while females are 500 gram (1lb 1$^1/_2$oz). Rats live for about up to three years. Rats too are able to reproduce at six weeks but are better bred at three months. After a pregnancy of 20-23 days 10-12 pink and blind young are born. With some experience it is possible to discern the nipples on females after two weeks. The distance between anus and vulva of females is about 15mm ($^5/_8$in) with females and about 40mm (1$^1/_2$in) with males. Males are rarely aggressive towards each other.

Breeding

Breed rats as with mice. About three adults and their offspring can be accommodated in a laboratory cage of 60 x 38 x 20cm (24 x 15 x 8in). Rats smell much less than mice. Pick rats also up by the base of the tail but set them down again quickly.

Feeding as prey

Only feed live rodents to terrarium animals if the predator is fully active but even then rodents can harm terrarium animals. For this reason it is safer to feed rodents immediately after killing them. If either vitamin D$_3$ or A is being fed to rodents, this must not be combined with the other food for the terrarium animals. Offer young mice and rats as food as soon as possible after they have been removed from their mother because the presence of their mother's milk provides valuable nutrition and it is only at this time that the calcium-phosphorus proportion is 1:1. The skeleton at this time has absorbed little in the way of minerals.

Newly born mice can live for 24-48 hours after being removed from their mother but if not eaten remove before 24 hours have elapsed, kill it and store in a freezer.

OTHER VERTEBRATES

Guppies, swordtails, and such like can be quickly raised in a hard water aquarium with plenty of current and water at 25-27°C (77-80.6°F). Feed these fish vegetable matter (frozen spinach).

Chicks

Day old chicks (deep-freeze cat food) are of low nutritional value and should only be given as part of a diet.

MIXED WILD INSECTS

Feeding a collection of flies, grasshoppers, spiders, midges, ants, bees, hover-flies, and bugs provides a healthy and varied diet.

Collection

Reinforce a butterfly net with e.g. the frame of a tennis racket. It is also possible to glue a length of air hose that has been cut open around the rim. Push or draw the net through a high dry verge or through grassland. In addition to the creatures mentioned above you will also collect grass seeds and other plant material. Place the items collected in one or more jam jars. Of course this type of food should not be collected from alongside busy

Rack with laboratory cages for rats and mice.

Only give day-old chicks as additional food. This is a Tupinambis teguixin (CITES B).

Collecting wild insects.

Insects can be captured in winter with a tree band.

Assorted wild insects are healthy food.

Slugs and snails can be found in the morning and after a shower of rain.

highways or anywhere where poisons have been sprayed, such as agricultural land and flower beds.

Feeding as prey

Remove any insects that should not be fed to the terrarium (spiders and wasps) and place the jar in the terrarium. The insects leave the jar and are eaten. Remove the jar with its plant material the following day but make sure no terrarium animals are in it. Vitamin and mineral supplements are not usually sprinkled over collections of wild animals. Such a collection can be kept in a refrigerator for about a week.

Midges can be captured from February, springtails on wood, daddy-long-legs inside houses and other buildings, spiders and grasshoppers in autumn in order to provide prey. Wasps, bees, and hover-flies can often be captured in large numbers on flowers. Once indoors in the terrarium room they will all fly to the window where they can be collected with tweezers and shared with the insect-holding terrariums for praying mantids.

Slugs and snails are ideal food for many tortoises, lizards, and amphibians. They can be most readily collected in the morning or after a shower of rain. They can be kept and bred in a moderately ventilated box at 15-20°C (59-68°F). For slugs provide 100mm (4in) of leaf mould and for snails garden soil and peat. Feed slugs with all manner of cooked vegetables and snails with stale bread. Provide shelter for them with pieces of bark. Clean out a breeding container every eight weeks.

TREE BANDS

Generally no insects are collected in winter for feeding to the terrarium yet tree bands can provide small natural food for creatures such as poison dart frogs.

Fixing a tree band.

Tubifex worms.

Capture

Tree bands consist of a strip of corrugated cardboard covered with a folded sheet of waterproof paper and then by a fairly large piece of hessian (see illustration). This band is fastened to the tree with strong steel wire with the open side of the band facing downwards. The band provides a fine warm and dry shelter for many over-wintering insects. The bands are fastened to fruit trees and oaks (which give the best results) in about July with their locations noted so that they can be collected in January.

Insects creep inside the band up to winter. The bands can be brought in at any time when the weather is dry. Pull the bands apart over a bucket, remove unwanted specimens and then feed the catch to the terrarium.

Yield

Examples of yields from one tree band are: (apple tree with normal stem) – 200 spiders, 200 millipedes, 100 beetles, and 35 bugs *(Orius* sp.); (standard-grown apple) – 11 moths, 24 beetles, 1 bug, 36 spiders, and no millipedes.

Each band collects countless small creatures of less than 5mm ($^3/_{16}$in).

PLANKTON

Plankton includes all manner of microscopic and extremely small water organisms such as water fleas, red and white midge larvae, and tubifex worms.

This provides a good source of food for aquatic living amphibians such as terrapins and other freshwater turtles. The midges which emerge from the larvae are eaten by insectivorous animals but bear in mind that the infamous midges which sting emerge from the black larvae.

Tadpoles are excellent food for banded snakes but remember that frogs, toads, their spawn and tadpoles are protected in The United Kingdom and a number of other countries.

Capture, buying, and storing

Water fleas *(Daphnia)*, single-eye shrimps *(Cyclops)*, black and white midge larvae can be found in ditches and ponds. Sweep a fine net gently in a figure of eight through the water. Make sure that the bottom is not disturbed to prevent all the muck being caught instead of plankton. Black midge larvae hang from the surface and quickly shoot to the bottom when disturbed.

Pour the catch through a sieve when you get home and remove any large predatory specimens such as dragonfly larvae and beetles. Leave the filter for up to an hour to prevent any specimens being lost in the filter. A surplus of water fleas can be stored in trays or containers with a large surface area with gentle oxygenation by means of an air pump. Place in partial sun at a maximum temperature of 25°C (77°F). Feed them with a little milk, yeast, fish meal, or powdered egg.

Red midge larvae and tubifex worms (thin red worms) are found in polluted sediments and these can be bought cheaply from aquarium shops. Do not feed these organisms more frequently to your own specimens than twice per week. Red midge larvae must not be brownish red, dried out and lifeless. Keep them in moist newspaper in a refrigerator. Tubifex worms showing greyish-white patches in the mass are of doubtful to poor quality. Place tubifex worms in a shallow tray with slowly running water and keep at 10-20°C (50-68°F). Feed them with a slice of cooked potato or other organic material. Tubifex worms can be stored in a net hung in the cistern of the WC or in a shallow tray of water in a refrigerator.

Red midge larvae.

Brine shrimps *(Artemia salina)* are small crustaceans which can be fed in place of water fleas (e.g. in winter). They are purchased as eggs from aquarium shops. Oxygenate water to which 20-25 grams (approx. ³/₄oz) of salt is added per litre and sprinkle a few eggs into it. The larvae or nauplii emerge from the eggs in 24-48 hours. If the air supply is turned off they will sink to the bottom from where they can be siphoned off. The indigestible egg cases float. The shrimps can be fed with a little yeast or powdered nettle.

Meat

Meat and vertebrate animals are readily eaten by many terrarium animals (lizards, tortoises, and amphibians). An excess of animal foodstuffs though can create kidney and other problems.
Canned cat and dog food often contains bonemeal and is a relatively complete food in terms of vitamins and minerals. It needs to contain no colourings and be low in fat content. There is usually some 0.2-0.3% calcium and slightly less phosphorus in these foods and often high levels of vitamin A (2,500-17,000 IU/kg) and fairly substantial vitamin D₃ (100-400 IE/kg). Enhance canned pet food with a little calcium lactate to achieve the correct ratio of calcium to phosphorus but do not use vitamin and mineral supplements to avoid an overdose of vitamins A and D. Do not allow canned pet food to form more than fifteen per cent of the food given to your animals. The same is true of soaked dried cat food. Because this does not contain the 80% moisture of canned food the proportion of calcium is about 1% and slightly less for phosphorus. Ox heart contains one hundred times more phosphorus than calcium, with only 2mg calcium per 100g (3¹/₂oz) of meat. Heart also contains virtually no fibre but very high levels of protein. For these reasons it is best not fed to terrarium animals. Liver has similar problems and also contains high levels of waste matter.
If raw chicken is fed there is a chance of infection with *Salmonella entiritidis*, even if the poultry has been frozen.
Infertile eggs contain ovidin which depletes the body of biotin (vitamin B complex, see page 41).

Vegetable food

Wash all green vegetables and fruit well, slice it finely, and mix together. Feed the mixture in a dish and if necessary place this on some linoleum if a lot of soil still gets taken in with the food.

When feeding vegetable matter such as fruit and vegetables bear the following points in mind.
– The proportion of calcium to phosphorus (see tables). The starting point is 1.5 times more calcium (Ca) than phosphorus (P). Poor ratios can be improved with multivitamin and mineral supplements. The general values in the table (based on

Terrapins (and many lizards) are keen on canned cat food.

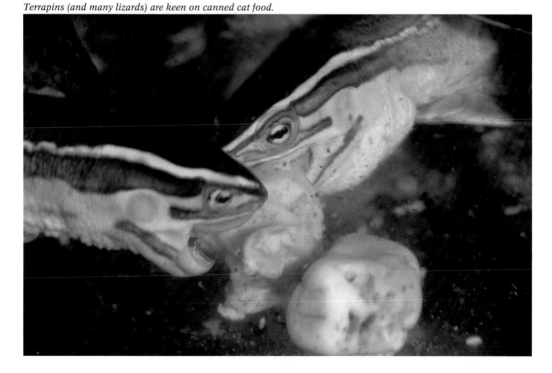

Iguana varia) may vary in other tables due to different analysis methods. The Ca:P ratio of green cabbage is shown for example as 2.9-7.5:1. In addition there are many different species of vegetables and fruit, each with a different value.

- The fibre content (see tables). Animals always need ample fibre for good digestion.
- The protein content. For animals that mainly eat vegetable matter this needs to be high and especially so for young animals and breeding females (see tables). Tofu can also be provided as a high protein food.
- Vitamins. All fruit contains vitamin C, carrots contain vitamin A, and beanshoots contain vitamin B.
- Variety. Some plants contain harmful substances (see the following remarks). By providing a wide variety animals naturally compensate overdoses. Feed as varied a diet as possible with introduction of new fruits, vegetables, or meadow plants.
- Oxalic acid depletes the provision of calcium for bone development. It can also cause blood circulation problems. Rhubarb, spinach, parsley, purslane, carrots, and broccoli are high in oxalic acid.

Many flowers can be fed but do not pick them alongside highways.

- Nitrate reduces the blood's capacity to absorb oxygen which can cause cramp. Comfrey and spinach contain concentrations that are too high.
- Tannin is dangerous so never feed peas or broad beans because of their high levels of tannin or avocados, which are also toxic.
- Cyanide can cause throat problems for tortoises for instance so limit the amount of cabbage.
- Never collect food from alongside busy highways or where spraying may have taken place.

TABLE

The table gives the values of various fresh raw vegetables and fruit

Vegetables	Ca mg/100g	P mg/100g	Cc:P	Fibre g/100g	Protein g/100g	Remarks
Bean shoots	13	54	0.2:1	1.8	3.0	
Broccoli	48	66	0.7:1	3.0	3.0	high in oxalic acid
Brussels sprouts	42	69	0.6:1	4.2	3.4	
Carrots	27	44	0.6:1	3.0	1.0	high in vitamin A and oxalic acid
Cauliflower	22	44	0.5:1	2.5	2.0	
Celery	40	25	1.6:1	1.7	0.8	
Chicory	19	26	0.7:1	3.1	0.9	
Chinese cabbage	105	37	2.8:1	1.0	1.5	++
Courgette	15	32	0.5:1	1.2	1.2	
Dandelion leaf	187	66	2.8:1	3.5	2.7	++
Endive	52	28	1.9:1	3.1	1.3	
Kale	135	56	2.4:1	2.0	3.3	++
Leek	59	35	1.7:1	1.8	1.5	
Lettuce, Cos	68	25	2.7:1	1.9	1.3	
Lettuce, Iceberg	19	20	1:1	1.4	1.0	
Lettuce, Webbs	32	23	1.4:1	1.0	1.3	
Oxheart cabbage	47	23	2.0:1	2.3	1.4	
Paksoi	105	37	2.8:1	1.0	1.5	++
Parsley	138	58	2.4:1	3.3	3.0	high in oxalic acid

Vegetables (continued)	Ca mg/100g	P mg/100g	Cc:P	Fibre g/100g	Protein g/100g	Remarks
Potato, peeled	7	46	0.2:1	1.6	2.1	
Red cabbage	51	42	1.2:1	2.0	1.4	
Rhubarb	86	14	6.1:1	1.8	0.9	
Savoy cabbage	35	42	0.8:1	3.1	2.0	
Spinach	99	49	2.0:1	2.7	2.9	high in oxalic acid
Turnip tops	190	42	4.5:1	2.4	1.5	++

Fruit	Ca mg/100g	P mg/100g	Cc:P	Fibre g/100g	Protein g/100g	Remarks
Potato	14	19	0.7:1	2.3	0.6	
Apple, unpeeled	7	7	1.0:1	2.7	0.2	
Aubergine	7	22	0.3:1	2.5	1.0	
Banana	6	20	0.3:1	2.4	1.0	
Fig cactus	56	24	2.3:1	3.6	0.7	
Dates, dried	32	40	0.8:1	7.5	1.9	
Grapes	11	13	0.9:1	1.0	0.7	
Peas	25	108	0.2:1	5.1	5.4	too much tannin
Kiwi	26	40	0.7:1	3.4	1.0	
Coconut	14	113	0.1:1	9.0	3.3	
Cucumber	14	20	0.7:1	0.8	0.7	
Maize	2	89	0.02:1	2.7	3.2	
Mandarin	14	10	1.4:1	2.3	0.6	
Mango	10	11	0.9:1	1.8	0.6	
Papaya	24	5	4.8:1	1.8	0.6	
Paprika	9	19	0.5:1	1.8	0.9	
Parsnip	36	71	0.5:1	4.9	1.2	++
Pear, unpeeled	11	11	1.0:1	2.4	0.4	
Peach	5	12	0.4:1	2.0	0.7	
Plumbs	4	10	0.4:1	1.5	0.8	
French beans	37	38	1.0:1	3.4	1.8	
Tomatoes	5	24	0.2:1	1.1	0.9	
Broad bean	22	95	0.2:1	4.2.1	5.6	too much tannin
Figs	35	14	2.5:1	3.3	0.8	
Water melons	8	9	0.9:1	0.5	0.6	

In addition to the vegetables and fruit mentioned in the above tables, alfalfa, blackberries, grape leaves, chamomile, raspberries, morning glory, shepherd's purse (minor and major), cherries, clover (leaves and flowers), kohlrabi (leaf and grated bulb), rape (especially the flowers), herbs, nasturtiums (flowers), dandelions (leaf and flowers but not stem), pumpkin, violets, watercress, and plantain can all be given as food.

Allow beans, lentils (orange), sunflower seeds, and other seeds germinate or soak them before feeding. Newly sprouting lentils, lucerne (alfalfa), rape seed, radish, wheat (and similar grain), and sunflower are first class foods.

Arthropoda, the group of arthropods: segmented bodies and jointed limbs

The group or phyllum, to use the scientific classification, of Arthropoda consists of about three-quarters (975,000) of all known species of animals and represents a tremendous diversity of both form and colour. This group of invertebrate creatures includes the sub-phylla Chelicerata (with first pair of feeding structures known as chelicerae from which the group name is derived) which includes horseshoe crabs, scorpions, spiders, and mites; Crustacea, including shrimps, lobsters, crabs, water fleas, and wood lice; and Uniramia, comprising centipedes, millipedes, and insects.

Praying mantis in Southern Cameroon.

APPEARANCE

All arthropods have segmented bodies and jointed legs in pairs with an external exoskeleton instead of the internal bone structure of vertebrate animals. The exoskeleton is produced from protein and chitin to form a strong but slightly flexible 'skin' that is toughened in places by phenol to form sclerotin, containing minerals such as calcium. The hardened plates are joined together by flexible cuticular membranes. The 'armour plating' serves as protection, is waterproof, and can grow to provide all manner of useful tools. Arthropods need to lose their hard outer shells from time to time in order to grow. They crawl from their old shell to reveal a new one already in place. Air is pumped into the body in order to expand it and stretch the new skin. The skin then dries and hardens with the muscles fastening themselves to the new plates. While this process is being completed, the creatures are extremely vulnerable.

Arthropods have either simple or compound eyes (the latter consisting of a number of elements or facets). The other senses are stimulated through feelers, hairs, and ears) to receive smell, taste, and sound information. The nervous system runs through these animals like a rope ladder with co-ordination of the central nervous system in the head.

Blood flows freely throughout the body and is kept circulating by a dorsal heart.

REGENERATION

The shedding of the outer exoskeleton provides arthropods with the opportunity to replace lost limbs after about three moults. The legs often have weak spots but if a leg breaks off the wound seals itself rapidly so that little bodily fluid is lost.

COLLECTING SKINS OR DEAD SPECIMENS

The outer skin or shell contains all the external characteristics of its previous occupant. The skins remain flexible for one to two days after being shed and can be set into a good shape by use of pins. Within a week the old exoskeleton has dried and can be kept for ever.

Dead arthropods can be kept in the same way.

The exoskeleton of a praying mantis.

Allow those with hard outer shells (e.g. beetles) to dry naturally. Spray others with 70 to 100 per cent alcohol and allow them to dry. Large lightly armoured animals or parts of them such as the rear body of a tarantula are best emptied out. Fill the cavity with some cotton wool or urethane foam.

DISTRIBUTION

Arthropods are to be found over almost the entire earth, with the greatest variety in the tropics.

DISEASES

Arthropods can suffer infections from viruses, bacteria, and moulds. These are normally ingested with their food. There is often no external sign of disease so that the animals dies inexplicably. For this reason maintain the highest standards of hygiene possible, washing vegetable matter with water. Specimens captured wild can suffer from internal parasites such as the larvae of the ichneumon fly. Nothing can be done to treat this with the animals often dying within a few weeks. Worms too can cause death.

Insects can be infected with larvae from the Phoridae family. The maggots eventually emerge from the host insect.

Take care with insecticides and other toxic substances which are often to be found on newly purchased house plants, in fresh compost, and in treatments for blood mites for reptiles, in cork, and in plants gathered from beside highways and agricultural land.

Let dead arthropods like this praying mantis dry out in the correct position.

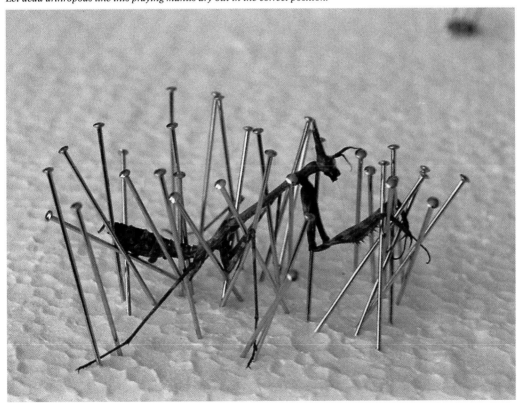

Female Heteropteryx dilatata *shedding her skin.*

The class Insecta (Hexapoda) or insects

Insects can be the cause of much nuisance. Think of wasps, midges, and insects that plague agriculture. Because of this many people are unaware of the beauty, peculiarities, and novelty of this group of creatures.

APPEARANCE

The diversity between this largest of all classes of creatures is enormous. At present zoologists recognize 26 different orders with about 850,000 of the millions of species being codified and described. Man only knows much about a few thousands of these species with little more being known about the rest beyond their scientific name. An insect's body consists of three parts: the head, the chest or thorax, and rear body or abdomen. The appendages that form the mouth are the mandibles, labium and maxillae. The labium or lower lip has feelers on it. The maxillae are often very hard through sclerotization and grind or tear the food and act as knives. The upper jaw (mandibels) help to push the food into the mouth. With butterflies and moths the mandibles have evolved into a tube and with flies to a tongue that can lap up moisture. The upper lip is the labrum. The antennae on the head respond to both smell and touch and take all manner of forms, including spring-like. Insects have two compound eyes which consist of thousands of smaller eyelets and/or several simple eyes (ocelli). Praying mantises and related animals also possess three ocular cells on the head.

The thorax comprises three segments, the prothorax immediately behind the head, the mesothorax, and finally the metathorax. Each segment of the thorax bears one pair of legs and the rear two segments generally carry two pairs of wings with most adult insects. The thorax is mainly filled with muscle.

The legs are in three segments (but five recognisable parts). From the body the first part is the coxa or hip (which is usually short), then a very short trochanter or thigh joint, followed by an elongated femur or thigh, a long tibia or shin, and tarsus or foot. The flexible foot consists of one to five articles, a pair of claws with sucker pads between them to grip. This end of the foot is known as the pretar-

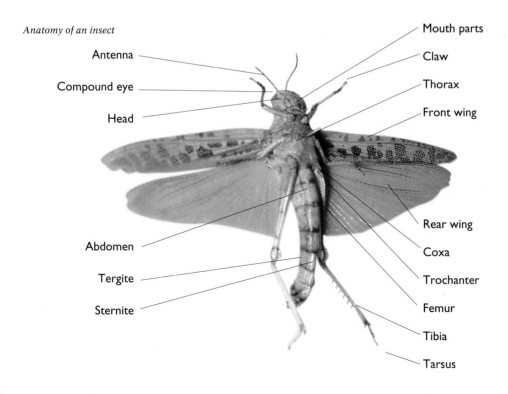

Anatomy of an insect

Antenna
Compound eye
Head
Abdomen
Tergite
Sternite

Mouth parts
Claw
Thorax
Front wing
Rear wing
Coxa
Trochanter
Femur
Tibia
Tarsus

sus. Some insects develop specialized legs for jumping, digging, swimming, catching, or holding their prey. Insects have either no wings or two pairs. If there are wings then the large filmy rear wings are often hidden beneath the sturdy front wings. In addition to flying, wings are used to produce sound, ward off enemies (warning colours), for camouflage, and for protecting the body. Insects wings are not extended limbs which have developed as with birds but entirely new appendages. The abdomen contains the organs responsible for digestion of food, reproduction, and breathing. Insects do not have lungs and breathe via a system of tubes or tracheae. The breathing apertures or stigmata are often in the sides of the abdomen. The stigmata are closed by valves.

REPRODUCTION

Most insect reproduction is by sexual means but populations of some species produce young from eggs which have not been fertilized, known as parthenogenisis.

Most insects lay eggs but a few produce young which hatch at time of birth. Eggs have a shell of chitin and are adapted in both shape and colour to the surroundings in which they are laid. With winged insect orders the offspring either closely resemble the adults or are totally different. Young that resemble the adults are known as nymphs which are hemimetabolous, meaning they undergo only a partial metamorphosis. After shedding their skin several times they are adult and do not shed their skin again. The wings unfurl at the time of the final shedding, as is the case with grasshoppers and stick insects. The other category of insects produce larvae which eventually pupate after several moults. The adult insect emerges from pupation after a total metamorphosis, as occurs with butterflies and beetles.

HANDLING

The defence mechanisms of insects and method of handling them is given per insect order. It is important to be aware that humans can be allergic to

Stick insects do not undergo full metamorphosis. The wings can be seen with this nymph.

The larvae of insects that fully metamorphose first pupate before emerging as adults.

virtually every insect with symptoms such as hay fever resulting.

The order Phasmida, stick insects

The five families and 16 sub-families of stick insects and Phyllidae family of leaf insects together form the order Phasmida. The name is derived from the Latin 'phasma' meaning 'phantom' or 'apparition'. These are almost exclusively nocturnal animals that rely by day on camouflage to protect them as they remain motionless.

Many people only know the one species of these insects, *Carausius morosus,* sometimes known as Indian stick insect. Some 2,600 species have been described world-wide and it is estimated there are about 4,000 species in all. About 100 species are kept in Europe and enthusiasts collect new species each year in the tropics and attempt to breed them in captivity.

Appearance

Stick insects mainly look like a branch or twig with fairly robust bodies mimicking the look of bark while leaf insects resemble a leaf. This camouflage is often reinforced by an unusual manner of movement so that the insect appears to be moving in the wind.

Carausius morosus, *best known stick insect.*

The two segments of the thorax at the rear are extremely long with stick insects. Each pair of legs is developed to move together. The abdomen consists of ten segments with the first of these often fused with the rear thorax segment.

The majority of these insects have wings, some species have fully-developed wings on both males and females, while others see only rudimentary wings on females with fully-developed wings on males. There are also species with no wings at all.

Distribution

Phasmida are distributed throughout the tropical and sub-tropical regions of the world with the greatest variety of species in South-East Asia and South America. Mainly reed-like 'blades of grass' are found in Africa, where the species predominantly eat grass. European species are limited mainly to Southern Europe where species of the genera *Bacillus, Leptynia,* and *Clonopsis* are found. The last of these is found as far north as Brittany.

Accommodation

An insectarium for stick insects needs to be at least three times taller than the longest insect to allow for shedding of skin. Tall enclosures also reduce the frequency at which the specimens have to be fed because larger branches of food plants can be provided with many more leaves.

Insectariums to consider are:
– an upright aquarium with either the top or part of a side covered with mesh, depending on the amount of ventilation required;
– a standard terrarium with five sides of glass and a sixth of part glass and part perforated aluminium;
– all manner of plastic pots, and containers with nylon stocking covers;
– mesh cages, which provide plenty of ventilation.

Ensure a daytime temperature of 21-28°C (69.8-82.4°F) by means of a small tungsten filament lamp. Switch this off at night to maintain 17-22°C (62.6-71.6°F). Stick insects eat more when the temperature is higher and the life cycle is completed more rapidly. These insects will be too warm if placed in the full sun or with heating. Many of these insects

Rumulus sp. 'grass stem' in Chad.

An insectarium with stick insects.

like to drink and a high humidity eases the shedding of their skin. Spray with a plant sprayer once each day, preferably with rainwater and in the evening, especially with young specimens. If water droplets are too large to form puddles small nymphs can become stuck and drown. The water must evaporate within a few hours to prevent illness and infections from moulds. Ensure ventilation therefore with at least one side that allows fresh air in but draughts can cause problems for moulting. Place stems of the food plants in a jar of water but fill the jar with aquarium filter pads so that the insects will not drown. You can add one tablespoon of sugar per litre of water so that the plant stems last longer and replace the food plants immediately when they have been eaten or are wilting.

For those species which lay their eggs in moist soil (such as species of *Aretaon, Eurycantha, Haaniella,* and *Heteropteryx*) provide at least 50mm (2in) of moist old compost or cactus compost mixed with sand. The eggs of most other species are sensitive for mould and need to be laid on dry ground, although this should be sprayed from time to time. Too much in the way of decoration causes a problem with the weekly replacement of the food plant material but a rear cork wall does provide additional climbing opportunities. If you observe a number of insects with damaged legs this is a sign that the insectarium is too full.

Moulting

When a stick insect remains for some time in the same place and makes curling motions, it will shortly shed its skin. The skin splits immediately behind the head and the neck or prothorax is pushed outwards. The head and antennae follow followed by the rest of the thorax and then the abdomen drops down from the skin.

The tip of the abdomen remains in the old skin and the legs still have be removed it. Finally the insect dries for several hours before it will move again. Before moving, the insect will often eat its old skin. Females shed skins about six times but males normally only five.

A number of things can go wrong during the process.

1. The place in which the insect is housed is too moist so that the old skin is too weak or the place in which the insect hangs itself up is too slippery. This causes the shedding insect to fall to the ground where the shedding cannot proceed as normal. If discovered soon enough the insect can be attached by its claws to a branch with a clothes peg. If too late feed the specimen to an insectivorous animal such as a tarantula, praying mantis, or lizard, or kill it by freezing.

2. Alternatively the place is too dry and the new skin starts to dry before the insects has managed to fully separate itself from the old one. It is usually impossible to remove the old skin for the animal and despatching the insect is the best solution. Prevent this disaster by spraying the terrarium immediately before moulting.

3. There is an obstruction because the terrarium is too full or too low, or because the stick insect has chosen a bad place. The animal dries out in the wrong position and usually cannot be saved. If the deformation is not too serious (e.g. just one unusable leg) then this can be rectified at the next shedding. Lost limbs are fully regenerated after the third moult.

4. The terrarium is too full so that the stick insect is disturbed by others while shedding its skin. This can also lead to the insect falling to the ground (see 1 above) or being injured. Spraying with water while shedding can also prove a fatal disturbance.

Stick insects of different species which require the same conditions of care can be housed together. Big heavy types with sharp 'weapons' can injure more vulnerable species. Leaf insects in particular are often eaten by other species within the order Phasmida.

Millipedes, wood lice, grasshoppers, and newly-emerged praying mantises can be combined with stick insects. Bear in mind that praying mantises will prey on animals up to twice their own size.

Bramble leaves can be picked in winter too. Cut away the brown edges.

Three types of evergreen oak.

Feeding

Stick insects eat fresh leaves. Some species only eat one type of plant, but others have a wider choice.

Most species will eat bramble leaves *(Rubus* sp.) and the green leaves of these plants can be found in hedges and woods in winter, even under snow. Any brown edges to the leaves will not be eaten by the insects and must be cut away. The edges of other types of leaves which are too hard for small nymphs (e.g. *Rhododendron)* can be cut away or eaten by larger stick insects. With *Rhododendron* the sticky shoots and flower buds should be removed. Certain species will only eat if there is movement of the air, which can be created by a small fan.

There can be problems with bramble leaves in spring, when the old leaves have died off and the new foliage is too high in toxins. Some species will accept evergreen oak, *Rhododendron*, ivy, dwarf medlar *(Cotoneaster)*, and *Viburnum rhytido-phyllum*, all of which are evergreens that can usually be found in parks. Other alternative food plants are indicated with the species descriptions. The best plant is given first with the others only being eaten by semi-mature or adult insects.

Botanical names of less well known plants are: firethorn *(Pyracantha)*, croton *(Codiaeum variegatum)*, cherry laurel *(Prunus laurocerasus)*, and bay laurel *(Laurus)*.

This is not a complete list of food plants. Other plants can be tried with each species that are eaten by related species.

Do not collect food plants close to busy highways, industrial areas, and agricultural land (where agricultural chemicals are used). Remove the lowest thorns, if there are any, with a knife and trim the stems, also removing the lower leaves which will decay in water. Check carefully for spiders and rinse away any dirt.

Sex determination

With populations resulting from sexual reproduction the males are always smaller and thinner than the females. With winged species the males often have longer wings. Females are mainly unable to fly.

Males have a reproductive opening on one of the two rearmost segments of the abdomen inside which is the aedeagus or ventral penis. This often looks like a swelling.

The male also has two claspers which precisely fit apertures in the female's abdomen. Claspers will only fit females of the same species to hold her firmly during copulation thereby preventing cross breeding.

The ovipositor is often already visible with female nymphs on the underside of the last three segments of her abdomen. Some species also produce gynandromorphs which are part male and part female.

Mating and parthenogenisis

TThe insects are sexually mature about two weeks after the final moult. During mating the male rides on the female, twisting his rear body around her to make contact with the underside of her body in order to pass spermatophore to the female. This is often still visible on the female after paring. Empty

Rear ends of Aplopus sp. *during mating. Note the female's ovipositor.*

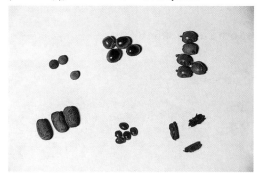

Eggs of Lopaphus caesius *(top left),* Eurycantha calcarata *(bottom left),* Phobaeticus serratipes, Baculum thaii *(bottom left), and two undetermined species.*

spermatophores can sometimes be seen on the ground after mating. Mating can last from hours to days. The female can store sperm so that she can fertilize eggs for several months after mating.

Most species can reproduce by parthenogenisis if there are no males with offspring being produced from unfertilized eggs, but only females. Incubation is generally longer and the survival rate somewhat lower than with fertilized eggs. With some species of *Carausius* and *Siploidea* there are no disadvantages of parthenogenic reproduction.

The eggs of *Carausius morosus* (and others) that reproduce parthenogenically can produce high proportions of 'males' with high temperatures (28-30°C/82.4-86°F) but these are in reality females with male characteristics. These specimens even attempt to mate but no fertilization occurs. This strange occurrence is known as gynandromorphism.

Egg laying

Two to four weeks after the final moult a female, having eaten well and filled out, starts to lay eggs. Depending on the species, this usually varies from three to fifteen each night but can be one per week. Again depending on the species, females lay between fifty and a thousand eggs. The hard-coated eggs are often camouflaged so that they resemble plant seeds or excreta. Sperm enters the egg through the micropyle, a tiny opening through the layers of the egg's shell. One or more of these can be seen as a drip-shaped, oval, or elongated patch. The opening by which the nymph emerged is known as the operculum.

- Most species allow the egg to fall (such as *Carausius morosus*) or they flick it away with the rear of their body (such as *Exatosoma tiaratum*). The egg covering of these species sometimes has a lid or capitulum. This attracts ants which drag the tasty disc to their nest, thereby helping to distribute the eggs.

– Species in particular from colder climates insert their eggs into the ground (such as *Eurycantha* and *Heteroopteryx*).
– Some species attach their eggs to leaves, back walls, and sometimes even to other stick insects (such as *Sipyloidea sipylus)*.

Leave the eggs in the terrarium or place them at 22-24°C (71.6-75.2°F) in a mixture of one part sand to three parts old compost or cactus compost with the same moisture level as fresh compost. Place eggs which are inserted into the ground in little wells in the mixture with their covering just above the ground. Spray at least once per week. Eggs will suffer from mould in soil that is too moist. Springtails (Collembola) help to prevent mould.

The nymphs emerge, depending on the species and environmental factors, usually after two to twelve months. Check for emergence regularly and make sure there is food for the nymphs. It is quite normal for not all the eggs to succeed in hatching.

At a temperature of 17-20°C (62.6-68°F) the European species in particular undergo a temporary cessation in development (diapause) lasting from three months to a year.

Rearing

It is fascinating to see how a relatively large nymph drags itself out of a quite small egg. After emergence part of the shell may remain stuck to a leg of the delicate nymph but do not go to its aid for the shell will fall off naturally. The small creatures often run around a lot in the first few days.

Spray a fine mist each evening. Young stick insects drink quite a but make sure they don't get stuck to the glass by water droplets.

Clip off the hard edges of leaves if the nymphs cannot break them off for themselves (e.g. *Rhaphiderus scabrosus* on *Rhododendron)*. If necessary place the nymphs with other stick insects that can gnaw away the hard edges of leaves. Stick insects do not undergo a full metamorphosis. The nymphs become fully mature after usually five sheddings for males and six for females, normally achieved in a period of three to six months. The adult insects survive for between three months and three years.

Stick insects defend themselves in the following ways.
– Camouflage – (merging with the background and becoming part of it) plus a nocturnal life.
– Mimicry – the nymphs of *Extatosoma tiaratum* resemble an Australian species of ant that bites, and the adult *Eurycantha* sp. have the appearance of a scorpion.
– Playing dead – when disturbed many species fall into a cataleptic trance in which they appear to be dead.

An egg about to be flicked away by the abdomen of Extatosoma tiaratum.

A female Eurycantha calcarata *inserts her eggs in the ground.*

Eggs of Sipyloidea sipylus *attached to a bramble leaf.*

An Extatosoma tiaratum *nymph emerges from its egg.*

An Extatosoma *sp. nymph resembles a biting species of Australian ant.*

Female Acrophylla titan.

Heteropteryx dilatata *in threatening stance. She rasps her wings to produce sound.*

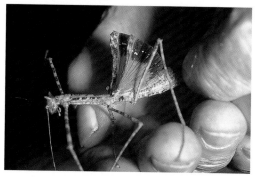

Orixines macklottii *tries to frighten predators with bright colours when disturbed.*

- Attack – *Eurycantha* and *Heteropteryx* species in particular have spikes on their hind legs with which they can squeeze fingers in a pincers grip.
- Warning colours – many species display their brightly coloured rear wings when disturbed, such as *Orxines, Aplopus,* and *Creoxylus.*
- Stridulation – a female *Heteropteryx dilatata* makes a hissing sound by rasping her wings.
- Chemical deterrent – some stick insects can eject acid from their neck. *Anisomorpha buprestoi-* des is the best known example. The acid taste foul, stinks, irritates the mucous membranes, and makes breathing difficult. It causes inflammation of open wounds. Protect the eyes from such attacks. *Eurycantha, Orxines,* and *Sipyloidea* eject a chemical deterrent when confronted with danger.
- Escape – some species can move rapidly.
- Self-mutilation (autotomy) – species such as *Phoebaeticus serratipes,* and species of *Acrophylla, Siploidea,* and *Orxines* quickly shed a leg when handled or captured.

Handling
Either let a stick insect walk onto you hand or pick them up by means of a jar. If required hold them carefully but never pulled them away abruptly. They can be picked up by normal forceps but not with ultra lightweight ones. Those with spins should be held firmly between the centre and back legs. It is not essential to wear gloves for handling the 'acid' spurters but certainly best to protect the eyes. Nymphs can be picked up with either a pencil or lightweight forceps (tweezers).

ACROPHYLLA SPECIES

Appearance
Acrophylla wuelfingi females are up to 180mm (7in) long and brown or brown-green. Her body is 10mm ($^3/_8$in) thick and there is a white patch on her front wings. The darker rear wings have transparent brown banding. The wings cover about three-quarters of her body and there is a long ovipositor. Both the thorax and legs are covered with spiky protruberances like thorns. The much more slender males are 110-130mm ($4^1/_4$-$5^1/_8$in) and have similar colouring. The males can flutter about. Both genders have small rear feelers or cerci.
Acrophylla titan has the same appearance as *A. wuelfingi* but the female is 230mm (9in), the males 130mm ($5^1/_8$in). The females have a short ovipositor and both genders have long cerci.
Phasma gigas resembles the previous species. The females become about 200 mm (8in) with bodies

15mm (⁵/₈in) wide. The female has a flap on the back of the sixth segment and very spiky mesonotum. The red-orange rear wings have many black stripes. The wings cover half of the abdomen. Both males and females have large, flap-like rear feelers that are larger than *Acrophylla wuelfingi*, and the female has no ovipositor. The smaller, more slender male can fly.

Distribution
The *Acrophylla* species live in arid *Eucalyptus* forests in Queensland, Australia. *P. gigas* comes from Papua New Guinea.

Food
Leaves of bramble, *Eucalyptus* sp., and hazel. *P. gigas* also eats evergreen oak.

Reproduction
The 4mm (⁵/₃₂in) eggs of *Acrophylla* species are flicked away by the abdomen. The eggs hatch after 6-12 months. The 20mm (³/₄in) nymphs are green. The males alone have a white stripe on their backs. Keep both *Acrophylla* species fairly warm and dry and keep all three species in a spacious insectarium. *Phasma gigas* eggs are large, black, and spherical. The incubation period is relatively long. Keep this species at 25-28°C (77-82.4°F) and in a reasonably high relative humidity.

ANISOMORPHA BUPRESTOIDES

Appearance
Females are about 70mm (2³/₄in), the males 40-50mm (1⁹/₁₆-2in). Both sexes are shiny brown-black with yellow-brown stripes and wingless. When threatened a stinking, tissue irritating, and breathtaking liquid is ejected up to 50cm (20in) from a gland in the neck. This can even cause temporary blindness. Adult males pair with one female and remain with her for the rest of their life, in other words they are monogamous.

Distribution
This species is fairly diurnally (daytime) active among dry shrubs in the USA (Florida).

Food
Rhododendron leaves.

Reproduction
The 4mm (⁵/₃₂in) eggs resemble the excreta of this

Female Anisomorpha monstrosa.

stick insect. The female lays up to ten eggs in holes she digs herself. The 15mm (⁵/₈in) young emerge after 3 months with the nymphs resembling the adults. This species does not tolerate long periods of moisture well so keep them dry, spraying the soil only seldom if at all or never. Do not combine this species with another because their chemical deterrent is also harmful for other stick insects.

ANISOMORPHA MONSTROSA

Appearance
Females grow to 70mm (2³/₄in), the males 40mm (1⁹/₁₆in). Both sexes are shiny black with reddish-brown markings and are wingless.

Distribution
Belize.

Food
Privet leaves.

Reproduction
Nymphs of 15mm (⁵/₈in) long emerge after 3-4 months from the 4mm (⁵/₃₂in) eggs. Keep this species fairly dry but spray a little water on the soil at the bottom each evening.

Male of Aplopus *species display their rear wings when threatened.*

Mating Anisomorpha bupresoides.

Aplopus *species during mating.*

A *pair of* Aretaon asperrimus.

APLOPUS SPECIES

Appearance
At present only two of the nineteen *Aplopus* species have been bred in Europe. Both species resemble each other closely. The females are green or brown, and 120-170mm (4³/₄-6³/₄in) long, with 15mm (⁵/₈in) long wings. The females have an ovipositor at the rear of their body. The wings of the 95mm (3³/₄in) long male cover about two-thirds of his abdomen. When threatened he unfolds his wings so that the burgundy colouring of the rear wings can be seen. His body is green or brown, the legs always green. Both sexes have six spiky protruberances on the thorax and two on their heads.

Distribution
Trees and shrubs in the Dominican Republic.

Food
Leaves of rose, bramble, *Eucalyptus* sp., may, oak, raspberry, and dwarf medlar *(Cotoneaster).*

Reproduction
One species lays large eggs with a substance to attract ants, the other eggs of 4 x 2mm (⁵/₃₂ x ¹/₁₆in) without the substance. The eggs hatch in 4-6 months producing female nymphs of 26mm (1in) and male ones of 22mm (⁷/₈in). Keep these species fairly moist.

ARETAON ASPERRIMUS

Appearance
The 80-90mm (3¹/₈-3¹/₂in) long females are brown with a lighter underside and they have an ovipositor at the rear. The thinner males grow up to 60mm (2³/₈in) and are dark brown with light lateral stripes on the back and sides. Both sexes have no wings. The males in particular have spiky protruberances.

Distribution
Sabah, Borneo.

Food
Leaves of bramble, oak, hazel, firethorn *(Pyracantha)*, rose, raspberry, dwarf medlar *(Cotoneaster)*, beech.

Reproduction
The females insert 5mm (³/₁₆in) thick eggs into the soil. The 15mm (⁵/₈in) nymphs emerge after 2-6 months. Keep this species moist by spraying each day.

BACILLUS ROSSIUS

Appearance
Females are 65-105mm (2⁹/₁₆-4¹/₈in) long. The bottom of the femurs are red on the inside and black on the outside. Males are 50-80mm (2-3¹/₈in) long. Both sexes are wingless and either brown or green. The antennae consist of 20-30 segments (only 12-15 with *Clonopsis gallica).*

Distribution
Bacillus rossius lives in Southern Europe and North Africa. There are at least nine species of *Bacillus* in this region.

Food
Leaves of bramble, rose, plum, apple, dwarf medlar, may, pear, bilberry, *Eucalyptus*, and broom.

Reproduction
Some populations reproduce sexually, others parthenogenically. The blue eggs are 2.4mm (³/₆₄in) in diameter and spherical. Fertilized eggs emerge after 2–3 months at 25°C (77°F) and a high humidity. Others emerge after 3–9 months. The nymphs are 10mm (³/₈in) long and green with brown antennae. Keep at 20-22°C (68-71.6°F) and at about 70% humidity but never spray the insects themselves.

BACULUM EXTRADENTATUM

Appearance
Females become 90-110mm (3¹/₂-4⁵/₁₆in) while the males reach 70mm (2³/₄in). The middle legs of

Mating pair of Baculum extradentatum.

Baculum extradentatum *nymph.*

Pair of Baculum thaii.

the females have small lobes and there are two spikes between the eyes. They are brown with darker and more yellow patches without wings.

Distribution
Shrubs in Vietnam.

Food
Leaves of bramble, may, *Pyracantha*, oak, hazel, rose, strawberry, and *Geranium Ribes.*

Reproduction
Baculum species eggs are extremely varied, often flat or cylindrical. Those of B. extradentatum are spherical and 3mm ($^2/_{16}$in) in size. Nymphs of about 10mm ($^3/_8$in) emerge in 2-6 months. This species also reproduces parthenogenically.

BACULUM THAII

Appearance
Stick like females of 105-115mm ($4^1/_8$-$4^1/_2$in) mainly green, but can be brown with two forward-facing flattened 'horns' on the head. Slimmer males are about 80mm ($3^1/_8$in) long and brown. Both wingles.

Distribution
Thailand.

Food
Leaves of bramble, *Eucalyptus* sp., may, oak, firethorn *(Pyracantha)*, rose, plum, birch, rowan, and bird cherry.

Reproduction
The flat, angular brown eggs are at least 3mm ($^2/_{16}$in) long. Nymphs of 15mm ($^5/_8$in) emerge after 6-12 weeks. Spray this species daily. They can also reproduce by parthenogenisis.

CALYNDA BROCKI

Appearance
The females of this stick like species grow to 140-180mm ($5^1/_2$-$7^1/_8$in) long and are green or yellow-brown. They have a 15mm ($^5/_8$in) long ovipositor at the rear and two 'horns' on their head. The much thinner males are 80-100mm ($3^1/_8$-4in) long and are usually brown. The male's claspers are large. Neither sex has wings.

Distribution
Costa Rica.

Food
Bramble, firethorn, rose, oak, and dwarf medlar.

Reproduction
The eggs are 4 x 2mm ($^5/_{32}$ x $^1/_{16}$in) in size and emerge after 4 months. The insects mature another 4 months later.

CARAUSIUS ABBREVIATUS

Appearance
The females are about 110mm ($4^5/_{16}$in) and brown. There are long lobes on the front and middle legs and a number of spikes. The males of 80mm ($3^1/_8$in) have less pronounced lobes but have a broad thickening of about 5mm ($^3/_{16}$in) of the penultimate body segment. Neither sex has wings. Striking features are the short hind legs which are attached to the fourth segment of the female and seventh abdominal segment of the male.

Distribution
Sarawak and Sabah, Borneo.

Food
Leaves of bramble, *Eucalyptus* sp., may, firethorn, raspberry, and rose.

Reproduction
The nymphs emerge from the eggs after 3 months.

Pair of Calynda brocki.

Female Carausius abbreviatus.

Female Carausius morosus *and gynandromorph.*

CARAUSIUS AURICULATUS

Former name *Phenacephorus auriculatus.*

Appearance

Females grow to 75mm (3in) and are brown with long lobes on their legs. There are remarkable flaps on the female's head. The thinner males reach 65mm (2⁹/₁₆in) and are brown-green. Both sexes are stick like and wingless.

Distribution

Brunei.

Food

Leaves of bramble, rose, firethorn, and *Eucalyptus* sp.

Reproduction

The eggs emerge after about 5 months. The females can be determined after the first moult by their flaps, while the males are smooth.

CARAUSIUS MOROSUS

This 'common' Indian or Laboratory stick insect is the best known with many already being cared for in home terrariums.

Appearance

Females become 70-80mm (2³/₄-3¹/₈in), are stick-like, and brown or green. The insides of the front legs are red with mature females. Eggs held at 28-30°C (82.4-86°F) for the first month can produce many gynandromorphic offspring (see page 65). These grow to 55mm (2³/₁₆in) and are brown or green. Not only the front legs but also the thorax

Female Carausius auriculatus.

has red colouring. In India true males emerge from populations of sexually reproduced *C. morosus.* Both females and gynandromorphic 'males' are without wings. The species plays dead in the event of danger.

Distribution

India.

Food

Bramble, privet, ivy, may, firethorn, rose, *Forsythia,* lilac, oak, hazel, *Rhododendron, Tradescantia, Ficus, Narcissus,* umbrella plant, avocado, *Abutilon, Nepenthes,* parsley, potato, *Croton, Geranium* (not *Pelargonium*), and many others.

Accommodation

This exceptionally easy to care for insect can be kept at room temperature.

Reproduction

Reproduces parthenogenically in captivity. The brown eggs of 1mm (¹/₆₄in) have a substance that attracts ants for food and emerge in 3-8 months.

CLONOPSIS GALLICA

Appearance

The females become 62-70mm (2¹¹/₁₆in-2³/₄in) with gynandromorphs about 50mm (2in). These green or brown insects have the usual stick form and they have no wings.

Distribution

Southern Europe.

Food

Leaves of bramble, broom, plum, may, rose, strawberry, and oak.

Reproduction

This species reproduces by parthenogenisis. Place the eggs at 4-10°C (39.2-50°F) for several months during winter. Green nymphs emerge from the 3mm (²/₁₆in) eggs in April. Keep this species dry, spraying only very occasionally. Do not keep this species too warm.

CREOXYLUS SPINOSUS

Appearance

The females grow to 50-70mm (2-2³/₄in) and are green or brown. They are fairly thick in proportion and have very small under-developed wings. The

Clonopsis gallica.

Dares validispinus *females*.

Dares verrucosus *females*.

thinner males that are 50mm (2in) have the same colouring. They also have grey wings which cover their entire abdomen. Both sexes have two small 'horns' on their heads. The female has eight spikes on her thorax to the male's two. When threatened they play dead but the males can also use warning colours by displaying their wings.

Distribution
Bushes in Trinidad.

Food
Leaves of bramble, may, firethorn, ivy, oak, raspberry, rose, and hazel.

Reproduction
The females push their eggs into the surface layer of the soil with their short ovipositor. Greyish-brown nymphs emerge from the light brown eggs that are 2.5mm ($^3/_{64}$in) after 3 months. The nymphs have yellow and brown stripes on their legs.

DARES SPECIES

Appearance
Females of species of this genus grow to 40-50mm ($1^9/_{16}$-2in) long and are stockily built. Egg laying females have a broadening of the centre of their abdomen. The thinner males grow to 35-40mm

Creoxylus spinosus *females*.

($1^3/_8$-$1^9/_{16}$in). These insects are often dark brown and spiky, with the males resembling Epidares nolimetangere. Neither sex has wings. These species hide away beneath bark and such like during the daytime.

Distribution
Dares ulula and *D. validispinus* originate from Sarawak and *D. verrucosus* comes from Sabah.

Food
All species eat leaves of bramble and oak. *Dares ulula* also eats firethorn and raspberry. *D. validispinus* can cope with all these and also eats may, cherry laurel, beech, birch, alder, and dwarf medlar.

Reproduction
Females lay just two or three eggs each week but they live for two years. The eggs of *D. ulula* and *D. validispinus* have little hair on them but those of *D. verrucosus* are fairly hairy. Leave the barrel-shaped eggs, that are about 4mm ($^5/_{32}$in) high, laying on the ground. At a temperature of about 24°C (75.2°F) these emerge after 4-6 months. The nymphs are 7-15mm ($^4/_{16}$-$^5/_8$in) long and dark brown.
Keep these stick insects moist and without too much ventilation by spraying every day.

DYME SPECIES (EXCEPT D. RAROSPINOSA)

Appearance
Females of species within this genus except *D. rarospinosa* are rod like without wings. The be-

Dyme *species female.*

Dyme *species female.*

Eurycantha calcarata *male.*

come 105mm (4¹/₈in) long and are green. When threatened the front legs are splayed to display the bright red mouth and blue-green lower legs.

Distribution
Ecuador.

Food
Leaves of bramble and rose.

Reproduction
These species reproduce by parthenogenisis with 18mm (³/₄in) nymphs emerging from the eggs after 5-6 months.

EPIDARES NOLIMETANGERE

Former name *Dares nolimetangere*

Appearance
Females grow to 45mm (1³/₄in) and are entirely dark brown except for an orange-brown stripe on the back. The abdomen of egg-laying females is obviously distended. The males are 35mm (1³/₈in) long and shiny brown with dark green or black markings. Both sexes are without wings and have a number of spiky 'thorns' on their backs. These are red-orange with the males.

Distribution
Low vegetation in the rain forest of Sarawak (Borneo).

Food
Leaves of bramble, raspberry, oak, firethorn, rose, and hazel.

Epidares nolimetangere *female.*

Reproduction
Each week the females lay hairy eggs of 4 x 2.5mm (⁵/₃₂ x ³/₆₄in) in size on the ground. Leave these where they lay. Nymphs of about 7mm (⁵/₁₆in) emerge after about 4-6 months when the eggs are kept at about 24°C (75.2°F). Keep the humidity at 85-95% relative humidity by spraying every day.

EURYCANTHA CALCARATA

Appearance
The females of this robust species are 125-150mm (4⁷/₈in-5⁷/₈in) and they weight 20 grams (approx. ³/₄ oz). They possess a 15mm (⁵/₈in) ovipositor at the rear of the body (photo page 66). The males are 105-120mm (4¹/₈in-4³/₄in) and have a 10mm (³/₈in) spike on each of the femurs (third segment) of the hind legs. When threatened these insects stand with the abdomen raised and with the legs spread from the body but are then slammed together from time to time which can be painful for the fingers. Both sexes are shiny brown, without wings, and possess spiky 'thorns' on the rear of their legs. *E. calcarata* males do not have the fairly large spikes on the rear-leg tibiae that are found on the close relative *E. horrida*, which also has five rather than two rearward-facing spikes on the abdominal segments.

Distribution
Trees and shrubs in the rain forest of Papua New Guinea. During the day they hide beneath and between flaps of bark.

Eurycantha calcarata *males have a sturdy spike on the hind legs.*

Food

Leaves of bramble, may, oak, rose, beech, pear, apple, alder, hawthorn, hazel, cherry, cherry laurel, elm, rowan, knotweed, Guelder rose, sorrel, vine, and species of *Cotoneaster, Rhododendron Croton,* and *Tradescantia.*

Reproduction

The female inserts barrel-shaped eggs of 8 x 4mm ($^5/_{16}$ x $^5/_{32}$in) in the ground. Nymphs of 15-20mm ($^9/_{16}$-$^3/_4$in) that are usually brown but can be green emerge after 4-6 months. Provide a hiding place such as a piece of cork bark or a box and also a shallow water tray with cotton wool to prevent drowning. Do not keep too moist.

EURYCANTHA CORIACEA

Appearance

Eurycantha coriacea resembles the previous species but is less pronouncedly spiky. The spikes on the body are green and those on the legs brown. Females are 110-120mm ($4^5/_{16}$-$4^3/_4$in) long and the males 70-80mm ($2^3/_4$-$3^1/_8$in). Mature specimens are all shades of brown. The males are thinner than other Eurycantha species and do not have thickened rear-leg femurs.

Distribution

Papua New Guinea (Irian Jaya).

Food

Leaves of bramble, raspberry, ivy, oak, *Rhododendron,* firethorn, dwarf medlar, hazel, and *Viburnum.*

Reproduction

Females insert lightly-coloured eggs of 7 x 4mm ($^9/_{32}$ x $^5/_{32}$in) into the soil. Brown-green nymphs of 25mm (1in) emerge after 4 months.

EXTATOSOMA TIARATUM

Appearance

The 140mm ($5^1/_2$in) females are light brown or brownish-green and they are moderately covered with spikes and have lobes on the legs and abdomen. The female's wings are short (15mm/$^5/_8$in). The much thinner males are 90mm ($3^1/_2$in) with dark brown bodies without spikes but they have wings which cover almost the entire abdomen.

Eurycantha coriacea.

Extatosoma tiaratum *male.*

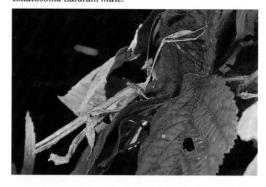

Extatosoma tiaratum *female.*

Distribution

Arid forests of Australia and New Guinea.

Food

Leaves of bramble, *Eucalyptus* sp., may, oak, rose, beech, birch, elm, hazel, apple, dwarf medlar, guava, sorrel, lettuce, and *Citrus* sp.

Reproduction

Extatosoma tiaratum can reproduce by parthenogenisis. The spherical eggs are shiny and white with brown markings and are coated with a substance that attracts ants. Nymphs of 20mm ($^3/_4$in) emerge after 6 months. These are black-brown with an orange head, orange-brown legs, and a white patch on the neck until the first shedding. They resemble species of Australian ants *(Leptomyrmex* sp.) and are unattractive for insectivorous creatures. Spikes can be seen on the females by the second nymph phase. Spray the small nymphs each day. Raise this species in a spacious cage, preferably not with any other species.

HAANIELLA SPECIES

Appearance

This sturdily built stick insect mimics leaf mould on the floor of primeval forest. They are chiefly dark brown. There are spikes on the body and legs, especially with the males where they are often greenish-blue. Both sexes have short wings which are partially cream-coloured with some species. When threatened they raise the abdomen and

Haaniella echinata *female in threatening posture.*

Haaniella dehaanii *female.*

HAANIELLA DEHAANI

Appearance
Females of this dark brown species are about 90mm (3¹/₂in) and males about 65mm (2⁹/₁₆in).
Distribution
Sarawak, Serapi mountain (Borneo).
Food
Bramble, ivy, oak, firethorn, raspberry rose, and hazel.

HAANIELLA ECHINATA

Appearance
Females become 100-110mm (4-4⁵/₁₆in), males 75mm (3in). During threat display a blue-green colour is visible between the plates of the abdomen.
Distribution
Sabah, low-lying rain forest (Borneo).
Food
Bramble, may, oak, *Rhododendron*, rose, rowan, apple, hazel, *Berberis,* and *Mahonia.*

HAANIELLA GRAYII

Appearance
Females become 90-120mm (3¹/₂-4³/₄in) long, males 70-90mm (2³/₄-3¹/₂in).
Distribution
Sarawak, the Seraphi Bengoh and Santubong mountains in Borneo.
Food
Leaves of bramble, ivy, oak, firethorn, raspberry, rose, and hazel.

Egg *in the ovipositor of a* Haaniella *species.*

strike out with the legs, rasp the wings, and eject a chemical deterrent.
Distribution
Haniella species originate from tropical rain forest in Borneo (Sabah, Sarawak, and Brunei), but *H. muelleri* comes from Malaysia. The insects hide away beneath bark by day.
Food
These animals are not fussy about their food. Offer a mixture of hard and soft leaves. Suitable leaves are bramble, ivy, *Rhododendron*, rose, raspberry, oak, may, hazel, firethorn, apple, and pear.
Reproduction
The females lay on average one egg per week during the first year and less after this. Eggs of the larger species are 11 x 7mm (⁷/₁₆ x ⁴/₁₆in) and those of the smaller species 7 x 5mm (⁴/₁₆ x ³/₁₆in). They are buried several centimetres deep in the ground and when kept in a moist mixture of sand, compost (or cactus compost) will emerge after 6-18 months. The early stages of the ovipositor can be seen on young female with some difficulty. The nymphs of about 30mm (¹³/₁₆in) grow slowly and mature at between eight and eighteen months. The females then live for about a further two years. Provide semi-mature and mature specimens with a water tray with a sponge in their terrarium. Keep Haaniella species moist, spraying the terrarium each day. Ensure a daytime temperature of 23-26°C (73.4-78.8°F) and one of 17-20°C (62.6-68°F) at night.

Haaniella echinata *male.*

Haaniella grayii *female*.

Haaniella grayii *male*.

Haaniella muelleri

HAANIELLA MUELLERI

Appearance
Females become 85mm (3³/₈in), males 60mm (2³/₈in). Both sexes are grey-brown with green tinges and light patches.
Distribution
Forests of Western Malaysia, Sumatra.
Food
Leaves of bramble, rose, oak, beech, ivy, firethorn, dwarf medlar, hazel, and Guelder rose.

HAANIELLA SAUSSUREI

Appearance
Females become 90mm (3¹/₂in), males 60mm (2³/₈in).
Distribution
Forests in Sarawak, Borneo.
Food
Leaves of bramble, rose, oak, ivy, raspberry, and species of *Eucalyptus*.

HAANIELLA SCABRA

Appearance
Females become 85mm (3³/₈in), males 55mm (2³/₁₆in).
Distribution
Sabah and Kinabulu mountain, Borneo.
Food
Leaves of bramble, oak, and hazel.

Haaniella saussurei *female*.

Haaniella saussurei *male*.

Haaniella scabra *female.*

Haaniella scabra *male.*

HESPEROPHASMA LOBATA

Zoologists are currently carrying out studies to determine if this species is properly designated.

Appearance
Females become 60mm (2³/₈in) long and have no wings. The colour varies from green to brown. The seventh segment of the abdomen is cream-coloured. There are two flaps on the head. The males grow to 55mm (2³/₁₆in) and are dark brown. Both sexes have flaps on their legs.

Distribution
Panama.

Food
Leaves of bramble, oak, firethorn, and raspberry.

Reproduction
The eggs are laid on the surface of the ground.

Hesperophasma lobata.

HETEROPTERYX DILATATA, JUNGLE NYMPH

Appearance
Females Are 150mm (6in) long, weigh 45-65 grams (1¹/₂-2¹/₄oz) making them one of the heaviest insects. Adult females are green to green-yellow with wings that cover a third of their abdomen. Males, of 5-15 grams (¹/₆–¹/₂oz), grow to 90mm (3¹/₂in), are much thinner and brown, with light brown stripes on the front wings. The unfurled rear wings are red with black veins. Both raise their back legs when threatened and slam them together when anything comes between them. Females rasp their wings loudly but males flap their wings open.

Distribution
Tree and shrub dweller of Western Malaysia.

Food
Bramble, cherry laurel, may, ivy, oak, laurel, rose, beech, elm, pear, apple, plum, dwarf medlar, Guelder rose, hazel, guava, rowan, and *Rhododendron.*

Accommodation
Ensure a temperature of 23-28°C (73.4-82.4°F) and spray once or twice each week. Lay about 100mm (4in) of moderately moist old compost or a peat and sand mixture on the bottom of the terrarium. Keep the soil at about 21-23°C (69.8-73.4°F).

Reproduction
The female inserts the 10mm (³/₈in) thick barrel-like eggs up to 40mm (1⁹/₁₆in) into the ground. Nymphs of about 20mm (³/₄in) emerge after 8-12 months but the incubation period can last 3¹/₂ years. Nymphs hide by day behind withered leaves, which needs to be borne in mind when replenishing leaves and also hang in clusters of leaves by day in a sleeping position. Light abdominal segments and indentations between them can be seen quite early with the males. The females have an ovipositor from the start and change from brown to green in the final three stages of development. *Heteropteryx dilatata* mature to adulthood after 1-1¹/₂years.

Heteropteryx dilatata, *male.*

Heteropteryx dilatata, *female after the last moult.*

Pair of Libethra regularis *mating.*

Distribution
Caribbean Islands (Trinidad).
Food
Leaves of bramble, may, firethorn, ivy, oak, elm, hazel, raspberry, broom, rose, and *Tradescantia.*
Reproduction
Nymphs of about 24mm (2³/₈in) emerge after five to six weeks from spherical eggs 4 x 2mm (⁵/₃₂ x ¹/₁₆in). The nymphs are straw-coloured but they quickly become green or brown once they have eaten.
Keep this species fairly moist.

LONCHODES SPECIES

Both the males and females of the many species of this genus all have wings. These are long, thin, stick-like insects. There is often a kink in the body by the middle legs.

LONCHODES AMAUROPS

Appearance
The females grow to 90-110mm (3¹/₂-4⁵/₁₆in) long, the males to 75-90mm (3-3¹/₂in). Both sexes have a spike on the fifth abdominal segment, although it appears to be on the fourth because the first abdominal segment is fused with the thorax. There are also several spikes on the legs and two on the head. The females have a warty knob on their sixth abdominal segment and they are dark or light brown, or grey, while the males are either green or light brown with green.
Distribution
Rain forest in Sarawak.
Food
Leaves of bramble, may, privet, firethorn, raspberry, rose, ivy, and oak.
Reproduction
Brown-green nymphs emerge after three to four months from the 3.5mm (⁵/₆₄in) diameter spherical eggs. The 'wart' on the females is visible from the fourth stage and a forked rear end becomes apparent too at this stage.

LEPTYNIA HISPANICA

Appearance
Females become 50-60mm (2-2³/₈in) and are pale green or grey-brown with a white stripe on the side. This species is wingless.
Distribution
Mediterranean Sea area (Spain, Portugal, South of France).
Food
Leaves of rose, strawberry, rosemary, sun rose *(Helianthemum* sp.), and *Dorycnium suffruticosa.*
Reproduction
This species mainly reproduces by parthenogenisis. The 4mm (⁵/₃₂in) long eggs are laid in the ground or attached to something. The green-grey nymphs of 10mm (³/₈in) emerge in mid May. The white stripe can be seen after the third stage. Keep this species dry and hardly ever spray.

LIBETHRA REGULARIS

Appearance
Females become 50mm (2in) and are brown with yellow-brown colouring. A triangular marking is usually visible on the upper side. The skin has a rough texture. The abdomen becomes clearly distended during egg laying. The males are up to 45mm (1³/₄in) long, thinner, and brown with white patches on a green side stripe. Neither sex has wings.

Lonchodes amaurops *female.*

Lonchodes brevipes *male.*

The black nymphs have white banding on the legs. After several stages the olive green males are slimmer than the brownish females. Keep this warm (24-26°C (75.2-78.8°F)) and moist.

LONCHODES HOSEI

Appearance
Females are 120-140mm (4³/₄-5¹/₂in) and are coloured in a variety of brown-cream shades with black markings. The thinner males become 95mm (3³/₄in) and they are mainly brown with a sheen. The females in particular tend to have spiky legs with lobes while the males have two side-protruding spikes just in front of the back legs.
Distribution
Borneo and Java.
Food
Leaves of bramble, may, privet, firethorn, and rose.
Reproduction
Nymphs that are 15mm (⁵/₈in) long emerge from the eggs after two to three months.

LONCHODES MODESTUS

Appearance
Females are 105-120mm (4⁷/₈-4³/₄in) long and brown or green. The bottoms of the legs are red and the legs are also slightly lobed. There are two spikes between the eyes while the seventh abdominal segment has short appendages. Males grow to 90mm (3¹/₂in) and vary from green to brown.

LONCHODES BREVIPES

Appearance
The females grow to about 120mm (4³/₄in) and the males about 90mm (3¹/₂in). The female is dark brown, sometimes with lighter flecks and her front and back legs can also be green. Males are dark brown with dark green legs. This species has a knobbly appearance. There is a small hook at the sixth segment of females and there are several spikes and lobes on the legs.
Distribution
Malaysia and Sumatra.
Food
Mixed *Rhododendron* and bramble.
Reproduction
The 2.5mm (³/₆₄in) eggs emerge after 3-5 months.

Lonchodes brevipes *female.*

Lonchodes hosei *female.*

Lonchodes modestus *female*.

Lopaphus perakensis *male*.

Neither sex has wings. When threatened they pretend to be dead.
Distribution
Sabah and Kalimantan (Borneo).
Food
Leaves of bramble and ivy.
Reproduction
Nymphs of 20mm ($^3/_4$in) emerge from the 3.5mm ($^5/_{64}$in) eggs after four to six months.

LOPAPHUS CAESIUS

Appearance
The stick-shaped females grow to about 120mm ($4^3/_4$in) long and they are light brown in colour. The rear feelers are large and flattened. The female's small front wings are light brown with a darker fleck. The rear wings of both sexes are transparent with light brown margins and these cover slightly less than half the abdomen.
Males grow to 95mm ($3^3/_4$in) and they are thin. The thorax of the predominantly brown male is blue-green and the knees are black.
Distribution
Vietnam.
Food
Bramble and cherry laurel.
Reproduction
The spherical eggs are 3mm ($^2/_{16}$in) in size and grey. Breeding this species is not possible.

LOPAPHUS PERAKENSIS

Appearance
Adult females are 90mm ($3^1/_2$in) long and they are dark brown to olive green and stick-like. There are a number of grey to white irregular flecks on the body. The 70mm ($2^3/_4$in) adult males are thinner but also stick-shaped. The males have green-brown markings. Adult specimens of both sexes have red mouth parts and are both wingless.
Distribution
Western Malaysia.
Food
Bramble leaves.
Reproduction
The eggs of 2mm ($^2/_{32}$in) hatch after 8-12 weeks. Bury the bottom of the eggs in sand if required, to increase the percentage that hatch. The nymphs

are 15mm ($^5/_8$in) and are green with a purple stripe on their backs.

NEOHYRASEA MAERENS

Appearance
The adult females are 75-85mm ($3-3^3/_8$in) and they are brown with a green side stripe. There are spikes on the back up to the third abdominal segment and also on the sides of the legs. The adult males are 50-65mm ($2-2^9/_{16}$in) and they have a darker stripe on their brown bodies.
Distribution
Vietnam.
Food
Leaves of bramble, ivy, oak, rose, raspberry, and species of *Rhododendron*.
Reproduction
Nymphs of 13mm ($^5/_8$in) emerge from the eggs of 2.5mm ($^3/_{32}$in) after five to six months.

OREOPHOETES PERUANAS

Appearance
The up to 70mm ($2^3/_4$in) long females are black with a bright yellow-orange head and seven black patches. The places at which the legs are connected to the rear abdominal segments are also partially yellow-orange. The body has pale yellow stripes. Adult males are 60mm ($2^3/_8$in), dark red, with black legs and antennae. *Oreophoetes peruanas* is often active during the day. A stinking white substance is emitted when the insect is threatened.

Pair of Neohyrasea maerens.

Oreophoetes peruana *mating.*

Orxines macklotti *male.*

Distribution
Undergrowth of mountainous forests in Peru and Ecuador.
Food
Ferns only; those bought from shops will be full of insecticides for quite some time.
Accommodation
Ensure a temperature of 20-25°C (68-77°F) and a fairly high relative humidity. Spray the terrarium and the ferns in it once each day. Eggs hatch well on moist soil.
Reproduction
This species reproduces both sexually and by parthenogenisis. The females drop on average one 3.5 x 2mm ($^5/_{32}$ x $^2/_{32}$in) eggs per day on the ground. With the temperature at 20°C (68°F) and a high relative humidity nymphs of 15mm ($^5/_8$in) that are black and orange emerge after nine to twelve weeks. If the air is too dry the eggs either do not hatch or the nymphs have deformed limbs. A dark 'Y'-shaped patch can be seen on the underside of the females from the third stage but with the males just a black spot. The male's red colouring only appears after the final shedding.

ORXINES MACKLOTTI

Appearance
The female grows to 70-80mm ($2^3/_4$-$3^1/_8$in), the male to 55mm ($2^3/_{16}$in). Both sexes resemble lichens on trees with their black-brown, brown, and green colourings. There are two horns on the head and both sexes have 55mm ($2^3/_{16}$in) long antennae. The rear wings cover half of the abdomen and when threatened they are opened to display orange colouring with black and white (photo page 67).
Distribution
Mountain forest in Java.
Food
Leaves of *Rhododendron* species.
Reproduction
The 50mm (2in) long thin eggs are pressed into fissures in moss and cork and such like or in the ground. With a temperature of 23-25°C (73.4-77°F) and high humidity the eggs hatch after four

to nine months. Provide the 15mm ($^5/_8$in) long nymphs with a high relative humidity of 85-95% and spray water regularly. The nymphs in particular shed their legs readily when threatened.

PARAHYRTACUS GORKOMI

Appearance
The females are 95mm ($3^3/_4$in) and they are green or light brown with paler bands between the segments. The rear end is pointed. The thinner males are 60-70mm ($2^3/_8$-$2^3/_4$in) and they are light brown with a darker strip on the side of the thorax and two light stripes on the head. Neither sex has wings and they both have 65mm ($2^9/_{16}$in) long antennae.
Distribution
The Philippines.
Food
Leaves of bramble, raspberry, hazel, firethorn, dwarf medlar, guava, and species of *Eucalyptus.*
Reproduction
Eggs that are cylindrical and 4mm ($^5/_{32}$in) long emerge after 5–6 months at 20°C (68°F) and after 7 weeks at about 27°C (80.6°F). The 20mm ($^3/_4$in) long nymphs are dark green with yellow-green stripe.

PARAMENEXENUS LAETUS

Appearance
Females are 100-110mm (4-$4^5/_{16}$in) long and are bright green on top and dark green underneath.

Parahyrtacus gorkomi *female.*

Paramenexenus laetus *female.*

Parapachymorpha spinosa *female.*

Phaenopharos herwaardani *female.*

There is a white lateral stripe on their sides. The female has an ovipositor. The males are 75-85mm (3-3³/₈in) and are similarly coloured. There are six to eight black spikes on the thorax. Neither sex has wings.

Distribution
North Vietnam.

Food
Leaves of bramble, rose, and ivy.

Reproduction
After about three months pale green nymphs 20mm (³/₄in) long emerge from the 3.5mm (1³/₁₆in) spherical eggs. These become grey-green and do not change back to green until the final stage.

PARAPACHYMORPHA SPINOSA

Appearance
Females are about 60mm (2³/₈in) long, males 50mm (2in). Both sexes are olive green to light brown, have about 10mm (³/₈in) long antennae and are without wings. The females in particular have many spikes on the body and legs.

Distribution
Thailand.

Food
Leaves of bramble, ivy, firethorn, rose, raspberry, and hazel.

Reproduction
Brown nymphs 7-8mm (⁴/₁₆-⁵/₁₆in) long emerge from eggs that are 2 x 1.5mm (³/₃₂-¹/₁₆in) after four to five months from moist soil at 20°C (68°F).

PHAENOPHAROS HERWAARDANI

Appearance
The stick-like females of this red 'micro-wing' are 130mm (5¹/₈in) long and they are beige to dark brown with darker patches. The 3mm (²/₁₆in) long fiery-red wings are opened in display when threatened. The male is 70mm (2³/₄in) and similarly coloured.

Distribution
Thailand.

Food
Leaves of bramble, oak, raspberry, rose, ivy, hazel, firethorn, Guelder rose, and species of *Eucalyptus*, and *Rhododendron*.

Reproduction
Nymphs 22mm (⁷/₈in) long emerge after 4¹/₂ months from the 4mm (⁵/₃₂in) long oval eggs.

Phaenopharos herwaardani, *red micro-wing.*

Phaenopharos herwaardani *male.*

Phenacephorus cornucervi *female.*

Pair of Phobaeticus serratipes.

Distribution
Sabah.
Food
Leaves of bramble, ivy, rose, hazel, raspberry, and firethorn.
Reproduction
The eggs hatch after about five months. The females can be distinguished after the first stage by their flaps (the males are smooth).

PHOBAETICUS SERRATIPES

Former name: *Pharnacia acanthopus.*
Appearance
At 230-330mm (9-13in) body length the females are the longest stick insects. Their overall length is 400-570mm (15³/₄-22¹/₂in). The females have no wings. The males reach 160-180mm (6¹/₄–7¹/₈in) with wings of 30mm (1³/₁₆in). Both male and female are stick-like and green or brown, sometimes with white patches on the back. The legs have indentations. When threatened this species either plays dead or sheds its legs. Although they can live with only two legs, this species needs to be handled very carefully.
Distribution
Western Malaysia, Java, Sumatra, and Borneo.
Food
Leaves of bramble, oak, beech, and hazel.
Reproduction
Nymphs emerge after five to six months from the flat 5mm (³/₁₆in) eggs. The nymphs are 30mm (1³/₁₆in) with an overall length of 60mm (2³/₈in).

PRISOMERA MALAYA

Appearance
The stick-like females grow to about 100mm (4in) long and are light to dark brown. The males are thinner and only 85mm (3³/₈in) long. The middle legs of both sexes are moderately lobed.
Distribution
Low-lying land and rain forest in Singapore.
Food
Leaves of bramble and oak.

PHENACEPHORUS CORNUCERVI

Appearance
The fairly thick, brown female becomes 75mm (3in) long and she has several flaps on her body, and a plant seems to grow out of her head. The legs are lobed. The thin, olive green males reach 65mm (2⁹/₁₆in) and often adopt an angular posture. Neither sex has wings.

Prisomera malaya *female.*

Rhapiderus scabrosus *female.*

Reproduction
The female lays one or two large brown flat eggs each week. Keep the eggs moist during the long incubation period and keep the nymphs moist too.

RHAPHIDERUS SCABROSUS

Appearance
Females are 70-85mm (2³/₄-3³/₈in) and are pale green to yellow-green. On the thorax there are six to twelve yellow 'thorns' with brown tips. The much slimmer brown males are 50-65mm (2-2⁹/₁₆in). Neither sex has wings.

Distribution
Moist areas on Réunion.

Food
Rhododendron species.

Reproduction
Pale green nymphs of 15mm (⁵/₈in) emerge after three to six months from eggs of 3mm (²/₁₆in). If there are no larger specimens in the terrarium to bite away the edges of the *Rhododendron* leaves for them clip them off. Provide a temperature of 20-25°C (68-77°F) and for the nymphs in particular create a high humidity level. This species can reproduce by parthenogenisis.

SIPYLOIDEA SIPYLUS

Appearance
Females are 90-100mm (3¹/₂-4in). Males of 60-65mm (2³/₈-2⁹/₁₆in) are found in the wild in South-

Sipyloidea sipylus *female.*

East Asia but only gynandromorphs are known in captivity. Both sexes are straw coloured and have wings that cover almost the entire abdomen.

Distribution
South-East Asia; introduced to Madagascar where they reproduce by parthenogenesis.

Food
Leaves of bramble, rose, may, firethorn, oak, beech, birch, alder, hazel, elm, St. John's wort, maple, rowan, species of *Rhododendron*, *Geranium* (not *Pelargonium*), and *Buddleja*.

Reproduction
This species reproduces by parthenogenisis in captivity. The females stick the 4mm (⁵/₃₂in) long eggs

Sipyloidea sipylus *female.*

to leaves, rear wall of terrariums etc. (photo page 66). The eggs almost always hatch under any conditions in two-and-a-half to four months. The green nymphs are 20mm (^{3}/$_4$in). Keep *Sipyloidea* species fairly dry but spray lightly each evening.

SIPYLOIDEA SPECIES

Appearance
The 90-100mm (3^1/$_2$-4in) long females are olive green to beige. The green males are 65mm (2^9/$_{16}$in) long. Both sexes have wings that cover not more than two-thirds of the abdomen and they can both fly. The wing margins of the male are red.

Distribution
Thailand.

Food
Leaves of bramble, raspberry, rose, firethorn, hazel, cherry laurel, and species of *Eucalyptus.*

Reproduction
The females drop 3.4 x 2mm (^{5}/$_{32}$ x ^{2}/$_{32}$in) eggs onto the ground from which 12mm (^{7}/$_{16}$in) long pale green nymphs appear after about three months.

Sipyloidea *species male and female.*

PHYLLIUM SPECIES, LEAF INSECTS

The Phyllidae family of leaf insects are separate from the phasmids and consist of three genera. Only the genus *Phyllium* has been successfully cared for in terrariums.

Appearance
Insects of the *Phyllium* species imitate leaves, even down to nibbled edges. Both sexes have broad folds of skin on their bodies and legs. The abdomen of the female is hexagonal. The outer wings are wide and cover two-thirds of her abdomen. The rear wings are usually absent. The antennae are shorter than the head. The males are lancet-shaped and smaller than the females but they have longer antennae. The outer wings are short (max. 15mm or ^{5}/$_8$in) but their small, almost transparent lower wings reach as far as the rear of the abdomen. The antennae reach beyond the front legs. Both sexes are green, brown, or green with brown patches.

Distribution
Tropical and sub-tropical forests of Asia.

Accommodation
Ensure a daytime temperature of 20-25°C (68-77°F) and 18-22°C (64.4-71.6°F) at night with ventilation. Use a terrarium largely made of mesh with a small fan for example. Plenty of light is impor-

Phyllium bioculatum *females.*

Mesh insectarium for leaf insects.

Young leaf insects often will only eat oak and not bramble.

PHYLLIUM BIOCULATUM

Appearance
Females of this relatively less difficult species are 70-85mm (2³/₄-3³/₈in). The broad part of her abdomen is typically trapezoidal (smaller at the rear). Males are 50mm (2in) and nymphs are 17mm (¹¹/₁₆in) long.
Distribution
Tropical mountain forests on Java, Borneo, Sumatra, The Seychelles, and Ceylon.

PHYLLIUM CELEBICUM

Females are 90mm (3¹/₂in) and have lobes on their legs that are smaller than those of *P. bioculatum*. The broad part of the abdomen is rectangular. This species has well-developed rear wings. Males are 60mm (2³/₈in). The 17mm (¹¹/₁₆in) long nymphs are reddish-brown with white flecks.
Distribution
The Seychelles, The Philippines, Celebes, Laos, Vietnam, Thailand, and Malaysia.

PHYLLIUM GIGANTEUM

Females are 100-110mm (4-4⁵/₁₆in) but gynandromorphs only 80mm (3¹/₈in). The dark red nymphs have a square abdomen.
Distribution
Western Malaysia.

Nymphs of leaf insects are often initially reddish-orange.

tant. Ensure a strict hygiene regime and place crumbled peat or floor covering on the bottom of the cage or terrarium. Ensure a relative humidity of 80-90% by moistening the terrarium every day but never spray the insects directly. The nymphs can easily become stuck by water droplets.

If required accommodate the semi-mature males at a cooler temperature of 18-20°C (64.4-68°F) because they become adult one or two phases earlier than the females and only survive as an imago (fully-grown adult) for a few weeks. The semi-mature male nymphs can be distinguished quite quickly by the longer wing joints and longer antennae.

Do not combine leaf insects with other Phasmidae or too many other of their own kind or they are likely to be eaten.

Voeding
Many require very fresh oak leaves, especially when they are young. Refresh these frequently. The percentage of failure is lower with oak than bramble. For winter supplies, acorns can be sown but there are also evergreen oaks such as *Quercus ilex* (Holm oak). If no evergreen oak is available try bramble from the third or fourth stage on. In the wild these insects chiefly eat guava *(Psidium guajava). Phyllium celebicum* will also eat dwarf medlar and hazel. Rinse all the food thoroughly with water before feeding it.

Reproduction
Parthenogenic reproduction is possible. The females whip the angular eggs far and wide with their tail. Reddish-orange nymphs of 15-20mm (⁵/₈-³/₄in) emerge from moist peat with an ambient temperature of 23-28°C (73.4-82.4°F) emerge after three to six months *(P. celebicum)*, six months *(P. bioculatum)*, or six to eight months *(P. giganteum)*. The nymphs quickly change colour to green after they have eaten. Spray 2-3 times each week.

Accommodation

Ensure a temperature of 26-30°C (78.8-86°F) and spray the terrarium daily.

Reproduction

This species reproduces parthenogenically so that gynandromorphs occur.

PHYLLIUM PULCHRIFOLIUM

Females are 70-90mm ($2^3/_4$-$3^1/_2$in), males 50-60mm (2-$2^3/_8$in).

Distribution

Tropical forests of Western Malaysia.

The order Mantodea, praying mantis

The approx. 2,500 species of praying mantis (also known as praying mantid) are distributed between in excess of 400 genera. Enthusiastic amateurs rarely deal with more than five species at the same time because of the time and numbers of prey insects required.

The name mantis originates from the Greek and means a prophet or soothsayer.

Appearance

Praying mantises have three striking characteristics.

1) A large triangular head with large eyes. The considerable amount of movement of the head is exceptional in the world of insects. They look directly at a prey or at their partner and are able to judge distance extremely well.
2) A long prothorax or neck to which the arms used for capturing prey are attached.
3) Substantial and spiky arms for catching prey.

Acanthops falcata *from Venezuela.*

Nymph of Coptopteryx argentina *from Argentina.*

The coxa is almost as long as the femur and the tibia. The spikes on these last two sections of the legs fit together precisely.

In repose, when the praying mantis waits for a prey, its posture resembles that of a person praying, hence the name. When a prey comes close enough the catching arms strike with lightning speed.

Most species are perfectly camouflaged as a withered leaf, flower, bark, or desert floor so that neither their prey or their enemies see them. The smallest of them are about 15mm ($^5/_8$in) long and the biggest are about 250mm ($9^7/_8$in).

Distribution

Praying mantises are found in warmer moderate climates, the sub-tropics, and tropical regions. *Mantis religiosa* is found in southern parts of Europe, as far north as Southern Germany. These insects live in a wide variety of biotopes from desert to tropical rain forest and from high in trees to scampering over hot desert sand.

Accommodation

Almost all praying mantises need to be kept on their own because of their cannibalistic behaviour. Certainly this is necessary if you want as many insects as possible to survive. Species of the *Empusa* genus and related species can be housed successfully in groups.

Large suitable terrariums are often too big for the

space available if some twenty of these animals are to be kept. Terrariums need to meet the following requirements. Firstly, in common with other insects that shed their skins, the insectarium needs to be at least three times taller than the length of the insect (see Moulting, p64).

Secondly the praying mantis needs a good place to sit and to hang by providing a branch in the insectarium that bends horizontally at the top. With too many branches there is a risk that the praying mantis will catch up on one so that it does not dry out in the correct position after shedding its skin.

Thirdly there must be ventilation at all times. Sealing the insectarium with nylon stocking or fine mesh is usually sufficient.

Finally the terrarium will need to be heated for certain species. Praying mantises are true sun-worshippers with their optimum temperature 25-30°C (77-86°F). Colder temperatures increase the time between each stage of development but can be fatal. Insects that are kept at too low a temperature sit in the warmest spot they can find, as high as possible in the terrarium. If the temperature is too high the young praying mantises in particular will need to drink more than usual.

Old lemonade bottles, pots, and jars covered with nylon stocking or fine mesh are suitable to keep these creatures in. Place these containers if necessary in a heated terrarium or cage. Praying mantises like plenty of light but make sure you do not overheat the terrarium. Spray lightly with water between once to seven times each week, depending on the species, making sure that nymphs will not be at risk of becoming stuck by water droplets. Cigarette smoke can be harmful for insects and spiders. For example, some three-quarters of newly emerged praying mantises died several hours after a party at which lots of people smoked. The praying mantises were in the same student room where the party was held.

Food
Praying mantises are gluttonous prey-seeking creatures. They lie in wait for their prey in the characteristic praying position. When a prey

One praying mantis per bottle.

Praying mantises eat all manner of insects, including their own kind.

Adult females are larger, often longer, and have six belly segments to the males eight.

comes within reach it is grabbed by the enlarged front legs within $^1/_{100}$-$^1/_{10}$th of a second. Only very hungry praying mantises actively hunt their prey; several desert-dwelling species chase theirs.

All manner of arthropods and vertebrates that are smaller than praying mantises or not more than one-and-a-half times their size are taken as prey. Praying mantises do not kill their prey before starting to eat them with their powerful jaws.

Feed with a variety of insects but do not overfeed. Dead insects will also be taken if they are offered in motion on the end of forceps. Adult females need more nourishment than males because of egg production. The catching legs of all the flower-like praying mantises *(Creoboter, Hymenopus,* and *Pseudocreobotra)* are fairly weak and have almost no indentations, so it is best not to feed crickets to species of these genera.

A well-nourished, fat praying mantis does not catch any more food until several days after shedding its skin. Make sure there are no prey still present in the terrarium when this occurs because they can disturb the process. Occasionally a praying mantis will stop eating without any obvious reason. If this happens increase the temperature. push a fragment of prey in its mouth and watch what happens.

Provide some ripe fruit in the terrarium so that prey such as house flies, fruit flies, crickets, and mealworms survive longer and are of higher nutritional value. It can also help them breed to provide a source of more food. Keep the terrarium clean and hygienic.

Sex determination

The sex can be determined after the fifth stage with most species. The females has six sternites (belly segments) compared with the male's eight. The first of these is partially hidden beneath the hind legs. The additional sternites enable the male to arch his rear during mating in order to reach the female. The final, more pointed, sternite of the female alone has a groove in it.

Adult females are larger than adult males, have shorter wings, shorter antennae, and a much bigger appetite.

In those species where the males are much smaller than the females, the males mature much earlier. They also only live for a few weeks or months. In order to get their maturity to coincide with the females, keep the males at about 15°C (59°F) and feed slightly less than normal.

Mating

A well-known story about praying mantises is that the female rips the male's head off during mating and eats it with the male's body continuing to copulate prior to the rest of it being eaten too. The thorax and abdomen continue to be impelled by nerve endings and the male provides the protein for his own offspring. This ritual is rarely seen in captivity because the females are usually extremely well-filled out.

One or two weeks before the final stage the males actively seek out a partner, attracted by the scent of the pheromones released by the female. The males, which are usually smaller, can fly well. The male has to take care not to be eaten before the mating occurs so that his approach to her can last for several hours.

Feed the females well before mating so that they are sated in order to reduce the chance of cannibalism.

Place one male and one female together in a spacious terrarium or on a large plant at least two weeks after the final shedding of both male and female. Check regularly to see if they mate. If this

Female Hierodula *sp. eats her mate.*

does not occur within 24 hours try again a week later. To help things along, allow the female to walk past the male. A male that is ready to mate which quickly become aware and will not let her out of his sight. His antennae will start to vibrate.

Very backward males can be helped by giving the female a cricket. The male can then see that the other praying mantis is a female as she moves and that she is not dangerous because she is busy with prey. This method can encourage the males of *Sphodromantis* and *Hierodula* species to mate within five minutes but the males of Hymenopus species usually need longer.

Once a male has leapt on a female it can take some time before he sits upright on her. The males vibrate their antennae (or in the case of *Hymenopus* species, their catching arms) against the neck plates of the female to calm her down.

A female that is ready to mate remains calm. The male moves backwards and arches the back of his body to make contact and pass the spermatophore to the female. Mating usually takes four to seven hours. Sometimes the white spermatophore can be seen in the sexual orifice of the female.

The males of most species then leap off the female and fly away in search of another female but with others such as those of *Hymenopus* the male remains on the female to prevent the spermatophore of another male from fertilizing her. One mating can be sufficient for the eggs to be fertilized.

Mating of Hierodula parviceps *from The Philippines.*

Female Hierodula *sp. makes an egg case.*

Cross-section of a dried egg case.

Emergence of Sphodromantis gastrica *from an egg case.*

Parthenogenic reproduction can occur with *Brunneria borealis*, *B. subaptera*, *Miomantis* sp., *Parasphendale affinis*, *Sphodromantis viridis*, and *Tenodera sinensis*. Only female offspring result from parthenogenisis, and these are often weak.

Egg laying

If a female has eaten well enough she will create an egg case in which she will then lay some 30 to 300 eggs. The case is fashioned by a foamy mass that she excretes from the rear of her body, which then hardens and protects the eggs against drying out and other potential dangers. The more she has eaten or the more nutritious her food the larger is the egg case. Most species create three to six egg cases but some produce as many as twenty.

Remove the egg packet from the female either by removing it from her or her from it. The main factor for successful hatching is the humidity. They might be sprayed too little or not placed in a sufficiently humid position. If the eggs become too moist they will rot or suffocate. It makes little difference how often the eggs are sprayed with some species.

Sphodromantis species hatch if sprayed once each day but can also be successful if not sprayed, provided the humidity where they are kept is at least 70%.

Place the container with the eggs in a larger container with e.g. a wet sponge or wet sand. If necessary put the eggs in a moist terrarium but bear in mind that crickets, flies and other insects can eat the egg cases.

Never seal an incubation container with adhesive tape because praying mantises get everywhere and are certain to get stuck on the tape. Small nymphs can also drown in condensation or the water in a drinking tray.

Emerging praying mantis nymphs slide down a mucous thread. The strange-looking creatures shed their skin immediately and then run away from their brothers and sisters in every direction. Normally they all hatch at the same time but a few species emerge in daily batches spread over up to two months *(Coptoperyx)*.

Most eggs emerge after five to six weeks at 23-30°C (73.4-86°F) but those that are kept fairly dry and cool can suspend development until conditions permit their emergence.

Rearing

Small praying mantises can start to eat on the day they emerge. Make sure that a jar of fruit flies is available. Alternative or smaller prey includes aphids (available from April to September), springtails, and similar.

Many praying mantises are cannibalistic from their first day. If some loss is not a problem, and this is usually not a problem with some 100 or so emerging at one time, provide a large terrarium for the young with plenty of climbing branches or plants and provide plenty of food. This saves both time and space.

House the young separately once there are still about 25 of them left of a reasonable size.

Moulting

Depending on the species, males shed their skin through seven to nine stages and females eight to ten times, with the first change taking place immediately upon emergence from the egg. They are extremely vulnerable to predation, too much moisture, or if conditions are too dry.

Praying mantises do not eat for several days before shedding their skin and they move about very lit-

Tenodera aridifolia *in threat posture.*

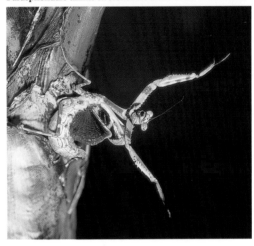

Parasphendale affinis *stretches its arms when threatened.*

tle. Usually they will hang by the head from somewhere in the top of the terrarium.

The moulting of praying mantises occurs in the same manner as with stick insects and is exposed to the same dangers. A praying mantis leaves its old skin hanging with precisely the same shape as the insect formerly had.

Defence

Praying mantises have many enemies in the wild (they are favourite food of chameleons). They rely as the first line of defence on their camouflage and calm swaying motion that imitates the effect of the wind. Certain species take on a camouflage posture when threatened, imitating Popa species of withered branches by stretching their catching arms out in front of them. Many others try to fly or run away, or allow themselves to fall. Only the mature males can fly away.

Hierodula parviceps *shedding its skin.*

When threatened Hierodula parviceps *females show off fine colours.*

Finally many species adopt a spectacular stance when threatened. The catching arms are held against the body (when even the brown *Hierodula* species displays purple and yellow) or stretches them out, and a pair of wings are often opened too and even red jaws opened wide.

Handling
Praying mantises are not dangerous because they have no poison. Only a few species grasp hold with their catching arms but this can be painful and difficult to get free from.
Praying mantises are best handled by allowing them to crawl onto a hand. Never grab hold of them. Let the nymphs walk into a jar. Escaped insects can often be found by the window.

CREOBOTER **SPECIES**

Appearance
The females of this species of praying mantis are 30-40mm (1³/₁₆-1⁹/₁₆in) long, the males 30mm (1³/₁₆in). Both sexes are green with white markings. The various species all have an eye patch with a different shape on the wings. For instance *C. pictipennis* has an oval white patch on the wings ringed with black edging. During threat display it is apparent that the rear wings are basically pink with a black warning patch.

Pair of Creoboter pictipennis.

Creoboter meleagris.

Distribution
Creoboter species mainly lie in wait in flowering shrubs for insects seeking nectar. *Creoboter pictipennis* originates from Sri Lanka and Southern India. *C. gennatis* hails from Thailand.

Verzorging
Ensure a daytime temperature of 25-32°C (77-89.6°F) and 17°C (62.6°F) at night. Lightly spray with water each evening. Specimens of the same size exhibit little cannibalism if they are well fed.

Reproduction
Females produce about five flattened egg cases about 20-60mm (³/₄-2³/₈in) long. These are white or brown, and pointed and contain 25-50 eggs. These hatch after 4¹/₂-6¹/₂ weeks if kept at 28-32°C (82.4-89.6°F) and sprayed twice each week. Newly emerged offspring are brown or black but later this becomes white mixed with green and pink, making them sometimes difficult to differentiate from flowers.

DEROPLATYS **SPECIES**

Appearance
Species of *Deroplatys* are various shades of brown and they imitate dead leaves. The neck plate is well-developed, especially in the case of females with which the broadening of the sides of the prothorax terminates in a point at the back. The females also have a broader abdomen and lobed

Almost fully-adult Deroplatys dessicata.

Deroplatys truncata nymph.

legs. Females of *D. desiccata* are 75-80mm (3-3^1/$_8$in) with the males remaining about 10mm (^{3}/$_8$in) smaller.

During threat display *D. lobata* unfurls its wings and spreads its catching legs. The upper parts of the outer wings are brown-orange and the lower parts pink. The pink areas are flecked with dark patches. The rear wings are black with white veining. The catching arms spread next to the body are a fine orange with a row of white dots and a black patch.

Distribution
Deroplatys species live on the floor of tropical rain forests. *D. dessicata* originates from Indonesia and Malaysia, *D. lobata* from Malaysia, and *D. truncata* from Malaysia, Borneo, and Sumatra.

Care
Use a terrarium with a reasonable sized floor area (150 x 150mm/6 x 6in) and cover this with a 50-100mm layer of leaf mould. Provide a stem, thick branch, or piece of cork bark. Keep the ground moist by thorough spraying.

Almost adult Empusa pennata.

Reproduction
About three egg cases are laid in splits in wood from which 20-40 offspring emerge after about seven weeks if kept at about 28°C (82.4°F).
The newly-emerged insects do not have the broad pro-thorax plate. This increases in size with each stage.

EMPUSA PENNATA

Appearance
Females are up to 65mm (2^9/$_{16}$in) with the males 5-15mm (^{3}/$_{16}$-^{5}/$_8$in) shorter. With their slender bodies and pro-thorax plate these insects are not readily spotted in grass. There is a large conical projection on the head which is larger with females than males. The males on the other hand have larger spring-like antennae with which to find a female by her scent. Both characteristics can be discerned by semi-mature specimens. Adults of this species are brown and have green wings.

Distribution
This species lives in hot, dry grassland and scrub throughout the Mediterranean region.

Verzorging
E. Pennata rarely eats one of its own kind of the same size and so they can be kept in groups. Provide at least one spot for them that is 30-35°C (86-95°F) by day. Spray the terrarium once each week.

Reproduction
Leave the final-stage nymphs at 10-15°C (50-59°F) in December and January to over-winter. These nymphs will become adult in spring. About 40 larvae emerge from the egg cases after about five weeks at 32°C (89.6°F).

Male Idolomorpha lateralis, *close relative of* Empusa, *from Chad.*

Male and female nymphs of Gongylus gongylodes.

Hierodula tenuidentata.

Female Hierodula parviceps *in The Philippines.*

GONGYLUS GONGYLODES

Appearance
Both sexes of this bizarrely-shaped species are 85-100mm ($3^3/_8$-4in). The prothorax is very elongated and narrow. Both the body and legs are lobed, and the head is pointed. The female is brown and she has wings that cover three-quarters of her abdomen. The wings of the darker male cover his entire abdomen and his antennae are broader and feathery.

Distribution
Southern India and Sri Lanka.

Verzorging
Keep this species at 30-35°C (86-95°F) although it can survive up to 60°C (140°F). Spray with water three times a week but for short duration. This species is not cannibalistic and can be kept in groups in a spacious terrarium (minimum 40 x 40 x 50cm/16 x 16 x $19^3/_4$in).

Reproduction
The female lays up to ten egg cases from which 30-40 nymphs emerge after five to seven weeks if kept at 30-40°C (86-104°F) and sprayed three times a week.

HIERODULA SPECIES

The species of this genus are very similar to *Sphodromantis* species and they are regularly confused with them.

Appearance
Hierodula species are of the classic praying mantis form. They are green or brown but can also be reddish-brown or yellow-green. Females of *H. membranacea* are 90mm ($3^1/_2$in), the males 80mm ($3^1/_8$in). With H. parviceps the females are 65-70mm ($2^9/_{16}$-$2^3/_4$in) and males 55-60mm ($2^5/_{32}$-$2^3/_8$in). Both sexes possess wings that cover the entire abdomen.

Distribution
The species of this genus inhabit shrubs and trees of hot and humid climates in South-East Asia.

Reproduction
The females are fairly aggressive towards the males. The method of introducing a cricket to the female to give the male confidence works well provided the female has been adult long enough (it can need four weeks). Each female lays up to six blue or white egg cases which quickly become brown. If kept at 25-30°C (77-86°F) 100-200 young emerge after five-and-a-half to six weeks.

HYMENOPUS CORONATUS, ORCHID PRAYING MANTIS

This praying mantis, which is very difficult to breed, is often regarded as the finest looking.

Appearance
Adult females are about 60mm ($2^3/_8$in) and are white with a green haze over the wings and brown markings. Adult males are no larger than 30mm ($1^3/_{16}$in) and they are marked with white and

Almost fully-matured Hymenopus *nymph.*

Hymenopus coronatus *newly emerged.*

brown. The immature specimens are pink, white, or whitish pink. There are semi-circular folds of skin on the walking legs and the eyes are pointed.

Distribution
This species hides between large white or pink flowers, frequently orchids, in Western Malaysia and Sumatra. They lie in wait for flower-seeking insects.

Accommodation
Provide a temperature of 25-30°C (77-86°F) and relative humidity of 80-90%. It is important to spray two or three times each day and ventilate well with a fan.

Feeding
Feed copiously with flower-seeking insects such as bees, butterflies, and flies. These can be dusted with a vitamin and mineral supplement or with pollen. Poor food is one of the reasons why breeding this species frequently fails.

Reproduction
The male is not easily manipulated into mating with the female so place him in a large terrarium with a female that has been adult for least two weeks. During mating the male regularly and audibly drums on the female with his catching arms.

Each of the five or so egg cases are about 60mm (2³/₈in) long and 10mm (³/₈in) across and is white. These egg cases require fresh air and high humidity of 80-90%. Spray twice each day. About 100 bright red and black nymphs emerge after 44-46 days if kept at 23°C (73.4°F) by day and slightly

Mating attempt by Hymenopus coronatus.

cooler at night. After their first moult the nymphs are pink-white.

Rearing
Care for the young of this species in the same way as the adults. Males if kept in the same conditions will mature much earlier than their sisters. By the time the females are adult, the brothers are probably all dead. If the males are required to breed with hatchlings from the same cluster of egg cases as themselves then separate the sexes as early as possible. The young males have larger wings than a female of the same size. Place the males at a temperature of 20°C (68°F). The females on the other hand need to develop as fast as possible.

MANTIS RELIGIOSA

This well-known species is the classic praying mantis form. Females are 45-80mm (1³/₄-3¹/₈in)

Mantis religiosa *female.*

long, males 40-65mm ($1^9/_{16}$-$2^9/_{16}$in). Both sexes are green or brown. There is a white patch on the inside of the coxa of the catching arm.

Distribution
Mantis religiosa occurs in Germany, where it is protected, but is rare. It is more commonplace elsewhere in southern parts of Europe and they are also found in other parts of the world, such as North America.

Accommodation
Keep at a temperature of 20-30°C (68-86°F) and spray once per week.

Reproduction
The egg cases are produced in later summer or autumn, usually beneath stones, where they over-winter. The 80-200 offspring emerge in May or June.

MIOMANTIS SPECIES

Appearance
Miomantis species are 35-45mm ($1^3/_8$in-$1^3/_4$in), and are light brown or green. Males are often 5mm ($^3/_{16}$in) longer than the females and they have feelers that are twice as long. The lighter weight males can fly very well with their large, transparent wings. The wings of females are coloured. *M. pharaonica* is distinguished by black dots on the coxae of the catching arms.

Distribution
Miomantis paykullii comes from North and East Africa, *M. pharaonica* from Egypt, and *M. abyssinica* originates from Tanzania. All the species live among shrubs and savannah.

Miomantis pharaonica *of Egypt, mating.*

Miomantis pharaonica *of Egypt, mating.*

Miomantis abyssinica *from Tanzania, cleaning herself.*

Accommodation
The temperature range of these praying mantises if 22-35°C (71.6-95°F). Keep them in reasonably humid conditions (60-70%) by spraying twice each week.

Reproduction
Miomantis species are easy to breed provided there is sufficient food available (springtails, aphids, and small fruit flies). A well-nourished female will lay twenty egg cases. These are light brown, triangular, and about 20-30mm ($^3/_4$-$1^3/_{16}$in) long. If kept at 25°C (77°F) the 20-50 nymphs will emerge as quickly as about thirty days. The nymphs are 5mm ($^5/_{32}$in) long.
Some species also reproduce by parthenogenisis.

PARASPHENDALE AFFINIS

Appearance
Females are 50mm (2in) and light brown with pale grey markings. The wings cover three-quarters of the abdomen. The inner sides of the front wings are a bright brown with black markings with the rear wings being mauve. The inside of the catching arms also display brightly-coloured brown. *P. affinis* shows this readily when adopting the threat stance (photo p91).
Males are up to 35mm ($1^3/_8$in), have greater contrast in their markings, and have long wings.

Parasphendale affinis *female.*

Distribution
Trees and shrubs in Ethiopia, Kenya, and Somalia.
Accommodation
Spray three times a week; keep at 25-30°C (77-86°F).
Reproduction
The up to six egg cases contain about 150 eggs which emerge in about six weeks at 25-30°C (77-86°F). The nymphs are black at first and later marked with brown.

PHYLLOCRANIA PARADOXA

Appearance
This species has an asymmetrically formed leaf-like protruberance on its head. There are lobes on the legs and abdomen and the segment protecting the prothorax is broadened to form a square. Females are about 45mm (1³/₄in) long and dark brown. The rear wings are transparent with dark brown patches. The males are 50mm (2in) and are dark to light brown, occasionally olive, with transparent grey-brown wings, and their antennae are much longer than those of the female.
Distribution
Open scrub and woodland in eastern parts of Africa from Somalia to South Africa.

Female Phyllocrania paradoxa *above her eggs.*

Popa undata nymph in camouflage stance.

Mating pair of Popa undata.

Accommodation
Ensure a temperature of 25-30°C (77-86°F) and spray four to seven times each week.
Reproduction
The thin egg cases are about 40mm (1⁹/₁₆in) long and at first are white. About 25-30 young emerge after five weeks at 25°C (77°F). This species is not very aggressive and they can be reared together.

POPA UNDATA

Popa species mimic dead branches and are completely dark brown. When older, the fore-end and first segment of the abdomen are lighter brown. *P. undata* has purple and *P. batesi* yellow colouring on the insides of the catching arms. Females are about 65mm (2⁹/₁₆in) and have wings about 28mm (1¹/₁₆in) long with a light diagonal stripe through the middle. The thinner males are 55cm (2⁵/₃₂in) long and have 35mm (1³/₈in) long. The rear wings are darker in colour.
When disturbed they immediately adopt a camouflage stance with the catching arms extended and remain motionless.
Distribution
Popa undata originates from the Transvaal in South Africa. *Popa batesi* lives in southern parts of Madagascar.
Ensure a temperature of 25-30°C (77-86°F) and spray once per week.

Reproduction

When disturbed *Popa* species immediately adopt the camouflage stance and it is difficult to interest them in these circumstances in mating. Place a male and female together therefore in the same terrarium and leave them in peace and quiet. The females are extremely aggressive.

Each week the female lays about one egg case approx. 20 x 16 x 7mm ($^9/_{16}$ x $^3/_8$ x $^5/_{16}$in), laying about five in total. These emerge after five to seven weeks at a temperature of 30°C (86°F) if they are also sprayed once per week. The 100 or so nymphs are pitch black, crooked, and about 7-8mm ($^5/_{16}$in) in size. The nymphs are prone to cannibalism from day one. Semi-mature females can be recognized by a small lobe on the rear walking legs. The females also have a number of spikes on their abdomen.

PSEUDOCREOBOTRA SPECIES

Appearance

These praying mantises are white or pinkish white with broad green markings. There are black and white roundel markings on the wings with a blue centre and the abdomen and walking legs are extensively lobed. During threat display the yellow of the opened rear wings can be seen.

Pseudocreobotra wahlbergii grows to 40-80mm (1$^9/_{16}$-3$^1/_8$in) and they have a thorax that is wider than it is long. *P. ocellata* is 40-50mm (1$^9/_{16}$-2in) with a thorax longer than its width. In addition the indentations of its catching arms are less coarse than those of *P. wahlbergii*.

Distribution

These flower-dwelling praying mantises are mainly found on flowering shrubs. *P. wahlbergii* is found in East Africa, to the east of the East African high plateau with its great lakes, and from Somalia to South Africa. *P. ocellata* originates from west of the East African plateau.

Accommodation

Ensure 25-32°C (77-89.6°F) and spray with water each evening.

Reproduction

The dark brown egg case is 30-80mm (1$^3/_{16}$-3$^1/_8$in) long 5mm ($^3/_{16}$in) wide, and 3-5mm ($^2/_{16}$-$^3/_{16}$in) thick

Female Pseudocreobotra ocellata *with her egg case.*

with a flattened shape. They are extremely well camouflaged on a branch. Some 35-70 nymphs emerge after about six weeks with a temperature of 25-30°C (77-86°F) and spraying twice each day. After several stages they are an attractive pinkish white with green and have a remarkable appearance because of the many lobes and curved abdomen.

PSEUDOHARPAX UGANDANUS

Appearance

Both sexes are 20-25mm ($^3/_4$-1in) long and they are green with pale yellow undersides. The eyes are pointed.

Distribution

Forest and agricultural areas of Rwanda, Uganda, and surrounding countries.

Accommodation

Ensure a temperature of 25-30°C (77-86°F) and spray twice each week.

Reproduction

This species is not very aggressive and mating is easy. The female produces up to fifteen egg cases, each with ten to sixteen eggs which emerge after five weeks. The nymphs are 4mm ($^5/_{32}$in) long.

SPHODROMANTIS SPECIES

These are the most widely kept form of praying mantis and they closely resemble *Hierodula* species. The *Sphodromantis* species though have a bump against the eyes, between the eyes and the antennae.

Pseudocreobotra ocellata *eats a fly.*

Pseudoharpax ugandus *mating.*

Sphodromantis gastrica *mating*.

Stagmatoptera hyaloptera *mating*.

Appearance
Sphodromantis species are green or brown with typical praying mantis appearance. Both sexes of the most widely kept species *(Sphodromantis centralis, S. lineola, S. gastrica,* and *S. belachowski)* are 60-80mm (2³/₈in-3¹/₈in), and S. viridis is 100mm (4in). Both the male and female have long wings with a small white or yellow 'eye'.

Distribution
This genus is found in large parts of West and East Africa below the Sahara. *S. viridis* lives in North Africa and is found along the Mediterranean coast.

Accommodation
Spray once or twice each week and ensure a temperature of 22-30°C (71.6-86°F).

Reproduction
Mating usually passes off easily. A female lays up to six white egg cases that quickly turn brown. Between 70 and 400 nymphs emerge after six weeks if kept at 25-30°C (77-86°F) and sprayed once or twice each week. Nymphs are born tan with dark eyes but turn brown after the first stage.

STAGMATOPTERA HYALOPTERA

Appearance
The female is 57mm (2¹/₄in) with feelers of about 10mm (³/₈in). Her coloured wings match the length of her abdomen. The male is the same size but he has 27mm (1¹/₈in) long antennae. His trans-

Taumantis ehrmannii *mating*.

parent wings are 7mm (⁴/₁₆in) longer than his abdomen. Both sexes are grass green and they have a 4mm (⁵/₃₂in) 'eye' on their wings that are black-brown with a white eye.

Distribution
Argentina.

Reproduction
This species is extremely aggressive. The egg cases over-winter in Northern European summers. The young emerge daily for some weeks which makes rearing them difficult. Keep this species in moderate humidity and at 25°C (77°F).

TAUMANTIS EHRMANNII

Appearance
Grass-green female's wings cover three-quarters of abdomen. Females reach 50mm (2in) compared with 33mm (1⁵/₁₆in) for transparant green-blue males whose wings are 27mm (1¹/₁₆in) projecting 5mm (³/₁₆in) beyond body.

Distribution
Shrub dweller of north-eastern parts of Africa.

Reproduction
Females are aggressive towards males who are sluggish but can fly when confronted with danger. Lumpy egg case is 250x140x100 mm (9¹³/₁₆ x 5¹/₂ x 4in) with 15mm (⁵/₈in) shank. Nymphs emerge after six weeks at 28°C (82.4°F) with weekly spraying. Keep at 25-30°C (77-86°F) and spray twice each week.

TENODERA ARIDIFOLIA SINENSIS

This species is widely used in both China and North America for the biological control of pests.

Appearance
This long thin insect has a small spike on the femur of the four walking legs. Females grow to 85–100mm (3³/₈-4in) long, males 80-95mm (3¹/₈in-3³/₄in). There are green lateral stripes on the predominantly brown wings.

Distribution
Tenodera aridifolia sinensis inhabits grassland in moderate climates. They originate from China but were introduced into the USA. The eggs over-winter.

Reproduction
Tenodera species are easy to breed. Females lay about five egg cases from which 125-400 nymphs emerge after five to six weeks if the temperature is kept at 25°C (77°F) and the eggs are sprayed three times each week. The egg cases are about 35mm (1³/₈in). The nymphs mainly have straight abdomens.
Provide this active species with plenty of space. They can be kept at 20-26°C (68-78.8°F) and provide humidity in the range of 60-65%.

Tenodera aridifolia sinensis *mating.*

Tenodera fasciata *from India is up to 85mm (3³/₈in).*

The order Blattaria, cockroaches

Until recently cockroaches formed, together with praying mantises and termites the order Dictyoptera. The order Blattaria consists of five families: Blattidae, Blaberidae, Blattellidae, Polyphagidae, and Cryptocercidae. At present about 3,500 of these insects have been fully described with new ones being discovered every day, as with all insect orders.
Only about fifty species are a pest for mankind, of which half of these are found in homes. The most ubiquitous form in Western Europe is the German cockroach *Blattella germanica.*
Cockroaches can spread about forty different infections. These are mainly transmitted via the skin but they also regurgitate their food sometimes to mix enzymes from food previously eaten with the new food which also spreads germs. Cockroaches kept in a terrarium will be exposed to little infection.

The German cockroach, Blattella germanica.

Appearance

Cockroaches have a long oval and flattened body which enables them to live in small cracks. Many species can fly but most can run fast on their powerful legs. The downwards facing head is entirely hidden beneath the neck shield or pronotum. The legs are spiky. The soles of the feet have pads to adhere to surfaces. Like many other insects they remain white for some time after shedding their skins until the salt in their new armament has oxidized. The old skin is usually eaten.

The largest cockroach is *Megaloblatta blaberoides* from Central and South America with a 100mm (4in) body and wing span of about 180mm (7^1/$_{16}$in). The burrowing *Macropanesthia rhinoceros* from Queensland in Australia is 15mm (^{5}/$_8$in) shorter but heavier at about 35 grams (1^1/$_4$ oz). Cockroaches are nocturnal creatures. When threatened, many species rasp their legs against their bodies to create sound with *Nauphoeta cinerea* being able to create 60 decibels. Cockroaches live for between three months and two years.

Distribution

Cockroaches are found throughout the world with the greatest variety and numbers being found in the tropics. These nocturnal animals live in every manner of biotope with a few living semi-aquatically. Cockroaches respond to touch all around themselves (thigmotaxis), preferring to live in the narrowest of holes and cracks.

Accommodation

Most cockroaches prefer a warm and moist climate. Provide a temperature of 28-32°C (82.4-89.6°F) and relative humidity of 70-90%. Tropical species will slowly die at below 20°C (68°F) or above 35°C (95°F). At 25°C (77°F) a generation of *Blaptica dubia* will exist for at least six months and at 30°C (86°F) this is only one-and-a-half to two months. Several hundred cockroaches can live in a dark terrarium of 50 x 50 x 30cm (20 x 20 x 12in) if there are sufficient hiding places. Provide hiding places with flower pots, cork tiles, and egg boxes. Place 50mm (2in) of moist peat, old compost, or leaf mould, mixed with sand, on the bottom. Make the container 'cricket proof' (see crickets, page 42).

Insectarium for cockroaches.

Under side of the abdomens of a pair of vibrating cockroaches.

Blaberus cranifer *forms an egg case.*

Feeding

Cockroaches eat virtually any organic matter (e.g. dried cat food, bread) but provide sufficient fruit and vegetables (not in excess to prevent mould). There is no need of a water tray. Clean the breeding terrarium before it starts to smell.

Cockroaches sometimes hunt insects smaller than themselves and cannibalism does occur, which is advantageous in times of food shortage when population numbers need to be controlled.

Many species can easily go without water for a month. Cockroaches often harbour small mites that do them no harm.

Sex determination

The smaller, thinner males have eight abdominal segments, the last of which (with no division) has two additional thin rear feelers between the cerci or other feelers. Females have only six abdominal segments, the last of which has a slight division but there are no additional feelers. The males also sometimes have wings that are clearly longer than those of the female.

Mating

Mating takes place after mutual exploration with the feelers and raising of the wings. The insects remain attached to each other throughout. One species reproduces by parthenogenisis.

Egg laying

Adult females lay between one and fifteen egg cases with 16-45 eggs in each. The egg case is white

Egg case of Blaptica dubia.

while being formed in the body but the soft case turns brown and hard when exposed to the air. The case is partially expelled from the body. Nymphs emerge from the eggs after between two weeks and three months, but usually after two months. The nymphs shed the embryonic skin immediately.

– Most species retain the eggs within the body. After the egg case is formed it slips back inside the body where it is retained in a brood chamber. The nymphs emerge within their mother and then often remain hidden beneath her until the chitin shell hardens. The nymphs of *Byrsotria fumigata* even remain until after the second stage.

– Other species that carry the eggs inside the body also retain them in a brood chamber but eject the egg case several hours before the eggs hatch.

– Species that lay eggs hide the egg cases several hours or days after it is formed in a safe place, such as a crack.

– One species, *Diploptera punctata*, bears live young which are nourished from the mother's body, as opposed to those retained in eggs which derive their nourishment from the egg.

Rearing
Nymphs, which are often 6-12mm ($1/4$-$1/2$in) long can be left with their parents. Depending on the species they mature into adults after five to eleven stages. This development can last for between 50 and 275 days.

Defence and handling
Cockroaches are rarely to be seen because they are timid and nocturnal. In danger they flee and some species are very fast. Escape cannot be wholly prevented, especially if a container with many small cockroaches is opened. Care for cockroaches therefore in a bare unfurnished area (such as a shower cubicle) to make it easier to catch specimens that escape.

Many species rasp their legs to create a hissing sound or give off a noxious odour which also irritates the skin. Those who are not allergic can pick cockroaches up with bare hands. Hold them firmly on both sides.

A plague of cockroaches is often caused by failure to keep an area clean. Try to prevent this happening by leaving no food remnants or moisture for cockroaches and keep everything clean. Glue traps work well but poison does not. If necessary contact the pest control department of your local council. Escaped specimens of tropical species will not create a plague.

BLABERUS CRANIFER

Syn. *Blaberus fuscus.*

Appearance
Females are 55-65mm ($2^5/_{32}$-$^{29}/_{16}$in) long, the males slightly smaller. Adults are light brown with a dark patch on the neck shield. There is also a brown-black patch on the wings. This cockroach is extremely quick on its feet but never flies.

Distribution
Inhabitant at ground level of tropical forests in Central and South America.

Reproduction
Nymphs of about 7mm ($^4/_{16}$in) emerge after three-and-a-half weeks. They are dark brown with tan markings.

BLAPTICA DUBIA

Syn. *Blaberus dubia.*

Appearance
Both sexes are 40-45mm ($1^9/_{16}$in-$1^3/_4$in) long and they are black-brown with lighter brown markings. Only the males have long wings

Distribution
Argentina.

Reproduction
The female produces an egg case every six weeks with 15-30 eggs. The nymphs are sexually mature after four to six months.

Female Blaberus cranifer *and nymph.*

Blaptica dubia.

Euryotis floridiana.

Panchlora nivea *with egg case.*

EURYOTIS FLORIDIANA

Appearance
Females are about 45mm (1³/₄in), males slightly smaller. Both sexes are dark brown with reddish brown markings and neither has wings. When threatened they exude a stinking and irritating defensive discharge.

Distribution
Florida and the West Indies. This species mainly lives on dead wood.

Reproduction
This species lays eggs.

GROMPHADORHINA PORTENTOSA

Appearance
This wingless cockroach is about 60mm (2³/₈in) and brown. The more thickly protected parts are black. The wingless body is very flat.
These nocturnal insects are lethargic. Confronted with danger they pull the abdomen in and blast air out of the trachea to produce a hissing sound of 90 decibels.

Distribution
Tree dwellers of the tropical rain forest of eastern Madagascar.

Sex determination
Males have longer, broader antennae and two large battering lumps on the neck shield. Territorial disputes between males are settled by shoving and making a hissing sound.

Feeding
Mainly fruit but also other organic matter.

Gromphadorhina portentosa *male.*

Reproduction
This species carries its eggs internally and produces 20-40 offspring each time. The gestation period lasts for a maximum of seven months.

PANCHLORA NIVEA

Appearance
Females are about 20mm (³/₄in), males remain 5mm (³/₁₆in) smaller. Both sexes are green with a yellow lateral strip on each side. The wings are transparent and adults can fly well. *P. nivea* is nocturnal.

Distribution
Tropical forests and plantations from Mexico to northern parts of South America and the Antilles.

Accommodation
Keep this species at 28-32°C (82.4-89.6°F) and at a relative humidity of 80-100%, ensuring adequate ventilation. Lay a 20cm (8in) moist mixture of leaf mould and sand on the bottom of the terrarium and do not allow it to dry out. The nymphs live in this soil until their final stage. This cockroach can be combined with fruit beetles.

Feeding
Fruits (bananas), honey, nectar (for aviary birds), and dried pet food.

Reproduction
Young specimens of this species which retains eggs in its body are brown or black. The nymphs must not dry out. They mature after about three months and then live from six months to one year.

PERIPLANETA AMERICANA, AMERICAN COCKROACH

Appearance
Females are 40mm (1⁹/₁₆in), males 30mm (1³/₁₆in) and both sexes are shiny red-brown. This potential plague insect can run very fast.

Distribution
This ground-living insect is found throughout the world in warm and moist conditions.

Periplaneta americana.

Reproduction

The egg case with a maximum of 40 eggs is placed in a crack. The nymphs emerge after five weeks and are adult after nine to thirteen stages. This species can be very harmful and form plagues.

Achrimandrita tesselata.

Blaberus atropos.

Byrsotria fumigata.

Byrsotria *sp. from Cuba.*

Elliptorrhina chopardi.

Leucophaea maderae.

Other types of cockroach			
Species	*Origins*	♂ *(mm/in)*	♀ *(mm/in)*
Achrimandrita tesselata	Central and South America	70 (2³/₄in)	60 (2³/₈in)
Blaberus atropos	Central and South America	53 (2¹/₁₆in)	45 (1³/₄in)
Blaberus discoidales	Central and South America	55 (2⁵/₃₂in)	50 (2in)
Byrsotria fumigata	South America	55 (2⁵/₃₂in)	45 (1³/₄in)
Byrsotria sp. female with part wings, male full wings	Cuba	55 (2⁵/₃₂in)	45 (1³/₄in)
Elliptorrhina chopardi	Madagascar	50 (2in)	40 (1⁹/₁₆in)
Leucophaea maderae	throughout tropics	50 (2in)	40 (1⁹/₁₆in)
Nauphoeta cinerea	throughout tropics	35 (1³/₈in)	30 (1³/₁₆in)
Princisia vanwaerebeki	Madagascar	50-80 (2-3¹/₈in)	70-90(2³/₄-3¹/₂in)

Nauphoeta cinerea.

Well-camouflaged Acrida bicolor *of West Africa.*

Princisia vanwaerebeki.

Terrarium for grasshoppers or stick insects.

The order Orthoptera (Saltatoria), grasshoppers and crickets

A characteristic feature of this order is the back legs which usually have developed into efficient jumping legs. The males are usually able to stridulate to make the well-known 'chirrup'. The order consists of two sub orders, Ensifera and Caelifera. Caelifera, sub order of shorter antennae grasshoppers, includes the true grasshoppers. They have short, thick antennae of 5-20 segments. The males in particular make a sound by rasping a row of pins on the inside of the femur against the hairy veins of the front wings. The ears are usually side on to the abdomen and are usually covered by the wings.

The Ensifera have longer antennae and includes crickets. Except for the mole cricket they all have antennae longer than their bodies. Males produce sound by rasping teeth on the veins of the front wings against a hardened area of the other wings. The ears are on the tibiae of the front legs. The females have an easily visible ovipositor on their abdomen.

Caelifera, *short antennae grasshoppers*

With the exception of *Proscopia* species, all the species of short-antennae grasshoppers belong to the family Acrididae, of field grasshoppers.

Appearance

True grasshoppers vary widely in colour. While one species adopts camouflage, another uses bright warning colours. The nymphs often have totally different colours from their parents. The body is usually elongated and laterally flattened. Most species have full wings but only a few species can fly long distances. The front wings are always thicker than the rear ones, which lie folded beneath the front wings. Determination of the species is difficult because of the wide variation in species and close resemblance to each other. Often the form of the male sexual organ provides a clue.

Distribution

Caelifera are found throughout the world. Field grasshoppers are predominantly found in open and reasonably dry areas on herbs and grasses. They exist in profuse numbers.

Accommodation

Grasshoppers hang themselves up to shed their coats and therefore need a terrarium that is at least three times higher than the longest specimen (see stick insects p64). Provide a temperature of 25-37°C (77-98.6°). A good example of a terrarium is a one metre (40in) high container that is well-ventilated as illustrated on p105. Fix a light-box at the top above the mesh with a spot lamp and incandescent lamp. Spray about twice each week. Provide at least 100mm (4in) of a moderately moist mixture of old compost or peat with sand. Cover the entire bottom with this or place in a jar.

Grasshoppers can be ideally combined with other grasshopper-like species, stick insects, or small praying mantises.

Feeding

Place branches of food plants (often bramble) in a jar of water. Provide grass eaters with grass gathered together with a rubber band so that old grass can be removed easily. A well organized breeding set-up has a big demand for food. The adults are especially fond of thistle flowers and rose hips.

Sex determination

Females have an ovipositor at the end of their abdomen which when viewed from the side appears to be a series of backward facing segments. The rear end of a male has the appearance of a raised up bow of a boat. Viewed from below, the final segment of the male abdomen is one piece but is divided with females.

Mating

Adults mate regularly with the male arching his abdomen around that of the female.

Many grasshoppers, like Chondracis rosea, *eat bramble leaves.*

Eggs of Locusta migratoria.

Egg laying

Grasshoppers lay tens of eggs in a foamy mass in the soil. The female pushes her rear end into the soil to do so. The ground must be as moist a fresh compost. The foamy egg mass quickly hardens and protects the eggs.

Rearing

Nymphs emerge between two weeks and six months after the eggs are laid. The membrane which protects them as they crawl through the soil is immediately discarded once they reach the surface. Nymphs are often a totally different colour from their parents and they often remain together in groups.

Place the nymphs in the same container as the parents. The initial phase is critical but once the third skin has been shed the further development is straightforward. Most grasshoppers live for two to six months as adults.

Handling and defence

Catch small nymphs with a jar. Semi-mature specimens are strong enough to be grasped by the sides of their thorax. Adults can be held by the wings and hind legs. Grasshoppers often regurgitate their food when held and others exude a deterrent substance.

AULARCHES MILLIARIS

Appearance

Females are 70mm (2³/₄in), males 50mm (2in) long. Both sexes are an attractive green, yellow, black, and white, with red markings. There are several lumps and spikes on the neck segment. This species makes no sound.

Distribution

Hot, reasonably dry areas in Indonesia and Malaysia.

Food

Bramble leaves in captivity, silkweed *(Asclepias sp.)* in the wild.

Rearing

The eggs emerge after about four months. The nymphs are black with bright red spots and a broad white lateral stripe from head to base of the hind leg.

Defence

When threatened *A. milliaris* exudes a foamy defence substance from the bottom of its hind legs.

Defence

This beetle can give a nasty bite and spurt a defensive acidic fluid which is directed at the face. This burns painfully and can be dangerous for the eyes.

The Scarabaeidae family, (scarabs, chafers, tumblebugs)

This family consists of sub families such as Cetoninae (garden chafer and some 100 *Pachnoda* species), Goliathinae (with *Goliathus* and *Eudicella)*, and Dynastinae (rhinoceros beetle and *Dynastes).*

All the members of this family have antennae that consist of moveable flattened plates. These are used to sense with and play an important role in partner recognition.

The insects of this family are diurnal, spending the night mainly underground. Cetoninae and Goliathinae are unable to fold away their covering plates for and during flight and hence they make a buzzing sound as a result of the wings hitting the plates.

CETONINAE AND GOLIATHINAE, CHAFERS

In addition to the well-known garden chafers, this group includes the small colourful Goliathinae.

Dicronorrhina micans *of central Africa.*

Eudicella ducalis *of Burundi.*

Mounted Smithi (Euthalia) bertherandi *from southern Africa. The true* Eudicella smithi *is not certainly a species and cannot be kept in captivity.*

Eudicella woermanni woermanni *from Zaire.*

Smaragdestes africana africana *is green but* Smaragdestes africana smaragdina *is yellow.*

Appearance

Chafers are usually 20-40mm ($^3/_4$-1$^9/_{16}$in) long. The size can vary widely depending on the circumstance (moisture, food etc.). *Pachinoda marginata peregrina* for instance can range from 2-25mm ($^3/_4$-1in). These insects vary in colour through yellow, black, emerald green, blue, purple, white and or red, and either shiny or dull.

Some Goliath beetles *(Goliathus* species) from West Africa can be about 100mm (4in) and weight 110 grams (3$^3/_4$oz).

Distribution

Chafers are widely found in the tropics, especially in forests, plantations, and gardens. The adults are active during the day searching for ripe fruit, flower nectar, and sap from trees.

Accommodation

A well-ventilated 40 x 30 x 30cm (16 x 12 x 12in) terrarium is sufficient for a large group of 30mm (1$^3/_{16}$in) of these beetles. Lay 100mm (4in) of leaf

111

Smaragd africana oertzeni *from Tanzania.*

Gymnetis holocerica *from Bolivia.*

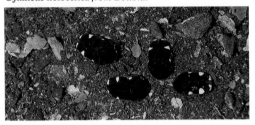

Pachnoda ephippiata *from Tanzania and Kenya.*

Pachnoda flaviventris *from South Africa.*

Pachnoda marginata aurantiaca (gold), P. m. marginata *(dark), and* P. m. peregrina *(brown/yellow). All are from the west coast of Africa (Senegal to Angola).*

mould, woodland soil, or old compost on the bottom, with similar moistness as new compost. Do not make the soil too moist or allow it to dry out, so do not use any bottom heating. Provide climbing opportunities and keep the temperature at about 25°C (77°F) and spray once per week.

Feeding

Feed ripe or overripe fruit, and canned peas. The larvae eat rotten wood and decaying leaves but some species depend on them (e.g. *Dicronorrhina micans*).

Sex determination

The males of *Eudicella* and *Dicranorrhina* species are larger than the females and have a Y-shape nose plate.

With many species such as those of Pachnoda the males have a groove from front to back on the underside of their abdomens.

Pachnoda marginata marginata.

Stephanorrhina guttata *from western and central Africa.*

A pair of Pachnoda marginata peregrina.

Larvae of Pachnoda marginata peregrina.

Female rhinoceros beetle (Augosoma centaurus) *in Cameroon.*

Egg laying
After mating the female lays one to three eggs each day in the ground. The larvae emerge after two to four weeks.

Rearing
Larvae of chafers resemble caterpillars but are grubs. They crawl underground on their back to fruit and other food laying on the surface. A 40cm (16in) long terrarium can house 30 adult *Pachnoda marginata* and about 150 larvae. The animals will consume two bananas and half a tin of peas each week. Larvae from some species are cannibalistic so that with these it is best to rear the larvae separately. They pupate after three to four months in black earthen cocoons in the soil (see photo p62). Pupation takes one to two months.

Some *Pachnoda* species breed so quickly that their larvae can be used as food for insectivorous terrarium animals.

Dynastinae, rhinoceros beetles

Rhinoceros beetles are usually fairly large and mainly brown or black in colour. The thorax plate of the males have one to five horns. With Dynastes hercules from Peru these can be up to 90mm (3¹/₂in) long. These beetles eat fruit and their larvae consume rotten wood or humus. Bag up oak

Male rhinoceros beetle (Augosoma centaurus) *in Cameroon.*

and beech leaves in autumn and feed them as soon as they start to disintegrate. Rotting sawdust can also be given as food. The larvae stage last for one to four years. The adult beetles live for three to six months after pupating, which takes one-and-a-half to two-and-a-half months.

XYLOTRUPES GIDEON

Appearance
Females are 45mm (1³/₄in), males 65mm (2⁹/₁₆in). Both sexes are lustrous brown-black.

Distribution
Various subspecies live in Thailand and Indonesia. The beetles inhabit trees where they seek both food and partners. The larvae live underground.

Accommodation
A well-ventilated 50 x 30 x 30cm (20 x 12 x 12in) terrarium is adequate for a pair or trio of these insects. Lay 150mm (6in) of reasonably moist leaf mould mixed with some rotten wood on the bottom. Provide some climbing opportunities. Maintain a temperature of 25-28°C (77-82.4°F) with a lamp and spray once each week. Do not allow the bottom to dry out, so do not use bottom heating.

Feeding
Feed the beetles ripe or overripe fruit.

Reproduction
Reproduction is largely as per chafers. The larvae of rhinoceros beetles are also grubs and below

Pair of Xilotrupes gideon *which have very short horns.*

113

ground they eat rotten oak or beech wood, never coniferous wood. They pupate after ten to twelve months in black earthen cocoons in the soil. The pupation last one to two months and the beetles then live for another six months.

The sub-order Heteroptera, bugs

This diverse sub-order belongs, together with cicadas and aphids to the Hemiptera order of insects with snout-like projections. The species are sucking and piercing insects that all have a clear rostrum or tube extension to the mouth. Many species feed on sap of plants but the predator bugs of the Reduviidae family are of most importance for terrarium keepers. Larvae of this mainly diurnally-active group often camouflage themselves with all manner of materials. They lie in ambush for their prey or actively hunt them down.

PLATYMERIS SPECIES, PREDATORY BUGS

Appearance
Platymeris biguttatus is a 10-40mm ($^3/_8$-1$^9/_{16}$in) long black bug with two white dots on its wings. There is a yellow band on each leg. Young nymphs are reddish brown. Shortly after shedding their skin these insects are bright red-orange with yellow legs.
Platymeris rhadamanthus resembles *P. biguttatus* but has red spots instead of white ones.
Distribution
Platymeris biguttatus originates from West Africa, *P. rhadamanthus* from East Africa (including Tanzania and Kenya). Both species inhabit the floor of the rain forest.
Accommodation
Fairly large groups of these animals at each stage of development can be kept in a 30 x 20 x 20cm (12 x 8 x 8in) terrarium. Provided there are sufficient hiding places from cork, wood, or stones there should not be too much problem with cannibalism. Provide a temperature of 24-30°C (75.2-86°F) and relative humidity of 60-80%. Spray once per

Platymeris rhadamanthus.

A male bug has a conical thickening of his abdomen.

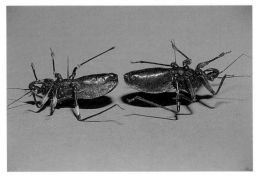

A semi-mature predatory bug during the shedding process.

week. Lay a moderately moist base of peat and sand mixture or old compost of 50mm (2in) thickness.
Feeding
Provide a variety of insects, such as crickets, cockroaches, and mealworms. These are hunted down, held with the forelegs and sucked out. The prey are paralysed quickly by poison injected by the bug.
Sex determination
Only the males have a conical thickening of the last belly plate of the abdomen. This plate is flat and divided in two with females.
Reproduction
Parthenogenisis occurs in addition to sexual reproduction.
If properly nourished and the conditions are right, the females will lay a few small black-brown eggs each day, letting the eggs, with their white covering, drop to the ground. The eggs need to lay in moderately moist soil and they hatch after one to two months.
Rearing
The young remain red-brown through several stages of development. At first they eat the larvae of buffalo gnats, and small crickets. They only indulge in cannibalism if there is too little food and water.
Defence/handling
A sting from a predatory bug is painful and can

Platymeris biguttatus eats a cricket.

cause annoying infections. Poison is excreted or spurted out and can be squirted in the eyes, because the piercing snout can be directed.

Take care at all times and do not handle with bare hands. These animals are best handled with long forceps with two pieces of draught strip stuck to each side and wearing safety glasses.

The order Lepidoptera, butterflies and moths

Approximately 150,000 species of butterflies and moths fly in the entire world. They have two large wings attached to the thorax. Butterflies in particular have very beautiful colourings and markings on the upper sides of their wings.

THE GENUS *HELICONIUS*, PASSION-FLOWER BUTTERFLIES

Appearance
Heliconius species often have longer fore-wings, resulting in a wing span of 60-85mm (2³/₈-3³/₈in). These butterflies are multi-coloured, often black with yellow, red, or orange markings. The butterflies live three to eight months.

Distribution
There are more than 500 species of this genus. They originate from wet forests in the southern parts of USA, Central, and South America.

Accommodation
With a few butterflies it is quickly necessary to

have a large (mesh) insectarium (2 x 1 x 1 metre or 6ft 6in x 3ft 3in x 3ft 3in for small species such as *Heliconius* spp.) or a greenhouse with a double door. Drape the inside of the greenhouse with horticultural netting to prevent the insects hurting themselves against the glass. Butterflies and moths will hurt themselves quickly in small terrariums as well. Create an insectarium of mesh and wood, providing sufficient ventilation if a number of walls are airtight.

Provide a daytime temperature of 25-30°C (77-86°F). 20°C (68°F) at night, and spray the terrarium three times each day or use a misting system for 80-90% humidity. Provide lighting for butterflies and their caterpillars for 14-16 hours per day to encourage plenty of eggs to be laid. Plant host plants in which the butterflies can deposit their

Heliconius charitonius.

Heliconius hecale.

eggs. Sometimes this will be the only plant the caterpillars eat. With *Heliconius* species this is *Passiflora* species plants.

Plagues of insects such as white fly, aphids, and red spider mites can be biologically controlled with ichneumon flies and predatory mites. Hummingbirds eat spiders.

Feeding

Nectar plants will rarely provide sufficient nutrition. Provide supplementary food for butterflies with 2 spoonfuls of nectar for aviary birds, 2 teaspoons of honey, and 2 teaspoons of pollen in 500ml (17fl oz) water. Provide this in tubes hidden in the middle of flowers painted on acrylic sheet.

Sex determination

Males have scent reflectors, which are the glinting parts at the front of the rear wings. This feature is usually beneath the front wings.

The best way of determining sex is generally by studying the side of the belly of the pupa.

Mating

A female attracts a male with sex pheromones, sitting with opened wings and raise abdomen on a plant. The male tries to make contact as he flies in.

Egg laying

The eggs of *Heliconius* species are often yellow and bottle-shaped. They are laid on plants of the genus *Passiflora* and the larvae emerge after six to eight days. It is best to remove the eggs from the butterfly cage and to rear the caterpillars in a separate cage. The caterpillars are often prickly. The caterpillars are immune to the toxins in the passion flowers but this makes them poisonous and the butterfly is also poisonous.

Rearing

The caterpillars need a lot of ventilation. Ensure there are always fresh stems of the food plant and add one tablespoon of sugar per litre to the drinking water and protect this to prevent the caterpillars from drowning. It is also possible to place entire plants in the breeding area. Especially during their final stage the caterpillars eat a great deal. Provide a temperature of 25-30°C (77-86°F) and lightly spray the terrarium each day but never the caterpillars themselves. During their development the caterpillars change colour and hair covering extensively. Caterpillars go through about five changes and *Heliconius* caterpillars pupate after two weeks.

Heliconius melpomene *hybrid just before mating.*

Pupa nursery.

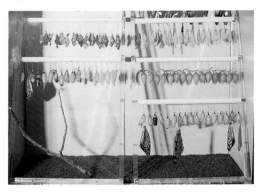

Atacus atlas *mating.*

Immediately before pupating the caterpillars search the terrarium for a good place to pupate. Provide several branches for them. Pupation takes seven to ten days. Regularly introduce new blood from unrelated specimens to prevent the risk of the population suddenly crashing.

Handling

In principal the butterflies should never be handled. It is better to move the eggs, caterpillars, and pupae. Hairy caterpillars often possess hairs that when touched cause irritation and inflammation rather like nettle rash.

OTHER BUTTERFLIES

The following butterflies can be cared for in a broadly similar manner.

ATACUS ATLAS

Appearance

These brown moths with light brown markings can have wing spans up to 220mm (8⁵/₈in). The antennae of the males are large and spring like. They live for a maximum of fourteen days.

Distribution

South-East Asia.

Reproduction

The eggs are laid in the wild on the Tree of Heaven *(Ailanthus glandulosa)* or on privet in captivity. The larvae emerge after 10–14 days and are initially white and woolly; feed privet. The caterpillars pupate after 12–16 weeks when about 120mm (4³/₄in), and pupation takes two to six weeks.

Heliconius melpomene *hybrid at the feeding point.*

Caligo atreus.

Atacus caesar *on its cocoon*.

CALIGO MEMNON

Appearance
This brown butterfly that is active at twilight is marked with yellow and brown has a wing span of 90-110mm (3$^1/_2$-4$^5/_{16}$in). The reverse sides of the wings reflect blue light. They live for three months.
Distribution
Tropical rain forest from Mexico to the Amazon region.
Reproduction
The eggs are laid on banana trees (*Musa* spp.) and emerge after fourteen days. The caterpillars eat the same plants and they pupate after eight to ten weeks, hanging in a dark place. Pupation lasts for three weeks. Feed the butterflies with overripe bananas supplemented with water and rum or sprinkled with pollen.

DRYAS JULIA

Appearance
This butterfly is related to those of the genus *Heliconia* and is orange with brown-black lines surrounding and on the wings. The wing span is 40-45mm (1$^9/_{16}$-1$^3/_4$in). They live for a few months.
Distribution
Moist forests from the southern parts of USA to the south of South America.

Caligo memnon.

Female common windmill, Atrophaneura polyeuctes, *is poisonous.*

Reproduction

The eggs, which are laid on plants of the *Passiflora* genus, emerge after 7 days. Feed the caterpillars with the same plant. The larvae pupate after 2 weeks with pupation lasting 7-9 days.

PAPILIO SPECIES

Papilio species enjoy CITES protection. *P. chikae, P. homerus,* and *P. hospiton* are in list A, with *P. benguetanus, P. esperanza, P. grosesmithi, P. marabo, P. morondavana,* and *P. neumoegeni* in list B.

Appearance

These butterflies are often black with white, yellow, red, or orange markings. The wing span is generally 60-100mm ($2^3/_8$-4in) and there is usually a 'swallow tail' on each of the rear wings. They live for 2-6 weeks.

Distribution

Moderate to tropical parts of Asia.

Reproduction

Several species lay their eggs on citrus fruit trees and the larvae emerge after fourteen days. Feed the caterpillars, which are generally green, leaves from citrus trees, carrot foliage, dill, rue, and parsley. They pupate after two weeks with pupation lasting two to six weeks.

This Papilio polytes *female is not poisonous but mimics the common windmill butterfly.*

119

Aphonopelma bicoloratum.

The class Arachnida, or arachnids

Spiders and their related cousins do not enjoy a good image. Perhaps this is due to their many legs, their hairiness, predatory lifestyle, and the way the male is killed after a mating that has more in common with a rape. The media, especially films, have hardly helped improve the spider's image. Consequently the beauty and tremendous variety of colour, shape, and behaviour of these creatures is unknown to most people.

The class Arichnida contains some 90,000 species that have been described, contained within the following orders:
Araneae/Araneida (true spiders)
Scorpiones (scorpions)
Uropygi (whipscorpions)
Amblypygi (tail-less whipscorpions, whip spiders)
Solifugae (windscorpions)
Pseudoscorpiones (pseudoscorpions)
Opiliones (harvestmen)
Acarina/Acari (acari mites, ticks)
Ricinulei (small, slow-moving arachnids)
Palpigrada (microwhipscorpions)
Schizomida (short-tailed whipscorpions/schizomids)

The body of most arachnids consists of a combined head and chest segment (prosoma, also known as cephalothorax) and the rear part of the body (opisthosoma abdomen). There are virtually always 4 pairs of walking legs attached to the prosoma, the jaw feelers (pedipalps) and the jaws (chelicerae). Other external characteristics will be dealt with per order.

MOULTING

Arachnids are invertebrate arthropods so that they too must shed their exoskeleton in order to grow (see p58). During the hormone-controlled preparation for the moult the arachnid eats nothing for several days up to several weeks and keeps itself quiet. Once the new 'skin' is formed beneath the old one, the archnid acquires a dull appearance and bare patches of skin darken in colour.
During this moult body fluids in the opisthosoma increase pressure within the body. The jaws push the dorsal shield free from the prosoma (combined head and chest) and sometimes the rear part of the body (opisthoma) splits open. The arachnid then crawls out of its old exoskeleton. Even the book lungs, and parts of the gullet, anus, and places where the muscles are attached to the dorsal shield are replaced. The body is now pumped up with air and with fluid from the opisthoma.
During the hardening of the slightly larger new exoskeleton the arachnid is again quiet but once the new plates harden, within anything from a few hours to weeks, the fasting stops. Arachnids that have lost limbs can replace them within three to four moults.

POISONOUS ARACHNIDS

Although the majority of arachnids are completely harmless, a number of species are kept in terrariums that are fairly venomous. Examples are the black widow spider, *Phoneutria* species, the 'violin spider', and several scorpions.
The toxicity of a bite or sting depends on the type of arachnid, its size, sex, time since its last meal, and amount of toxin injected. During a defensive bite, during which little or no venom is injected, the arachnid withdraws its jaws quickly. With an attacking bite, the arachnid keeps its jaws clamped longer and more toxin is passed. The risks of death from a bite with the types referred to is 1-5% but children, older persons, or persons with lowered resistance due to illness and those with allergic reactions are at greater risk.
Poisonous arachnids are kept in terrariums because of the interest of studying the species but al-

Brachypelma smithi is the best known tarantula kept in terrariums.

Pterinochilus murinus is an aggressive and quite venomous tarantula.

A black widow for sale at a show.

Spider with pincer jaws.

so because people get a kick out of keeping a venomous creature.

Bear in mind that everyone may forget to close a door occasionally. A 30cm (12in) pair of forceps may well prove a useful tool. Handle the specimens as little as possible and be certain precisely which species are present. Dangerous and harmless arachnids can closely resemble each other. If there is any doubt then take care.

Never ever make a show of bravado for the benefit of friends. This is not the point of this hobby.

Do not work with your arachnids if you are off colour or have had a little bit too much to drink. The speed and assuredness with which arachnids strike their target is impressive and slow reactions can be punished. Take care with pets and children. Write down instructions for others against the chance that something might go wrong. Never underestimate the danger.

Most countries have legislation about the keeping of dangerous animals. In the United Kingdom this is the responsibility of both central and local government.

The Araneae order, spiders

The order Araneae is sometimes called Araneida. The 40,000 or so known spiders are part of the infra-orders and sub-orders Araneomorphae or Labigidognata (most common spiders), Mygalomorphae (includes tarantulas), and Mesothelae (rare primitive spiders of the family Lipistiidae). By the infra order Mygalomorphae and sub-order Mesothelae (known in older books as Orthognatha, or straight jawed arachnids) the chelicerae are more or less parallel to each other and the line of the body, closing together from above to below. With Araneomorphae these fangs close in against each other.

The infra-order of tarantulas and related arachnids consists of 15 families, including that of tarantulas themselves (Theraphosidae), several families of trapdoor spiders, and the Atypidae or purseweb spiders. Examples of this final family are also to be found in Europe.

Appearance

The prosoma or combined head and thorax consists of a dorsal shield (carapace), two belly plates (sternum with small labium or bottom lip) and six pairs of appendages. The ocular tubercle or eye

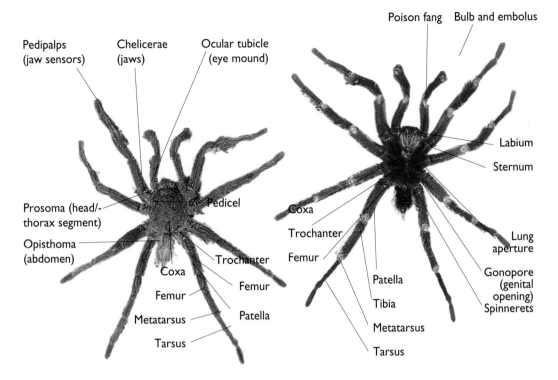

Pedipalps (jaw sensors)
Chelicerae (jaws)
Ocular tubicle (eye mound)
Poison fang
Bulb and embolus
Labium
Sternum
Prosoma (head/-thorax segment)
Pedicel
Coxa
Opisthoma (abdomen)
Trochanter
Lung aperture
Trochanter
Femur
Coxa
Femur
Patella
Gonopore (genital opening)
Spinnerets
Femur
Tibia
Metatarsus
Patella
Metatarsus
Tarsus
Tarsus

mound is positioned on the prosoma, with eight small, symmetrically positioned eyes. Despite this the field of vision is quite limited. Prey are principally captured by touch. Various sensory hairs play an important role, especially those on the jaw feelers and front legs. The little pit in the dorsal plate (known as central apodeme, tergal apodeme, dorsal groove, median fovea, or thoracic groove) is important for the connection of muscles for the legs and the chelicerae.

The legs consist from top to bottom of a hip (coxa), thigh joint (trochanter), thigh (femur), knee (patella), shin (tibia), the basal joint of the foot (metatarsus), and foot (tarsus). There are often two claws on each foot which can be withdrawn. With many species there is a bristly pad or scopula on the end of the tarsus (pretarsus). These pads enable some spiders to walk up glass.

The pedipalps are extended mouth parts and they consist of six segments. They are principally used to feel things and to grasp prey. They are further extended in males and play a role in mating.

A chelicera consists of a basal segment with venom fang. The venom glands are located in the basal segment, and the venom duct leads to an opening in the fang. The mouth opening is sited between the chelicerae, leading to the gullet.

The less robust rear part of the body (opisthoma) is linked by the thin pedicel (also known as petiolus and peduncle) to the head/chest segment (prosoma). It contains the circulatory, respiratory, reproductive, and digestive organs. Most spiders have two book lungs and one or two tracheal apertures for breathing. Book lungs are so called because of the way the tissue resembles pages of a book. Tarantulas have four book lungs and no tracheae. The reserves of food in the abdomen (opisthoma) can be so large that a spider can go without food for weeks, even months.

The openings of the lungs are visible on the underside of the opisthoma. At the extremity of the abdomen there are two short and four long spinnerets. The anus is immediately above these.

Distribution
Spiders are to be found throughout the world in the most varied biotopes, from tundra to mountain tops, and from desert to rain forest.

Accommodation
Virtually all spiders are cannibalistic and can therefore only be kept on their own. For ground dwelling species provide a terrarium that is at least three times as long and as wide as the spider's length.

Burrowing species will also need a layer of soil that is at least twice as thick as the body's length. Tree dwellers have no specific needs regarding the soil but need enough space to make a burrow. Web-spinning spiders need sufficient room to spin their web in a well-ventilated mesh terrarium.

A Mexican red-kneed tarantula eating a baby rat.

Feed no more than one prey to fat and dull-coated spiders.

Adult male with embolus on the pedipalps.

Lay a mixture on the bottom of 50% old compost (or granular peat) and 50% sand on the bottom. Provide hiding places for those specimens that require it, e.g. hollows under stones or wood. No stone should be able to fall on a spider while it is burrowing.

Heat the terrarium for tropical species to a temperature of 22-28°C (71.6-82.4°F) with a lamp bearing in mind that burrowing kinds remain quite cool. Bottom heating is not natural and it also cause the soil to dry out quickly. Terrariums can be furnished with a few plants, such as species of *Scindapsis*.

Feeding

Spiders eat all manner of living prey that is smaller than themselves. In terrariums this is usually insects but new-born rats and young mice are also suitable for the larger types. Pieces of steak or boneless chicken offered with forceps is also taken sometimes. Variety is less important than with reptiles and amphibians provided they are not fed mealworms for months on end.

Feed a spider a little and often, of the order of one to three prey each week. Spiders do not eat for some days or even weeks before a moult. Many prey animals can disturb or even harm a moulting spider. For this reason feed a fat but dull-coated spider only one prey and make sure that all crickets are removed from the terrarium and are not hiding behind the back wall.

Male spiders may be eaten occasionally by the females after mating, providing useful protein for the offspring.

Spiders mainly catch their prey with cobwebs or by falling on their prey with lightning speed. Struggling prey are held fast with several legs and then the fangs are sunk into the victim. The spider spurts enzymes into its prey and these are mixed by the jaws with the prey's tissue to dissolve it.

Because spiders have a very thin digestive tract they can only take in food in liquid form. Indigestible parts such as chitin plates are removed by the spider to a far corner of the terrarium away from its dwelling place. Prey that are not eaten immediately are spun into a web.

Sex determination

Adult males carry sperm in a shiny pear-shaped bulbous protrusions on the end of the pedipalps. The body of this secondary sex organ is known as the bulb. Some species, such as tarantulas only acquire these bulbs after the final moult. With wolf spiders and *Polybetes* species they already exist in immature males and are regenerated with each moult. Even when folded away, as is usually the case, they remain visible as swellings on the tips of the pedipalps. The neck of the bulb, known as embolus is a specific shape which acts as a key of sorts that engages precisely in the genital opening of the female, to prevent cross-breeding. The genital opening of both sexes is found on the underside of the abdomen, close to its connection to the head/thorax segment.

Adult males have a smaller abdomen and longer legs than adult females.

When females are ready to mate their genital opening often dilates slightly. There are two lines between the genital opening and the link with the combined head and thorax.

The area between is the epigynal plate, which is rectangular and flat with males but trapezoidal and often swollen with females. With smaller spiders this is extremely difficult to see.

Two seminal receptacles (spermathecae) can be seen with quite young animals on the inside of an old skin. The receptacles are sited above the genital opening and look like two little clubs or an curled up roll of skin which can take many forms. The male deposits his sperm in the seminal receptacles during mating. With tarantulas of the *Poecilotheria* genus these seminal receptacles consist of very thin and uniformly adhering skin which can easily be overlooked.

A male tarantula has a dark area some 0.5-3mm ($^1/_{51}$-$^2/_{16}$in) in size both inside of the flap and out, above the genital opening. The opening itself is surrounded by two brush-like whorls of bristles.

Males moult until reaching adulthood and then never again. Fertile females live somewhat longer and moult at regular intervals at which point the store of sperm is usually also lost. This means a female has to mate again after moulting.

The sperm receptacles of dead males are often a determining factor in properly sexing spiders, which is just one reason why it is so difficult.

Mating

Adult male spiders have only one aim in life: to fertilize female spiders but they can only mate once the sperm receptacles are filled. This occurs from a week to a month after the final moult and is more fully explained in the section on tarantulas. They then actively seek out a female.

During mating the male spider empties the embolus into the genital opening of the female on the underside of her body. Adult males have a short life.

Egg laying

Some time after mating, the female spins a white eggsac and lays her eggs in it. This cocoon is either carried around by the female or guarded in her territory until the young spiders emerge from it.

Rearing

Each of the young needs to be reared separately to prevent cannibalism but it is less time consuming to keep them in a group. They can be reared in a smaller version of the parent's terrarium.

Handling

Although some spiders can be handled and held it

These spermathecae (of Theraphosa blondi) *look like curled flaps of skin.*

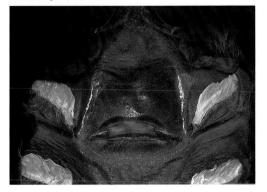

Curly-haired tarantulas with the dilated genital opening of the female and black line above the male genital aperture.

Brachypelma smithi *mating.*

is always better to place a small container over the spider and slide the lid underneath. Long forceps are also useful for handling spiders but they need some draught strip stuck to their ends to prevent them from having the spider.

Sickness

Spiders that do not eat or are rather thin may be too dry, too cold, or suffer from an infection. Those that do not eat can sometimes be encouraged with a smaller spider after which the usual prey may be accepted again.

Old or ill spiders often become weak, move very little, and refuse food. The abdomen also become wrinkled.

A terrarium that is too dry can cause moulting to go wrong. Using cotton buds, moisten the old skin and try to remove this from the spider. If this fails and the spider cannot eat its death is virtually a foregone conclusion.

Killed by mould.

Haplopelma albostriatum *captured wild, with mites.*

A terrarium that is too moist with inadequate ventilation causes mould growth. This manifests itself as increasingly large patches of white or grey on a spider. Badly affected spiders become apathetic in behaviour and inactive. Place affected spiders in a newly-established terrarium with sufficient ventilation. The mould, which has a musty smell, often begins to grow on the soil. In this case too the spider should be moved to a new terrarium. Fungal growth should be treated with benomyl available from garden centres. No insecticide must be incorporated with this fungal agent.

Specimens caught in the wild in particular are often plagued by mites. These suck out the body fluids and will eventually kill the spider. Remove the mites as well as possible with cotton buds dipped in 70% alcohol before placing the spider in a new terrarium. Keeping terrariums clean prevents many problems. Too much moisture also contributes to plagues of mites. The predatory mite *Hyoaspis miles* can be used to get rid of other mites. Mites around the jaw are harmless parasites that even help to clean up.

Broken limbs present difficulties for the following moult. Grasp the femur of the leg involved with forceps, of which the tips have been protected with aquarium hose, and give a sharp pull. The spider is able to release the leg because of a natural break in the coxa. The wound will usually heal within a few hours.

If a large tarantula falls onto a hard surface from a height of more than 30cm (12in) its fat abdomen can split open. Small splits can be treated with petroleum jelly. With much bigger splits it is kinder to place the spider in the deep freeze to prevent suffering.

Spiders that are kept in conditions that are too cold or moist, or too hot and dry become listless and apathetic. Cleaning agents and insecticide treated items like flea collars can also be harmful for spiders.

Take care when buying a spider that you do not purchase an adult male, unless you want one (see Sex determination). Older females are often quite large but they can live for several years. Those with a wrinkled abdomen have only a short life expectancy. There should be no irregular patches, bumps, or swellings on the abdomen and the mouth parts must be complete.

Theraphosidae family of tarantulas

There are about 92 genera of tarantulas and some 850 species in total. The name tarantula is strictly reserved for a limited number of spiders of an entirely different family, but North American usage prevails among both lay persons and experts. For this reason, the term is used here and elsewhere in the book to indicate members of the Theraphosidae family, which more properly ought to be known as 'bird-eating' spiders. Keeping most species of tarantula is fairly straightforward provided attention is given to a few matters.

Appearance

Most tarantulas are of the order 50-80mm (2-3^1/$_8$in) long, with a few species however being up to 110mm (4^5/$_{16}$in). Most of them are densely covered with bristles and have sturdy legs.

Tarantulas do not spin webs to catch their prey. Instead sensitive bristles on the legs assess the direction to their prey and its size. Many types spin 'tripwires' by their burrow so they can sense the presence of a prey.

The tarsus and metatarsus are often covered with a dense layer of gripping hairs (the scopula). The ad-

Megaphobema velvetosoma.

hesion of these enables tarantulas generally to be able to walk up a sheet of glass. The abdomen of many (North American) species have urticating defence bristles with barbs which cause irritation of the skin and mucous membrane for days after contact with them. The effect of these urticating bristles should not be underestimated. Some species can shoot the bristles into the air with their legs. The pedipalps and first walking legs contain bristles that can sense a prey by smell.

Many tarantulas can make a hissing sound by stridulation of the jaws, coxa, trochanter sensors, or the front walking legs.

Tree-dwelling tarantulas in particular spurt their excreta against the panes of their terrarium.

Distribution
Tarantulas are found in most sub-tropical parts of the world, in both rain forest and desert. Bear these origins in mind when preparing a terrarium for them and also in the care regime.

These spiders can be divided into three groups.

– Tree-dwelling spiders have relatively small abdomens and large feet with which to grasp onto smooth surfaces. These types, with long, dense bristles, jump from their tree in danger and spread their legs to glide to somewhere safer. Tree-dwellers create a cocoon in which to hide, moult, and eat.
Examples are *Avicularia* and *Psalmopoeus* species from South America and *Poecilotheria* species from Asia.
– Ground-dwelling spiders are generally compact creatures with fairly sturdy legs and an ovoid rear body. They often sit just in front of or inside their burrows and go in search of their prey at night.
– Underground-dwelling spiders live in underground burrows (between roots) that can be dug out to several meters below the surface. They generally lie in wait for prey just in front of or just inside the entrance. This group generally has shorter bristles and plainer colourings. *Citarischius crawshayi* and *Theraphosa blondi* are burrowing spiders that are rarely on view in a terrarium.

Tree-dwelling Avicularia *sp. 'Purple' from Peru.*

Burrowing spiders usually have shorter bristles, tree-dwellers longer ones. These are the legs of Citharischius crawshayi *and* Avicularia metallica.

Burrowing spiders like this Citharischius crawshayi *are rarely seen outside their lair.*

Accommodation
A terrarium of 30 x 30 x 20cm (12 x 12 x 8in) is adequate for ground-dwelling spiders of 60-80mm (2³/₈-3¹/₈in). If the terrarium is too large there is less chance that prey will be caught and spiders can fall and hurt themselves in terrariums higher than 40cm (16in). Ventilate with a perforated grille that is ¹/₃ to ¹/₂ of one side. Normal mesh can cause spiders to get their legs trapped in it and both spiders and crickets can bite through it. Semi-mature spiders can also gnaw a hole in the boxes generally used to keep crickets in. If the lid is too light, these spiders can push it aside.

Make sturdy hiding places with stones, cork, bark, parts of plant pots, or wood. Make sure that a spider cannot hurt itself by burrowing under a stone or such like that might fall on it. Burrows provide an even temperature.

Spiders sometimes climb and can hurt themselves if they fall on a prickly plant such as a cactus or lava.

Heat the terrarium during the day to 24-27°C (75.2-80.6°F) with a lamp but keep burrowing spiders somewhat cooler at 20-24°C (68-75.2°F) e.g. by placing their terrarium at floor level. Keep the night-time temperature at 20°C (68°F) with a minimum of 15°C (59°F). It appears that a sharp

Terrarium for 1 tree- and 4 ground-dwellers.

How a hobby can grow.

Avicularia versicolor *with cricket.*

temperature gradient between day and night (15-17°C/59-62.6°F) can stimulate desert and plain-dwelling species to reproduce. Do not provide under-floor heating since this is not natural and dries the soil out too quickly. Provide a small tray of water and replenish it regularly. Humidity should be 60-85% with the highest end of this range for tree-dwelling species. Spray part of the terrarium regularly, in the case of tree dwellers once per week. Never directly spray on a cobweb or the spider itself. Terrariums that are too dry cause moulting problems. Provide a soil bottom of 50-100mm (2-4in) with a mixture of sand and spent compost or peat and keep this only slightly moist for species from arid regions. It should not be moist to the touch. Those specimens that originate from rain forest biotopes can be kept slightly damper. Provide a rear wall covering.

Spiders do not demand much by way of maintenance. Regularly remove food remnants deposited in one corner and wash excreta and spun web from the panes with warm water without any cleaning agent. If the spider seems to be permanently ill at ease then replace the soil and decorative material, since these symptoms clearly show the spider does not feel well.

Toxic materials

Fresh compost with weed-killer is harmful for spi-

Small trays with young spiders.

ders. Glued cork sheet contains substances that are toxic for spiders and newly-purchased plants often contain insecticide. These should not be used until they have been thoroughly rinsed off a number of times.

If for example a snake is having to be treated against blood-sucking mites in the same hobby room as spiders they will need to be moved and care should be taken with any insecticide.

Sand alone, shingle, or vermiculite encourages growth of unwanted bacteria, mites, and moulds.

Feeding

Tarantulas eat prey that is slightly smaller than themselves. After a moult it is possible to overfeed a tarantula or allow it to fast for months. Neither are ideal. Feed one to three portions regularly each week until the spider is ready for the next moult. Remove uneaten remains from a satisfied spider. North American species often eat nothing in late autumn and winter.

Moulting

Very young tarantulas moult every one to two months. An adult male does not moult further and fertile females moult about one to three times each year.

Ground-dwelling species spin a 'mat' on the soil or in their hollow and lie on this on their back. The mat is sometimes strengthened with urticulat-

A tarantula on its back, ready to moult.

The spider has pulled its legs from the old skin.

The prosoma and opisthosoma split open.

The spider rests beside its old skin.

ing bristles. Tree-dwellers moult in a tube-like web.

The prosoma and opisthosoma split open and the old skin is then pushed by the legs. The moult can last for anything between half an hour to 36 hours. The spiders must have the space in which to stretch out their legs fully.

The bare area that was covered with urticulating bristles is quickly covered with them again. Spiders that are out of condition can even become smaller during a moult. Adult tarantulas do not eat for about two weeks after a moult.

Sex determination
First read the information about sexing for the order Araneae (p124), of which tarantulas form part. Further differences between the sexes for tarantulas are as follows.
– Adult males of many species have a single or double tibial hook on the shins of their front legs which they use to grasp the female at a safe distance during mating.
– Males mature between after fifteen months (inc. *Lasiodora parahybana, Brachypelma angusta*) and up to four years; females mature one to two years later. Once adult, a male lives for about one year. Fertile adult females of African and Asian species live a further five to ten years, and North American species even twenty years once they are ready to mate. They moult from time to time

to regenerate lost of injured limbs and other body parts.
– In some species the males and females are differently coloured and marked, such as some *Poecilotheria species* and *Aphonopelma seemanni*.

Mating
A male has to fill his sperm receptacles before he can mate. About one to three months after his final moult, the male spins a sperm web for the first time. This is a mat on the ground with another just off the ground into which he creeps, on his back between the webs. Using the epiandrous glands he

The right-hand skin has a spermatheca and is hence from a female.

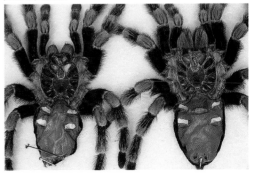

Tibial hooks on the front legs of an adult male
Brachypelma smithi.

A Theraphosa blondi *male under his sperm web.*

forceps at least 150mm (6in) long to guide the male and assist him if the female becomes aggressive. Some species such as those of *Ceratogyrus* climb right up forceps unless they are first smeared with glycerine in water.

When the male touches the front legs of the female she lifts herself up at the front. The male holds her chelicerae up (using his tibial hooks), pushes her further backwards and creeps under the female, who is frozen rigid. He vibrates his sensing legs against her belly plate and then inserts the tip of an embolus (or both of them) in her gonopore and eposits his sperm in the seminal receptacles (spermathecae). The actual mating lasts between half a minute and a quarter of an hour. Afterwards the male releases the female and flees from the usually aggressive female. It is essential that there is sufficient space for him to escape or otherwise that help is forthcoming from the terrarium keeper. With species of the *Avicularia, Pachistopelma, Psalmopeus, Stromatopelma,* and *Tapinauchenius* genera the male and female can be put together for a week after week without danger. Females of certain species only mate once but many more mate a number of times over a few weeks.

Male tarantulas are mainly eaten when they are old and unable to correctly produce the specific sound signal of the species. Spiders that refuse to

spins a closed patch of silk onto which he then deposits a droplet of sperm. The spider then crawls onto the upper web and sucks the droplet into his sperm receptacle. The sperm web is then destroyed but remains of them can be seen. The process last for several hours. Tree-dwelling male spiders usually create different structures, often inside their home cocoon. The male is now ready to mate and is at his most fertile for the first six months. Females can produce an eggsac each year until their death.

Do not use too old a male for breeding. A fertile female adult can be mated several days after moulting but it is better to wait until she is eating again. It is not advisable to mate her just before a moult since females lose the sperm they have stored during the moult.

Males that are ready to mate stamp their legs to produce bursts of buzzing or knocking interspersed with pauses. This special sound can also be heard by humans. A female that is ready to mate answers with the same sound. This approach process during which the male slowly approaches the female can last for several hours. If both animals are in the same cage or container, place the male opposite the female's territory. This can be done before any drumming of feet has occurred. Control the mating, using sticks (chopsticks) and

Brachypelma albopilosum *just before mating.*

Avicularia metallica *mating.*

mate can be stimulated by placing them so that they can hear their future partner.

Tarantulas in the wild are affected by the seasons. Adult males can be found in northern parts of South America most certainly in August and September and this natural life rhythm can also be observed in terrariums. The young of *Theraphosa blondi* are mainly for sale during the winter months, following mating a few months earlier. Species from Argentina and Chile (many of the *Grammostola* species) benefit from winter hibernation at temperatures of 10-15°C (50-59°F).

The spider in this enclosed web probably has an eggsac.

Avicularia versicolor with eggsac.

Egg and first stage nymph.

Research is still needed to determine the best time for mating of tarantulas.

Egg laying

Fertilized females have until the next moult to produce an eggsac and frequently this is not done so that the supply of sperm is lost. The female then has to be mated once more.

If all goes according to plan the fertilized female has an enlarged appetite although she usually stops food intake a few weeks before laying her eggs. From three weeks to twelve months after mating she busies herself spinning in her hiding place. The females can develop into real digging machines at this time. Tree-dwelling females often enlarge the living cocoon, creating a closed off 'nursery', first spinning a thick, round bowl. Depending on the species, the female lays 30-2,000 eggs in this receptacle that are usually 3-5mm ($^2/_{16}$-$^3/_{16}$in) in size. The eggs are fertilized as they leave the body. The female then spins a mat of silk covering for the eggs and separates the receptacle from the base. She then surrounds it a number more times with spun silk to form a round eggsac complete with urticulating hairs incorporated, that is reasonably protected against both dryness and predators. The female remains enclosed in her hollow or burrow with the eggsac, or carries it with her for weeks on end to a place with the right temperature and humidity. She regularly turns the sac and protects it from enemies. In between she rarely eats but the eggsac may be put down for a while. When the offspring emerge she guards her brood for a few days before abandoning them.

Never disturb a spider while she is carrying the eggsac and if possible shield her territory. If she is disturbed in any way the female will often stop caring for her eggs or even eat the eggsac.

The tiny nymphs emerge from the eggs after two to four weeks. At this stage they have little mobility

First nymph stage.

Opened eggsac of Avicularia versicolor.

Second stage Poecilotheria *sp. nymphs. One is already a spiderling.*

Removing the eggsac from Avicularia versicolor.

and are without bristles and have almost no joints in their legs. These first-stage nymphs shed the first skin at about three weeks when they start the second nymph stage. At this point they resemble a small bald spider but they still have little movement. The nymphs usually then crawl out of the eggsac and are still protected by their mother. Their skins are moulted again outside the eggsac one to two weeks later (sometimes 12) to become true spiderlings, usually about 8mm ($^5/_{16}$in) in size and similarly coloured to their parents. The spiderlings begin to eat after several days.

Depending on the species and temperature the nymphs usually emerge some six to twelve weeks after the eggs are laid. Remove the eggsac after four to five weeks though because:

– the female sometimes eats the eggsac (if disturbed, a noisy location);
– the female can sometimes not find the right conditions within the terrarium so that the nymphs decay or dry out in the eggsac. By removing the sac the surviving nymphs can be saved;
– if not the nymphs will have to be recovered from all over the terrarium;
– rearing the young in this way is usually straightforward.

Try to remove the eggsac carefully with forceps, using a stick to separate the mother from the sac if she becomes alarmed, bends herself over the eggsac, or puts her chelicerae into it.

Offer the mother another empty sac filled with cotton wool and sewn up. This calms her down quickly and causes less stress.

Carefully tear open the eggsac that has been removed and place the young in a clean, dry place at 23-27°C (73.4-80.6°F) with humidity of 70-80 per cent.

Most females moult once more after the young have emerged from the eggsac but *Poecilotheria* species and *Psalmopoeus cambridgei* exceptionally produce a second eggsac, about 4 months after the first.

Rearing

In the wild, the death rate is high among the young spiders (about 95%). Almost all the young can be successfully reared in terrariums.

Rear the spiderlings separately or in groups but in the latter case regularly sort them to limit cannibalism. Use small plastic containers with ventilation openings. With young of tree-dwellings species, push a wad of cotton wool through an aperture in the container and soak this with water.

Use the same soil mixture as with adult spiders but make sure it does not dry out completely. Provide a hiding place with e.g. half a film cassette canister or a piece of thin PVC pipe (for tree dwellers).

Feed the young once per week with some fruit flies and small crickets. Provide a little fruit for the prey to keep them alive longer, increase their nutritional value, and to encourage them to breed. Take care though to prevent mould from growing.

Depending on the species, males mature after one to four years, which is earlier than their sisters, who are adult after three to five years (and an additional one to two moults).

Defence

The North American tarantulas in particular have urticulating bristles on their opisthosoma which cause irritation and inflammation of the mucous membranes and skin. These bristles can also cause a strong tendency to cough, and itching for many weeks. The severity of these symptoms varies from person to person. Generally it is just the skin between the fingers that is affected but do not underestimate this weapon. Washing the hands does not help because of the barbs in the bristles. Sometimes just opening the terrarium can be sufficient to cause their discharge. Check first in a pet shop or specialist supplier if you are allergic for these

About 2,000 nymphs of Lasiodora parahybana.

A container with a young tree spider.

Bald rear end of a spider that has defended itself.

animals. The living quarters, eggsacs, and other webs are often furnished with these bristles. Some species throw a cloud of these bristles into the air with their back legs. This leaves the opisthosoma devoid of bristles but they are replaced at the next moult.

Many people think that all tarantulas are aggressive and deadly. In reality they are primitive spiders with primitive toxins. Not one single tarantula is able to kill a healthy person.

If a tarantula bites, the result depends on the type, amount of venom, and the sensitivity of the person bitten. The outcome is often relatively mild but a bite can lead to severe pain and swellings. A strong bite though is always painful because of the large chelicerae and can lead to nasty wounds and infections. Therefore always take care.

The venom of most species affect the muscles and heart. The aggressive *Heteroscodra, Stromatopelma,* and *Pterinochilus* species have neurotoxins that affect the brain.

After a bite visit a doctor or hospital. Small children and persons with lowered resistance can die. Allergies for bites and urticulating bristles can become worse over a period of time.

Handling

Anyone who has to or wants to handle a tarantula must bear in mind that the 850 species vary widely in their aggression, activity, and toxicity.

A number of North American tarantulas such as *Brachypelma* and *Grammostola* species are very quiet and do not readily bite but are quite capable of doing so!

Tap the spider before letting it walk on the hand so that it knows something is to happen and that the hand is not an approaching prey. Hold the hand in front of the spider and let it walk onto it by tapping the rear legs. Never panic or drop the spider. The weak opisthosoma is pressurised and can burst open. Never allow a spider to walk on your clothing because the little hooks on the feet can become trapped.

Another way is to place a container over the spider and to slide the lid beneath it. This enables the

Aphonopelma moderatum *dribbles venom.*

The experienced person can handle aggressive spiders like this pair of Theraphosa blondi *this way.*

Lots of spiders bred in captivity can be bought at shows.

spider to be viewed from every angle and this method does not cause much stress. With lively species, the following method is more suitable.

Press the spider to the ground by pushing the index finger on the prosoma, then hold the spider between thumb and middle finger between the second and third walking legs. The spider usually curls its legs inwards. This method is used by experienced terrarium keepers, sometimes even for quite aggressive types. Other species initially adopt the threatened stance (front legs raised and chelicerae displayed) before they bite. Examples are *Theraphosa blondi* and *Poecilotheria* species. These spiders can be guided into a container with a 30cm (12in) stick that has soft protection of its tip and then the lid can be carefully put in place. Never pick up spiders with forceps because it is easy to apply too much pressure which can injure the spider. The most aggressive spiders, such as *Stromatopelma* and *Pterinochilus* species do not threaten but bite immediately. Handle them likewise with a container and lid.

African and Asian species do not have urticulating hairs but are often aggressive. These are also the most venomous types *(Harpactira, Harpactirella, Heteroscodra, Pterinochilus,* and *Stromatopelma* species). Their bite is very painful and causes inflammation of the area bitten. The South American *Acanthoscurria* species and those of *Haplopelma* from Asia cause similar bites.

Tree dwelling species are often more readily frightened and very fast. In fleeing they can jump off somewhere. These spiders are recognisable by an opisthosoma that is fairly small in proportion and their legs are often densely covered with bristles. Examples of these are *Avicularia, Poecilotheria, Psalmopoeus,* and *Tapinauchenius* species.

Handle these spiders if possible in a room with few if any hiding places such as the bathroom or on the floor.

When transporting tarantulas, pack them in a container with soft paper so that the spider is not in contact with the sides of the box. Do not provide any food or moist substances.

Escaped specimens should be found as quickly as possible. Start at first beneath the terrarium and if necessary hunt at night with a torch. Hang a notice on the door to warn others to check the floor as they enter and leave.

Acquiring the first tarantula

– Look for a female, they live longer.
– If the spider is to be on show then choose from the genus *Brachypelma* because they are very calm.
– Buy one that is brightly-coloured rather than dull (i.e. one that has just moulted) because they are generally stronger.

- The age of adult specimens is unknown, so they could be very old.
- A healthy tarantula can lift its own body weight and is very lively if disturbed.
- Make sure if the specimen is adult or almost adult that all its limbs are intact.
- Do not buy on price. Cheaper specimens are often the more aggressive types that are rarely seen in terrariums

Species

Precise identification of species is extremely difficult and is not dealt with in this book. Shed skins from the female, dead males, and the origins of the specimens are important aids to determination and the proportion between length and breadth of various parts of the body and amount of bristles are widely used aids.

The spiders are listed alphabetically by their scientific name but bear in mind that these can change. The most recent former names are also given. The length indicated concerns the body length (of both prosoma and opisthosoma).

There are a number of sub-families within Theraphosidae:
- Aviculariinae (American tree dwellers including the genera *Avicularia*, *Psalmopoeus*, and *Tapinauchenius)*;
- Grammostolinae (American, including species of the genera *Aphonopelma*, *Brachypelma*, and *Grammostola)*;

The male embolus is an important aid in identifying species.

A species of Schizopelma.

Acanthoscurria antillensis.

- Harpactirinae (African 'baboon' spiders, including species of *Ceratogyrus*, *Harpactira*, and *Pterinochilus)*;
- Poecilotherinae (Asian, including species of the genus *Poecilotheria)*;
- Theraphosinae (American, including the genera *Acanthoscurria*, *Lasiodora*, *Megaphobema*, *Pamphobeteus*, *Phormictopus*, *Theraphosa*, and *Xenesthis*.

ACANTHOSCURRIA ANTILLENSIS

Appearance
This 70mm (2³/₄in) long spider is brown with a coppery sheen. In addition to one or two tibial hooks on the front legs, Acanthoscurria males also have tibial hooks on their pedipalps.
This genus includes some fairly aggressive species. A number of them stand up on their legs, turn themselves around hurl bristles and spray excreta towards the threat.

Distribution
Most of the 41 species of *Acanthoscurria* originate in Brazil. *A. antillensis* is a burrowing kind from the lesser Antilles and Martinique.

Reproduction
Acanthoscurria eggsacs contain up to 800 nymphs.

APHONOPELMA SPECIES

Many of the 90 *Aphonopelma* species formed parts of the *Dugesiella*, *Eurypelma*, and *Rhechosticta* genera. They originate mainly from southern parts of USA and Central America. These are often slow developing spiders.

Acanthoscurria geniculata.

Aphonopelma borelli *from Paraguay.*

Aphonopelma caniceps *from Mexico and USA.*

APHONOPELMA CHALCODES

Appearance
The highly-arched prosoma and the legs of this 80mm (3¹/₈in) long species are light brown while the opisthosoma is lightly bristled and brown. The sturdy legs are fairly short. This moderately aggressive spider rarely ejects hairs or excreta.

Distribution
This strong burrowing species originates from Mexico and Arizona.

Accommodation
Keep dry (60-70% humidity) and at 27-29°C (80.8-84.2°F).

Reproduction
Approx. 500 nymphs emerge after six weeks.

136

Aphonopelma chalcodes.

APHONOPELMA HENTZI

Former name *Dugesiella hentzi.*
Appearance
Aphonopelma hentzi is a spider of 60-70mm (2³/₈-2³/₄in) with dark brown opisthosoma with grey bristles. The prosoma is red-brown. The legs are black-brown with grey bristles.

Distribution
This burrowing species originates from southern USA (Texas, Arizona).

Reproduction
The 500-1,000 nymphs emerge after seven to nine weeks and develop slowly.

APHONOPELMA MODERATUM

Former name *Rhechosticta moderatum.*
Appearance
This 70mm (2³/₄in) spider has a highly-arched prosoma. The legs of this generally grey-brown spider are alternately grey-black and brown-orange. The carapace is golden brown. *A. moderatum* is aggressive and one of the spiders that already drips venom while in its threat stance.

Distribution
This ground-dweller originates from Texas.

APHONOPELMA SEEMANNI

Appearance
Different populations of this species can vary in colour. The basic colour of this 65mm (2⁹/₁₆in) long spider is often black-brown to dark grey. There are yellowish orange bristles on the opisthosoma but these are reddish orange on the underside. There are white, pink, or orange later stripes

Aphonopelma hentzi *female.*

Aphonopelma moderatum.

Aphonopelma seemanni.

Aphonopelma texense.

on the patellae, tibiae, and metatarsi of both the pedipalps and first and second legs. The femur is almost entirely black. The joints have white rings. The markings disappear before each moult. After the final moult, the males are uniform dark brown to black.

A. seemanni spiders are prone to stress and are quite aggressive.

Distribution
This ground-dweller originates from (rain) forests from Panama to Texas and California.

Accommodation
Keep the terrarium moderately dry (60-80% humidity) but spray regularly.

Reproduction
The nymphs emerge after eight weeks.

AVICULARIA SPECIES

The genus *Avicularia* contains some 35 known species of tree-dwelling tarantulas. When a large spider was seen to eat a small hummingbird, the spider was named *Avicularia* from the Latin avis or bird.

Appearance
Spiders of the *Avicularia* genus are 50-70mm (2-2³/₄in) long and densely bristled. Their tarsi and metatarsi are densely packed with millions of tiny hairs. The last pair of legs are longer than the first pair. Many species have a reflective sheen on the legs and dorsal plate, especially after a moult. The opisthosoma of certain species (e.g. *A. versicolor*) has a shiny 'mirror' patch with urticulating bristles. Young specimens exhibit tiger-like markings on the opisthosoma, which is often orange and black.

These non-aggressive spiders will quickly panic and attempt to flee when disturbed or chased. A few of the species move their rear end backwards and forwards to release the barbed bristles which can penetrate the skin.

Distribution
Species of the *Avicularia* genus are found from Panama to Bolivia and on some Caribbean is-

137

Avicularia zarodes *from Brazil.*

Avicularia aurantiaca.

Avicularia hirsuta *spiderling.*

lands. Most of them are found in central parts of Brazil. They inhabit trees, houses, the tubes of bromelias etc. Some species have adapted to man and inhabit pineapple and banana plantations.

Accommodation

Spiders of this genus will often build their living cocoon close to a lamp, which is best not installed within the terrarium. Provide a day-time temperature of 25-28°C (77-82.4°F) and 2-23°C (68-73.4°F) at night. Keep the terrarium moist at all times (70-80% humidity) and spray once or twice each week. *A. versicolor* often thrives best though in a dryer terrarium but this also requires a lower temperature.

Reproduction

A mature pair that are able to mate can be kept together for a certain amount of time. The 50-200 eggs emerge after three to five weeks at 27°C (80.6°F). The nymphs shed their first skin four to five weeks later and about a week later they leave the eggsac. Young of this genus are generally not cannibalistic up to the first moult but do not rear them in too small a terrarium or they are likely to stop eating. Separate the nymphs of *A. versicolor* and *A. purpurea* after the first moult.

AVICULARIA AURANTIACA

Synonym: *A. magdalenae.*

Appearance

These 50-70mm (2-2³/₄in) brown-grey spiders become black just before a moult. They have ochre bristles on the prosoma and brown-white ones on the legs and opisthosoma. *A. aurantiaca* has yellow banding on the legs compared with *A. walckenaeri* with its orange bands. Both species have otherwise slightly varying fovea (the groove in the prosoma).

Distribution

Peru.

AVICULARIA HIRSUTA

It is possible that specimens are *Pachistopelma concolor* but further research is required to classify these spiders with certainty.

Appearance

Avicularia hirsuta has a dark wide, lateral strip on the opisthosoma with yellowish bristles on the sides. The dorsal plate has grey-yellow bristles. These spiders are 50-60mm (2-2³/₈in) and they are very active and fairly aggressive.

Distribution

Rain forest in Brazil.

AVICULARIA METALLICA

Appearance

This 70mm (2³/₄in) long species is often offered for sale. It is dark black which has a blue metallic sheen immediately after a moult. The ends of the bristles on the body are greyish white and the feet are pink. *A. metallica* is often confused with *A. avicularia.*

Distribution

Northern parts of South America and Central America.

Adult Avicularia hirsuta.

Avicularia metallica *spiderling.*

Avicularia metallica *mating.*

Avicularia miniatrix.

AVICULARIA MINIATRIX

Appearance
This 40mm (1⁹/₁₆in) spider is pinkish brown with black and orange grids on the opisthosoma, rather like the markings of the young of many species. The feet are dark with lighter tops.
Distribution
This species inhabits bromelia plants among others in Venezuela.
Accommodation
Do not keep this species too moist (maximum 75% humidity).
Reproduction
A typical brood of *A. miniatrix* consists of about 40 nymphs.

AVICULARIA PURPUREA

Appearance
These 50mm (2in) long black spiders have a purple sheen and dark grey bristles on their legs. The toes are yellow-orange.
Distribution
Ecuador.
Reproduction
The 70-120 offspring are bluish in colour for the first few months.

AVICULARIA VERSICOLOR

Appearance
This species is black with a purple tinge, 60mm (2³/₈in) long, and also has dark grey bristles on the legs. The charcoal grey legs are covered with reddish-brown to purple bristles. There is a greenish

Avicularia purpurea.

'mirror' on the reddish-brown opisthosoma (see photo. p131).

Distribution

Martinique and Guadeloupe.

Reproduction

Unlike most other *Avicularia* species, the male has no tibial hooks. Despite this the female is fairly aggressive during mating. The 80-160 nymphs are a superb blue colour with light-blue grid pattern on their opisthosoma until after the fifth or sixth moult.

AVICULARIA WALCKENAERI

Appearance

This species looks like *A. aurantiaca* but has orange banding on the legs.

Distribution

Brazil.

BRACHYPELMA SPECIES

Legal status: all the species of this genus are CITES B.

There are fourteen species in this genus, including the most popular tarantulas. The name *Brachypelma* is often incorrectly used as a synonym for *Euathlus* species. Many species (in particular *B. smithi*) are captured en masse for export to the USA and Europe. This is why these species are now protected by CITES legislation (see The law). Many species of *Brachypelma* are quiet and calm

Avicularia versicolor *spiderling.*

Avicularia walckenaeri.

Brachypelma baumgarteni *of Mexico.*

Brachypelma angustum.

spiders that are easy to handle but they do fire urticulating hairs into the air to defend themselves.

Reproduction

Some 500-900 nymphs emerge from the eggsac after eight to ten weeks at 25°C (77°F).

BRACHYPELMA ALBOPILOSUM, CURLY-HAIRED TARANTULA

Appearance

This up to 80mm (3$^{1}/_{8}$in) long spider has a brown-black ground with golden curly hair or bristles on the legs and opisthosoma and a golden sheen on the prosoma (see photo. p130). *B. albopilosum* is very calm.

Distribution

In wet forests from Guatemala to Costa Rica.

Accommodation

Keep this spider, that is ideal for beginners, reasonably humid at 70-80%.

Reproduction

This species is easy to breed. The 500-900 nymphs emerge from the eggsac after eight to ten weeks and grow quickly to become adult at two to three years.

BRACHYPELMA ANGUSTUM

Appearance

This 70mm (2$^{3}/_{4}$in) spider closely resembles both *B. sabulosum* and *B. vagans.* There is a light brown rim to the black carapace and the equally

Brachypelma auratum.

Brachypelma emilia *of Mexico.*

black opisthosoma has erect red bristles. The legs
are blue-black. With *B. vagans* the red bristles are
slightly curly and the legs are more charcoal grey
(with recently moulted specimens).

Distribution
Costa Rica.

BRACHYPELMA AURATUM

Appearance
This spider is up to 80mm (3¹/₈in) long and is basically black with a light rim to the carapace. The
upper part of the patella is bright red. The patellae,
tibiae, and metatarsi each are marked with white
rings. *B. auratum* is regarded as a highland form
of *B. smithi* but is darker in colouring, slimmer,
and can stridulate slightly.

Distribution
Moderately humid highlands in Mexico.

BRACHYPELMA BOEHMI

Appearance
This 60-70mm (2³/₈-2³/₄in) species has a copper-
coloured carapace. This does not have the black
triangle found with *B. emilia.* The opisthosoma is
black with beige bristles and the femur is black.
Patella, tibia, and metatarsi are reddish orange. *B.
boehmi* is a nervous types that quickly resorts to
defensive bristle throwing.

Distribution
Arid areas of Mexico.

Brachypelma boehmi.

Accommodation
Allow these spiders a dry period of several months
each year.

BRACHYPELMA EMILIA

Appearance
This 70mm (2³/₄in) species has a black base
colouring with reddish orange bristles on the
opisthosoma. The carapace is brown-orange with
a large black triangle from the front to centre of the
carapace. The fifth leg segment (tibia) is orange
while the others are black. Males are slightly darker coloured.

Distribution
This ground-dwelling species is found in semi-
desert areas of Mexico and Panama. The spiders of
the Panamanian population are darker, with more
sharply defined markings and do not have the
lighter crease in the dark carapace triangle.

Reproduction
This species is widely bred. The offspring develop
very slowly.

BRACHYPELMA KLAASI

Appearance
The corkscrew appearance of the male embolus
and the sperm receptacles are different with this
species to the other *Brachypelma* types, so that
this species is sometimes regarded as part of the
Brachypelmides genus. *B. klaasi* is a black spider,
65mm (2⁹/₁₆in) long, with reddish orange bristles

Brachypelma klaasi.

Brachypelma pallidum *of Mexico is now called*
Aphonopelma pallidum.

Top (left to right): 1. (B. vagans *x* B. albopilosum) *x* B.
albopilosum, *2.* B. vagans *x* B. albopilosum, *3.* B. vagans
from southern Mexico, centre: B. angustum, *bottom left:*
B. vagans *from northern Mexico, right:* B. sabulosum.

on the opisthosoma and fourth to sixth leg seg-
ments. It resembles *B. emilia* except for the fourth
leg segment.
Distribution
South-West Mexico.
Accommodation
This species benefits from cooler night tempera-
tures of 15-17°C (59-62.6°F).

BRACHYPELMA SABULOSUM

Appearance
This species cannot be differentiated from *B. vagans* with the eye alone and this is made even
more difficult by geographic colour variations, differences in colour depending on the length of time
to the next moult, and natural crosses between the
many *Brachypelma* species. Both *B. vagans* and *B.
sabulosum* are brown-black with a light rim on the
dorsal plate and red bristles on the opisthosoma.
Distribution
Guatemala.

BRACHYPELMA SMITHI, MEXICAN RED-KNEE

Appearance
This 70-80mm (2³/₄-3¹/₈in) has a basic black
colour with the dorsal plate edged with beige and
white and orange bristles on the legs and opisthosoma. The patellae and bottom half of the tibiae
are bright orange (see photo. p121).
Distribution
These ground-dwellers burrows down to about
50cm (20in) to create a 1.5 metre (5ft) long chamber in semi-desert parts of Mexico. The spiders remain in their burrows from March to October
during the hot and wet season (daytime up to
35°C/95°F, night-time 25°C/77°F, humidity 85-
95%). The rest of the year is dry.
Accommodation
Allow these spiders a drier period of a few months
from time to time. Males are adult after four to five
years and females after six to seven.
Reproduction
The difficulty is in getting a male and female ready to
mate at the same time. The 500-1,000 nymphs emerge
from the eggsac after 10–12 weeks at 25°C (77°F).

Brachypelma vagans.

BRACHYPELMA VAGANS

Appearance
Like *B. angustum* and *B. sabulosum*, this 70mm
(2³/₄in) spider is a third tarantula with a reddish
opisthosoma. This species has a basic black colour
with long red bristles on the rear of the body and
there is a thin beige border to the prosoma.
Distribution
This species lives in relatively moist parts of southern Mexico through to Honduras.
Reproduction
The 300-500 nymphs emerge after eight to nine
weeks and grow rapidly.

BRACHYPELMA RUHNAUI

This spider was given this name by G. Schmidt in
1997. Previously it was named *Aphonopelma* sp.,

142

Brachypelmides ruhnaui.

Ceratogyrus cornuates.

Rechostica sp., *Chromatopelma californicum*, and *Delopelma californicum*.

Appearance

This 70mm (2³/₄in) black spider has red bristles on its opisthosoma and uses bombardment as a defence. The dorsal plate is golden and the legs are charcoal grey.

Distribution

Ground-dweller from Arizona.

Accommodation

Ensure its terrarium is fairly dry and not too hot (max. 25°C/77°F).

CERATOGYRUS **SPECIES**

Appearance

Ceratogyrus species have a horn where other spiders have the central apodeme on the prosoma. Food is stored in the horn so that the spider can survive dry periods. With *C. bechuanicus* this horn leans over to lie flat, while that of *C. brachycephalus* points forward, *C. darlingi* points backwards but is short, compared with *C. cornuates*, which is similar but longer.

Females are 50-70mm (2-2³/₄in) long and are grey-brown flecked with black. There is often a star marking on the dorsal plate. The slightly smaller males are often darker.

All spiders of this genus are aggressive.

Distribution

Seven species live in southern Africa where there burrow to 70cm (27¹/₂in) in dry grassland and

Ceratogyrus darlingi.

woods. These spiders spin large living cocoons and are rarely seen.

Accommodation

This species cannot withstand drought. Keep the soil of their terrarium lightly moist with humidity of 80% and temperature of 25-30°C (77-86°F).

Reproduction

The eggsac is not carried around but hung in the living cocoon. The 80-250 nymphs emerge from the eggsac after five to six weeks at about 25°C (77°F) and grow rapidly to become adults in one to two years.

CITHARISCHIUS CRAWSHAYI

Appearance

Citharischius crawshayi is a striking reddish brown spider of 90-100mm (3¹/₂-4in) with very short, velvety hair. This plus the sturdy 7mm

Citharischius crawshayi.

Chromatopelma cyanocubescens *of Venezuela, formerly* Delopelma cyanocubescens.

Cyclosternum fasciatus.

(⁴/₁₆in) thick back legs of the female points to an underground life style. The male is only 30-50mm (1³/₁₆-2in) and he has thinner legs with longer hair after his final moult. There are also tibial hooks. This aggressive spider stridulates loudly.

Distribution
This species is found in bushes in Kenya, Tanzania, and Uganda. They dig 50cm (20in) deep hollows ending in a chamber.

Accommodation
Provide them with a minimum of 200mm (8in) of slightly damp (never wet) sandy soil and maintain a temperature of 20-24°C (68-75.2°F). Leave the burrowing spider alone so far as possible. *C. crawshayi* almost never lets anyone see it for three months at a time. Never dig this spider out from curiosity for this causes severe stress.

Reproduction
About 1,000 nymphs emerge after six to eight weeks and these take four to five years to reach adulthood.

CYCLOSTERNUM FASCIATUS

Appearance
This up to 40mm (1⁹/₁₆in) spider has a copper-coloured dorsal plate with a lighter patch in the middle that is often rubbed bald. There are five diagonal orange stripes on the black opisthosoma and brown-orange bristles on the black legs. Adult

males have tibial hooks. *C. fasciatus* is shy, nervous, and moderately aggressive.

Distribution
Moist mountain forests from Costa Rica to Guatemala.

Accommodation
Provide a fairly humid terrarium (70-80%) for this spider and they must have burrowing possibilities.

Reproduction
Some 300-500 nymphs emerge from the eggsac after five to eight weeks.

CYRIOCOSMUS ELEGANS

Appearance
The carapace of this up to 10mm (³/₈in) long spider is copper-coloured with a black triangle. The black legs are silvery on their upper sides. There are brownish stripes on the sides of the black opisthosoma and a heart-shaped coppery patch on the top of this rear part of the body.

Distribution
Burrows in Bolivia, Brazil, Trinidad, and Venezuela.

Reproduction
The male needs to placed with the female for a fairly long period of time. Feed the nymphs with small fruit flies and very small crickets.

Cyclosternum kochi *from Venezuela, formerly* Chaetorrhombus kochi.

Cyriocosmus elegans.

EPHEBOPUS MURINUS

Appearance
This 50mm (2in) type has a black base colouring. The prosoma is a light beige and there are light beige lateral stripes on the legs which cause this species to be regularly confused with *Aphonopelma seemanni*. These spiders are moderately aggressive.

Distribution
Ephebopus murinus is a burrowing species from Brazil, French Guiana, and Guyana. Their principal habitat is among tree roots.

Reproduction
The female is not aggressive towards the male.

EPHEBOPUS VIOLACEUS

Appearance
This species is 60mm (2³/₈in) long and has a shiny golden dorsal plate. The opisthosoma is black with reddish brown bristles. Each femur is dark blue, and the patella through to the tarsus is brown. There are white stripes on the legs. This spider is not aggressive.

Distribution
These climbing spiders inhabit tropical rain forest from Brazil to Ecuador.

Accommodation
Provide high humidity (85%).

Cyrtopholis majum *from Cuba, formerly* Cyclosternum majum.

Ephebopus murinus.

Encratoscelus pachypus.

Grammostola alticeps *from Brazil and Uruguay.*

EUATHLUS VULPINUS

Synonyms: *Phrixotrichus auratus* and *P. roseus.*
Appearance
These 50-60mm (2-2³/₈in) spiders are easily confused with *Grammostola cala* and *G. rosea. Euathlus vulpinus* though has a stridulation organ on the coxae of the pedipalps and front legs, which *Grammostola* species do not have. *E. vulpinus* is brown and pink to brown/orange with a clear pink-gold sheen on the dorsal plate which *Grammostola* also does not have. *E. vulpinus* is a calm spider.

Distribution
Ground dweller from Chile.

Reproduction
This species benefits from winter hibernation at a temperature of 10-15°C (50-59°F).

EUCRATOSCELUS PACHYPUS

Appearance
These 50mm (2in) long spiders have a darker rear body and their back legs are stout and densely covered with long bristles. *E. pachypus* is aggressive.

Distribution
These spiders live in deep burrows in Tanzania.

Accommodation
Provide *E. pachypus* with moist soil and maintain high humidity.

Grammostola cala.

Grammostola chalcothrix.

Grammostola mollicoma.

Grammostola pulchra.

GRAMMOSTOLA CALA

Appearance
This 50mm (2in) long spider has many geographical colour variations. It can be bright reddish brown to pink with darker feet.
Distribution
A ground-dweller from woods in Chile and western Argentina.
Reproduction
These very calm spiders are not difficult to breed from but their offspring develop very slowly.

GRAMMOSTOLA CHALCOTHRIX

Appearance
This 60mm (2³/₈in) long spider is blue-black after a moult but becomes more dull later. The bristles are light brown and there is a 'mirror' on the opisthosoma. *G. chalcothix* closely resembles *G. argentinensis* of western Argentina but this latter species is less blue with more dense bristles, so that the 'mirror' is less apparent.
Distribution
A calm ground-dwelling spider from eastern Argentina.
Reproduction
In common with all *Grammostola* species from Argentina and Chile, this species benefits from winter hibernation at 10-15°C (50-59°F).

GRAMMOSTOLA MOLLICOMA

Appearance
This black spider has blue-grey bristles on the legs and a blue sheen on its carapace. There are red bristles on the opisthosoma and light curved lines. Males have very long legs of 280mm (11in) span. In the wild this species is specialized in catching young rattlesnakes.
Distribution
Ground dweller from Brazil to Uruguay.
Reproduction
Some 200 nymphs are found in the eggsac.

GRAMMOSTOLA PULCHRA

Appearance
This 70mm (2³/₄in) long spider has a basic black colour with dark purple sheen.

Distribution
Grammostola pulchra inhabits pampas areas in southern Brazil and Uruguay.
Accommodation
Always keep the soil moist and the humidity at 70%.

GRAMMOSTOLA PULCHRIPES

Appearance
This up to 110mm (4⁵/₁₆in) long dark-brown and grey spider has ochre bristles on the opisthosoma and legs. There is also a shiny lighter patch on the abdomen. *G. pulchripes* is not aggressive.
Distribution
Lives on the pampas and in the woods of Argentina, Paraguay, Uruguay, and Brazil.

Grammostola pulchripes *male*.

Grammostola rosea.

Haplopelma lividum.

GRAMMOSTOLA ROSEA

Former names: *G. spatulata* and *Phrixotrichus roseus*.

Appearance
This 60mm (2³/₈in) long spider is dark brown, beige, or reddish brown but lighter than *G. cala*. Furthermore *G. rosea* has hard red spiky bristles on the coxae of the pedipalps and first pair of legs. *G. rosea* males have a pink sheen on their dorsal plate, which also has short, dark lateral stripes. There are long reddish brown bristles on the legs and each femur, patella, and tibia has two light-coloured thin lateral stripes. The tarsus of each leg is dark.
These generally calm spiders rarely use bombardment in defence.

Haplopelma minax *in threat stance*.

Distribution
This ground dweller lives in shallow hollows in woodland in Chile.
Accommodation
Do not keep this species too moist.
Reproduction
Grammostola rosea is not difficult to breed. Many hundreds of nymphs emerge from the eggsac after eight weeks but they develop slowly, reaching adulthood in five to six years.
There is considerable confusion between the three species widely imported from Chile *(G. cala, G. rosea,* and *Euathlus vulpinus)* because of their similarity in appearance.

HAPLOPELMA ALBOSTRIATUM

Former name: *Melopoeus albostriatus*.
Appearance
This 60mm (2³/₈in) long spider has a generally dark brown-grey body and legs and there are dark markings on the opisthosoma. The legs have light-coloured lateral stripes. Males are sometimes lighter in colour (see photo. p126).
Distribution
These burrowing spiders inhabit bamboo woods in Burma, Cambodia, and Thailand.
Accommodation
Provide humidity of 80% for this aggressive species.
Reproduction
The female is aggressive towards the male during mating.

HAPLOPELMA LIVIDUM

Former name: *Melopoeus lividum*.
Appearance
These spiders reach adulthood at 50-60mm (2-2³/₈in) when they are grey-brown with a downy dorsal plate and blue-grey opisthosoma with indistinct black markings. Except for the silver-coloured coxae and trochanters, the legs have a metallic blue sheen. The smaller males are slightly more brownish in colour. Immature specimens have a lighter-coloured opisthosoma and are less blue. This slender spider has short bristles. They are very fast and aggressive.

147

Distribution

This burrowing species inhabits the edges of forests in Burma, Malaysia, Thailand, and Singapore.

Accommodation

Provide them with deep reasonably moist soil for burrows. Ensure a temperature of 20-23°C (68-73.4°F) with humidity of 89%.

HAPLOPELMA MINAX

Former name: *Melopoeus minax.*

Appearance

The 60-70mm (2³/₈-2³/₄in) females of this species have brown-black dorsal plates with an indistinct black marking on the opisthosoma. Her black legs are brown at the back. With the lighter brown and smaller males the femur of each leg is black and his feet are also dark. When threatened the red hairs of the chelicerae are clearly visible. *H. minax* is an aggressive spider.

Distribution

Forests in South-East Asia (Burma and Thailand).

Reproduction

Place the male in the proximity of the female and mate them after several days. The female lays 30-100 eggs.

HARPACTIRA GIGAS

Appearance

This 60mm (2³/₈in) long spider is black with reddish brown colouring with a star marking on the dorsal plate, a patch on the opisthosoma, long

Heteroscodra maculata.

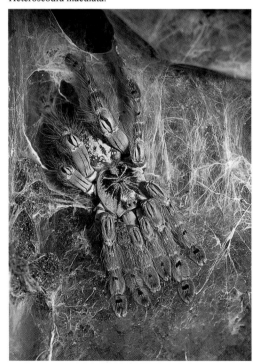

bristles on the lowest three leg segments. This closely resembles *Pterinochilus* species. Underneath they are black with an orange banding around the genital opening. *H. gigas* is fast, very aggressive, and stridulates a great deal. This spider covers the entire terrarium with its silken threads.

Distribution

Ground-dweller from South Africa but can climb.

HETEROSCODRA MACULATA

Appearance

This 60-70mm (2³/₈-2³/₄in) long spider is brownish grey in colour. There is a black star marking on the carapace and black patches on the opisthosoma. The femur of the rear leg is much thicker. This species is very aggressive.

Distribution

Ground-dweller from equatorial Africa.

Accommodation

Care for as *Avicularia* species.

HOLOTHELE INCEI

Former name: *Hapalopus incei.*

Appearance

These spiders are no more than 35mm (1³/₈in) long and have a golden star marking on a dark brown dorsal plate. There are six dark brown bands on the lighter brown opisthosoma. The legs are brown. The smaller males have dark brown feet.

Distribution

Burrowing spider from Trinidad and Tobago.

Accommodation

Provide a reasonably humid terrarium (70-80%).

Reproduction

The 30-40 nymphs emerge after 4 weeks.

HYSTEROCRATES GIGAS

Appearance

This 65mm (2⁹/₁₆in) long spider has reddish brown bristles with a brown-black to grey opisthosoma and legs. The carapace is charcoal grey. *H. gigas* is extremely aggressive.

Distribution

Burrowing species from equatorial Africa.

Holothele incei.

Hysterocrates gigas.

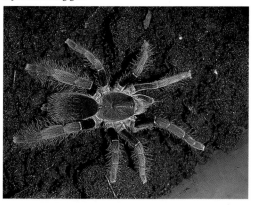

Lasiodora parahybana.

Lasiodora difficilis *from Brazil.*

Lasiodora striatipes.

Accommodation
Provide humidity of about 85% and a thick layer of moist soil. The nymphs in particular are very sensitive to dry conditions (humidity less than 65%).

LASIODORA SPECIES

The genus *Lasiodora* consists of 22 species mainly from Brazil. These are often large nomadic spiders, without a fixed dwelling place requiring a large terrarium (minimum 40 x 30 x 30cm/16 x 12 x 12in).
Lasiodora species spiders are aggressive, readily bombarding any threat with urticulating bristles.

Reproduction
The 2,000 or so nymphs emerge from the eggsac after 12 weeks and grow rapidly. The males often mature within 2 years and the females in 3.

LASIODORA KLUGI

Appearance
This 90-100mm (3¹/₂-4in) spider has a basic black colour with red bristles on the opisthosoma and brown-black legs and prosoma.

Distribution
Ground-dweller from Brazil that climbs a lot.

LASIODORA PARAHYBANA

Appearance
This up to 100mm (4in) long brown-black spider has a light margin around the dorsal plate and long reddish brown, slightly curly bristles on the opisthosoma and legs. There are two light-coloured lateral stripes on both tibiae and patellae.

Distribution
This ground dweller lives in the Brazilian rain forest.

LASIODORA STRIATIPES

Appearance
This 90mm (3¹/₂in) long spider is brown-black with many long but lighter bristles.

Distribution
Brazil.

LASIODORA STRIATUS

Former name: *Pamphobeteus wallacei.*

Appearance
This 80mm (3¹/₈in) long brown-black spider has whitish, orange, or reddish brown lateral stripes on the patellae, tibiae, and metatarsi. *L. striatus* resembles *Aphonopelma seemanni* but it is larger and has reddish brown bristles on its opisthosoma. This moderately aggressive ground dweller spurts excreta towards any threat.

Distribution
This ground dweller lives in the rain forests of Peru and Colombia.

MEGAPHOBEMA MESOMELAS

Appearance
This 50-60mm (2-2^3/$_8$in) long black spider has brown chelicerae. Patellae are orange-brown as are tibiae and femurs, though less bright. The bristles are short.

Distribution
Megaphobema mesomelas makes burrows in moist earth in the cool, humid mountain climate of the Monte Verde region of Costa Rica.

Accommodation
Keep this moderately aggressive species at 18-22°C (64.4-71.6°F) and fairly humid (75-85%).

Lasiodores striatus.

Megaphobema mesomelas.

Megaphobema robustum.

Reproduction
Place the anxious male with the female and leave them alone.

MEGAPHOBEMA ROBUSTUM

Appearance
This 90mm (3^1/$_2$in) long rust-coloured spider have swollen trochanters and femurs on the third pair of legs. The femur are black, the patellae, tibiae, and metatarsi are reddish brown. The rear legs are long. The carapace and opisthosoma are black to reddish brown and their are red bristles on the opisthosoma. The legs have lateral stripes.

Distribution
Rain forest in Colombia and Brazil.

Reproduction
This species is difficult to breed successfully.

METRIOPELMA ZEBRATA

Former name: *Crypsidromus zebrata.*

Appearance
This 50mm (2in) long species closely resembles *Cyclosternum fasciatus.* The first diagonal band on the opisthosoma however does not have a lower part. Furthermore the feet are not strikingly covered with orange-brown bristles. The male has no tibial hooks. *M. zebrata* is moderately aggressive.

Distribution
Costa Rica.

Megaphobema velvetosoma *from Colombia and Peru.*

Nhandu carapoensis *from Brazil and Paraguay.*

PAMPHOBETEUS SPECIES

Pamphobeteus is a popular genus with species that are generally aggressive (e.g. *P. nigricolor).* Although the females are mainly brown in colour, the males often exhibit fine pinkish purple colouring. Many species have two comma-like markings from the ocular tubercle to the central apodeme. Young specimens have an attractive orange opisthosoma with black 'Christmas tree' markings. Keep these inhabits of the rain forest at a humidity of 80%. Some 200 nymphs emerge from the eggsac.

PAMPHOBETEUS ANTINOUS

Appearance
This 100mm (4in) long, uniformly brown spider has reddish brown bristles on its opisthosoma. There are two comma-like markings from the ocular tubercle to the central apodeme. Adult males have a blue tinge to their dorsal plate and legs but

Pamphobeteus platyomma *female with eggsac.*

females and young specimens only have this on the femurs.

Distribution
Quite aggressive ground-dwelling species from the rain forests of Bolivia and Peru.

Pamphobeteus antinous.

Pamphobeteus ornata *female, from Colombia.*

Pamphobeteus platyomma *male.*

Pamphobeteus ornata *male.*

Pamphobeteus augusti *from Ecuador.*

Pamphobeteus fortis *from Colombia in dull colouring.*

Pamphobeteus ferox *from Colombia.*

Pamphobeteus insularis *from Brazil.*

Pamphobeteus nigricolor *from Bolivia, Peru, Colombia, and Ecuador. This is dull colouring (normally black).*

PAMPHOBETEUS PLATYOMMA

Appearance
This 80-90mm (3^1/$_8$-3^1/$_2$in) long spider is variable in colour and its taxonomy is still subject of research. Usually it is brown-black to reddish brown with lighter stripes on the patellae. The opisthosoma is dark brown. Adult males have a pinkish-red star on the dorsal plate and similar colour on the femurs.

P. platyomma is moderately aggressive.

Distribution
Ground dweller from Ecuador.

Reproduction
This species produces a maximum of 100 nymphs.

PAMPHOBETEUS VESPERTINUS

Appearance
This up to 70mm (2^3/$_4$in) long brown-black spider has purple bristles on its legs and opisthosoma, and a purple star marking on the dorsal plate.

This fairly aggressive spider readily bombards with its barbed urticulating bristles.

Distribution
Ground dweller from Brazil.

Reproduction
Pamphobeteus vespertinus has 100-120 nymphs.

PARAPHYSA HORRIDA

Appearance
This 80mm (3^1/$_8$in) long charcoal grey spider has a bright orange prosoma. It is aggressive.

Distribution
Brazil.

PARAPHYSA PULCHRIMAKLAASI

Appearance
This approx. 70mm (2^3/$_4$in) long spider is blue-black with orange leg stripes and golden 'mirror' on the opisthosoma. This somewhat nervous spider does not appear to suffer stress or become aggressive.

Pamphobeteus roseus, *95mm (3³/₄in) long.*

Pamphobeteus vespertinus *male.*

Paraphysa horrida.

Distribution
Ecuador.
Reproduction
Some 200 or so nymphs emerge from the eggsac.

PHORMICTOPUS CANCERIDES

Appearance
This 80mm (3¹/₈in) long brown-black spider has a golden star-shaped gleam on the dorsal plate. Before a moult these spiders are light brown but afterwards dark black. The long legs and opisthosoma are densely covered with orange bristles. The patellae and tibiae have two grey lateral stripes. *P. cancerides* is an aggressive bombarding spider.

Paraphysa pulchrimiklaasi.

Paraphysa pulchrimiklaasi.

Distribution
Ground dweller from rain forests on Haiti and the Dominican Republic.
Accommodation
Provide humidity of 80%.
Reproduction
The maximum of 150 nymphs emerge from the eggsac after five weeks. They grow rapidly with females becoming adult after about three years.

PHORMICTOPUS NESIOTES

Appearance
This 70mm (2³/₄in) long brownish-grey spider has golden coloured femurs and dorsal plates. *P. nesiotes* is aggressive and stridulates loudly.
Distribution
Ground dweller from Cuba.

Phormictopus cancerides.

153

Phormictopus nesiotes.

Poecilotheria formosa.

Poecilotheria rufilata *adult male from India.*

POECILOTHERIA SPECIES

Appearance

The genus *Poecilotheria* consists of fourteen species. These spiders are strikingly marked with grey-white and brown with lemon yellow undersides of the femur, tibiae, and metatarsi of the first and second pairs of legs. The yellow colour frightens enemies when the spider is in its threat stance. *Poecilotheria* species are moderately aggressive but very agile tree spiders which attempt to flee before resorting to biting. The venom causes fairly serious problems. In the wild these spiders mainly eat large moths.

Distribution

These spiders inhabit and spin quarters in holes and cracks in trees and houses, in India and Sri Lanka.

Accommodation

Provide sufficient climbing opportunities and high humidity (70-80%) for these spiders. Give them a piece of bark or bird nesting box as hiding place.

Reproduction

Once adult the males can be placed with a female without concern for him. The females too can be kept in groups, provided they are given enough to eat. The courtship can continue for some time before mating takes place. The 70-150 nymphs emerge from the eggsac after about six weeks and develop quickly.

POECILOTHERIA FASCIATA

Appearance

Poecilotheria fasciata grows to 60-70mm (2³/₈-2³/₄in) long. In the centre of the female's grey-white dorsal plate there is a dark pair of lateral stripes and there is also a grey-white zigzag lateral marking in the middle of her grey-brown opisthosoma, with indistinct dark diagonal stripes alongside. The underside of the body is reddish brown and the legs are alternately grey and brown-black. The lower side of the femurs are grey or lemon yellow in colour. The male is much browner with dark feet. This species resembles *P. regalis* but has slightly different dorsal plate markings.

Distribution

Monsoon forests in Sri Lanka.

Poecilotheria fasciata.

POECILOTHERIA FORMOSA

Appearance
There is an indistinct black central marking on the greyish-brown dorsal plate of the 60-70mm (2³/₈-2³/₄in) long female. A darker bottle-shaped marking also runs from the ocular tubercle to the central apodeme. The darker opisthosoma has a white/-brown lateral stripe and indistinct brown diagonal markings. Legs are alternately indistinct grey and brown-black markings. The brown male has a black ocular tubercle and darker feet.

Distribution
Southern India.

POECILOTHERIA ORNATA

Appearance
The 60-70mm (2³/₈-2³/₄in) long female is greyish-brown with a pair of black dorsal stripes. The darker opisthosoma has a white/brown lateral stripe with 8 black diagonal markings. There are fiery bright yellow to orange markings on olive-coloured legs with two orange stripes on the tarsi and one on the metatarsi of both sexes. The undersides of the legs are bright yellow but the undersides of the pedipalps of both sexes are red. The male is only a little bit smaller and grey-green in colour with reddish-brown bristles.

Poecilotheria ornata *female.*

Poecilotheria ornata *adult male.*

Poecilotheria regalis.

Distribution
Mountain areas of Sri Lanka.

POECILOTHERIA REGALIS

Appearance
This 70mm (2³/₄in) long spider closely resembles *P. fasciata* but has a light beige diagonal marking above the genital opening on the underside. Furthermore, the black diagonal stripes on the back are more clearly defined. The male too resembles *P. fasciata* but has a grey-white lateral stripe on its opisthosoma.

Distribution
India.

Poecilotheria subfusca.

POECILOTHERIA SUBFUSCA

Appearance
This 90-100mm (3 1/2-4in) long spider is grey-brown with light grey and black markings. The underside of the prosoma, tarsi, and metatarsi are black while the underside of the opisthosoma is dark grey. The upper side of the femurs of the back legs are black with white terminations (as opposed to *P. fasciata)*, and the underside of the femurs of all legs are entirely black.

Distribution
Monsoon forests in Sri Lanka.

PSALMOPOEUS SPECIES

The genus *Psalmopoeus* consists of agile, mainly tree-dwelling spiders with copious covering of bristles. The front legs are longer than the fourth pair (in contrast with the genus *Tapinauchenius).* Both genera also differ in the bristles on the pedipalps. *Psalmopoeus* species never have a shiny patch of urticulating hairs ('mirror') on the opisthosoma but always have short hairs on this rear part of their bodies.
Psalmopoeus species spiders are aggressive, quick, and customarily jump.

PSALMOPOEUS CAMBRIDGEI

Appearance
The carapace of this 70mm (2 3/4in) long grey-brown spider is tinged with green. The female, in contrast with the darker male, has an indistinct black check pattern on her opisthosoma and there are reddish orange stripes on the tarsi and metatarsi.

Distribution
This tree-dwelling spider spins enormous living cocoons in rain forests on Trinidad.

Accommodation
Do not keep this species too dry but at humidity of 70-80% with a temperature of 25-30°C (77-86°F).

Reproduction
This species is easily bred although the female is often aggressive towards the male. The 100 or so nymphs emerge after five to eight weeks and grow quickly. The female will often produce a second eggsac just before she moults.

Psalmopoeus cambridgei.

PSALMOPOEUS IRMINIA

Appearance
The up to 60mm (2 3/8in) long female is charcoal grey with eight orange segments on the opisthosoma and reddish orange stripes of the tarsi and metatarsi. The slightly smaller males are grey-brown.

Distribution
Venezuela.

Reproduction
This species is fairly easy to breed from. Spiderlings have a brown carapace, and black opisthosoma with yellowish orange patches and black legs. The metatarsi are yellowish orange.

PSALMOPOEUS REDUNCUS

Appearance
This 50mm (2in) long spider has a dark brown basic colour with a golden brown dorsal plate. The bristles are less dense than with *P. cambridgei,* with an opisthosoma that is fairly smooth in appearance but with longer bristles at the side. There are no urticulating hairs or stripes on the legs.

Distribution
This species creates underground burrows in Costa Rica.

PSEUDOTHERAPHOSA APOPHYSIS

Appearance
This imposing dark brown spider grows up to 110mm (4 5/16in) long. There is a large round dark patch on the opisthosoma. *P. apophysis* is an aggressive bombarding spider.

Pair of Psalmopoeus irminia.

Psalmopoeus reduncus.

Adult female Pseudotheraphosa apophysis.

Distribution
Ground dweller from Venezuela.
Reproduction
About 80 nymphs emerge from the eggsac.

PTERINOCHILUS SPECIES

Appearance
The genus *Pterinochilus* consists of 20 extremely aggressive species from Africa. These spiders are slimly built with a star marking on their dorsal plate and a marking on the opisthosoma. Every species is extremely aggressive and their venom is dangerous, especially for children.
Accommodation
Do not keep these spiders too moist (humidity of 60-

Pseudotheraphosa apophysis *spiderling.*

Pterinochilus meridionalis *from Malawi, Mozambique, Zambia, and Zimbabwe.*

70%). They build and spin a large system of chambers and passageways between decorative material in the terrarium and in the soil. Their webs combine living quarters, snare for prey, and escape route.
Reproduction
The eggsac is not carried but is made part of the main web. Some 150 nymphs emerge after about five weeks and develop quickly.

PTERINOCHILUS MURINUS

Appearance
This up to 60mm (2³/₈in) long reddish brown spider has a black star marking on the dorsal plate and black patches on the opisthosoma.
Distribution
Dry plains in coastal areas of East Africa (Kenya and Tanzania) close to rubbish tips, and hence in the proximity of humans. This species spins a lair in hollows beneath stones and shrubs.

PTERINOCHILUS SPINIFER

Appearance
This 55mm (2⁵/₃₂in) long spider has a black star marking on the brown carapace and a black patch in front of the ocular tubercle. There is an indistinct central line and black patches on the brown opisthosoma. The legs are brown.
Distribution
Woodland in East Africa (Tanzania).

STROMATOPELMA CALCEATA

Former name: *Scodra calceata.*
Appearance
This 55mm (2⁵/₃₂in) long spider is decoratively marked with brown, grey, and black. There are small black markings on the tarsi and metatarsi and a dark lateral stripe plus several other markings on the lighter opisthosoma. *S. calceata* has darker coloured femurs on the pedipalps. The front legs of *Stromatopelma* species are sturdy. The males remain 20mm (³/₄in) shorter. The subspecies *S. c. griseipes* has grey or greyish brown markings and the front legs are long with broad tarsi and metatarsi. The legs have fairly long bristles with black markings. The femurs of the pedi-

Pterinochilus murinus.

Pterinochilus spinifer.

Stromatopelma calceata *male*.

palps of *S. c. griseipes* are light in colour. *S. calceata* is extremely aggressive and quick. It is one of the African species that bites without warning and its venom is fairly strong.

Distribution
These tree dwellers from West and Central Africa build their cocoons in the crowns of shrubs and trees (such as palm trees).

Reproduction
The female is not aggressive towards the male. She lays 100-350 eggs which emerge as nymphs from the eggsac after 8 weeks and become adult in 1¹/₂-2 years.

TAPINAUCHENIUS GIGAS

Appearance
This 60mm (2³/₈in) long spider is light brown and densely covered with long bristles. There is a broad band of glistening bristles from top to bottom of the opisthosoma. Four little points are visible on the rear of the opisthosoma which are where the muscles are attached.

Distribution
Tree dweller from Colombia and French Guyana.

THARAPHOSA BLONDI

This spider is named for the researcher Le Blond and is often referred to as *T. leblondi*.

Appearance
This 100-120mm (4-4³/₄in) long spider has a max-

imum span of 250mm (9⁷/₈in). The species is dark brown with short bristles on the opisthosoma and longer ones on the legs.

T. blondi is usually aggressive and the urticulating hairs it throws in the air with its legs cause severe irritation. When threatened this spider stridulates quickly and loudly. These spiders are prone to gluttony and fat ones can acquire an opisthosoma as big as a tennis ball but this reduces their fertility.

Distribution
These burrowing spiders inhabit rain forests in northern Brazil and from Venezuela to French Guiana. They dig deep beneath the roots of the rain forest.

Accommodation
Provide this species with at least 100mm (4in) of soil and provide a good shelter with tree bark to enable the spiders to hide themselves away. Keep the humidity high at 75-80% but never spray directly on the spiders themselves.

Reproduction
The female is not aggressive towards the male, who has no tibial hooks. Keep a terrarium with an eggsac carrying female moist but not actually wet to prevent the eggs from rotting. The eggsacs contain 30-150 nymphs of 15-20mm (⁹/₁₆-³/₄in). The nymphs usually emerge after eight to nine weeks although development can take twenty weeks. The offspring grow rapidly.

Tapinauchenius gigas *female*.

Fully-grown Theraphosa blondi *female*.

Theraphosa blondi *mating.*

Xenesthis monstrosa.

VITALIUS ROSEUS

Appearance
This up to 60mm (2³/₈in) long spider is golden brown with light brown markings. The legs, which are partially brown-black, have pink to orange lateral stripes. This species rarely bombards in defence and is not aggressive.

Distribution
Brazil and Colombia.

Reproduction
About 400 nymphs emerge from the eggsac.

XENESTHIS IMMANIS

Appearance
This up to 70mm (2³/₄in) long spider has a black base colour with a red-to-pink star marking on the

Vitalius roseus.

Xenesthis immanis.

dorsal plate and brown bristles on the opisthosoma. This aggressive spider quickly throws all its bristles in defence, leaving itself bare.

Distribution
Ground dweller from rain forests in Colombia, Ecuador, Venezuela, Peru, and Panama.

Accommodation
Provide humidity of 75-80%.

XENESTHIS MONSTROSA

Appearance
This 80-90mm (3¹/₈-3¹/₂in) long charcoal grey spider has short bristles. X. monstrosa is aggressive.

Distribution
Ground dweller from Colombia.

Trapdoor spiders

In addition to those spiders we have called tarantulas in this book, the straight-chelicerae spiders also include some extremely venomous spiders such as *Atrax* species from Australia, the genus *Trechona* from South America, *Macrothele* species from southern parts of Europe, and a number of trapdoor spiders. A number of families of arachnids are termed trapdoor spiders, including Barychelidae, Ctenizidae, Nemesidae, and Actinopodidae.

Appearance
Most species, including spiders of the widely kept genus *Conothele,* are no bigger than 30mm (1³/₁₆in). The body is thickset with powerful legs. These burrowing spiders are virtually bald. *Conothele* species are overall golden brown with black lines on the legs and the margins of the dorsal plate. The opisthosoma is ochre with an indistinct grey cross marking. These spiders dig burrows in fairly loose soil in which they spin their cocoons, closely the entrance with a hinged and well-camouflaged trap door. Passing prey are captured during the night. Some species also make cavities beneath bark and such like.
Trapdoor spiders are extremely aggressive. Even specimens that appear dead can summon their last reserves to give a nasty bite. African and Australian species are very dangerous.

A trap door spider from Australia (Conothele sp.).

Distribution
Trapdoor spiders are found in the area around the Mediterranean Sea, from Africa through to Australia, and in Central and South America.

Accommodation
Care for these spiders as burrowing kinds of tarantula. Provide at least 250mm (9⁷/₈in) of loose earth such as a peat/sand mixture and keep this moderately moist.

Reproduction
The 25-150 young emerge from the eggsac after about 3 weeks.

Pincer-jawed spiders

The infra-order Araneomorphae (also known as Labidognata) of pincer-jawed spiders have the chelicerae articulated so that they close from outwards in, with the basal segments facing downwards.

The families Araneidae and Nephilidae, orb weaver spiders

Both the genera *Araneus* (includes the cross spider *A. diadematus)* and *Argiope* fall within the family Araneidae.
The principal genus of the family Nephilidae is *Nephila.*
Orb weaver spiders create a more or less circular web. First they spin the framework of support threads and then a wheel is spun with spokes and many sticky threads which together form a spiral. Some species such as those of *Argiope* reinforce their web with silken threads in a zigzag at the centre. The spiders either remain in the centre of the web or hide themselves at its rim.
The smaller males have to approach the female with care. European species over-winter as eggs and become adults in late summer. The sticky droplets can best be seen early in the morning when the web is covered with dew.

THE GENUS *ARGIOPE*

Appearance
Argiope bruennichi is a 11-25mm (⁷/₁₆-1in) long. The opisthosoma of the female is strikingly marked with diagonal black and yellow stripes. The dorsal plate is silver coloured, and the legs are banded with charcoal grey. The male is 4-7mm (⁵/₃₂-⁴/₁₆in) long and has an elongated, light brown opisthosoma.
Argiope lobata is alternately marked with beige, grey, black, or silver colourings. There are three to four lobes on each side of the opisthosoma.

Distribution
Argiope species often build their webs in vegetation. There is often a white zigzag beneath the spider in the wheel-shaped web. *Argiope bruennichi* is found from central and southern Europe to South-East Asia, China, and Japan.
Argiope lobata originates in southern Europe, Africa, and the Middle East through to southern parts of Asia.

Accommodation
Provide an adult female with an airy terrarium of at least 40 x 15 x 50cm (16 x 6 x 20in) with no fewer than two sides of fine gauze. Give the specimens several branches. Feeding can be done through a small aperture. Spray water lightly once per day and ensure a daytime temperature of 24-30°C (75.2-86°F) and about 20°C (68°F) at night. It is also possible to let this spider live freely in the terrarium room because they tend to remain with their web.

Reproduction
Place the male on the edge of the female's web and remove him if she does not react within 30 min-

Argiope bruennichi *with eggsac.*

Argiope lobata *in Chad.*

utes. The small brown male only mates with females that are fertile. The female lays several hundred eggs in autumn. *Argiope bruennichi's* eggsac
is large, downy, and hangs in the web. *Argiope lobata*]builds a large pear-shaped eggsac. Allow the
eggsacs from these European species over-winter.
at 10-15°C (50-59°F).

THE GENUS *NEPHILA*, GIANT ORB WEAVER

The spiders of this genus of 50 species can make
webs of up to 5m (16ft 5in) in diameter.

Appearance

Female *Nephila* spiders are up to 60mm (2³/₈in)
long. The opisthosoma is cylindrical and is usually
strikingly coloured (often red, white, and yellow).
The underlying colour of the body and legs is almost always black. The legs are extremely long, especially the front ones. The largest span measured
with these spiders is in the region of 200mm
(7⁷/₈in). The males are much small with bodies up
to just 10mm (³/₈in).

These spiders spend the day sitting in the centre of
their very strong wheel-like webs that are usually
of 1.5 metres (approx. 5ft) in diameter.

When disturbed they let themselves fall and pretend to be dead. They sometimes adopt a threat
stance and will bite when necessary but their venom is not very dangerous.

Distribution

Nephila species are found in all sub tropical and
tropical regions, mainly inhabiting moist woodland and savannah.

Accommodation

Provide an airy terrarium of at least 80 x 40 x 80cm
(31¹/₂ x 16 x 31¹/₂in) for an adult female. At least
two sides should be gauze. Provide several branches. Feeding can be provided via a small opening.
Ensure a temperature of 24-30°C (75.2-86°F).
Most species of *Nephila* are sensitive for drought
so spray a little water each day but make sure the
moisture has evaporated within a few hours. A
number of *Nephila* specimens can be kept together in a large terrarium and can also be allowed free
run of a sufficiently warm terrarium room.

A giant orb weaver makes a very large web. This is
Nephila maculata *in the Philippines.*

A Ugandan Nephila *sp. plays dead.*

A Philippines Nephila *sp. with catch and a male.*

Sex determination

The male is much smaller than the female and he
reaches adulthood much sooner which makes it
difficult to breed them, since by the time the females are adult, their brothers are dead.

Mating

Give the female a substantial prey and then place
the male on the edge of her net. The male will remain in her neighbourhood and regularly attempt
to mate with her. To prevent cannibalism remove
the male back to his own terrarium if he has not
approached her within 30 minutes.

Egg laying

Several hundred eggs are laid a few weeks after
mating. The eggsac is hung up in the net. Remove
the eggsac and keep it moist. The nymphs emerge
after one to five months but only go their separate
ways after shedding their first skin to become spiderlings.

Rearing

Raise the young spiderlings together in large terrariums with plenty of branches. The young eat
aphids and fruit flies. Spray water each day. Once
the males can be identified by their thicker pedipalps (the future sperm receptacles), set them
apart at 20-25°C (68-77°F) and give them minimal
food.

Feed the females well at 25-30°C (77-86°F) in order to attempt to get both sexes to adulthood at the
same time. It is also possible to raise half of the
brood slowly. In breeding results though in smaller and less healthy spiders.

Nephila clavata *(Philippines) with small brown male already in her net.*

Melanistic black form of Nephila maculata.

NEPHILA MACULATA

Appearance

Females are up to 45mm (1³/₄in) long with a span of 150mm (6in). The opisthosoma is black with yellow stripes or patches. The dorsal plate is silvery-yellow and the legs are black with a certain amount of orange marking. The 8mm (⁵/₁₆in) long brown male mates during hot wet seasons.

Distribution

Tropical rain forests and gardens from India to southern Japan and North Australia.

Other Araneae

The following types of true spiders from the order Araneae are also frequently kept in terrariums.

The Heteropodidae family, crab spiders

There are other families of crab spider but this is the best known.

Appearance

Crab spiders are flat creatures with small bodies and very long, thin legs. Their span can be more than 200mm (8in). They can move quickly to the side with their crab-wise legs. Crab spiders are fast and try to attempt before becoming aggressive. Most of them are active at night or during twilight. They do not build nets to trap prey.

Distribution

Crab spiders are found in all sub tropical and tropical regions where they principally live on walls, in buildings, on branches of trees, and in banana plantations.

Accommodation

House crab spiders in a terrarium without any chinks in it that is five times wider, deeper, and taller than the spider's span. Keep one side of a soil covering of peat and sand mixture moist. Ensure a temperature of 25-30°C (77-86°F) and keep humidity around 70-80% with a weekly spray.

Reproduction

The flat, cushion-like eggsac are characteristics of *Heteropoda* species. The eggsac is guarded by the female, and is either hung up in a rather rudimentary web or carried around beneath her. The nymphs hatch in about four weeks.

HETEROPODA VENATORIA

This spider often enters Europe in consignments of bananas, as do *Phoneutria* species.

Appearance

Heteropoda venatoria is an up to 25mm (1in) long brown spider with lighter banding at the front and back of the dorsal plate. The male remains 5-10mm (³/₁₆-³/₈in) smaller.

Distribution

Heterpoda venatoria originates from Sri Lanka but has now found its way through the sub-tropical and tropical world.

Male of a species of Heterpoda.

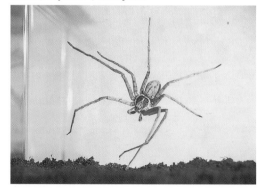

Female of a species of Heterpoda.

Polybetes pytagorica *female with eggsac and nymphs.*

POLYBETES PYTAGORICA

This spider also forms part of the Heterpodidae family.

Appearance

This up to 30mm (1³/₁₆in) long spider has a brown-black carapace. The opisthosoma is marked with ochre and brown, with a darker lateral stripe and there is a black cross marking on the underside of this rear part of the body.

Distribution

Wall and tree dweller from Argentina.

Reproduction

The male is smaller and when adult has clearly visible sperm receptacles. The eggsac is 30mm (1³/₁₆in) across and 10mm (³/₈in) thick. The 200 nymphs emerge after 30 days at 27°C (80.6°F) and humidity of about 70%. These shed their first skin to form spiderlings after a week. Allow some of them to escape from the breeding terrarium and capture them immediately to place them in a container of their own. This is best done somewhere unfurnished, such as a tiled bathroom. Spray the young at least twice each week. A wad of kitchen roll in their terrarium will absorb excess water and also provide water for the young spiders.

Pair of Polybetes pytagorica.

The Lycosidae family, wolf spiders

The best known wolf spiders are those of the genus *Lycosa.*

Appearance

Wolf spiders often have an elongated prosoma in comparison with the opisthosoma. The body and legs are usually covered in abundant dense short bristles and they are often marked with lateral stripes or banding – on the body. The four smallest eyes of Lycosidae are lined up in a row at the front of the head with two larger eyes behind them. The other two eyes are on the side of the head.

These small spiders are very shy and some South American species are somewhat dangerous.

Distribution

There are more than 3,000 species in about 100 genera spread throughout the entire world. Most of the species live close to the ground and sometimes inhabit holes in the ground.

Reproduction

Wolf spiders carry their round eggsacs with them. After the nymphs emerge they crawl onto their mother's back and remain there for several weeks.

Species of Lycosa *from Uruguay, with young.*

Species of Sicaria *from Argentina.*

Pair of Cupienius salei.

The Sicariidae family, sand spiders

SYCARIA SPECIES

Appearance
The females are up 15mm (⁵/₈in) long and they are fairly uniform in colour, which is either brown or greyish-brown. The opisthosoma does differ slightly in colour. The male is barely 10mm (³/₈in) long. Neither sex has much in the way of bristles.
These slow spiders often live hidden beneath stones or in burrows they create in sand from which they overpower passing prey. These spiders do not make webs and are unable to walk up glass. Sand spiders are extremely venomous and a bite will need surgical removal of the tissue involved.
Accommodation
Care for these spiders in the same way as crab spiders but keep them slightly dryer.
Distribution
These spiders inhabit reasonably moist micro-climates in dry areas of Argentina. Sand spiders are also found throughout southern Africa.

The Ctenidae family, comb spiders

Species of the genera *Cupienius* and *Phoneutria* which are widely kept form part of this family.

CUPIENIUS SALEI

Appearance
The 30mm (1³/₁₆in) long female is light brown with a broad brown lateral stripe across the body. She also has brown legs but at the back of the opisthosoma there are yellowish orange patches. Underneath is attractively orange with black markings. The 22mm (⁷/₈in) long male is almost uniformly brown. These very fast moving spiders do not make webs and they are extremely venomous.
Distribution
Tropical rain forest of Central and South America (Brazil).
Accommodation
Care for these spiders as crab spiders.

PHONEUTRIA SPECIES

Appearance
The females of the various species of *Phoneutria* (*P. fera, P. keyserlingii,* and *P. nigriventer*) are 35mm (1³/₈in) long with the males 10mm (35mm (³/₈in) shorter. These species are brown on top. *P. nigriventer* has a black fleck on its underside. *Phoneutria* species spiders do not make webs. They are quick, aggressive, and extremely venomous spiders. A mere 0.0003mg of the powerful neurotoxin per kilogram of the victim is sufficient to kill. Most victims die with six hours from respiratory problems.
Distribution
These spiders live on and in buildings and plants such as bananas throughout tropical and sub-tropical South America. Every spider found on bananas becomes dubbed a banana spider and this applies to *Phoneutria* species too.
Accommodation
Care for *Phoneutria* species in the same way as crab spiders.
Reproduction
The eggsacs are placed under stones and such like.

The Loxoscelidae subfamily 'violin' spiders

LOXOSCELUS SPECIES

Appearance
Loxoscelus species are light brown spiders of at

Phoneutria *species.*

Loxoscelus *species mating.*

A black widow (Latrodectus mactans) *is true to her name.*

most 13mm (¹/₂in) long (males) and 15mm (⁵/₈in) for females. There is a dark brown marking on the dorsal plate, which some say resembles a violin.

These spiders are nocturnal and they spin an untidy horizontal web. Their venom can be more dangerous for some people than that of the black widow spider. *Loxoscelus* species produce a tissue dissolving venom. Victims develop a scab on the wound area and when this falls off the wound beneath has become worse. The problem can take several months to heal and sometimes requires skin grafts.

Distribution

These spiders live under stones and in houses from the USA to South America. They are also found in Africa, Europe, and Asia.

Accommodation

Care for *Loxoscelus* species as crab spiders.

Reproduction

Mating follows quickly on from a certain amount of drumming on the female's web. The eggsac with its 100-150 eggs is guarded and the nymphs emerge after about 5 weeks.

The Theridiidae family

LATRODECTUS SPECIES, BLACK WIDOWS

Many believe that black widow spiders are tarantulas and that one bite is deadly. Both assertions are untrue.

Appearance

Latrodectus species females are 15-20mm (⁵/₈-³/₄in) long. The striking feature is their smoothly rounded and often glinting opisthosoma. Some species have a brown or white base colouring. A characteristic is the red 'egg timer' marking on the underside of the opisthosoma. The marking is different with a few species, e.g. a red triangle.

Adult males are 5mm (³/₁₆in) long and they are a lighter, cream to dark brown colouring with striped legs and lightly striped markings on the opisthosoma.

The widely offered *L. mactans* is entirely black except for the red 'egg timer' marking. *L. geomet-*

ricus, or the brown widow, is never entirely black. This species varies in colour but is often brown or grey-brown with several black dots on the sides of the opisthosoma. The 'egg timer' is reddish orange.

L. hasselti (the Australian redback) is dark brown with a red lateral stripe on the opisthosoma.

Distribution

The various *Latrodectus* species originate in North America, around the Mediterranean, in Africa, Asia, and Australia. They inhabit dry subtropical or tropical regions and live beneath all manner of matter, in shrubs, and fissures.

Latrodectus mactans originates from the USA but has been introduced to Australia. *L. geometricus* is found throughout all subtropical and tropical countries. *L. hasselti* is found in Australia, New Zealand, and Japan. Throughout the Mediterranean region, including Spain, Portugal, and large parts of France, the species *L. tridecimhuttatus* can be found, and *L. congoblatus* originates from Greece.

Black widow spiders do not survive in moist climates such as that of northern Europe.

Accommodation

House *Latrodectus* species in well sealed terrariums such as jars, with perforated lids. Greasing the lid with a little salad or vegetable oil prevents the spider from hanging on to the lid. Lay a base of

Latrodectus hasselti.

peat and sand mixture on the bottom and provide several upright branches for nest building. Those from moderate climates should be kept at 20°C (68°F) while tropical species require 25°C (77°F). Avoid bright light and keep the jar dry. Humidity can easily become too moist resulting in fungus forming.

Feeding
Feed small insects.

Sex determination
Males remain smaller and are lighter in colour and more colourful. The emboli are visible with adult males.

Mating
Place a male close to a well-fed female and leave them alone. The male is frequently eaten.

Egg laying
Females make about ten white to brown eggsacs of 15mm ($^5/_8$in) diameter which they hang in their web. The eggsac of *L. mactans* is round and yellowish. while those of *L. geometricus* are pure white apart from dots. The female rehangs the eggsac somewhere else if conditions are unfavourable. The eggsacs hatch in about one month.

Rearing
Remove all eggsacs and hang them in a well-sealed jar with ultra-fine mesh. The newly emerged white offspring of some species are smaller than young aphids so they quickly escape. Keep humidity between 50 and 70%. Keep the pot sealed so that most of the 100-500 young eat each other but when there are about fifteen left raise these in separate containers. It is possible to determine sex after about one month. The nymphs mature to adults in two to three months. The males die after about one to two months as adults but the females can live for a maximum of 3 years.

Defence
Only the females are potentially dangerous. At first they remain calm, try to fall, or flee. They only bite when all else fails. The females are more aggressive if they are protecting an eggsac.

The pain following a bite by *L. mactans* only becomes apparent after about ten minutes and can become unbearable as the venom spreads throughout the body. The symptoms (shock, fainting, nausea, vomiting, sleeplessness, breathing difficulty, and high blood pressure) can last for days or even weeks. A healthy adult has a 5% risk of dying if no antidote is administered. The venom is a neurotoxin (it affects the nervous system) and it is fifteen times more powerful than the venom of a rattlesnake. The amount of the venom though is much smaller. A bite of *L. geometricus* is much less severe but still painful.

Young black widow spiders are smaller than young aphids.

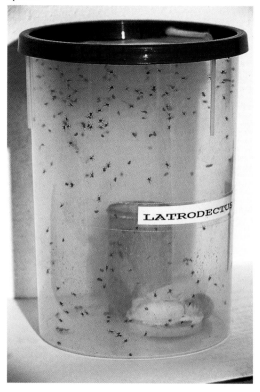

Pair of Latrodectus mactans.

Latrodectus geometricus *with eggsac.*

The brown widow (L. geometricus) *is often found under mattresses and chairs in Chad.*

Handling

Handle black widows by means of jars and never with bare hands. This generally calm spider can move rapidly when frightened.

STEATODEA PAYKULLIANA, THE FALSE WIDOW

Appearance

This spider is also part of the Theridiidae family and resembles the black widow. This species is also dangerous for humans. The 8-15mm ($^5/_{16}$-$^5/_8$in) long females have a brown-black prosoma and legs. The black opisthosoma is ringed with a pale yellow, orange, or red band and there is a dorsal stripe. Males are 4-6mm ($^5/_{32}$-$^1/_4$in) long and thinner. They are more clearly marked with a white banding around the rear of their body and have black banding on their legs.

Distribution

These spiders live under stones in buildings in southern parts of Europe as far north as Switzerland, North Africa, and western parts of Asia. They are sometimes imported among fruit. The ends of their threads are sticky.

Accommodation

Care for *S. paykulliana* as black widow spiders.

Reproduction

Mating and reproduction are the same as with black widows.

Steatodea paykulliana *female.*

The order Solifugae, wind scorpions/sun scorpions/ sun spiders

Wind scorpions, also known as sun scorpions, and sun spiders are sometimes offered for sale but they are fairly difficult to keep in captivity and have not yet been successfully bred.

Appearance

Wind scorpions bodies consist of a segmented head, a thorax of three segments and an abdomen of ten segments. The chelicerae have developed to enormous protruding gripping pincers that tear prey apart. The pedipalps and front legs are lengthy and act as feelers. These animals walk on the rear three pairs of legs. These insects are up to 70mm ($2^3/_4$in) long and their bodies are moderately covered with bristles of up to 50mm (2in) long. The yellow or ochre-coloured desert-dwelling species are nocturnal while the darker coloured species are diurnal, inhabiting grassland and woods. There are just two large eyes on the ocular tubercle. Wind or sun scorpions do not have book lungs and they breathe through tracheae.

Distribution

The around 900 species of wind/sun scorpions in their twelve families inhabit warm (and usually dry) regions of desert and plain throughout the world except Australia. There are two *Gluvia* species in Spain and species of *Galeodes* are found in Syria and surrounding countries, while *Eremobates* species are from the USA. These creatures dig long horizontal burrows up to 100mm (4in) deep in the ground, where it is comparatively cool.

Accommodation

These creatures are difficult to keep in captivity. Provide each specimen with its own 30 x 20 x 30cm (12 x 8 x 12in) well-sealed terrarium. These animals can walk up glass and will gnaw their way through mesh. Lay at least 100mm (4in) of sandy soil and keep it slightly moist. Create sufficient sheltering places and provide a water tray. Heat the terrarium during the day to 35°C (95°F) and at night provide under floor heating with cables to

Wind scorpion specimen in museum.

167

Wind scorpion.

Wind scorpion after formaldehyde.

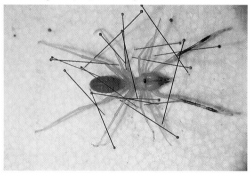

24-28°C (75.2-82.4°F) for half of the floor and allow the other side to cool to 15°C (59°F). Spray each evening to create night-time humidity of 70-90%.

Feeding
Feed all manner of arthropods and small rodents. Wind scorpions are quick, active hunters (and cannibals) with an enormous appetite.

Sex determination
Adult males are smaller, slimmer, and can be recognized by projections on the lower jaws, and by their larger 'teeth'.

Mating
Allow species from subtropical regions (e.g. *Galeodes*) six to eight weeks hibernation at 5-10°C (41-50°F). When male and female meet the male leaps on the female and bites her in the back. A female that is ready to mate will now become 'paralysed' and is laid on her back. The male kneads the genital area with his jaws and once this dilates he removes a drop of sperm from his own genital opening and deposits it in hers. He then holds her genitals shut before fleeing.

Egg laying
From several days to a few weeks after mating the female digs a 200mm (8in) deep chamber in which she deposits 20-200 eggs. Both the eggs and nymphs are guarded by the female until they transform into 'spiderlings'.

Rearing
Raise the extremely cannibalistic young separately in their own terrarium. These insects have a life span no longer than one year.

Defence
Wind scorpions are extremely quick movers and when cornered are extremely aggressive. The jaws are displayed during the threat display and the rear of the body is raised while the animal stridulates. These creatures do not possess any venom glands but their bite with large jaws are painful so never hold them.

The order Scorpiones, scorpions

Scorpions have a bad reputation, they have a gruesome appearance and people think that every species is deadly.

The 600-800 species of scorpion are divided into seven families: the Bothriuridae, Buthidae, Chactidae, Diplocentridae, Iuridae, Scorpionidae, and Vejovidae.

Appearance
A scorpion's body consists of a head section (prosoma) and rear body (opisthosoma). This rear section in turn consists of the mesosoma (the thick part containing most of the organs) and the metasoma (or tail). The venom barb on the end of the

Underside of a scorpion.

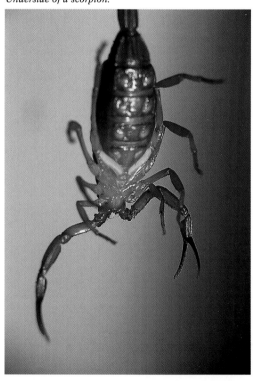

Scorpions grasp their prey with their claws. This is Buthus occithanus.

Pandinus imperator *eating a cricket.*

stinging apparatus (telson) is the fifth segment of the metasoma.

On the underside of the scorpion, from front to back, are found the belly plate (sternum), genital mound (genital operculum), the comb-like pectines, and five belly plates (sternites). The pectines are used to sense the soil and the scent of both prey and potential partners. On top behind the dorsal plate are seven tergite plates.

Scorpions too have four pairs of walking legs and a pair of pedipalps. The final segment of the pedipalps has developed into pincer like claws. Long bristles on these scissor-like claws and the body sense vibrations and warn of danger or an approaching prey.

Scorpions see with singular eyes (ommatidiae); there are two at the front of the dorsal plate (median eyes) and none to five pairs of lateral eyes on the dorsal plate. Scorpions do not see much.

The pincer claws are used to grasp prey, frequently an insect or spider, but can include mice. The venom barb is used by most species only for large and strong prey. It takes fourteen days for the venom supply to be replenished. The pincer like chelicerae eat the prey a bit at a time.

Some scorpions can stridulate with the coxae of the pedipalps and the front walking legs when they sense danger.

Scorpions have four pairs of book lungs with the spiracles (vents) of these being readily apparent on the underside of the last four segments.

Distribution
Scorpions inhabit all subtropical and tropical regions where these flat creatures live in fissures and holes. Some species dig underground chambers or burrows and a few others live in trees. Scorpions that live in desert regions are usually sand coloured while those from rain forests are generally darker in colour.

Because of their strong impenetrable skin and ability to live for a long time without food and to be able to store water, many scorpions can survive in the most arid regions on earth.

Accommodation
Provide a scorpion with a terrarium that is at least

three times wider than its overall length and twice as broad. Give it a shelter of stone, wood, or bark that is not too high, because scorpions like to feel protection against their back. Lay sand or sandy soil on the bottom for desert species and a mixture of peat, bark, and compost for forest dwellers. Provide burrowing kinds with at least 100mm (4in) of soil.

Always provide a shallow dish of water because scorpions drink a lot.

Scorpions are solitary creatures; house most species as individuals to prevent cannibalism.

The temperature and humidity requirements vary from species to species. For the tropical rain forest types ensure constant humidity of 70-80% and never allow it to fall below 50%. The desert dwelling species also need to have somewhere moist. If uncertain of the appropriate humidity spray just one side of the terrarium. The same applies to temperature: this generally needs to be 24-30°C (75.2-86°F). Those scorpions that originate from countries with hot dry summers and colder, wetter winters must have these circumstances recreated in their terrarium. For example with such types ensure 27°C (80.6°F) and 55% humidity in summer and 19°C (66.2°F) and 65% humidity in winter.

Feeding
Feed scorpions with insects sprinkled with a calcium preparation twice per week. Pregnant scorpions, those kept too cold, ones that are not hungry, and those about to moult eat less than usual.

Males are thinner (these are Euscorpius italicus).

Sex determination

Males can sometimes be recognized by their smaller and thinner bodies, longer tail segments, longer pectines or pectine 'teeth', a thicker sting, and longer and perhaps thinner pincer claws that may be hairier.

Mating

Once the male has cautiously approached the female he grasps her claws or chelicerae with his claws and 'dances' with her. When he finds a suitable place such as a flat stone, the male deposits spermatophore on the ground and then pulls the female over it. The spermatophore is only a few millimetres in size (with *Buthus* spp. 9mm/³/₈in) and with some species it resembles a dandelion seed without its plume. Usually the male deposits a pair of them linked together. When the male jerks her suddenly backwards the sperm flows into the female's genital opening. The male then releases her and makes good his escape. The male is only eaten exceptionally. The female can store the sperm and is able to produce several broods after mating. The empty spermatophore remain on the ground after mating.

Birth

Scorpions brood their eggs inside the female reproductive tract and give birth to live offspring. A female bears 8-35 eggs until they are born but does not feed the unborn offspring. The unborn young of species of the Scorpionidae family are able to absorb nourishment from the mother's body via their mouths.

Pregnancy can last up to 12 months. With highly pregnant females the segment plates of back and belly are separated as if they must explode. The embryos are carried in broodsacs. When the offspring are born the mother helps them out of the sac. The young then crawl onto their mother's back.

The female is extremely aggressive towards threats at this time and even her own young that fall from her back are likely to be chewed up. Try to allow mother's carrying young as much peace and quiet as possible.

Up to the first moult, the young scorpions live on the protein store of their egg. Then they leave their mother's back and start life on their own.

Rearing

There are often problems with the rearing of young scorpions. Try to avoid disturbing the mother or she may eat her young and never remove them from their mother's back.

Keep each new scorpion moist in its own container (65-85%) for if too dry there are problems with moulting. Spray the soil to keep it moist each evening and make sure the young can drink (but not drown). Ensure a temperature of 26-32°C (78.8-89.6°F). Give a varied diet and sprinkle the food with vitamin and mineral supplements. Calcium is required for the exoskeleton.

Moulting

During moulting, the prosoma splits open and the scorpion slides from its old skin. This is rarely seen because this happens at night in a hidden place. The old skin is then eaten.

During their first year the young scorpions moult four to six times, the following year two to three times, and in the third year just once. Adults moult once or twice each year. Some of the smaller species mature to adulthood after four to five moults but larger species need at least seven moults and three to seven years.

Very pregnant Buthus occithanus.

Pandinus imperator *carrying 16 offspring.*

Newly moulted Tytius species.

Toxicity

The venom of most species is not deadly, although its effects can vary from person to person. The sting is often extremely painful. Consult a doctor after a sting. Certain species cause inflammation and fever in addition to the sting.

The possible deadly species almost all are to be found in the Buthidae family. With the very dangerous types about 1% of all adults, 5% of school-age children, and 20% of infants stung die.

The various types all look so similar that it is essential to be cautious with all scorpions.

The most dangerous scorpions have long and slender pincer claws. The species known not to be dangerous have thick short claws but do not ever rely upon this.

Scorpions first try to hide from danger and only become aggressive when there is no escape. Pregnant females and those carrying their young on their back are more aggressive.

Hadruroides charcasus *from Peru.*

Handling

All species can be picked up by the tail with forceps with a little draught strip padding on their tips. Harmless large scorpions can sometimes be approached carefully from the rear with the sting or previous tail segment being held between two fingers. Never try this with the dangerous species. Scorpions should always be lively when they have been touched. Never purchase a specimen that is listless.

The family Bothriuridae

Some 70-80 species of this family are found in tropical and subtropical parts of Australia and South America. The sternum is wider than it is long with this family. The best known genus of *Bothriurus* comes from South America.

The Buthidae

This is the largest family with about 600 species in 45 genera, including the most venomous. The Buthidae are found on all the continents except Antarctica in warmer regions.

The most dangerous species are found in the genera *Tityus* (from America), Buthus (North Africa and the Middle-East), *Centruroides* (from southern USA and Central America), *Leiurus* (Africa and the Middle-East), *Androctonus* (Africa and

The correct way to handle a scorpion.

Brachysternus *species.*

Australia), *Centrurus* (America), and *Mesobuthus* (India).

BUTHUS OCCITHANUS

Appearance
Females of this sand-coloured to brown species are about 70mm (2³/₄in) long but the males are about 20mm (³/₄in) smaller. In common with all Buthidae the claws are fairly long and thin.

Distribution
Dry areas in the South of France, Spain, Portugal, North Africa, and the Middle-East. The North African population is much more venomous than the European ones and possibly dangerous for children.

Accommodation
Keep the daytime temperature at 35°C (95°F) and 25°C (77°F) at night. Give them a winter rest by lowering the temperature to 15°C (59°F) for European specimens and 20°C (68°F) for North African ones. They can be kept in groups.

Reproduction
The female gives birth to 25-40 young after a 5 month pregnancy. These reach adulthood after four to seven moults.

ISOMETRUS MACULATUS

Appearance
Females reach an overall length of 80mm (3¹/₈in), while the male, with bigger claws and relatively longer tail, is no more than 50mm (2in). These animals are light brown with darker brown markings.

Distribution
This species inhabits the ground and trees in Spain, Portugal, Africa, America, and eastern Asia through to Australia.

Giftigheid
The sting from this species is probably not deadly but is certainly painful.

Accommodation
Isometrus maculatus is very tolerant towards its own kind and can be kept in groups. Keep them on peat mixed with a little sand and at a humidity of 80%.

Reproduction
The female gives birth to 15-20 young after a two-

Buthus occithanus *just before mating.*

Isometrus maculatus.

and-a-half to three months pregnancy. The young leave their mother's back after about two weeks.

The Chactidae family

The 70-80 species of the thirteen genera of this family are found in the tropics and subtropics. The family is considered by some to be a sub family of Vejovidae.

EUSCORPIUS SPECIES

Appearance
Euscorpius species are about 30mm (1³/₁₆in) long with dark brown bodies and lighter brown legs. All species are not aggressive and not dangerous.

Distribution
The four different species live in southern Europe through to the Caucasus, and North Africa. *Euscorpius flavicaudis* is found in France and the United Kingdom.

Reproduction
The female gives birth to 20-30 offspring between June and August which leave their mother's back after about ten days.

The Diplocentridae family

The 30-50 species in this family are found in Africa, the Middle-East, and America (Mexico and the Antilles). These scorpions resemble Buthidae

Euscorpius italicus.

but they have shorter and thicker claws. All of them are harmless for humans and have a spike under the sting.

The Iuridae family

The five genera that form the Iuridae family were previously part of the Vejovidae family. Iuridae do not have a spike under the sting.

HADRURUS ARIZONENSIS

Appearance
These sandy- to light-brown coloured scorpions have brown-black bodies. They grow to 140mm (5¹/₂in) long and there are long bristles on the walking legs, claws, and tail.

Distribution
Desert-dweller from south-western USA and Mexico.

Accommodation
Keep each specimen of this species segregated for they are extremely cannibalistic.

Reproduction
Males have 34-39 'teeth' in the pectine but females only 28-30. Pregnancy last from six to eight months.

The Scorpionidae family

This family is found in the tropics and subtropics, principally in Asia and Africa but can also be found in Australia and Central America. The largest scorpions are found in the 150-175 species in 20 genera. These all have no spike under the sting.

PANDINUS IMPERATOR

Legal status: *P. imperator*, *P. dictator*, and *P. gambiensis* are CITES B.

Appearance
Females grow to about 150mm (6in) overall, excluding the pedipalps while males are somewhat smaller. The claws are 35 x 25mm (1³/₈-1in) and the sting is 20mm (³/₄in) long.
This species is not quick to sting unless it is a preg-nant female. Reactions to the venom vary from nothing through slight inflammation, to a severe bee sting.
The subspecies *P. imperator gigas* grows to 270mm (6³/₄in) and its sting is more painful due to a longer barb and greater amount of venom, resulting in localised pain for several days.

Distribution
Pandinus imperator comes from rain forest or wet savannah in West Africa (from Mauritania to Zaire).

Accommodation
Pandinus imperator can be kept in groups although this can lead to fighting in small terrariums. Keep the day temperature at 25-30°C (77-86°F) with high humidity of 70-85%.

Reproduction
The female gives birth to 10-25 pure white 15mm (⁵/₈in) long offspring after a pregnancy lasting one year. At first the female also provides a meal of finely shredded insects for her young. The offspring moult about seven times and are sexually mature after three to seven years.

HETEROMETRUS SPECIES

Appearance
Heterometrus species resemble *Pandinus imperator* but the claws are much smoother with fewer bristles. Most species are about 150mm (6in) long but *Heterometrus swannerdami* of India grows to almost 300mm (12in).
The sting is extremely dangerous, very painful, and causes headache, vomiting, balance problems, and heart difficulties. People have died from the sting of this species.

Distribution
Rain forest of South-East Asia.

Accommodation
Ensure a temperature of 24-27°C (75.2-80.6°F) with humidity of 75%. These species are sensitive to cold and they can be kept in groups.

Reproduction
Pregnancy last five to six months. The offspring moult about seven times and are sexually mature after one to two years.

Hadrurus arizonensis.

Heterometrus spinifer.

Scorpio maurus palmatus *with offspring.*

Pandinus imperator, *Emperor scorpion.*

Appearance
This species is 75-100mm (2³/₄-4in) long. The sub-species *Scorpio maurus palmatus* is light brown to yellow but the pincer claws are darker. *Scorpio maurus fuscus* is black.
Distribution
Scorpio m. palmatus lives in Egypt, *Scorpio m. fuscus* comes from Israel but both species live in arid areas.
Accommodation
This burrowing species can be kept in groups in fairly large terrariums with 100mm (4in) of sandy soil. They give birth to eight to thirteen offspring.

The Vejovidae family

The about 125 species in ten genera of this family are found in America and the Middle-East through to eastern Asia. Vejovidae species do not have a spike under the barb.

The order Uropygi, whipscorpions, vinegaroons

Mastigoproctus giganteus

The 130 or so species of whipscorpions previously

Mastigoproctus giganteus, *just before mating.*

belonged to the sub order Uropygi of the order Pedipalpi, scorpions, to which whipscorpions were formerly also part.

Appearance

Whipscorpions are 50-130mm (2-5^1/$_8$in) long. There is a definite boundary between the angular head/thorax segment (prosoma) and elongated segmented rear part of the body (opisthosoma).

The opisthosoma consists of the mesosoma with nine segments and the metasoma (tail) with three segments. To this is attached a long, thin, and segmented whip, where the venom barb or sting is found on a scorpion. The pedipalps have large cutting and grinding tools with which they can pinch severely.

Whipscorpions walk with the back three pairs of legs. The front pair of legs have developed into feelers with a number of sensory capabilities. Whipscorpions breath through two pairs of book lungs and they have two median eyes plus three to five pairs of lateral eyes (see Scorpions).

[Mastigoproctus giganteus] is black with brown-black pedipalps and they grow to 80mm (3^1/$_8$in).

Distribution

These animals are found in moist micro-climates in subtropical and tropical America and South-East Asia. By day they usually remain hidden beneath stones, wood etc. *M. giganteus* is principally captured in Arizona, Texas, and New Mexico but is also found in Central and South America.

Accommodation

Use a small terrarium of 30 x 20 x 20cm (12 x 8 x 8in) for a single specimen with a fairly dry mixture of sand and peat on the bottom. Make shelters with cork or stones and moisten these places three times each week. Provide a shallow dish of water. Do not expose to too much light and ensure a daytime temperature of 23-28°C (73.4-82.4°F) in summer with a slightly cooler night-time temperature.

Feeding

Insects and newly-born mice.

Sex determination

The male is smaller and sometimes has longer pedipalps.

Mating

In the wild, *M. giganteus* over-winters in cool and dry conditions under stones. When it begins to rain in May and June, they become active.

During mating, they grab hold of each other at the front and the male whips his tail vigorously. The male grasps the female's whip, steps over it, and pulls her behind him. The female grabs hold of the male's opisthosoma. Meanwhile two spermatophores are transferred, which resemble two white stems with a sperm sac at the top of each.

Egg laying

Several weeks after mating, the female lays 20-30 eggs which she retains within a membrane beneath her opisthosoma. Several weeks later during a period when it rains a lot (which should be imitated) the nymphs emerge. These initially white offspring remain on their mother's back until the first moult.

Rearing

The offspring seek a hollow of their own and then moult once per year until sexually mature after the fourth moult.

Defence

Large whipscorpions can bite hard with their pedipalp claws. They can also spurt a mixture of 85% acetic acid and 25% caprylic acid up to 50cm (20in) from the base of their tail, directed at

Mastigoproctus giganteus *mating.*

The twin stems of the spermatophores are left on the ground after mating.

A small whipscorpion with eggs.

their attacker. This is strong smelling, causes irritation, and can result in inflammation and watering eyes.

Handle them with jars, with forceps with draught strip attached, or with gloves.

The order Amblypygi, tailless whipscorpions

Tailless whipscorpions are rarely imported, although there are countless of them in tropical countries. One genus of this family is *Tarantula* and just as all Theraphosidae are wrongly known as tarantulas, so some give the name too to all Amblypygi. The true tarantulas are wolf spiders such as *Lycosa tarentula* from Italy.

Appearance

The more than 60 species have bodies of 10-70mm ($^3/_8$-$2^3/_4$in). All tailless whipscorpions have a flattened form with a broad dorsal plate and rounded opisthosoma. The legs are extremely long with the front pair developed into elongated feelers or whips. These are four times the body length because the tibiae are divided up into 25-35 segments and the tarsi even more. A whipscorpion that is 40mm ($1^9/_{16}$in) long has a span of its extended whips of about 250mm ($9^3/_4$in). The tarsi are subdivided into one to five tarsal segments and a pretarsus or foot. This usually has two claws and a tiny lobe. The pedipalps are large and heavy gripping legs that are held closed in front of the chelicerae. These can be either long and thin or shorter and broader. These end in some species with scissor-like pincers. The whipscorpion catches its prey with the pedipalps, holds its firmly with them, and uses them to clean itself.

The prosoma is clearly separated from the opisthosoma by a narrow pedicel.

Whipscorpions are unable to spin like spiders because they have no spinneret.

Whipscorpions are very fast and can run easily sideways up a wall. They breathe through two but sometimes one pair of book lungs. The Amblypygi are subdivided into two families. Whipscorpions with bristles on the tarsi of the second pair of legs fall within the Charontidae family. Those without

Whipscorpion from Guyana.

Damon species of tailless whipscorpion.

Newly moulted whipscorpion.

these bristles are part of the Tarantulidae, which in turn consists of three sub families. With the sub family Phrynicinae the tibiae of the fourth pair of legs are one entity whereas with Damoninae there are two parts and with Tarantulinae, three parts.

Some of the better known genera are *Damon* (from tropical West Africa), *Phrynus*, *Admetus*, and *Tarantula* (from North America).

Distribution
Amblypygi are found throughout the world in tropical and sub-tropical areas, especially in Africa through to Israel and Crete. They are not found in either Australia or on Madagascar.

They are often found in profusion on rocks, in caves, and houses, under fallen bark and leaves, and hollows. These nocturnal creatures never burrow a hole for themselves.

Accommodation
Provide a moderately humid terrarium fitted out as described for the tailed-form of whipscorpion. This needs to be four times as long as the diameter of the whipscorpion, twice as wide, and five times as high. Cover the back wall with cork bark and spray each day.

Voeding
Feed any type of insect.

Sex determination
The femurs and tibiae of the pedipalps of the male are longer than with females.

Mating
The male lays a spermatophore on the ground (like scorpions) and guides the female over it by touching her 'whip' lightly. She then takes the spermatophore into her.

Egg laying
The female lays 20-40 eggs in a sturdy, flattened recess in her opisthosoma.

The young emerge after three to four months and remain on their mother's back for four to fourteen days until they moult.

Rearing
Care for the offspring as the parents. Feed them fruit flies, tiny crickets, and aphids. A whipscorpion crawls from the burst prosoma when it moults, leaving the old skin of the opisthosoma intact.

Amblypygi are adult after 8 moults in about 1-2 years.

Defence
Tailless whipscorpions are not aggressive and they have no venom. Their principal defence is rapid escape but they can nip severely yet generally never do. Whipscorpions sometimes pretend to be dead.

Pill millipede: probably Globotherium *sp. from Madagascar.*

Subphylum Myriapoda (Uniramia), myriapods

Of the four classes that comprise the subphylum (or group) of myriapods known as Myriapoda (but now considered part of the subphylum Uniramia) the most interesting for terrariums are the Diplopoda millipedes and Chilopoda or centipedes. The other two are Symphyla and Pauropoda that have no common names, which are virtually never kept in terrariums.

Appearance

The body of a myriapod (many legs) consists of a head and a trunk. There are two antennae on the head, a pair of upper jaws and one or two pairs of lower jaws. The trunk consists of 8-240 segments, each with one (Chilopoda) or two (Diplopoda) pairs of legs.

The class Chilopoda, centipedes

The 3,000 species within this class are divided into five orders. The most frequently encountered genus of *Scolopendra,* of which there are 30 species, falls within the order Scolopendromorpha.

Millipede from Peru.

Appearance

Scolopendra species are quick and agile creatures. The legs of the first body segment have developed into strikingly large maxillipeds or poison claws. The body consists of 22-25 pairs of segments and is laterally equipped with one pair of legs per segment. There are usually four singular eyes on either side of the head. Centipedes breathe via tracheae. The colour varies considerably but is often golden brown, yellow, orange, green, and purple. The colour usually has a metallic sheen.

Males of *Scolopendra cingulata* grow to 110mm ($4^5/_{16}$in) long, the females 170mm ($6^{11}/_{16}$in). Females are olive green to brown with the males being lighter. They can live for about seven years.

Tropical species of *Scolopendra* are often larger, up to 300mm (12in) long. Classifying the species is extremely difficult.

Distribution

Centipedes inhabit almost every type of biotope, from relatively dry to fairly moist. These biotopes are however never either extremely wet or bone dry. During the day these creatures hide away beneath stones and in fissures in the ground.

Scolopendra cingulata originates from southern parts of Europe and Asia. *S. gigantea* (260mm/$6^1/_4$in long 25mm/1in thick) originates from tropical Central and South America, *S. heros* lives in southern parts of the USA.

Accommodation

Keep these cannibalistic animals apart in their own terrarium that needs to be at least twice as long as their body length and as least as wide as they are long. Place at least 70mm ($2^3/_4$in) of (sandy) soil, always mixed with peat, leaf mould, or good garden loam. Never allow the soil to dry out completely. Provide shelter and prevent bright lights. Ensure a daytime temperature of 23-30°C

Scolopendra gigantea.

Scolopendra cingulata *female.*

The male (with red head) of these Argentine species has a larger pair of back legs.

Centipede from Thailand.

Centipedes have large venom fangs and are aggressive and quick-moving.

(73.4-86°F) and about 17°C (62.6°F) at night.
Keep the humidity around 50-70% and spray half the terrarium each week with plenty of water. The fairly soft chitin skin of centipedes cannot withstand drought (i.e. humidity below 40%). A constant high humidity though causes mould infections and facilitates invasions of mites.
Seal the terrarium well of these aggressive, fast, and venomous creatures.

Feeding
Feed all manner of arthropods, snails and slugs, worms, and newly-born mice. The prey is first held by the front legs and then bitten. A hungry centipede can also hold more prey with its other legs.

Sex determination
The adult male is smaller than the female and he has a larger final pair of legs. A single segment between the rear legs is enlarged and serves for making the web on which the spermatophore is deposited (but this is difficult to see).

Mating
For species from moderate climates let them have eight weeks hibernation at 10°C (50°F).
Place a well fed pair together in a terrarium that is at least four times longer than the centipedes. They mainly mate at night and below ground. The male approaches the female, spins a web on the ground and deposits his bean-shaped spermatophore on it. The female then takes the spermatophore with her legs and works it back to her genital opening. Mating can last several hours.
In addition to sexual reproduction, parthenogenic reproduction also occurs.

Egg laying and rearing
Several weeks after mating the female lays about 20 eggs in a circle that she forms with her body, in a hollow or hole. In this way she protects the eggs from predators, mould, and infection, by among other things, licking them. Removal of the female results in mould forming on the eggs because the female's body also exudes a disinfecting substance. When the young emerge after one to two months, they remain in the hollow for a few days, protected by their mother. If a female is disturbed she may eat her eggs or nymphs.
At birth the nymphs are white but they have all their legs. Once they start to move around rear them separately from each other. They become sexually-mature after six to twelve months.
Moulting takes place in a hiding place, usually at night. Afterwards centipedes eat their old skin.

Defence
Treat these aggressive and extremely venomous creatures with respect for they are dangerous. The venom of *S. cingulata* can cause fever to 39°C (102.2°F) in humans together with swelling, inflammation, general debility, dizziness, and breathing and heart difficulties. The symptoms usually disappear after two days. Cleaning the wound with medical alcohol and iodine can help.
If the skin comes into contact with a centipede all manner of allergic reactions can occur and they can also nip severely with their final pair of legs.
When disturbed, centipedes are frenzied with the front half of the body swishing from side to side.

Bear in mind that a centipede can stand erect and is able to climb out of tall terrariums, many even being able to walk up glass.

Handling

Place a jar or container over the centipede and slide the lid underneath. If necessary pick them up with forceps softened with some draught strip but do not touch them with your hands. The draught strip makes it possible to hold the centipede without harming it.

The class Diplopoda

There are 10,000 species in the class Diplopoda of which only the subclass Chilognatha interests keepers of terrariums. The small subclass Penicillata comprises small bristly millipedes.

Chilognatha have a calcium reinforced exoskeleton. These are mainly long but thin ground dwellers. The thrust of two pairs of legs per segment, hardened skeletal plates, and powerful mouth parts enable these animals to survive amid rotting wood and in hard soil.

The class includes the infraclass Pentazonia (Opisthandria or pill millipedes) and the infraclass Helminthomorpha (Proterandia). There are eleven orders that form the infraclass Helminthomorpha but the rest of this section deals with the superorder Juliformia of 'true' millipedes.

This superorder contains three of the eleven orders. With all three of them both pairs of legs on the seventh segment have developed into reproductive organs. With the order Spirobolida there is a vertical seam across the forehead and these tropical species are often beautifully coloured. The largest millipedes are found in the equally tropical order Spirostreptida, being up to 300mm (12in) long. The front pair of male legs have also developed into a sexual organ. The order Julida contains smaller species from moderate climates but these are less frequently seen in terrariums.

Appearance

A millipede consists of a head, a trunk, and a tail (telson). If there are eyes these are found on the side of the calcium-hardened head with the antennae, and mouth parts of mandibles. Millipedes are active at twilight and during the night and mainly rely on their short and thick antennae for orientation. These antennae are six to eight segments in length and serve as sensors for touch and smell. The 1-90 lateral ocelli that form the eyes are sited close by the antennae.

The generally elongated and cylindrical trunk is smooth, hairy, prickly, or knobbly. The trunk consists of a thorax, then an abdomen, and a growth zone. The thorax comprises a single neck segment or collum without legs and three double segments which each bear three pairs of legs. From the abdomen each segment has two pairs of legs which results in more than 200 legs in certain species with the record of 375 pairs of legs being held by *Illacme plenipes* (of the order Siphonophorida). The minimum number of pairs of legs is thirteen.

Behind the abdomen there is a growth zone with specimens that have not fully matured. This is a short region of about three segments without legs which are gained after a moult. After moulting new legless segments appear. Some species continue to grow even when they reach sexual maturity.

The telson is the two final segments of which the last incorporates the anus for excreting waste matter.

The belly and dorsal segments of most millipedes are fused into a ring. Each ring or somite consists of two segments fused together. The front one of these or prosomite is supple and is largely hidden beneath the previous segment. The rear segment or metasomite is entirely hardened with calcium salts etc. The segments can close on each other perfectly.

The legs consist of eight segments: the coxae, trochanters, femurs, postfemurs, tibae, tarsi, and claw. Each leg makes its own shuffling movement but does so just before the one in front. This causes a ripple through the body from back to front.

Millipedes breathe through tracheae. The tubes are behind each leg joint with the body. Millipedes can live for ten to fifteen years. The known types of millipede bulldozer their way through the

Millipede from Nigeria.

earth. Other types open the soil by pushing their heads into a crevice and then open it up with their legs. Others 'bore' by pushing themselves into the soil and then contract their segments into one another.

The smallest millipedes are less then 3mm (²/₁₆in) long while the biggest are up to 280mm (11in) and 20mm (³/₄in) thick, such as *Archispirostreptus gigas* (formerly *Graphidostreptus)* from woodland in southern Africa and *Scaphistostreptus seychellarum* from The Seychelles.

The main species offered for terrarium are from the genera *Julius* and *Spirostreptus*. Because classification is extremely difficult they may often be wrongly named with nice sounding names such as *Spirobolus* sp.

Distribution

Almost all millipedes are ground dwellers. They mainly eat rotting vegetable matter (dead leaves) but also fresh vegetables and fruit. During the day they hide in the soil or beneath stones or fallen timber. Some species are good climbers. With their permeable skins most species inhabit moist biotopes (e.g. woodland) but certain species live in humid microclimates within dry biotopes such as deserts. These species have a waxy layer on their skin which reduces the evaporation of moisture.

These ecologically important animals, that often number in the tens per square metre, make large quantities of organic material suitable for further break down by bacteria and moulds.

Species from moderate and subtropical climates hibernate. The 140mm (5¹/₂in) long, dark-brown with yellow stripes *Orthoporus ornatus* from northern Mexico hibernates at temperatures below 20°C (68°F). They hide away in hollows, ants nests, beneath stones etc. They reappear in mid May. In the five months that follow they will be active early in the morning and late in the day if it rains from time to time. When the temperature is above 35°C (95°F) they take shelter.

Accommodation

Provide a terrarium of at least 60 x 40 x 40cm (24 x 16 x 16in) for a group of one species. Lay a minimum of 100mm (4in) of leaf mould/woodland soil on the bottom preferably with leaves from ash,

maple, birch, beech, and or oak. Mix calcium additive to some of the soil (e.g. bone meal). A layer of gravel under the soil aids drainage. Millipedes that have burrowed are either moulting or with their eggs and must on no account be disturbed. Provide hiding places of cork bark and if desired plant the terrarium.

Light the terrarium for 10-12 hours each day and keep the soil and air at 20-26°C (68-78.8°F) for rain forest species. Spray half of the terrarium twice per week (humidity at least 75%). If the humidity is high enough the millipedes will also be seen in the daytime. Make sure the ventilation is sufficient. Provide water with a shallow drinking tray.

Millipedes can be readily combined with stick insects, various types of beetle, and the smaller praying mantises.

Feeding

Feed dead and rotting leaves from beech, birch, ash, maple, hazel, and oak. In addition provide variety with fibre-rich manure, vegetables, and overripe fruit, some raw potato, pasta, all manner of pet food, some occasional meat, and decaying wood. Enrich the feed with a calcium supplement. Remove uneaten remains of food, preferably each day.

Sex determination

After the moult into adulthood, the male's first (and sometime also second) pair of legs on the seventh segment have developed into a pair of hooks or gripping implements (gonopods). These vary between the species and fit rather like a key in a lock in the female genital opening. After the fifth moult the gonopods are visible as nodules against the belly. Viewed from the side it looks as if the seventh segment has no legs.

The legs and antennae are both longer with males. The internal sexual organs of both sexes open out by the second pair of legs.

Millipede from the forest floor of Cameroon.

Julidae species from Argentina (Chaco).

With the male the legs of the seventh segment develop into little hooks: the gonopods.

Graphidostreptus sp. from Kenya, mating.

Mating

The male approaches the female, curls himself around the front of her body, and uses the gonopods to place a spermatophore in her genital opening. With the 150mm (6in) long Kenyan millipede pictured during mating on this page, the spermatophore was a milk white packet about 3mm ($^{3}/_{16}$in) in size. With some species, the male places the spermatophore on the ground and the female picks it up.

With some species the male moults after mating with the gonopods appearing as nodules. These are usually restored after a second moult. Such a period of sexual inactivity increases life expectancy, especially in adverse weather conditions. Certain species also reproduce by parthenogenisis.

Egg laying

The females of most species dig themselves into the ground before laying their eggs and hide themselves in a dome they create. Other females lay their eggs one at a time in a chamber of its own. The chamber of the larger species are about 5mm ($^{3}/_{16}$in) across with walls about 1mm ($^{1}/_{64}$in) thick. Either dome or chamber are often strengthened with excreta. The eggs of 2-5mm ($^{1}/_{32}$-$^{3}/_{16}$in) are white/yellow in colour. Some species lay up to 700 eggs over 12-30 days. The eggs hatch after about six weeks.

Rearing

The egg laying and first development stage are usually not seen so that suddenly young millipedes are seen. The newly emerged offspring only have three legs and only a few segments more. These increase with each moult. Once they can walk they leave the nest. At first the young millipedes moult about every couple of days. The offspring can remain with their parents and they become adult after two to three years. Desert dwelling species that are only active for a short time each year can take nine years to become sexually mature.

Millipedes rest for several weeks before and after a moult. Many species seek out a hiding place for this period, others burrow a chamber underground which is sometimes reinforced with excreta.

During the moult the old skin splits along the side of the belly and the millipede then wriggles out of it. The old skin is usually eaten. The new skin takes several days to harden before the millipede leaves its hiding place.

Defence

The first line of defence is to curl up. Laying in a spiral, the millipede protects its vulnerable belly segments and legs with an armour of hard dorsal plates that are strengthened by calcium salts.

If this is not sufficient, noxious chemicals can be released from lateral glands. The mixture varies with the species but aldehydes, quinones, phenols, and hydrogen cyanide are produced when a precursor and an enzyme are mixed together. The substances kill bacteria, and also irritates skin, mucous membranes, and eyes. The skin first turns yellow, then red or black, can blister, and in the most serious case comes away, leaving scarring. Rinse an area that has been sprayed with running water. The longer the millipedes are held in captivity the less toxic they become and less readily they release this defence. If in any doubt, handle all millipedes with gloves on.

Never put a number of millipedes together in a small container with little ventilation. The defensive substance quickly turn gaseous and can prove deadly for the animals themselves.

183

Sickness

Millipedes can be infected by moulds and fungi, viruses, and bacteria. There are also parasitic flies and worms which prey upon them.

Mites are fairly harmless, affecting mainly the head and where the legs join the body. This can be treated with a cotton bud, dipped in alcohol rather than water provided care is taken to avoid sensitive apertures in the body.

Never drop a millipede since the hardness provided by the calcium salts means they are brittle and easily injured. Such injuries do not readily heal and are prone to infection. A seriously injured animal is best placed for 24 hours in a deep-freeze or in chloroform or ether.

The superorder Pentazonia, pill millipedes

Pill millipedes are part of the class Diplopoda, having much in common with the more generally recognized millipedes.

With this superorder, consisting of three orders, the final pair of legs of the male have developed into clasping tools. The order Glomeridesmida comprises small, blind, primitive millipedes which cannot roll themselves up. The order Glomerida consists of pill millipedes from the northern hemisphere that can roll themselves into a ball. They have 17 pairs of legs and are at most 20mm (³/₄in) long. The best known is *Glomeris marginata* from European woods. The second and third dorsal plate of Glomerida species are fused into a single large plate.

The order Sphaerotheriidae is a source of interesting large pill millipedes for the terrarium. These originate from the southern hemisphere and have twenty-one pairs of legs. Glomerida and Sphaerotheriida are sometime collectively known as Oniscomorpha.

Appearance

Pill millipedes have sternite (belly) plates that are subdivided. Sphaerotheriida have thirteen segments and grow to 100mm (4in). There are two

Rolling up to protect themselves. Species from Peru.

Julidae species from Argentina (Sierra de la Ventana).

pairs of legs to each segment. The first segment has no legs though and the second to fourth segments only have one pair of legs. Just as other millipedes, pill millipedes have singular ocelli eyes, orientating themselves mainly by using their short, thick antennae. They also have a telson consisting of three plates that act like valves that open when the anus excretes waste matter.

There are five genera: *Sphaerotherium* and *Globotherium* from Africa, *Sphaeropoeus* and *Arthrospaera* from Malaysia and the East Indies, and *Cyliosoma* from Australia. Of the approx. 50 species of the genus *Sphaerotherium*, the smaller ones (from 10mm/³/₈in) live in mountain areas and the larger ones (up to 60mm/2³/₈in) live closer to the coat in wooded sand dunes. None of the species is found in arid areas.

Among the species found on Madagascar is *Globotherium* (formerly *Zoosphaerium*). The specimens illustrated may belong to this genus. The largest example was 80mm (2³/₈in) long and 45mm (1³/₄in) wide.

Distribution

See above. These animals are mainly nocturnal.

Accommodation

Pill millipedes are rarely kept longer than a half year in captivity. The following suggested housing and feeding provides potential for greater success.

Provide a group of large pill millipedes with a terrarium of at least 60 x 40 x 40cm (24 x 16 x 16in). Cover the bottom with a minimum of 100mm (4in) of moist leaf mould/woodland soil, with a preference for dead and rotting leaves of ash, maple, birch, beech, and or oak. Mix some calcium additive into part of the soil and lay a layer of gravel at the bottom for drainage. Provide hiding places of cork bark and if wished, plant the terrarium. Light the terrarium for ten to twelve hours each day and keep the soil and air during the day at 20-26°C (68-78.8°F), reducing to 17-20°C (62.6-68°F) at night. Spray the terrarium every day (humidity of 60-90%). Make sure there is adequate ventilation. Provide water with a shallow drinking tray with a sponge in it. Lay beside it a piece of rotten timber and a clump of fibre-rich (horse) manure. Also provide a bowl of sand with sea water added and sure there is a small patch of clean sand because some species ingest sand to aid digestion.

Feeding
The most important source of food is provided if the accommodation is correctly established. Supplement this with dishes of ripe fruit, green leaves, moss, lichen, mushrooms, and pieces of meat.

Sex determination
Determining the sex of healthy pill millipedes by sight is difficult because they curl themselves up when disturbed.

With the males, the last three pairs of legs develop gonopods with the final pair incorporating clasping tools which are not present on females.

The genital opening of the male is by the second pair of legs but this is difficult to find. Males are virtually always smaller than females and the final large segment (pygidium) looks like a saddle with males. The female has an oval or pear-shaped organ of tiny platelets on the back of both hips (coxae) of the second pair of legs which is missing with in males.

Mating
The male holds the female with his claspers during mating. He is able to stridulate by using a comb on the claspers.

Mating takes place at night and is easily disturbed by light etc. The male approaches the female, walking backwards, and turns her over as he stridulates with the comb on his claspers.

The female who has rolled herself up unrolls in recognition of the sound. The male now manoeuvres himself over the female so that he can grasp her by the front using his claspers. Once they are belly to belly, a spermatophore appears in the male's genital opening. This is about 1mm ($^1/_{64}$in) in size and in a matter of seconds it is passed to the female's genital opening a little further along. They both lay still for a time afterwards. The mating lasts for 4-7 minutes. The female takes the spermatophore in her mouth after the event, perhaps to eat the empty case after the sperm has done its job.

Egg laying
The eggs are laid in chambers beneath the surface of the soil. The larvae of the European species of *Glomeris* emerge from the eggs in 30 days. They have three pairs of fully developed legs and several legs that are not fully developed. Once the larvae have seven body segments and eight pairs of legs they leave the birth chamber. Pill millipedes moult below ground in a chamber.

Defence
When disturbed, pill millipedes roll themselves up into a perfect ball. The dorsal plates are slightly smaller at their fronts and can slot into the broad opening at the rear of the previous segment. The legs are flattened so that they can lay against each other without taking up much space when the millipede rolls itself up. The calcium reinforced plates protect the rest of the body. Neither ants or water can penetrate. Once danger has gone away the millipede will unfurl itself.

Glomeris species also possess a deterrent alkaloid which tastes even more bitter than quinine. The large tropical species do not appear to have any chemical deterrents.

Give pill millipedes a varied diet.

A banded pill millipede from Madagascar.

Keep pill millipedes moist. They drink a lot.

Pair of Calumma parsonii.

The class Reptilia, reptiles

The around 7,000 species of reptiles are divided into four groups:
1. Snakes and lizards (approx. 6,700 species)
2. Tortoises, turtles, and terrapins (approx. 250 species)
3. Crocodiles (23 species)
4. Tuataras (2 species), which are primitive lizard like reptiles.

Crocodiles are not really suitable for keeping in terrariums and Tuataras are extremely rare and protected (CITES A) which prevents them from being kept in captivity by hobbyists.

SKIN

Reptiles have thin plates of horn-like substance in the form of scales on their thick skin. This horny scale is virtually impenetrable which enables reptiles to withstand drought well but reduces the ability of the skin to breathe. With crocodiles and tortoises, the under layer of scales forms as bone and with tortoises the bone forms the shell.

Young reptiles shed their skins every two to four weeks, while the intervals are longer with adults. Most reptiles will shed their skin after coming out of hibernation and before laying their eggs or giving birth. Healthy snakes slither out of their old skin, leaving it whole, rather like an old pair of tights but with lizards and tortoises the skin is shed in sections. Several days before it is shed, the old skin becomes slightly loose resulting in the animal acquiring a duller colouring.

SENSES

With the exception of snakes, most reptiles have good eye sight. With snakes and some geckos the eye lids have grown to form a transparent but unmovable film.

Most reptiles do not have good hearing. The ear openings or ear drum are visible and both sides of the head. Snakes have no ears and are more or less deaf.

Many animals have an additional olfactory or smelling organ in their palate known as the Jacobson organ. This is so highly developed with all snakes and some lizards (e.g. monitors) that they make active use of it in their sense of smell. Their tongue collects scent molecules and presses them against the Jacobson organ in process of tonguing. Because both the forked tongue and the organ have left and right parts, the animals can smell 'in stereo' to help them locate their prey.

ORGANS

A reptile's heart consists of one chamber and two atria. A crocodile heart comprises two chambers and two atria. Most reptiles solely breathe by means of lungs. The lung is a bag with honeycomb like walls. Except for a few, snakes have two lungs. Reptiles have a terminal part of the gut known as a cloaca into which the alimentary, urinary, and reproductive systems open. Cloaca is the term generally used for the opening from the body.

REPRODUCTION

Fertilization of the female takes place internally with all reptiles. Snakes and reptiles have a two part reproductive organ known as the hemipenises. Tortoises, turtles, terrapins, and crocodiles have a single penis and monitor lizards have no such sexual organ.

The eggs are usually fertilized immediately after copulation but they can be stored in a sperm receptacle (sometimes for years) for later fertilization.

Most reptiles lay eggs with a leathery shell containing chalk which in the case of tortoises and

A tuatara at a Berlin zoo.

Reptiles, like this Burmese python, have scales on their skin.

The hemipenis of a yellow ratsnake (Elaphe obsoleta quadrivittata).

The shell of most gecko eggs are hard. Two gecko eggs with a newly emerged hatchling.

their ilk and many geckos harden off. The leathery shell eggs continue to grow up to 25 % during the development of the embryo by absorbing water. The eggs are laid in dry conditions in a hole or burrow, a natural hollow, or hidden behind bark or attached to a leaf. Incubation is either by the warmth of the sun or natural warmth created by rotting organic matter. Crocodiles and pythons are virtually the only egg-laying reptiles that care for their offspring. A number of lizards and snakes give birth to live young rather than eggs. All young reptiles are independent from the moment of their birth.

BREEDING IN CAPTIVITY

Determination of the sexes of reptiles is dealt with in each animal group. The following matters are also of importance for breeding:
– choice of partner
– hibernation
– mating
– egg laying
– incubation of the eggs
– rearing the young.

CHOICE OF PARTNER

With certain species not every male will mate with any female and vice versa. Exchanging specimens with someone can sometimes work but try to avoid inbreeding and maintain the breed pedigree.

HIBERNATION

Many animals require certain stimuli to make them ready to mate and to produce eggs. These processes are controlled by hormones. Reptiles from areas that have a winter often mate in spring. Many species from these parts of the world are prompted to mate by a cool winter period and hibernation although other species from moderate climate zones reproduce for a number of years without hibernating (e.g. tortoises, *Elaphe guttata*, and *Thamnophis* species). Animals manage to survive the cold winter months when food is scarce by hibernation. During this period the animals eat little or nothing and are wholly or virtually inactive. The temperature at which animals hide themselves away to hibernate differs from species to species. If the temperature is slightly higher many of these animals slow down to very little activity and eat nothing. If temperatures rise above a certain maximum a number of species become inert to conserve themselves through a drought.

Only animals that are healthy can be allowed to hibernate. Weak animals die or wake up. Try to ensure the animals are in good condition and well fed or otherwise miss a year. It is normal with very young reptiles to avoid hibernation or limit its duration.

Hibernation demands a certain amount of preparation and care.
– With the lamps still on, reduce the amount of food and reduce the length of day over a period of one month. Many reptiles notice that the days are getting shorter and naturally eat less.
– Stop feeding at least two weeks before the temperature is reduced. Everything remaining in the gut during hibernation will not be digest-

The intestines must be empty during hibernation. The remaining matter will be excreted after a bath in lukewarm water. These are Moroccan spiny-tailed lizards (Uromastyx acanthinura).

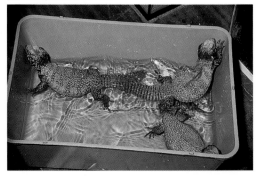

ed because of the lower temperature and can rot.

- To be certain bath the animals in luke-warm (hand hot) water. This will usually result in any remaining matter being excreted.
- After this the temperature is then usually gradually reduced by using a dimmer switch or replacing the bulbs each week with ones of lower wattage. The reptiles will become increasingly sluggish and will eventually crawl away to a hiding place. Do not feed them! Restless animals are probably not in good condition, so check this. If in doubt they should not hibernate.
- Also gradually reduce the period of time the lights are on each day. Climate information for the region of origin of the species is valuable in determining the right duration.
- Put the animals in a darkened place at the reduced temperature for eight to twelve weeks so that they can hibernate or rest. Places such as a cellar or even a refrigerator are suitable. The reptiles must be able to hide themselves in loose leaf mould or shredded peat and have access to fresh water.
- Check once or twice each week. Some species will emerge in the terrarium from time to time but do not feed them.
- After this cold period the temperature is usually gradually raised. This can result in the animals not eating for some time. Absorption of body fat during this period of not eating until the ideal temperature is reached again cause toxins to be released that can give liver and bacterial problems as a result of no food intake. It was suggested by Denardo (1996) that the temperature should be abruptly raised to the optimum in a matter of days. No harm is done by this and in nature reptiles that have just emerged from hibernation in spring can become very warm through sunning themselves and become very active and search for food.

A hibernation box for a pearl lizard (Lacerta lepida). *An artificial burrow surrounded by clean sand has been created in this polystyrene box. There is also a water dish.*

Terrapins that one day are laying in cold mud might be sunning themselves on a river bank a day or so later. The same can be true in late autumn provided the gut is empty. Terrapins lay in cold mud one day but may sun themselves on the river bank the next. The same applies to the drop in temperature in autumn (after a period of fasting), provided the gut is empty.

Certain reptiles from tropical and sub tropical climates are stimulated to mate by gradually reducing night temperature for one-and-a-half months and increasing the daytime temperature. Change the day-night difference for example from 30-26°C (86-78.8°F) to 32-20°C (89.6-68°F), so that on average the animals are kept at a cooler temperature. This sequence can be reversed after mating has taken place (source: F. de Groot, *The Terrarium* 13-3). The rainy season in the rain forest can be imitated by gradually reducing both day and night temperatures a few degrees and increasing spraying a fine mist. This too can stimulate mating.

The same is true of a period of drought, changing day lengths, or several months reduced food or different food. During the rainy season some omnivorous lizards mainly eat green foliage, flowers, fruits, and insects while they consume dry vegetable matter during periods of drought. Some reptiles mate throughout the year.

MATING

Mating will usually take place either immediately or a few weeks after providing the stimulus. The differences that are characteristic of certain reptiles is dealt with in the sections on the different groups. The mating period can last from a few days to several months.

EGG LAYING

That egg-laying is about to happen can be observed through:
- swellings in the belly
- a rapid increase in weight
- tendency to dig and/or restless behaviour
- not eating
- skin shedding.

Boa constrictor.

Make sure that egg-laying females have somewhere suitable to lay their eggs e.g. somewhere with loose and moist soil. If there is nowhere suitable to lay the eggs the female can retain them, causing serious harm and even death. This can sometimes be aided with an injection by a vet of calcium in suspension and hormones (oxytocin), or even an operation.

IINCUBATION OF THE EGGS

Remove the eggs once they have been laid as quickly as possible. Never turn the eggs because the embryos are not attached by a membrane as in the case of birds, so that egg turning can harm or kill the embryos.

Artificial incubation enables better control of the circumstances and it is often both too dry and cold in a terrarium for the eggs. Older animals also tend to eat the hatchlings when they emerge. Allow the female to complete her nesting procedures (e.g. closing the burrow) before removing the eggs. The female can become distressed even two months later if she discovers changes to the place where she laid her eggs. Fertilized eggs are smooth, mainly white all over and have a small exit disc on their top, except in the case of tortoises and their ilk.

A bearded dragon digs a hole in moist sand in which to lay her eggs.

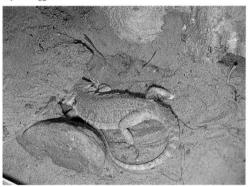

Eggs of a bearded dragon (Pogona vitticeps).

Keep good records for the incubator. One egg needs to be removed.

Important considerations for incubation are:
– the temperature of the substrate. For the majority of subtropical and tropical species this should be a minimum of 26°C (78.8°F), maximum 33°C (91.4°F). Try to maintain an even temperature with a variation not greater than 1°C. Eggs are usually incubated at 30°C (86°). The temperature influences a number of matters such as:
a. the proportion of males to females. Depending on the species a higher temperature will produce more offspring of a certain sex. Sometimes both high and low temperatures produce more females and temperatures in between more males. Generally with lizards, more females hatch at approx. 27°C (80.6°F) and more males at 32°C (89.6°F). Temperatures in between produce a more evenly match group of both sexes.
b. The incubation time: higher temperatures lead to quicker development. If the temperature is too high or too low for a length of time it will kill the embryos.
c. The size and growth: lower temperatures often produce larger and stronger offspring.

d. Deformed offspring often result from too high a temperature.

e. Pigmentation: the colouring can also be affected by the temperature.

– The humidity of the air: this should be 80-100%.

– The humidity of the substrate. It makes little difference if the eggs are in vermiculite, sphagnum moss, peat, or sand. Vermiculite, which is used by plant growers, has good moisture-retaining properties and is therefore widely used. For the right humidity for most species thoroughly mix 100 grams (3¹/₂oz) fine vermiculite with 80-100 grams (2³/₄-3¹/₂oz) of water, or use sphagnum moss wrung out as much as possible. If the eggs start to fail moisten the substrate around the eggs with the incubator already at its correct temperature. If the substrate becomes too moist the eggs will absorb too much, causing the pressure in the egg to increase and the embryo to die.

– Micro-organisms on the egg: healthy eggs are of a good clear colour and can withstand much. Soft-shelled eggs continue to grow in size. By shining a light through the egg (take care not to overheat it) the formation of blood vessels or darker colouring can be seen. Slight browning of the shell is not always harmful but try to ensure good hygiene, although only remove rotten eggs if they present a danger to the others. If in doubt

place the affected eggs in a separate tray. If an affected egg is stuck fast to other eggs it can be sucked dry with a syringe to limit the risk of mould growth and such problems.

– Remove maggots or worms from the eggs with a small brush without turning the eggs and place them on a new substrate. Always open failed eggs that have been removed to ascertain the cause of failure. Unfertilized eggs or ones that die quickly consist of a cheesy mass. If fully-developed offspring fail to emerge from the eggs the causes are: the substrate was too moist, the temperature was not correct, or the parents suffered from vitamin deficiency.

– Movement of the eggs: never turn the eggs. The embryo is not fixed within the egg and can be harmed by turning it. This is less of a problem in the first 24 hours. Mark the top of the egg with a pencil and if an egg is accidentally disturbed place it back in its original position.

– The amount of oxygen and carbon dioxide surrounding the egg: ventilate sufficiently, ensuring the required temperature can be maintained.

The appropriate requirements can be achieved with several types of incubator.

– A former hospital incubator, though these are rarely available and expensive.

A former medical incubator is ideal for reptile eggs.

Commercial 'bain marie' incubator.

Home-made 'bain marie' incubator.

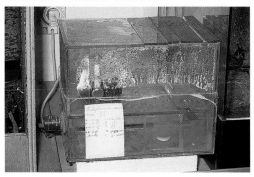

Home-made incubator.

– A 'bain marie': water is heated by e.g. an aquarium heater or heat pad so that the air above the water is 30°C (86°F). This also ensures high humidity. A tray is placed on the water with the reptile eggs. Sphagnum moss is better with such wet incubators because vermiculite can absorb too much water. Cover the egg tray to prevent hatchlings falling in the water and ensure ample ventilation.

– The air in an insulated box, cool box, or old refrigerator can be heated by means of heating elements, heat pad, or at least three lamps (e.g. 3 x 15 watt for a 40 x 30 x 30cm (16 x 12 x 12in) box. A dish of water, protected by nylon stocking to prevent drowning, ensures high humidity.

– A combination of the previous types of incubator.

– Professional incubators designed for reptile eggs. Experienced terrarium keepers can advise the best makes.

Do not scrimp on the acquisition of a hatchery for the money spent will be well rewarded. Homemade incubators can be ventilated with a computer fan. A thermostat is needed to control temperature and a hygrometer connected to a switch to a fan can control the humidity. Use digital display controllers with which it is possible to set both maximum and minimum values. Be vigilant to prevent condensation from dripping onto the eggs. Prevent this by fixing a sheet of glass at an angle above the glass, placing covers over the eggs, or fixing a cloth to catch the moisture. The eggs must never be directly sprayed with water.

With tall incubators, the temperature at the top is hotter than lower down. Take advantage of this is different eggs require varying temperatures.

Place half of each egg in the substrate. Do not separate eggs that are stuck together but incubate them in their original position.

The incubation time varies with the species (see by the species descriptions). Never help a hatchling from its egg. It is not uncommon for it to take between 24 hours and 2 weeks for an offspring to crawl from its egg after it has made the first hole

with its egg tooth. In the meantime the young animal is busy consuming the protein inside its shell.

Soft-shelled eggs cave in just before they hatch. Sometimes, as with spiky-tailed lizards, they sweat. If the young has not made an incision within 24 hours after this, hold the egg carefully by its middle or close to the middle with forceps. Make a small incision with a scalpel and then carefully enlarge the hole with nail scissors. Afterwards, leave the egg alone and never pull the young animal from the egg. Signs of breathing may not be apparent for several hours. If the occupant pulls back its head it is a sign that it is on its way.

It is questionable whether offspring that are not strong enough to break their way out of an egg should be kept alive. It is not abnormal for some of the eggs not to hatch, both in nature and among professional breeders. The first brood laid by a female often fails.

Some species of young lizard either only drink droplets of water or prefer to. Spray them regularly, like this lizard.

REARING YOUNG

The things to bear in mind in raising young reptiles are:
- Their terrarium should be a smaller version of that used for the older specimens of the species, with the same temperature, slightly more humid, and be easy to keep clean.
- Young reptiles are susceptible to drying out. Many desert-dwellers are born during the wet season, so spray young reptiles at least once each day provided there are no signs of stress (fleeing from the water). Supplement drinking water with vitamin D_3 and calcium. Make sure there is a moist area in the terrarium with e.g. sphagnum moss.
- It is often a few days before young reptiles start to eat. They mainly eat the same, finely sliced, food as their parents but usually need more protein. It is better to feed a little three times each day than too much in one go. Too many crickets drive the animals wild and can damage the youngsters.
- If animals see one of them eating, they follow suit. For this reason many reptiles are kept in a group until their territorial urges take over. With some lizards only a maximum of a pair can be kept together or stress results. Food intake in young snakes can be checked by keeping each snake separately, especially as young snakes are prone to cannibalism.
- Pay careful attention to providing vitamin and mineral supplements (especially vitamin D_3 and calcium).

Do not drag the young animals in containers to shows in order to sell them because this causes stress. Try instead to sell the animals from your home.

SICKNESS

Unfortunately it is still the case that a sick reptile is soon a dead reptile. There is little information available for hobbyists about reptile illness and disease. Fortunately much more research is being

A healthy snake sheds its skin at once. Its old skin remains virtually in once piece. (Note the 'spectacles'.).

Eyes that are partially closed indicate a problem.

done and more information is being published. There has also been increased interest among vets in reptile healthcare. Associations can usually direct you to a vet with an interest in reptiles. Although experienced enthusiasts have successfully diagnosed and treated animals this usually results in unnecessary losses when done by beginners. The five paragraphs about reptile sickness do not provide a comprehensive guide of all complaints, rather some important matters to consider are provided. These are particularly useful in helping to choose a healthy specimen from a shop or dealer. Try to prevent sickness by not acquiring doubtful specimens. This will include any specimen captured in the wild, those kept in dirty terrariums or ones with little room to hide, and avoid any animal that looks unwell.

A healthy reptile...
is alert, active,
difficult to catch,
has clear eyes,
does not have sunken eyes,
has no swollen eyelids,
has good skin,
ideally has no remains from an old skin,
has a clean cloaca,
has no warts or spots,
has firm stools,
has no slime in the mouth or nose,
bears no signs of mites,
has a mouth that closes,
(in principal) eats.

Try to keep new animals in quarantine at first for 4-18 weeks, observing them well, checking their droppings, and treating if required. Accommodate animals in well equipped terrariums with the appropriate numbers and correct feed. Specimens that will not eat may be being kept at too low a temperature. Allow the animals some peace and quiet, especially in the early days. Only handle terrarium animals if strictly necessary, for they are not pets. Avoid loud music (deaf snakes can still feel the vibrations) and only observe them at night with a torch.

The symptoms, causes, and remedies for some of the reptile illnesses that can occur are indicated in the following section.
– Also read the main section on vitamins and minerals.
– Semi-closed eyelids and lack of activity indicate in general terms that something is wrong.
– Have the excreta of new or suspected animals checked out quickly. A vet can help in this respect. Once more experienced it will be possible to recognize certain parasites yourself but the diagnosis of most parasites remains extremely difficult, so if in any doubt call the vet. Incorrect treatment ('It must be worms') can make matters worse, since all medicines are in principal toxic. Only treat one illness at a time and wait at least a week before starting a further course of treatment.

Fresh stools, no older than 24 hours, are used for microscopic examination. The faeces are mixed with water and a few drops placed on a slide. The stools may also be mixed in a tube with sodium nitrate of copper sulphate. After a sieve has been placed on the tube, the liquid is topped up until

it reaches the top of the tube. Place a slide on the top and examine this under a microscope after 15 minutes. Internal parasites will have floated to the top and be on the slide.
– Roundworm eggs are usually oval with a darker centre or are each filled with a tiny worm. Roundworm can be treated with 10mg fenbendazol or lavamisolphosphate per kilogram body weight, given by mouth for five days.
– Flagella, micro-organisms with long tails that can be clearly seen under a microscope at an enlargement of x 400. Symptoms of flagella are not eating, vomiting, messy and slimy excreta, and lethargic animals.
– Amoebas (an irregular, transparent, slowly moving cell) appear as dark cores in clear protoplasm. They can be coloured with a solution of 1 gram iodine and 2 grams potassium iodide made by adding water as droplets and then adding further water to make 100 ml. Mix one drop of the solution with stools and water. Amoebas are most prevalent with snakes and are passed on by insects and human hands.

Signs of amoebas are a dirty and bloody cloaca and blood in the stools.
Both amoebas and flagella can be treated with 50-75mg metronidazol or 10-20mg ronidazol per kilogram body weight to be given by mouth for ten days. These substances can easily cause harm through overdoses so weigh and calculate with care. If necessary, a maximum one-time dose of 250mg metronidazol per kilogram can be administered (so take great care).
With snakes, a blue patch and bumps which can be felt immediately in front of the cloaca is an indication of amoebic infection. Such animals cannot be treated and must be separated from all others to limit spread of the infection. If the remaining specimens are treated quickly enough they have a chance of survival.

White tapeworm segments (100mm long, 1mm in diameter/4in long ¹/₃₂in in diameter) on the fresh stools of a spiky-tailed lizard.

Some things needed to check stools.

This thin Boa constrictor *will shortly shed its skin.*

This red ratsnake is having difficulty shedding its skin. The terrarium is too dry or there is a deficiency of vitamin A.

Basiliscus vittatus with abscess.

– Reduced appetite, weight loss, and diarrhoea (with blood) are symptoms of coccidiosis. Coccidia are a parasitic protozoa and sometimes small round or dividing cells can be found in the stools. Treat (and prevent) with sulphonamides available from a vet.

– Excessive mucous in the mouth often indicates lung problems.

Collect a sample with a swab and protect in a tube to take to a vet for analysis.

– A healthy reptile mouth is generally a clear whitish pink. Inflammation of the mucous membranes of the mouth (stomatitis) is initially seen as lightly swollen mucous membranes in and around the mouth and nostrils, with red markings plus pale yellow cheese-like decayed tissue in the mouth. It is most prevalent in weakened snakes and reptiles (through import for instance), or in association with lung and intestinal disorders.

Clean the mouth each day with a 3% solution of hydrogen peroxide on a swab. First remove decayed tissue. Rinse with 6ml of hydrochloric acid per litre. Also administer a course of wide-spectrum antibiotic concurrent with this treatment, in consultation with your vet, which will also aid the likely lung, stomach, or intestinal infection.

– Pneumonia manifests itself with excessive mucous in the nostrils and mouth and a whistling sound with heavy breathing. Breathing will be with an open mouth. This is often associated with stomatitis but can be found on its own with all reptiles. Turtles and terrapins often no longer float horizontally on the surface. The cause is usually draught. Place the affected animals for about ten days at a constant 30-35°C (86-95°F) and provide adequate food and water. Most tortoises suffering with pneumonia do not eat. Treat with antibiotics with the vet's help.

– Inflamed or weeping eyes point to a vitamin A deficiency. It is most common with terrapins. Feed foods rich in vitamin A (liver or carrot), either directly or via prey animals or provide a vi-

tamin A supplement. Give a dose of 2,000-10,000 IU per kilogram or get the vet to subcutaneously inject 15,000-20,000 IU/kg. An eye ointment is also advisable.

– Parts of the old skin remaining after the skin has been shed indicates either too dry a terrarium or a deficiency of vitamin A.

– Mites are parasites which suck reptile's blood. The dark red to black mites are 1mm (^{1}/₆₄in) across and they mainly hide in folds of skin (where limbs join the body and eye lids), beneath the scales, and in ear openings. Mites are often best recognized by the silvery dust on reptiles (the remains of the mites skin shedding). Snakes often lay in water when they suffer mites and the dead mites can be observed as small black balls floating on the surface.

Replace the substrate at the bottom of the terrarium with newspapers and treat with a preparation containing foxim. This not only eradicates all traces of the mites but gets rid of their eggs too. Dissolve 250mg in 1 litre water and dip the animal in the solution but protect its eyes, nostrils, mouth, and any wounds (with e.g. eye salve) and also protect yourself. Dry the animal thoroughly after treatment and then wrap it firmly in a bag to prevent it from licking itself. The terrarium should also be sprayed with the solution after removing as much of the decorative material as possible (which could be hiding places for the parasites). Rinse thoroughly with water.

Plastic strips treated with dichlorvos can be used to treat mites provided their size is adapted to the size of the terrarium and its occupants (carefully read the instructions). Place the strip in a perforated box which the reptile cannot get access to. Ticks are larger than mites but also suck blood. They are usually grey-brown to black. Remove ticks with a twisting movement and smear the wound with chlorohexidine.

– Pock marks are light-coloured skin blisters which result from either too moist or too cold living conditions. Place affected animals in a dry, hygienically clean container. The pocks can be dabbed with iodine. The problem can be cured within about three skin sheddings. Serious problems can be helped with a vitamin A injection by a vet followed by several skin sheddings in short succession. This problem is best prevented by ensuring at least one dry position in the terrarium (e.g. beneath a spotlight).

– Abscesses can be lanced with a scalpel, cleaned with a swab, and then smeared with an antibiotic cream.

– Coat wounds with betadine iodine.

– Rachitis or rickets manifests itself in crooked legs or tail, prominent hip bones, spontaneous fractures, weak shells, loose jaws, swollen toes, poor egg shells, high mortality, and small, weak, or deformed offspring. Rickets is caused by a deficiency of vitamin D_3 or calcium. It is difficult to do anything for fully grown animals and is therefore best prevented (see the main section on Feeding).

– All reptiles can suffer a prolapsed cloaca or hemipenis (the organ pushed out of the body) through blockage, illness, or pregnancy. Keep the revealed organ clean and moist, wrap with a moist bandage and take the animal to a vet. The vet will return the organ to inside the body without twisting it, with much patience and care, using ice-cold swabs,. Once this has been accomplished, the vet will stitch the area to prevent recurrence and tightly bandage the area around the cloaca aperture.

– Blockages of the intestines can be caused by sand or stones being ingested with food that was not in a tray, if there is too little to drink, or the food is too low in fibre. The affected animal no longer excretes, has a distended belly, and continually tries to push the blockage through. This can often be eased with sunflower oil, petroleum jelly, or glycerine (3ml/kg) administered through a silicon tube fitted to a syringe that is fed through the intestine into the stomach. Many large lizards and tortoises have extremely powerful jaws that are difficult to open. Push a flat object (e.g. a plastic or wooden spatula with smaller lizards) between the jaws and twist it vertically. Keep the spatula in position while a helper inserts the tube until they feel slight resistance then insert the liquid. The oesophagus or gullet is the upper, larger opening. If the mixture is inserted directly into the mouth there is a risk of a weakened animal suffocating through the liquid entering the windpipe. The windpipe is always behind the base of the tongue.

– Sometimes it is necessary to force feed reptiles. Do not recourse to this too quickly and always try to discover and remove the cause of the animal refusing to eat. Forced feeding is very stressful and should only be used in the last resort. With lizards and tortoises (and their ilk) a liquid feed can be administered in the same way described above for treating blockages. The feed should ideally incorporate easily digested soya baby food (available from supermarkets) of mashed and sieved food. Snakes should be fed dead, smooth prey.

Rickets in lizards. The lighter-coloured specimen has crooked legs and cannot lift its cloaca from the ground.

Rickets in green iguanas. The large animal is 3 years old, the smaller one 4 years but it has crooked shoulders and can barely climb.

A prolapsed cloaca with a spiky-tailed lizard (U. acanthinura) several weeks after laying its eggs. When the cloaca is massaged back into place there must be no twist or kink in the cloaca or intestine.

196

Animals need to be carefully weighed before giving them medicines. All medicines are toxic and too much can kill.

– It is usually unnecessary to clip ground-dwelling reptile's claws provided there are enough rough stones in the terrarium.

Do not treat animals yourself if you are still inexperienced but seek assistance from an experienced terrarium keeper who may often be able to help. Very few medicines are stocked that are suitable for reptiles. Only a few fractions of a millilitre may be required from a large ampoule of roundworm treatment intended for a pig. Medicinal doses are given in amounts of active ingredients. If you are not too hot in calculating let someone else work it out. The weight of the animal to be treated is of great importance. A miscalculation by a factor of ten is virtually always fatal.

The order Squamata, lizards and snakes

Lizards and snakes did not appear on the earth until a few million years ago, making them relatively modern reptiles.

THE HEMIPENIS

Squamata are characterized by the masculine sexual organ that consists of right and left hand hemipenises. This organ is located behind the cloaca, towards the tail. There is a gland which swells up behind the hemipenis compartment. During mating this gland pushes the hemipenis pouch open. The swollen hemipenis is able to make firm contact with the female during mating thanks to barbs and folds.

During mating by Squamata species the female's cloaca may be on the left or right-hand side. The two part penis is therefore beneficial since the male can use the left-hand hemipenis if the female's cloaca in on the left and vice versa. There are two sub orders (or orders) of Sauria (Lacertilia) comprising 17 families of lizards and four families of legless or worm lizards representing about

The sheltopusik (Ophisaurus apodus, CITES A) is a limbless lizard from the Balkans (the dark brown specimen) and former USSR (the yellow with brown flecks).

4,000 species and Serpentes (Ophidia) with ten families and about 2,700 species of snake.

Worm lizards (Amphisbaenia) are rarely kept in terrariums and are not dealt with further. They are sometimes treated as a separate order.

EGG LAYING OR BIRTH

Some lizards and snakes, particularly those from cooler climates, do not lay eggs (ovipary) but retain the young in eggs inside the body (ovovivipary) or within the body itself (vivipary), giving birth to living offspring. A female that reproduces by ovovivipary retains the eggs in her body up to the moment that the young emerge. The female does not have to leave her own territory to lay her eggs and can seek out the best possible environment for her young. The offspring are retained within a thin membrane or are born without any shell.

The unborn offspring of an ovovivipary species derive protein from the egg. The unborn young of vivipary species (such as mammals) derive their nourishment from their mother via the umbilical cord or an extension of the intestines.

The suborder Sauria, lizards

Approximately 3,000 species of lizard inhabit the world, especially in tropical and subtropical regions. The most important lizards are the Agamidae (iguana-like lizards with acrodont teeth), Chamaeleontidae (chameleons), Gekkonidae (geckos or gekkos), Iguanidae (basilisks and iguanas), Lacertidae ('true' lizards), Scincidae (skinks), and Varanidae (monitor lizards, Komodo dragons).

Accommodation

Male lizards are often aggressive in defence of their territory. Prevent stress by avoiding competition for food, females, hiding places, and egg laying sites. Place only one male per terrarium for example and ensure there is a place to shelter and a 'sun basking' spot for each lizard. Stress is often not noticed soon enough and its reduces resistance to worms and other parasites and can prove fatal.

The lizard must not be able to tip over the water tray so this needs to be heavy. The lizard must be able to see over the rim of its water tray.

Feeding

Most lizards are predators and omnivores but the amounts each species eats varies widely. Many small lizards mainly eat insects (fruit flies, house flies, wax moths, and other collected insects) but also like to lick fruit. The majority of larger lizards eat larger prey (crickets, grasshoppers, newly-born mice etc.) and fruit. Green iguanas and monitor lizards are solely carnivores. Horned lizards specialize in eating ants which are an essential part of their diet. Herbivorous lizards that chiefly eat vegetable matter in the wild suffer intestinal and kidney problems if they eat too much animal protein. The young of such lizards do need slightly more animal protein though.

Terrarium with a trio (one male, two females) of Paroedura pictus. *Because there are only two places with a thick layer of moist soil (the pots), all these geckos eggs can be found there.*

The male bearded dragon has larger femoral pores on his thighs.

Sex determination

Males often have

1. More elaborate means of display. Lizards are territorial and the males in particular display with for example bright colours, dorsal combs, throat pouches, and have more robustly built body and head. The display behaviour such as head bobbing and swaying can also provide a clue although the females of certain species also display.

2. A thickened base to the tail with the hemipenises being seen as a swelling behind the cloaca.

3. Larger femoral pores on the underside of the back legs and/or pre-anal pores in front of the cloaca. These markings or even fringes may only be more prominent in males during the mating season (compare a number of specimens). These pores exude a scent during courtship and mating. Skinks do not have femoral pores.

4. Spores behind the cloaca which resemble loose scales but are less common.

5. Probing is possible with lizards but inadvisable because of their wild behaviour. Probing is a method widely used with snakes and will be dealt with there.

6. Popping the hemipenises, which are just in front of the cloaca, can be done by carefully squeezing upwards but should not be done unless essential.

7. It is not possible to determine sex in young lizards. A fair chance of determining the gender can only be made when they are six to twelve months old.

6. Non dominant male lizards often resemble females but this is a tactic used to avoid conflict with dominant males. In contrast, some dominant females can appear like males. This all makes sex determination in lizards a tricky business.

The hemipenises of this male skink (Mabuya sp.) *have been pushed out (or popped). This causes stress and pain and should not be done unless strictly necessary.*

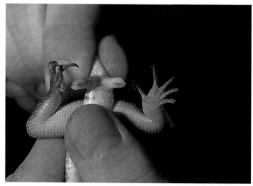

Mating skinks (Eumeces schneideri).

A two-week old lizard has drowned in 15mm(⁵/₈in) of water.

A water dragon laying eggs.

Mating

After the courtship display, the male grasps the female firmly with his mouth by her neck or side. This biting behaviour seems awful and can leave scars (another sign of gender) but this is natural behaviour. A female that is ready to mate allows the male to press his cloaca sideways against hers. Actual mating (with one hemipenis) can take from a few seconds to many minutes. Chameleons and others have different mating behaviour.

Egg laying

The majority of egg-laying lizards lay their eggs in a hollow in moist earth or sand. Dark soil can be sprinkled with silver sand so that it is easier to see where the female has dug. Look for the eggs if the female's flanks suddenly become slimmer.

Many geckos stick their eggs against something. The eggs have a leathery shell, although this hardens with certain geckos.

Females are sometimes mated very frequently and therefore often lay eggs but this can cause stress so separate the sexes.

Lizards can sometimes fail to lay their eggs as a result of too little calcium or vitamin D_3. The female also becomes stressed if she cannot find a suitable place to lay her eggs. A pregnant female who is suffering can be spotted by the way the tail and legs become slimmer and the lizard looks tired. Sometimes she will start eating again. Eggs that are not laid solidify.

Once it has been established that the female is pregnant a vet can inject substances that help to induce egg laying. If this fails the female will need to be operated on. This is a major operation which can entail removal of the female reproductive organs (ovaries) but the operation is essential or the lizard will die.

Rearing

Almost every young lizard looks like a strange cricket so rear them in separate terrariums, preferably individually. The offspring from some species can be raised in groups since they learn to eat from each other's example. Feed a little three times each day in preference to more once each day. For most species provide a very shallow water tray. In the photo above a young lizard of two weeks can be seen having drowned in (⁵/₈in) of water. Provided it does not cause stress, spray young lizards every day so that they can drink the water droplets.

Many lizards become sexually mature very early, especially if they are given plenty of protein. Young females though that lay eggs too soon never achieve normal body length and become quickly exhausted.

Thin after her brood: Basiliscus vittatus.

Day gecko with iodine deficiency.

This pearl lizard (Lacerta lepida) *has just ejected its tail.*

Sickness
A healthy lizard has...
– no withering of the base of the tail
– well-filled thighs
– licks something held in front of it
– does not have crooked legs and lifts its cloaca off the ground.

Wounds and missing toes and such like are not serious provided they heal properly.
Geckos and anoles particularly can suffer from iodine deficiency, which shows up as irregular thickening under the throat. Add 0.6mg of potassium iodide per litre of drinking and spraying water. With day geckos excessively calcium pouches that manifest themselves as white bumps behind the neck on both sides and behind the ear opening are benign.

Defence/handling
Most lizards can at worst inflict wounds in the following ways:
– biting (large and small lizards)
– scratching with their claws
– striking with their tail.
Capture large restless lizards with gloves, ensuring the wrists and arms are covered with substantial clothing. Bear in mind that many (small) lizards eject their tail and can flee quickly. Blood loss is limited by pressing muscles together. A new tail grows back after a few months. Larger lizards can lose their tails although these do not regrow.

The only venomous lizards are the Gila monster *(Heloderma suspectum)* and beaded lizard *(Heloderma horridum)* which are both covered by CITES B. These originate from Mexico, Central America, and western parts of the USA. Their venom is injected by chewing and can prove fatal. These rare warty creatures with their dark bodies and red to yellow flecks that grow to 600-800mm (24-31$^{1}/_{2}$ in) are never imported for the hobbyists terrarium.

A large, calm lizard can be lifted gently with both hands under its belly. Pick up a wilder specimen first with the left hand behind the head. Slide the palm of the right hand under its belly and position index and third fingers behind the head. The left hand can now be released to hold the base of the tail and hind legs.

Another option is to catch hold from above the head and front legs with one hand and base of the tail and hind legs with the other. Lizards do not remain as calm though with this method as the previous manner.

Head of a Gila monster.

Most large calm lizards can be picked up this way (Varanus exanthematicus).

Never pick a lizard up just by its tail. Place a flat hand quickly but gently on the body of a small lizard and grasp it gently by the neck between the thumb and index finger. The body will then lay in the hand.

Tricks to get a biting lizard to release its grip include offering it a surface on which to escape, holding it under water, covering its eyes, and if all else fails, dripping vinegar or spirits into its mouth.

Hold large lizards with paper and a linen bag or place them in a sturdy and well insulated box. Let chameleons sit on a branch if possible or place them in a linen bag. Transport small lizards in a plastic box with wads of paper in it.

The Agamidae family, agamids

Agamids (approx. 300 species in 30 genera) are widely kept in terrariums. They are sometimes considered to be a subfamily Agaminae of the Chamaeleontidae family.

Many agamids have a superficial resemblance to certain iguanas. With agamids though the teeth are fused in the jaw (acrodont teeth) whereas iguanas have pleurodont teeth at the side of the jaw.

Appearance
Agamids are characterized by their large triangular head with stubby nose. Many species have powerfully built bodies and the legs can sometimes be quite long. The tail is equal in length or longer than the body.

Agamids often have a dorsal comb and similar comb on the tail and/or spines on the tail, chin, or other parts of the body. The eyelids and eardrum membrane are readily apparent and the ear opening is large.

Those agamids with flattened sides are usually tree dwellers.

Agamids have a thick tongue that is often fairly long. Many species can change colour. Chameleons evolved from agamids.

They defend their territories by bobbing their heads, swaying with the front legs, or swishing their tails. The tail cannot be ejected. Agamids

Handling a small lizard like this tokay gecko.

Agama agama *male.*

are diurnal (active by day) and have good eyesight.

Distribution
Africa but not Madagascar, Asia, Australia, and one species *(Agama stellio)* lives in southern Europe. They are mainly found in arid regions.

AGAMA AGAMA, RAINBOW LIZARD

The rainbow lizard is attractive and fairly inexpensive although it requires plenty of space and is rarely bred.

Appearance
Males that are ready to mate are blue with an orange head and orange and/or white in their tail. Females (and some males) are brown with a bit of yellow or orange colouring. There are a number of subspecies of these very active 300-400mm (12-16in) long lizards with many different colour variations.

Distribution
Agama agama are plentiful in various arid regions in central and southern Africa, particularly around human habitation. These ground and wall-dwellers live in colonies of one dominate male, several females and their offspring.

Accommodation
Provide a large and dry terrarium with a large surface area (at least 200 x 60cm/79 x 24in) for one male and several females with climbing opportunities on the rear wall. Provide lots of hiding places

Agama agama *female.*

for these(initially) shy creatures. Ensure temperatures of 25-30°C (77-86°F) and 45°C (113°F) under the beam of the lamps. Provide ultra-violet lighting as well.

Feeding
These rapid hunters catch insects in the main. Feed a little fruit from time to time. Spray two to three times each week and provide a small water container.

Sex determination
Males have brighter colouring, larger pre-anal pores, larger bodies, and a bigger head.

Reproduction
This species is rarely bred. Ultra-violet lighting, good accommodation, and seasonal impulses are prerequisites. These lizards lay three to eight eggs.

Buying
All specimens offered for sale by the trade are captured from the wild and usually carry mites and the signs of them. They often are therefore in poor condition.

PHYSIGNATHUS COCINCINUS, ASIAN WATER DRAGON

A boisterous lizard that requires a large area of water with good filtration.

Appearance
The up to 800mm (31½in) long lizard (head and trunk 200-250mm/8-10in) is pale or dark green with darker stripes on the tail. There is a small

Male Agama agama *in Chad.*

Pair of Physignathus cocincinus.

Young water dragons already show swaying behaviour.

Water dragons are renowned for their mouth wounds. This one cannot be healed.

throat pouch beneath the large head and a comb on the back and tail.

Distribution
This tree dweller lives close to water in tropical rain forests throughout much of South-East Asia.

Accommodation
Create a riparium (bank terrarium) at least 150 x 50 x 60cm (59 x 20 x 24in) for one male and one or two females. This water loving animal requires a large water area with extremely clean (well-filtered and frequently renewed) water. Water dragons (especially specimens captured in the wild) are boisterous creatures that often jump against the terrarium glass. Because they defecate in the water any mouth wounds would quickly become infected in a normal tropical rain forest terrarium, even if the water was replaced every day. Such wounds can fester so badly the jaw becomes exposed and can prove fatal. Provided the water is well filtered the wounds will heal.

These lizards like to lay on a branch above the water. Heat this spot to 40°C (104°F) providing at least one spotlight per animal. The temperature elsewhere should be 28-32°C (82.4-89.6°F), with humidity of 80-90%.

Feeding
Feed insects, mice, earthworms, slugs and snails, tinned cat food and about 25% of the diet should be fruit.

Sex determination

From an age of one year the males have larger dorsal and tail combs, larger, more thick set head and body, a thickened base of the tail, larger femoral pores, and a larger throat pouch which is bluish-yellow.

Mating

Reproduction is enhanced by giving a winter rest period at 4°C (39.2°F) with 4 hours less lighting. Water dragons follow typical lizard mating behaviour with head bobbing and biting.

Egg laying

The 6-17 whites eggs are laid mainly early in the year (January-March), in a 100-250mm (4-9³/₄in) deep hole dug in loose, moist soil. Females compete fairly strongly for nesting sites. The eggs hatch after two months at 30°C (85°F) and 2¹/₂ months at 25°C (77°F).

Rearing

Newly emerged offspring are about 140mm (5¹/₂in) long overall. They have a relatively large head, are olive green to dark green in colour with light diagonal stripes but do not yet have combs. Provide the young with a large pool of water such as half the terrarium area 100mm (4in) deep. Filter the water well or replace the water daily. Feed in-

sects and earthworms. The males only start to grow larger after six months, when their territorial behaviour also commences.

Handling

Water dragons are not very calm by nature. Try to get them used to human contact by feeding them by hand and handling them from time to time. This provides benefits later on.

Sail-fin lizards

Sail-fin lizards of the genus *Hydrosaurus* need similar conditions to the water dragon but these easily grow to more than 1m (40in) so that they need a larger terrarium.

POGONA VITTICEPS, THE BEARDED DRAGON

This is a popular lizard with very interesting behaviour that is easy to keep and to breed, and easily tamed. A bearded dragon makes an ideal alternative for anyone for whom a green iguana is too big.

Former genus before *Pogona: Amphibolurus*.
Possible new genus: *Acanthodraco*.

Appearance

This 500-600mm (19³/₄-23⁵/₈in) long light brown to brown lizard has spines forming a beard under the head. The body is horizontally flattened and covered in soft spines.

Distribution

Semi desert and dry, open woodland in Australia. This ground-dweller is a good climber.

Behaviour

Bearded dragons are diurnal (active by day). Even the young communicate by slow leg swaying and adult females do this towards males.

In their threat stance they stand askew with flattened body and jet black beard puffed up. Sometimes bearded dragons open their mouths too. The mouth is also kept opened wide as a means of cooling themselves.

Accommodation

Provide a large desert terrarium for these active lizards, at least 150 x 50 x 50cm (59 x 20 x 20in) for a pair or one male and two females, of 100 x 40 x 40cm (40 x 16 x 16in) for a single specimen.

Young water dragons have a large head.

Pair of bearded dragons. Males have jet black beards during the mating season.

Male bearded dragons fighting. Place only one male in each terrarium.

Two week old bearded dragons.

Ensure temperatures of 30°C (86°F) to 45-50°C (113-122°F) beneath the spot lamps.

Male bearded dragons eventually become stressed in each other's company, even if they have grown up together. Fighting in these circumstances cannot be avoided and can be very fierce and it is far better to move the less dominant male as quickly as possible and check it for worms. Overpopulation also causes stress, aggression, injuries, and bitten off limbs and other body parts. Males can suddenly turn aggressive towards other species of lizard and harm them seriously.

Continuously ready-to-mate males hound the females, causing them stress. Continually pregnant females produce 4 broods each year but are barely able to recover. Remove the male under these circumstances to his own terrarium not less than 100 x 40 x 40cm (40 x 16 x 16in) and return him to a female several days before mating for a few days.

Feeding

Feed all manner of insects, small rodents, egg, tinned cat or dog food, vegetables, and fruit. Make the animal protein about 75% of the overall diet. An adult bearded dragon eats a great deal, at least about 25 crickets per week with the occasional mouse or baby rat. Bearded dragons digest their food rapidly and excrete a great deal of waste matter, making them renowned for their smell. Remove excreta regularly, sieve the sand, and replace all the sand twice per year.

Spray these lizards twice per week because they prefer to drink water droplets than from a water tray.

Sex determination

The sex of bearded dragons can be fairly successfully determined only when they are ready to mate. The males acquire larger and darker femoral and pre-anal pores and a somewhat more robust appearance. During the mating season the male bearded dragon's beard turns completely black. The females can also display a certain amount of black.

Mating

Provide a winter rest of 8 weeks with a daytime temperature of 20-25°C (68-77°F) and 15-20°C (59-68°F) at night. Mating sometimes follows head bobbing and biting. Remove an oppressive male if the female is probably already fertilized.

Egg laying

A fertilized female who is well nourished will fill out after several weeks and lumps can be seen in her underbelly. Provide a moist substrate in the terrarium of at least 100mm (4in) deep such as moist sand beneath a flat stone or plank of wood, or give a container of moist soil.

The female lays 10-30 eggs in a hole she digs herself, then she fills in the hole and firms the ground over the eggs with her flat forehead.

The offspring of 100mm (4in) long emerge after 55 days at 32°C (89.6°F) and 75 days at 28°C (82.4°F). The lower temperature produces many female offspring, the higher temperature more males.

Rearing

Care for no more than ten offspring of the same size in a terrarium 100 x 50 x 50cm (39³/₈ x 20 x 20in). Keep a close eye on them: in small terrariums in particular tales and toes can get bitten off if there is too little small insect food. If possible, rear the young individually.

Bearded dragon young fairly quickly start to eat vegetable food. It is important to spray them with water each day because they drink a great deal at this time. Supplement both water and feed with vitamins and minerals and if possible provide ultraviolet lighting (see Creating a terrarium). Bearded dragons are sexually mature after one to two years but too rapid growth and early reproduction are ill advised.

UROMASTYX ACANTHINURA, AFRICAN SPINY-TAILED LIZARD

Legal position: all *Uromastyx* species are covered in CITES B.

Spiny-tailed lizards (usually *U. acanthinura, U. aegyptia, U. hardwickii,* or *U. maliensis)* are not suitable animals for beginners but will tempt many a beginner to purchase them. The extremely calm lizards have an interesting appearance but are prone to stress and demand high standards in their care.

Appearance

Uromastyx acanthinura grow to 400-450mm (16-17³/₄in) long and they are grey-brown with green, orange, or yellow tinting. Their tortoise head is often almost black. The stocky, flattened body has sturdy legs and a thick tail. The scales on the tail are spiky and arranged in rows.

The three subspecies *(U. a. acanthinura, U. a. dispar,* and *U. a. geyri)* can be recognized by the number of bands on their tails and number of scales on the centre of their bodies.

Up to 1996 *U. maliensis* was widely imported, usually under the name *U. acinthinuria.* Both species can only be distinguished by very careful comparison and counting of certain scales by an experienced person.

Distribution

Morocco, Algeria, Tunisia, Libya, and Mauritania, in sunny and hot desert and semi-desert with little rainfall or vegetation. The diurnal spiny-tailed lizards dig deep holes in the hard ground. Each male needs a territory of several hectares within which he will find several females with their own territories.

Temperature

Uromastyx acanthinura survives where winters are 0°C (32°F) and it is 53°C (127.4°F) in summer. Temperatures can change during the day by 35°C (95°F). The ground can heat up in the sun to 80°C (176°F). Temperatures are more moderate

Uromastyx maliensis female.

Pair of Uromastyx acanthinura, *with female on top.*

Females too are territorial and can become stressed without it being noticed. This can lead to fighting, as here.

and constant in the deep burrows of these reptiles. The optimum body temperature is in the region of 40°C (104°F). Both colour and the animals changes of position give clues for temperature control and the reduction of fluid loss.

Excess salt is discharged through the nostrils and can be seen as white rims. Water can be stored in the skin, they can derive water from their urine, and in extended drought they can burn body fat to derive fluid.

Accommodation

Provide a hot desert terrarium of at least 150 x 50 x 50 (59 x 20 x 20in) for no more than one male and one female. More than one of the same sex causes stress which will manifest itself in worm infections.

Ensure 30-55°C (86-131°F) with the higher temperature beneath the spot lamps and a night-time temperature of about 25°C (77°F). Soil heating is required to keep the ground at 23-30°C (73.4-86°F) by day and 21-25°C (69.8-77°F) at night. These lizards can dig their own burrows in a minimum of 150mm (6in) sandy soil. If sand-pit sand is used, make sure that hollows are made with stones and or wood which can be readily checked.

The daytime humidity in North Africa is 10-30% and 60-80% at night. Therefore spray the terrarium each evening or morning with slightly more given in spring and autumn than in summer and winter.

Make sure with ample stones and pieces of wood that the occupants do not have to constantly look at each other.

Uromastyx acanthinura can be easily kept with the *Eumeces algeriensis* (Berber's skink) which comes from the same part of the world.

Feeding

Adult spiny-tailed lizards mainly eat vegetable matter but also insects and baby mice. The mainly eat leaves and flowers and are crazy about dandelions, clover, rape (leaf and flower), and orange lentils. Young specimens and adult females about

Spiny-tails are crazy about yellow flowers (dandelions).

The female closes up the hole thoroughly after laying her eggs.

Head of a male.

male will unhook himself after a time. If she is willing then customary lizard mating occurs, including firm neck biting.

Egg laying

Pregnant females are thicker and more aggressive. Provide them with a varied and highly nutritious diet. About four to six weeks after mating, in June or July, some 10-25 eggs are laid and buried in moderately moist soil at about 30°C (86°F). The female guards the closed up nest for weeks. At 30°C (86°F) and 95-100, the eggs hatch after 85-100 days. Do not keep the vermiculite too moist for the last few weeks.

Lay the eggs next to each other in a large container so that the first to hatch crawl over the other eggs and stimulate the others to emerge.

Rearing

Because of stress, do not place more than two youngsters together in the same terrarium, and then only with ample hiding places and food.

The offspring can be kept under the same conditions as their parents. Feed fairly small insects and spray a little water each day.

Place these animals on a bed of newspapers to prevent sand blockages.

A youngster if 70-80mm (2³/₄-3¹/₈in) long but they grow rapidly and become sexually mature after three to four years. The sexes can be distinguished at one-and-a-half to two years.

Defence

At signs of danger, spiny-tailed lizards crawls into a burrow with a narrow entrance so that their tail prevents intruders. They also puff themselves up.

Handling

Handle these animals as little as possible to prevent stress, regardless of how calm they are.

Other heat lovers

Chuckwallas *(Sauromalus* sp.), girdled lizards *(Corydylus* sp.), *Sceloporus* species, and desert iguana *(Dipsosaurus dorsalis)* are lizards that equally worship hot conditions as *Uromastyx.*

to lay and just after laying their eggs have a real need for animal protein.

Sex determination

This is difficult. During the mating season the femoral pores develop into fringes with males. Head bobbing and other courtship rituals are usually performed by the male. Adult males are slightly larger than females, they have a broader head, and often have a black underside and pointed nose. Females have lighter-coloured underside to the head and a stumpy nose. The male belly is flecked while the female's is more white.

Mating

Let *U. acanthinura* hibernate or have a winter rest at 15-20°C (59-68°F) with six hours lighting in December and January but this does not apply to *U. maliensis*. Provide one warm spot under a lamp of 35°C (95°F).

The pair have to get on with each other and both be ready to mate at the same time. Exchange with another specimen is sometimes required.

The males display to the female with head bobbing and by circling in front of the female and on her. This causes a white secretion to be deposited on the ground and on her back. If the female is not willing to mate she rolls onto her back and the

Chameleons are extremely interesting but difficult to keep.

The Chamaeleonidae family, chameleons

Legal position: all species except *Chameleo chamaeleon* (which is CITES A) are listed in CITES B.

The unusual appearance and interesting behaviour of chameleons make them very attractive. Most species though are extremely difficult to keep alive in captivity, let alone breed. Gain experience first with easier lizards. Get as much information as possible and give long and careful consideration before deciding to buy a chameleon and then plan for the animal before doing so.

Be aware that caring for chameleons is very time consuming and in practice demands daily caring. Anyone who fails to do this and thinks how nice it would be to have a chameleon that eats house flies among the house plants will soon seen the chameleon pine away.

Experienced enthusiasts have made great forward strides in the keeping of chameleons but there are many questions to which we still do not have answers.

Appearance

This book solely deals with the sub family Chamaeleoninae ('true' chameleons) and not Brookesiinae.

Chameleons are flat sided with a long, gripping tail. Many species have combs on the head, back, tail, beneath the throat, and on the belly. The five toes have fused together with two and three toes to form a little foot. The tongue is as long as the body and tail together, has a thickened end, and is used to catch prey. The eyes can move independently of each other and are housed in manoeuvrable turrets so that the body can remain motionless while the eyes move. The turrets are eye lids that have fused together so that only the pupils can be seen.

Chameleons are not necessarily as readily able to change colour as is generally thought. The ability to change colours is beneficial for imposing themselves or fighting rivals, the day-night cycle, frightening attackers, camouflage, and for mating. Pregnant females show by their colour that they no longer wish to mate and if a chameleon wishes to absorb more heat it makes its body darker. Conversely if it wishes to shed warmth it makes its body lighter in colour.

Chameleons in the wild do not grow very old. Although some species can survive for about ten years, others (mainly smaller species) grow no older than one to one-and-a-half years.

Distribution

The around 130 species of 'true' chameleons in four genera which inhabit very different biotopes throughout Africa, Arabia, India, and Sri Lanka. *Chamaeleo chameleon* (CITES 1) is found in southern Europe and North Africa.

Accommodation

Chameleons form territories and are sensitive to stress. Generally place only one chameleon in a fairly large terrarium and provide lots of horizontal and diagonal climbing branches with sufficient thickness to be grasped hold of, and plenty of plants. Most chameleons rarely come down to the ground. Lay plenty of branches on the ground (made of a peat-sand mixture or of artificial grass) so that the chameleon can quickly climb up again. Make sure the chameleon cannot become stuck anywhere between pots or other decor.

Good ventilation is essential but avoid draughts

Pair of Chamaeleo calyptratus.

Chamaeleo cristatus *from West Africa.*

and constant high humidity (normal is 70-80%). Standard shop bought terrariums are therefore entirely unsuitable.

Most chameleons and certainly the younger specimens must not be kept at temperatures above 30°C (86°F). Spotlights need to be placed above the branches but the chameleon must not be able to touch the lamps which would burn. Many species such as *Furcifer pardalis*, *C. jacksonii*, and *C. hoehnelii* like plenty of light for 12-14 hours per day. Use UV lamps by preference. Hang a few halogen spots for 'sunbasking'. In terrariums of at least 50cm (20in) high use at least two tubular fluorescent lamps and in larger ones use gas discharge lamps such as metal halide lamps from 35 watts upwards. Make sure that the temperature does not become too high.

Rain forest dwellers such as *C. parsonii* need a fairly high relative humidity, moderate light levels, and an even temperature (25-30°C/77-86°F), but slightly lower at night. Ventilate the terrarium with two large vents on the top and side.

Mountain species (e.g. *C. bitaeniatus*, *C. hoehnelii*, *C. jacksonii*, and *Furcifer lateralis*) need a well ventilated terrarium with two sides of mesh. Ensure 22-27°C (71.6-80.6°F) during the day and drop the temperature fairly sharply at night to 10-15°C (50-59°F) to ensure the animals get their necessary rest. This species can be kept in a well-planted outside terrarium in the summer, provided it has sufficient areas of shade. These named mountain species can even withstand temperatures around freezing and are able to live outside between May and late September. Heat them with spot lamps if it remains cold for any length of time. The best terrarium for many species is a room terrarium, greenhouse, or conservatory with good ventilation and day-night temperature gradient, providing it has the necessary humidity and lighting. Hang spot lamps over them and provide water regularly plus spray the plants every day. Chameleons mainly remain in their favourite place but can go for a walk in the room so take care. Burrowing females can cause a certain amount of mess before they lay their eggs. They can be placed

This 7.5 x 5 metre (24 x 16ft) conservatory is inhabited by Calumma parsonii, Furcifer pardalis, Chamaeleo calyptratus, C. quadriconis, *water dragons, helmet basilisks, girdled anoles, agamids, and* Python viridis. *The plastic roof lets UV light through and opens up in hot weather. Additional lighting is provided with halogen and 300 watt UV-B lamps. Automatic sprinklers spray water. There is a waterfall and also a 5 meter (16ft) long aquarium with miniature crocodile* (Paleosuchus) *and several terrapins.*

in a large terrarium to lay their eggs but not at the last moment.

Make sure that the greenhouse or conservatory does not become too hot, but also not too cold. Cooling with thermostatically controlled vents and fans and additional heating with powerful lamps will be necessary. Chameleons have their own territory and be extremely intolerant of each other. A single male can be kept with one or even several females in a very large terrarium provided there are adequate hiding places. Watch developments closely for the first few days after the animals are put together.

Chameleons can also be incorporated in a greenhouse or conservatory with other calm reptiles (including other species of chameleon) and amphibians, provided these are about the same size and will not fit in one or the other's mouth.

Feeding

Feed living self cultivated insects or ones collected

Chamaeleo dilepsis *in Chad.*

Calumma parsonii *eating a grasshopper.*

208

from nature. Although *Chamae* means lion, an adult *Furcifer pardalis* is satisfied with three adult crickets each day. Growing, pregnant, and sexually active specimens need more though. Too much food causes the animals to become fat. Some species also eat baby mice and rats.

The feed can be offered with the hand or forceps but many insects can be offered in a smooth-sided bucket. There needs to be a branch half in the bucket so that if a chameleon falls in it can climb out.

Provide a varied diet and do not forget vitamin and mineral supplements. Chameleon enthusiasts have a preference for 'Korvamin'. The appetite of chameleons that at little or nothing can be awaken by offering green insects such as 'sabre' grasshoppers.

Thirsty chameleons will often refuse food. Some chameleons eat some foliage, flowers, and fruit occasionally.

Water

The different species of chameleon have different levels of need for water. While *Calumma parsonii* drinks every day, *C. calyptratus* is satisfied with drinking twice per week. Vitamins and minerals such as calcium can be dissolved in the water.

Most chameleons will as a rule not drink out of a water tray. Water can be given in the following manner.

Missed!

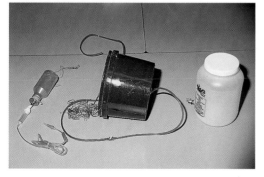

Various means of drip-feeding water.

This drip system used an air lift.

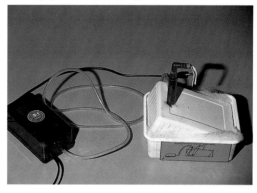

– Dribble water onto or into the mouth as droplets from a pipette. Most pipettes are small and only allow a few droplets to be administered before they are empty. This method is time consuming but does provide optimum control of what is given to the animals.

– Siphon water from a bottle or bucket with a length of air hose and let it drip into the terrarium. A bucket of water can dribble away for three days. Catch the water if puddles result. Syringes are also useful tools.

– Make a drinking water drip system using an air pump and some air hose to get air to bubble out under a plastic pipe. The pipe is placed in a container of water and the air bubbles lift water up the pipe and push it out of the top. Allow the water to drip down via a bend in the pipe so that it does not splatter upwards. Chameleons will drink from this dripping water. Excess water falls back into the container across a slanted surface (e.g. an upturned plastic container). This is important because chameleons can drown in the smallest of puddles. The water tray also needs to be filled with coarse gravel or other filter material but claws can get caught up in filter pads. The system should only be switched on during the day. Replace the water once or twice per week and clean everything thoroughly. With such a system it is important to be certain that the stools are free from parasites.

– Pump water up into a pipe and allow it to run down from the same pipe.

– Spray the terrarium with water each day, ideally in the morning, to imitate the dew that chameleons drink. Sprinklers can be set to operate by a timer in a conservatory.

– In very large terrariums a waterfall or indoor fountain can serve as drinking water provider.

Sex determination

The males often have striking characteristics for their courtship display, such as helmets, horns, combs, bright colouring, and larger size. The males also generally have a thickened base of the tail.

Only the male Chamaeleo calyptratus *has spurs on his hind legs.*

Brood of eggs from Chamaeleo calyptratus.

Male *C. calyptratus* for example have a spur growing as an extra toe between their claws and their two and three fused toes. This characteristic can even be seen in young animals.

Mating

Put animals of at least one year old in sight of each other each week. For attempted mating always place the female with the male. If the male is placed with the female there is a risk that he will not mate for some time although he may mate straight away. If the female reacts calmly and with muted colours to his display then she is prepared to mate. If she reacts with strong colours then the chances are that she is already pregnant. Mating follows after a short chase when the male grasps hold of the female with his front legs and climbs on her back an copulates. There are a number of variations to this mating behaviour. Many species mate several times over a number of days and the female then changes colour. Remove the male after two days.

The females eat copiously after mating and become more aggressive. Wild captured females are almost always pregnant. The females can store sperm and fertilize further broods with it.

Egg laying/birth

The species from cooler climates in particular tend to produce live young have carried the eggs. They give birth to 5-40 offspring which should be removed from the mother within a day. The females do not normally immediately eat their young but it can occur within a matter of hours or days. The forthcoming birth or egg laying is indicated by a reduced appetite and nervousness.

The types that lay their eggs are pregnant for one to five months. For them you should create a deep enough egg laying container that the female can dig down to at least half her overall length. Fill the container with a mixture of builder's sand, loose peat, and compost. The mixture should not collapse while the egg chamber is being excavated. Some species need to have the egg laying container heated (heating half will do).

Furcifer lateralis needs fairly hard, trodden down

A young Chamaeleo calyptratus *emerges from its egg and other is walking.*

and somewhat clay soil with something planted in it. This needs to be ready long before the egg laying. The soil of about 20cm (8in) should not be covered, not soaking wet, but not too dry, and about 24°C (75.2°F).

Eggs hatch in 90-380 days, depending on the temperature, if placed in moist vermiculite. Changes in temperature during incubation are extremely important for many egg laying species. *Furcifal lateralis* eggs need to be kept at 25-28°C (77-82.4°F) for the first 45 days, at 12-18°C (53.6-64.4°F) for the next 45 days, and then finally at 25-28°C (77-82.4°F) again until they hatch. With other species the cooler period of their area of origin needs to be imitated. Eggs of *F. lateralis* can also be incubated at a constant 25-28°C (77-82.4°F) but they then take five to six months to hatch.

Eggs of *C. montium* take four months to hatch at 24°C (75.2°F) and C. quadrocornis also require 4 months but at 22°C (71.6°F).

Rearing

Rearing of young chameleons can be quite successful and yet some of them virtually always die young. The entire brood can be kept in a large terrarium with plenty of plants and food for the first weeks. Prevent stress and losses by moving the young to their own individual and smaller terrarium before their territorial behaviour becomes apparent. In their own smaller terrarium they can easily find their food. The problem with small terrariums is that they are more prone to accidents, changes in temperature, and humidity.

Keep young specimens at the same temperatures as their parents. Spray enough water each day that it has evaporated after two hours and try to avoid spraying the animals themselves. Young chameleons easily drown in small puddles of water. The food should be a smaller scale version of the

Female Chamaeleo montium *from the mountain forests of Cameroon, West Africa.*

Chamaeleo quadricornis *from Cameroon.*

Rearing terrarium with young Chamaeleo calyptratus. *Halogen lamps without protective glass provide the required ultra-violet light.*

adults' food (aphids, fruit flies). It is a great pleasure to watch young chameleons discovering the power of their tongues and practising with them. Chameleons grow quickly with many species becoming mature in six months.

Sickness

Chameleons are very susceptible for illnesses. All manner of parasites *(Coccidia, Salmonella, Trichomonas,* and worms) that are mainly carried by specimens captured wild can become a problem through stress.

It is important that the eye socket is round and that both eyes can close at the same time. If a chameleon does not keep a watchful eye on its handler (has its eyes shut), this is a sign of stress. The eye turrets must also stand out and not be sunken. Thickened jaws or legs indicate a bacterial infection.

Keep a new chameleon in quarantine for at least six weeks before it comes into contact with other animals. Do not buy any females in advanced stages of pregnancy because the stress with cause her to fail to lay her eggs with all the consequences that entails.

Defence

Chameleons first line of defence in danger is to rely on their camouflage colour by hiding their body behind the branch on which they are sitting. Successively they use threatening colours, puff up their bodies and throat, open their mouths, and hiss. They can bite quite firmly. They are generally slow moving but can move rapidly when in danger.

Handling

Chameleons are very sensitive for stress and should be handled as little as possible. Allow the animal as much peace and quiet as possible. If pregnant females are stressed (e.g. by being handled) they are inclined to fail to lay their eggs with serious consequences.

To merely move a chameleon from one terrarium to another allow it to climb onto a branch and move the entire branch, if necessary in a reinforced insulated box.

Chamaeleo calyptratus *male.*

CHAMAELEO CALYPTRATUS, VEILED CHAMELEON

Legal status: CITES B.
This comparatively easy species is widely bred.

Appearance
Males of the subspecies *C. c. calyptratus* grow to 500mm (19³/₄in) long overall with a 60mm (2³/₈in) high helmet on their heads. Healthy and non-stressed males are a delightful turquoise colour with four yellow-green diagonal bands, blue flecks, and brown stripes. The males alone have spurs on their hind legs, even when they are young. Females grow to 350mm (13³/₄in) overall, and both their helmets and throat spines are smaller. They are mainly evenly coloured green with white flecks. Females live for three years and males for five years.
The subspecies *C. c. calcifer* is smaller (300mm/12in) and less attractively coloured. It is not certain that this is truly a subspecies.

Distribution
These chameleons originate from The Yemen and Saudi Arabia where they inhabit high wooded plateaux, well-vegetated river banks, lakes, and the hot coastal area. The climate is fairly dry.

Accommodation
Keep this species in a room terrarium or provide a mesh cage of at least 120 x 100 x 100cm (47¹/₄ x 40 x 40in) for one male with up to three females. Ensure adequate ventilation and daytime temperature of 28-32°C (82.4-89.6°F) with 35°C (95°F)

Chamaeleo calyptratus *female.*

under the spot lamps and 18-25°C (64.4-77°F) at night. Cover the bottom with sand and ideally provide ultra-violet light as well. Spray lightly with water every morning for humidity of 50-70%. Mimic a rainy season from April to September by increasing spraying. These chameleons will happily drink water from a water tray. Males are extremely aggressive towards other chameleons and certainly towards other males of their own species.

Feeding
This species is mainly carnivorous and growing specimens and pregnant females can easily manage five prey each day. They will sometimes eat foliage, flowers (dandelions), and fruit (dates and figs). Some experts suggest that *C. calyptratus* needs additional vitamin A so feed grated carrot to the crickets several hours before feeding them to the chameleon.

Mating
Males are usually ready to mate and will display as soon as they see a female. A female which is not prepared to mate changes colour totally to dark green and black with white and yellow flecks.

Egg laying
Eggs are laid 30-40 days after mating in a 30cm (12in) thick layer of moist sand. *C. c. calyptratus* lays 50-90 eggs but *C. c. calcifer* lays only 25-40 eggs. These emerge in 160-170 days if incubated at 26°C (78.8°F) in equal amounts of water and ver-

Young Chamaeleo calyptratus.

miculite. Make the substrate slighter wetter after 21 weeks (rainy season). The young chameleons are 70mm (2³/₄in) long and are green with white flecks. The male spurs are visible immediately on hatching. The female will normally be ready to mate two months after she has laid her eggs in ideal circumstances.

CHAMAELEO HOEHNLII, HELMETED CHAMELEON

Legal status: CITES B.
This species is relatively easy to keep alive but difficult to continue breeding through several generations.

Appearance
The males becomes 200-250mm (8-9³/₄in) long, females 150-200mm (6-8in). The male has a larger helmet on his head and larger protrusion on his nose than the female. The basic colour is olive green and/or brown with males often having yellow and blue tinges. There is a wide divergence in colouring between different populations. Some forms have orange cheeks and others blue heads.

Distribution
Helmeted chameleons inhabit woodland margins, shrubs, and savannah, roadside verges, and in gardens in the foothills and high plateaux of Kenya and Uganda, where there is a big difference between day and night temperatures.

Accommodation
A single chameleon requires at minimum a 50 x 50 x 40cm (20 x 20 x 16in) mesh cage and one of at least 60 x 60 x 80cm (24 x 24 x 31¹/₂in) is required for a pair. These chameleons can be kept outside during summer but ensure a minimum daytime temperature of 26°C (78.8°F) and 16°C (60.8°F) or lower at night. Spray each morning and evening.

Birth
This species retains its eggs in the body and gives birth to its young after a 5-6 months pregnancy. Breeding is reasonably successful but continued breeding through further generations is impossible even with ultra-violet light radiation.

CHAMAELEO JACKSONII, JACKSON'S CHAMELEON

Legal status: CITES B.

A female Chamaeleo hoehnelii *with baby on her back.*

Remove newly born young of Chamaeleo hoehnelii *from the female within one day.*

The information for this species is largely the same as *C. hoehnelii.*

Appearance
The major subspecies *C. j. xantholophus* is the most widely kept. It has a body of maximum 350mm (13³/₄in) long body and a large helmet, low, toothed dorsal comb, and is mainly green. Only the males have three forward-facing horns on the head.

With the other subspecies the females too have horns but these are smaller than with the males. They are more difficult to keep because of the desirable night-time temperature of 4-6°C (39.2-42.8°F) with a drier climate.

Distribution
The four subspecies inhabit the mountain forests up to 3,000 metres in Kenya and Tanzania.

Accommodation
Provide *C. j. xantholophus* with similar accommodation as *C. hoehnellii.* If the chameleon is housed in a terrarium it must be of mesh and at least 60 x 60 x 100cm (24 x 24 x 39³/₈in). These chameleons can be kept as pairs in really large terrariums.

Provide a daytime temperature of 35°C (95°F) with humidity of about 60%. This species needs a sharp drop in night-time temperature to 10-15°C (50-59°F). They can withstand temperatures down to 0°C (32°F). Keep them in an aviary in summer.

Male Chamaeleo jacksonii.

Reproduction

These chameleons mate between January and March at the start of the rainy season. Up to 40 young are born during a lesser rainy season from June to August. Breeding of subsequent generations is equally impossible with this species.

FURCIFER PARDALIS, PANTHER CHAMELEON

Legal status: CITES B.
Synonym: *Chamaeleo pardalis.*
This species is fairly easy to keep and to breed.

Appearance

The colour of this species is extremely variable. The males are usually green but can be brown with white or red flecks. Generally a pale lateral stripe is apparent. They grow to about 500mm (19³/₄in) long and have a small helmet on the head. The females grow about 350mm (13³/₄in) long and are more rounded and yellowish, grey, pink, or purple in colour. The throat pouch between the scales is mainly green with males and red-orange with females.

Distribution

This chameleon inhabits northern Madagascar and several hot island and coastal biotopes (woodland margins, bushes, and arable land) with high humidity. The rainy season is from November to March. These chameleons are found close to humans in all manner of open woodland and scrub but never in large numbers.

Accommodation

This species is pretty aggressive towards other chameleons and is often very active. House only one specimen in a terrarium of at least 50 x 50 x 100cm (20 x 20 x 40in) or several in a room terrarium or conservatory. Make sure there is good ventilation and a temperature of 22-28°C (71.6-82.4°F) and 35°C (95°F) under the spot lamps. Provide lots of lighting for these sun-worshippers and ideally include ultra-violet lighting. Spray at least every morning for humidity of 70-100%. The soil base for egg laying needs to be at least 30cm (12in) deep.

Reproduction

Females that are not prepared to mate immediately adopt a threat stance with opened mouth and puff up their body. Those prepared to mate are not aggressive for about the first three days of mating. The pregnant female assumes a bright colour a few days after mating.

The 16-44 eggs are laid three to six weeks after mating and they emerge after 170-362 days if kept at a constant 26°C (78.8°F). The new-born are dark brown but the males change grey in a matter of days while the females become a bright sandy colour. The tail roots of the males thicken after four months and they also acquire red belly patches. These chameleons become adult after nine to twelve months.

The Cordylidae family, girdled lizards

This South African family comprises about fifty species in ten genera. Most of them have large rectangular scales spread over the body in regular rows.

Appearance

The subfamily Gerrhosaurinae contains among others the genera *Gerrhosaurus* (plated lizards) and *Zonosaurus*. These have plates of bone beneath their skin making them rigidly built. To enable them to expand for breathing, pregnancy, of after eating, they have folds of skin between their

Cordylus giganteus.

Furcifer pardalis.

Gerrhosaurus major.

backs and the sides of their bellies. The head is not prominent and blends with the body.

The tail is rather fragile. The scales often form a line or ridge from front to back. The species of this subfamily lay eggs. The best known genera of the subfamily Cordylinae are *Cordylus* (girdled lizards, all CITESB), and *Platysaurus*. They have clearly separate heads, no folds of skin, and a sturdy tail. The scales are often very spiky or ridged. Almost all of the species (and certainly *Cordylus* sp.) carry their eggs to give birth to young lizards.

GERRHOSAURUS MAJOR, TAWNY PLATED LIZARD

A large sun-loving lizard that can become very tame.

Appearance
This up to 500mm (19³/₄in) long lizard that is yellow to dark brown resembles a skink. Sometime they have lateral black stripes and the males have femoral pores.

Distribution
Plains in East Africa and south-eastern parts of that continent.

Accommodation
Create a 'steppes' terrarium of at least 120 x 40 x 40cm (48 x 16 x 16in) for a pair or trio. Cover the bottom with at least 100mm (4in) of quarry sand for these burrowers. Make hiding places using stones and keep the temperature at 28-35°C (82.4-95°F) and up to 45°C (113°F) under the spot lamps but about 20°C (68°F) at night. Provide them a water tray they can get in completely and spray with water once or twice each week and let the lizards drink the spray water.

Feeding
Mainly feed vegetable matter (sweet fruit), but also insects, small rodents, and tinned pet food.

Reproduction
Breeding rarely succeeds. Mating takes place after six to eight weeks of dry, fairly cool (25-30°C (77-86°F) conditions. In the wild two eggs are laid following mating, usually in and old termite mound.

Gerrhosaurus major.

Basiliscus plumifrons *male.*

The Corytophanidae family, basilisks and related lizards

This Central American family with its three genera are part of the Iguanidae family. The characteristic features of these animals are slender bodies with long tails, long toes, and helmets on the head.

BASILISCUS SPECIES, BASILISKS

Basilisks ability to run on water has earned them the name in some languages of 'Jesus lizards'.

Appearance
Basilisks have flattened sides and are tree dwellers. The males have a large helmet on the head and dorsal and tail comb. There are membranes between their toes to enable them to walk on water and to swim. The body is about one third of their overall length.

Basiliscus basiliscus grows to 800mm (31¹/₂in) and is green-brown with white lateral stripes and dark lines on the flanks. The single helmet protrudes quite high and there are large dorsal and tail combs.

Basiliscus plumifrons, the double-crested basilisk, grows to 700mm (27¹/₂in) long, is bright green with blue-grey points and high dorsal and tail combs and double helmet or crest. [Basiliscus vittatus] is 750mm (29¹/₂in) long when mature and coloured brown. The comb is less pronounced than the other related species.

Pregnant Basiliscus plumifrons *female.*

Distribution

Rain forest in southern Mexico to northern parts of South America, often close to water.

Accommodation

These active lizards demand a rain forest terrarium of at least 150 x 60 x 180cm (59 x 24 x 71in) for three specimens. Provide ample climbing opportunities and a corner with dense and robust planting or artificial plants. Cover the bottom with peat, leaf mould, or beech bark and add a water tray big enough for the lizards to bathe in, ensuring clean water by filtration or fresh water daily, since these lizards usually defecate in the water. Ensure 27-32°C (80.6-89.6°F) with 40°C (104°F) beneath the spot lamps and 20°C (68°F) at night. The humidity should be 70-90% and the water should be heated to 25°C (77°F).

The males are territorial and fleeing animals can injure their mouths in skirmishes in the same way as water dragons, with similar consequences. Basilisks are sometimes combined with red-foot tortoises. Combing them with green iguanas or water dragons can cause stress because of their similar appearance.

Feeding

Feed mainly insects, rodents, and slugs or snails, with some occasional fish, earthworms, cat food, and soft sweet fruit. Provide each specimen with five to ten prey every two to three days.

Sex determination

Males have a higher comb and helmet. These can be damaged or no longer apparent with females following several rough matings.

Egg laying

The female lays four to fifteen eggs several times each year in loose and moist ground of at least 200mm (8in) deep. The eggs hatch after 55 days at 30°C (86°F), 80 days at 26°C (78.8°F) but can take up to 150 days.

Rearing

There are no special problems in rearing the 130mm (5¹/₈in) long offspring. A brood can be housed together for the first few months in a 100 x 40 x 40cm (40 x 16 x 16in) terrarium. Initially the young mainly eat insects and drink sprayed water.

An elderly pair of Basiliscus vittatus.

Less than 2 months old Basiliscus vittatus.

The sexes can be determined after nine to twelve months and they are sexually mature in two to three years.

Buying

Try to buy young captive bred specimens which will adapt better to terrarium life and be less inclined to injure their noses against the sides of the terrarium.

CORYTOPHANUS CRISTATUS, HELMETED IGUANA

Helmeted iguana can remain motionless the entire day so that some become bored with them, leading to neglect and death. Consider carefully before acquiring one. Specimens captured from nature often suffer stress and stop eating.

Appearance

These reddish-brown mottled iguanas have bodies of 100mm (4in) with 250mm (9⁷/₈in) long tails. They have a strikingly large helmet and throat pouches, especially when puffing themselves up when threatened. They also open the mouth when threatened.

Distribution

Rain forests of southern Mexico through to northeastern Colombia.

Accommodation

Housing and care are similar to basilisks but they are less fond of water but do require high humidity.

Reproduction

The males have a thickened base to the tail and larger helmet. These iguanas are rarely captive

Corytophanus cristatus.

216

bred. Clutches of five to ten eggs are laid through-out the year in shallow soil. These hatch in four to five months.

The Gekkonidae family, geckos

Anyone who has visited tropical and subtropical parts may well have seen small lizards catching midges and flies close to a lamp. These are geckos which form a popular family of mainly nocturnal lizards that climb. There are almost 700 species in about 80 genera.

Appearance
Geckos are mainly brown or grey with flattened bodies, large eyes, usually with broad, flexible toes with transverse lamellae which grip surfaces. Instead of acting as suction pads, these have tiny hooks and/or an electrical current to enable geckos to climb and even hang from smooth sur-faces.
The transparent eyelid does not move. Geckos have a long, fleshy tongue with which they lick their eyes clean. The scales doe not overlap each other and the old skin is eaten after it has been shed. Geckos often chirrup, whistle, and bark loudly. The well-known tokay gecko *(Gekko gecko)* and chikchak *(Hemidactylus frenatus)* derives their names from the sounds they make.

Distribution
All manner of tropical and subtropical biotopes.

Accommodation
Provide tall terrariums for climbing species, low ones for ground dwellers. Nocturnal species do not bask in the sun. Heat to 30°C (86°F) with tung-sten filament lamps.

Feeding
Geckos are mainly carnivorous. With the good eyesight, they constantly chase moving prey. Give them varied food but wax moths are a favourite. Many geckos like to lick soft fruit such as a banana, rose-hip syrup, or honey melted in water.

Egg laying
Almost all geckos lay eggs, usually two at a time. These can usually be seen as two bulges in the

Leaf-toed gecko.

Geckos usually lay two eggs each time. These are Phelsuma sp. eggs.

Geckos readily shed their tails (autotomy). This leopard gecko's tail is partly regrown.

female's belly. Many of them stick their eggs to the terrarium decor and rear wall.
Because the egg shells of most geckos only harden some time after they have been laid, they can be deposited in quite inaccessible places. Egg laying geckos need supplementary calcium. Hard-shelled eggs are pretty resistant to changes in temperature and humidity and will often hatch in the terrarium. Do not try to remove eggs that are stuck to some-thing, instead move them, complete with the substrate. Cover eggs left in a terrarium with a small plastic container or mesh (e.g. plastic tea strainer).

Defence and handling
Geckos in particular are quick to eject their tails (autotomy) if they are held. This also occurs in fights between males. The tail grows back in a few months but is shorter and has different scales. Given a chance, geckos will bite when being han-dled.
Their skin is thin and easily damaged.

EUBLEPHARIS MACULARIUS, LEOPARD GECKO

An ideal lizard for beginners.

Appearance
Appearance
The subfamily Eublepharine has movable eyelids and claws instead of hooked lamellae on its toes in contrast with most other geckos.

The leopard gecko (Eublepharis macularius) *on a heat rock.*

The thickened tail base of the male shows up as two small balls, visible behind the cloaca with leopard geckos. The femoral pores are also larger.

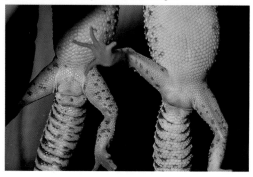

Leopard geckos grow to 250mm (9⁷/₈in) long. They have a white under colour with lots of brown or black flecks and lots of 'warts' on their body. The tail is slightly shorter than the trunk and head together and appears as if segmented. In common with many other ground-dwelling geckos, the leopard gecko is active in the twilight and at night.

Distribution
From eastern Iran through Afghanistan and Pakistan to north-western parts of India in semi-arid biotopes.

Accommodation
Use a 'steppes' terrarium of at least 60 x 30 x 30 (24 x 12 x 12in) for a pair. It is better though to house a larger group in a bigger terrarium. Males are often aggressive towards each other. Provide sufficient hiding places with e.g. pieces of flagstone and cover the bottom with sand. Heat the terrarium to 25-35°C (77-95°F) with a spotlight, tungsten filament lamp, and under-floor heating, reducing to 20°C (68°F) at night. For egg laying provide a tray (either with dark sides or keep it in the dark) with a moist substrate such as sphagnum moss.

Feeding
Feed lots of insects, baby mice and mice, baby rats, and some occasional finely sliced fruit. An adult gecko easily consumes ten insects, three times per week. Feeding of small rodents aids reproduction. There is a big demand for calcium. These geckos are active by twilight and night but can often be seen at feeding time during the day. Provide a water tray.

Sex determination
Adult males have larger pre-anal pores and a swollen tail base (two small balls behind the cloaca) and they are slightly more robustly built with broader heads.

Egg laying
Hibernation at 15-20°C (59-68°F) is not strictly essential. Two eggs with weak shells are laid from five to ten times each year in a moist mixture of peat and sand or sphagnum moss. Remove them regularly and incubate in fairly dry vermiculite. Mainly female offspring hatch after about three months at 28°C (82.4°F) but at 32°C (89.6°F) mainly males hatch after only one-and-a-half months.

Rearing
There are no particular problems in rearing this species. The 70-80 (2³/₄-3¹/₈in) long young geckos eat a lot – about five not too big insects every day. Make sure any crickets that are not eaten cannot grow to become so big that they can harm the geckos by biting them. Young geckos like to lay in a tray with fairly wet sphagnum moss. Sex can be determined after six to twelve months.

GEKKO GECKO, THE TOKAY GECKO

This popular gecko has a powerful bite and does not let go.

Appearance
These 350mm (13³/₄in) long steel blue and grey geckos have orange and pinks spots. From time to time they can be heard making their characteristic 'to-kay' sound from which their name is derived.

Distribution
Originated in South-East Asia but have been introduced to other tropical areas. The tokay gecko lives in buildings and woods and hides by day in holes and cracks.

Accommodation
Provide a high terrarium of at least 50 x 50 x 100cm (20 x 20 x 40in) for a pair. The males in par-

Newly emerged leopard geckos and an egg.

The tokay gecko, Gekko gecko.

ticular are aggressive towards each other. Ensure plenty of things to climb and provide, for example, a 50mm (2in) diameter bamboo or pipe for them to hide in. Make sure humidity if 50-75% with a temperature of 25-35°C (77-95°F), dropping to 20°C (68°F) at night. These nocturnal creatures do not bask in the sun. Place a heat mat for instance against the rear of the terrarium. Tokay geckos are often allowed free run of the house of hobby room but they do not get enough food this way.

Feeding
Food all types of insects and baby mice. Spray with water each evening as tokay rarely drink from a tray.

Sex determination
Males have larger pre-anal pores.

Egg laying
A well nourished female lays eggs about five times each year. The eggs are about 21mm (^{13}/$_{16}$in) and they are stuck to sites throughout the terrarium.
The young hatch after two to six months at 28-30°C (82.4-86°F). The bodies of the young are 50mm (2in) with 40mm (1^{10}/$_{16}$in) long tails that have black and white stripes.

Rearing
Rearing is not difficult and the young become adults in about twelve months.

Defence and handling
Tokay geckos open their mouths and bleat from the day they are born when threatened and once a

little older they will certainly bite if they get the chance if the threat comes closer. Tokay geckos are renowned for this behaviour. Only handle them if strictly necessary wearing gloves for they have a powerful bite and do not easily let go.

PAROEDURA PICTUS
These fairly small ground-dwelling geckos are easy to breed and are enjoying greater popularity.

Appearance
These geckos look rather like a spotted leopard gecko but they are smaller. The males grow to about 165mm (6^1/$_2$in), of which 70mm (2^3/$_4$in) is tail; females 125mm (5in), of which 45mm (1^3/$_4$in) is tail. There are a number of variations in colouring. The species is nocturnal.

Distribution
Forest in the southern half of Madagascar.

Accommodation
A terrarium of 70 x 40 x 40cm (27^1/$_2$ x 16 x 16in) is adequate for one male and several females. The males are aggressive towards one another. Place a dark pot with moderately moist vermiculite in the terrarium for the geckos to lay on and in which to lay their eggs. Cover the bottom with sand to a depth not exceeding 10mm (^{3}/$_8$in) so that the eggs will not be laid in it, making them difficult to find. These (predominantly) nocturnal geckos do not bask in the sun. Heat the terrarium to 25-35°C (77-95°F) dropping to 20-25°C (68-77°F) at night with

Newly-hatched tokay gecko already threatening.

Close-up of a tokay gecko foot with gripping lamellae.

Pair of Paroedura pictus.

Newly hatched Paroedura pictus.

Phelsuma madagascariensis.

a tungsten filament lamp and keep humidity around 60-70%, spraying with water twice each week.

Feeding
Feed mainly insects (crickets for adults). They lick soft fruit from time to time. Provide a shallow dish with water.

Sex determination
The males are larger, have broader heads (35mm/1³/₈in) than the females (18mm/³/₄in), and also a thicker base to the tail.

Mating
Provide a winter dry season at 20-25°C (68-77°F) for winter rest. Mating is quickly over; the females can store sperm with which to fertilize more than one clutch of eggs.

Egg laying
The females lay two eggs with hard shells every two weeks in moist vermiculite, sand, or compost, laying up to 60 eggs each year, so that care has to be taken to avoid the females becoming exhausted. The eggs hatch after 55-60 days at 30°C (86°F) and humidity of 80-90%.

Rearing
The young geckos have bodies 27mm (1¹/₁₆in) long with tails 20mm (³/₄in) long. There are no particular problems in rearing the young provided they can find somewhere moist. These geckos are sexually mature after nine months.

PHELSUMA SPECIES

Legal status: all *Phelsuma* species except *P. guentheri* which is CITES A are CITES B.
The popular *Phelsuma* day geckos are among the most colourful lizards, active by day, and not shy. Most day geckos originate from Madagascar, The Seychelles, and Comoros. Most of them are no larger than 150mm (6in) with *P. madagascariensis* Being one of the bigger species.

PHELSUMA MADAGASCARIENSIS

Appearance
Males grow to 300mm (12in) long, the females to 250mm (9⁷/₈in). Both sexes have a large head with bright green basic colour with white belly and throat. There are a number of bright red flecks and stripes of widely differing form on the side of the

head and body. These flecks are fairly circular in shape, often with a green centre, with the subspecies *P. m. sundbergi*. With *P. m. grandis* (max. 300mm/12in) and *P. m. madagascariensis* (max. 220mm/8⁵/₈in) these markings are irregular, with a green centre. This latter subspecies is slightly more blue than *P.m. grandis* and has a red line on the head running from the nostrils to the eyes. Another subspecies *P.m. kochi* (max. 240mm/9¹/₂in) is darker green and slightly more slender than these other subspecies.

Distribution
The north and east of Madagascar on smooth tree trunks and on leaves in open woodland, and sometimes in houses.

Accommodation
Set up a terrarium at least 40 x 40 x 80cm (16 x 16 x 31¹/₂in) for a pair, with ample smooth vertical things to climb (bamboo without foliage). If these are not available they will rest, sleep, and defecate on the vertical glass panels. Their thin excreta causes a great deal of mess. Bamboo is ideal for egg laying and to provide hiding places. Plant sturdy plants such as *Sanseveria* sp. that have smooth leaves in hydro-culture grains or peat.
The temperature should be 25°C (77°F) with 35-40°C (95-104°F) under the spot lamps. If no branch is placed high in the terrarium directly be-

Terrarium with smooth back wall of bamboo for day geckos.

Phelsuma standingi *with bent tail*.

Phelsuma laticauda.

neath the spot lamps, the geckos will most often hang from the ceiling and get bent tails as a result. Several tubular fluorescent lamps or plenty of daylight ensure healthy plant growth. Keep the terrarium fairly humid (60-80%). Many *Phelsuma* species are often kept too moist. Provide a waterfall and spray the plants with water three times each week and ensure ample ventilation.

To prevent stress put one male and ideally only one female in a terrarium together. *Phelsuma* species can sometimes be combined with other diurnal lizards of a similar size such as agamids.

Other species

Various other species of day geckos are found throughout Madagascar.

– *P. cepediana* (up to 150mm/6in) from Mauritius, likes it moist and hot. The species is dark blue-green with lots of red dorsal flecks.

– *P. laticauda*, 120mm (4³/₄in) long golden day gecko from large parts of Madagascar and Comoros. Keep hot with dry days and moist nights. The neck of this gecko looks as if it has been sprinkled with gold dust.

– *P. lineata*, 120-140mm (4³/₄-5¹/₂in) long, from Madagascar. This species is bright green with red flecks on the back at the base of the tail and often has darker lateral stripes.

– *P. quadriocellata*, up to 120mm (4³/₄in), inhabits eastern, central, and southern Madagascar. Likes

it humid, especially at night, and needs a winter rest at 10°C (50°F). This species has darker flecks surrounded by blue at the back of the front legs, and indistinct red patches on its green back.

– *P. standingi*, up to 280mm (11in) long, from the south of Madagascar likes it continuously dry and hot. These geckos are unremarkable brown in adulthood but are more colourful when young.

Feeding

Feed with insects twice each week (e.g. field collected insects, wax moth caterpillars, fruit flies and other flies and provide fruit (banana) and rose-hip syrup or water sweetened with honey once each week. Do not give too much fatty food (such as crickets) as this cause laziness, slowness, and reduces fertility. Let the geckos go without food for a couple of weeks from time to time. *Phelsuma* species have a major need for minerals and vitamins. Supplement their food by sprinkling a vitamin and mineral preparation on it and sprinkle crushed eggshell, cuttlefish bone, or a calcium additive in the terrarium. It is likely that calcium pouches may be noticed on the necks.

Phelsuma species rarely drink from a water tray. Spray water every day to which, ideally, in addition to vitamins and other minerals, 2ml of potassium iodide has also been added. Iodine is necessary for the production of the hormone thyroxine by the thyroid gland. The hormone is essential for the health and development of the skeleton, skin, and reproductive organs.

Sex determination

The males already have larger comb-like yellow pre-anal and femoral pores at six months and

Phelsuma cepediana.

Phelsuma quadriocellata.

Males have larger femoral and pre-anal pores.

One week old Phelsuma laticauda.

Day geckos skin is easily damaged by handling and like all geckos they quickly shed their tails.

slightly stronger colouring, with marginally wider head and slightly thickened base of the tail. Females have large chalk pouches (thicker cheeks).

Mating

A suitable pair (do not separate once established) will quickly mate and lay eggs following a courtship ritual. If the female flees during the male's biting behaviour she can become injured but the wounds heal quickly.

Egg laying

Females stick two (sometimes only one) hard-shelled round eggs five to ten times every four to six weeks somewhere in the terrarium. When laid the shell of the egg has not hardened and they can be placed in some inaccessible places.

Incubate the eggs, if necessary complete with substrate, at 28-32°C (82.4-89.6°F) and 70-90% humidity. The eggs hatch in about 60 days at 30°C (86°F). It is possible that the higher temperature will produce more male offspring. Eggs left in the terrarium at an average 25°C (77°F) will hatch after about five months. The 40mm (1⁹/₁₆in) long young shed their first skin immediately.

Rearing

The young are relatively safe between bamboo and *Sanseveria* sp. leaves in the parent's terrarium but it is better to rear them in a separate rearing terrarium.

Young *Phelsuma* species day geckos drown very easily in a large water tray. The young start to eat

after three to four days. Pay careful attention to vitamin and mineral supplements.

The young become sexually mature after 1¹/₂ years when they are also less tolerant of their own sex. Do not let young geckos mate too early, instead letting them fully mature first.

Defence and handling

Some species of day gecko can become extremely tame. Most animals though will at first try to escape. Day geckos also bite, though not severely. The thin skin of geckos quickly comes away when they are handled, leaving a visible scar after healing.

STENODACTYLUS PETRII

This small desert gecko can cheep like a mouse.

Appearance

These 100mm (4in) long, sandy-coloured and mottled geckos have no lamellae on their toes.

Distribution

This ground-dweller inhabits semi-desert from Israel to Algeria, where it is nocturnal, except when feeding.

Accommodation

Provide a small desert terrarium of 40 x 30 x 30cm (16 x 12 x 12in) for a small group. Create a temperature gradient with bottom heating and a small lamp of 30-40°C (86-104°F) by day and 20°C (68°F) at night. Create hiding places of flat stones or cork bark.

Stenodactylus petrii.

Feeding

These geckos eat lots of small insects such as crickets, grasshoppers or buffalo larvae fed with apple.

Sex determination

This is difficult with females also have a moderately thickened base to their tail. Acquire about six specimens to overcome this.

Mating

Allow them to hibernate in December and January at 10°C (50°F). They mate from March and egg laying is as *Paroedura*.

The Iguanidae family, iguanas

The Iguanidae family contains some 700 species in about 60 genera and four subfamilies: Iguaninae ('true' iguanas), Anolinae (anoles), Sceloporinae (spiny lizards), and Tropidurinae (lava lizards). These are lizards with striking signals incorporated into their bodies, such as combs, throat pouches (particularly tree dwellers), and helmets. These are usually more prominent with males. These lizards often have characteristic threat behaviour and impose themselves by devices such as head bobbing. The tails are about two-thirds of the overall length. Iguanas have short, thick tongues.

ANOLIS SPECIES, ANOLES

There are about 350 species of this genus, that are

Male Anolis carolinensis.

Male Anolis carolinensis.

mainly small diurnal lizards which are mainly found in southern parts of North America, tropical South America, and the Caribbean. Only a few species find their way regularly to terrariums.

Appearance and distribution

Anoles are slender climbing lizards with gripping lamellae on the claws and feet. They have a limited ability to change their colour. The throat pouch is quite large in males but only really visible when puffed up during display. The tail accounts for slightly more than half of the total length.

Anolis carolinensis, or red-throated anole, from the south-east of the USA (Florida), the Bahamas, and Cuba, is green or brown with an pink-red throat pouch. This inhabitant of trees, bushes, and gardens, grows to 200mm (8in) and it is a well-known 'beginner's lizard'.

Anolis equestris from Cuba and Florida gets to 550mm (21⅝in) long. This species lives in the tree canopy. Scales in the form of green squares reveal yellow skin beneath them which are said to resemble a harness (hence the name). Stressed and otherwise unhealthy specimens are darker in colour. There are yellow and white stripes above the front legs and under the eyes. The throat pouch is usually pink. The males in particular have large heads with a pronounced ridge between the top and sides. Both sexes have a low comb. This species can become very tame. There are many subspecies.

Female Anolis carolinensis.

Adult male Anolis equestris.

Male Anolis sagrei *displaying.*

Anolis roquet summus (newly named *Dactyloa r.s.)* is the best known of the six species of *A. roquet* found on Martinique. These inhabitants of the rain forest grow to 220mm (8⁵/₈in) long. The males are very colourful with an underlying emerald green while the females have lateral stripes.

Anolis (bimaculatus) sabanus is an up to 180mm (7¹/₈in) long lizard from Saba in the Netherlands Antilles. These inhabitants of rocky terrain and tree trunks have brown-black flecks on a light brown base colour that resembles a panther. The throat pouch is yellowish.

Anolis sagrei (no called *Norops s.),* originating from Cuba, Jamaica, Florida, and the Bahamas, is brown with both dark and light-coloured flecks. The females have a yellow dorsal stripe and two brown stripes on the flanks. The stumpy but highly-carried head has a large throat pouch that varies in colour from reddish-orange with a yellow breast to yellow with red flecks. Males grow to 180mm (7¹/₈in) long. females 140mm (5¹/₂in). This bush dweller stays close to or on the ground.

Accommodation

Provide a tall and well planted terrarium with lots of climbing possibilities which must not be smaller than 30 x 30 x 50cm (12 x 12 x 20in) for a pair or trio of small anoles. In order to breed *A. equestris* with one male and three females a terrarium of about 100 x 80 x 150cm (40 x 31¹/₂ x 59in) is ideally needed. The oppressive male then divides his attention be-

Providing a small tray for egg laying is the easiest way to find eggs in a simply furnished terrarium.

tween the females. Introduce all the females to the terrarium at the same time to prevent one of them establishing dominance towards the male which could happen if a new female is introduced.

Cover the bottom with a mixture of peat, sand, or leaf mould, perhaps mixed with sphagnum moss. Make the depth of the soil about half the length of the longest female.

Light the terrarium for 12-14 hours each day, keeping daytime temperatures between 20°C (68°F) and 35°C (95°F) – the hotter area under a spotlight – with humidity of 60-80% (but 80-100% for *A. r. rummus).* Keep the night-time temperature in the range 20-25°C (68-77°F) with humidity of 80-95%. The strongly territorial males will not tolerate each other but the females also need space. Stress resulting from an animal being dominated by another takes time to manifest itself when the animal goes off its food and becomes thin. Place such specimens apart from others.

Anoles can be combined with non aggressive lizards of their own size such as *Phelsuma* species or dif-

Adult male Anolis roquet summus.

ferent colour anoles, but also with small tree frogs (although these eat young anoles). *A. equestris* though is aggressive towards most other fellow inhabitants and smaller ones are likely to be eaten.

Feeding

Feed all types of insects, including spiders. *A. equestris* also eats baby mice and pieces of meat. Provide some soft and sweet fruit from time to time (*A. equestris* eats berries) and water sweetened with honey. Anoles rarely drink from a water tray so spray each day or provide a drip-feed system (see Chameleons). *A. equestris* drinks a great deal.

Sex determination

Males have pre-anal pores and generally have larger display pouches on their throats, thickened base of the tail, and larger body and head.

With *A. equestris*, the young females have yellow stripes on their flanks for the first few months. After this determining sex is difficult. Healthy males of one-and-a-half to two years have a thickened base of the tail (especially during the mating season) and clearly broader head. The males of *A. equestris* finish their head bobbing routine of vertical nods with a side to side movement. The females merely respond to this with a vertical bob of the head.

Mating

Let both *A. carolinensis* and *A. sagrei* have a winter rest of about two months at 20-24°C (68-75.2°F) with the lighting reduced to eight to ten hours each day. Reduce the food and spray twice each week. After eight weeks come slowly out of the rest period and spray every day.

If the winter rest period is given, the male will start to display himself, swaying and showing off his coloured throat pouch before mating. The mating season is usually from May to September.

Egg laying

One or two round eggs are laid every one to five weeks buried in moist loose soil 10-50mm (³/₈-2in) deep, often close to a plant. If the soil is strewn with silver sand it is easy to see when the female digs. Search for eggs when she has hollow sides. If not found seperate the cannibalistic older animals in another terrarium.

The eggs hatch after 40 days at 30°C (86°F) and 70 days at 25°C (77°F). This becomes 70 days at 24°C (75.2°F) and 90 days at 18°C (64.4°F).

Rearing

Raise the young on their own or at most as two in mini terrariums for they are quickly intolerant of each other. Feed them as their parents. A young *A. carolinensis* is 50-60mm (2-2³/₈in) long but they can easily drown in water trays. Spray them with water every day. The young of *A. equestris* are 120mm (4³/₄in) long. The offspring are sexually mature within one year.

CROTAPHYTUS COLLARIS, COLLARED LIZARD

A spirited lizard that has a powerful bite.

Appearance

The subspecies of these 200-350mm (8-13³/₄in) long lizards vary somewhat in colour. The basic colour is green, yellow, or brown. The body is 90-140mm (3¹/₂-5¹/₂in) long and it is often covered with light flecks and darker banding. There is a black and white 'collar' around the neck. These diurnal ground-dwellers have a large head. Collared lizards are shy, nervous, and inclined to bite but can become fairly tame.

Distribution

Semi desert, rocky plains, and open woodland from Utah to Missouri and Texas to Arizona, and northern Mexico.

The thickened base of the tail can clearly be seen with this male Anolis marmoratus.

Young pair of Anolis equestris. *The female has yellow stripes on her sides.*

Accommodation

Provide a large 'steppes' type terrarium of at least 100 x 40 x 40cm (40 x 16 x 16in) for a pair. These lizards run quite a lot. Temperature 25-35°C (77-95°F) with 45°C (113°F) beneath the spot lamps, reducing to 20°C (68°F) at night. The collared lizard is a true sun-worshipper. Provide sufficient hiding places with stones. These lizards can be combined with chuckwallas *(Sauromalus* spp.) in large terrariums.

Feeding

Feed insects, bay mice, some occasional fruit or foliage. In the wild they also eat other lizards, almost as big as themselves. Provide a tray with fresh water and spray each morning.

Sex determination

The male is more brightly coloured, has a larger head, is more heavily built, and has a thicker base to his tail. A sexually mature male has a blue-green or orange throat. Pregnant females have red-orange flecks and stripes on their neck.

Mating

Let them hibernate for two months at 10-15°C (50-59°F). These lizards mate from April to June. Pregnant females display some red colouring on their sides. The males can be aggressive towards one another in the mating season. This species is rarely captive bred.

Egg laying

Four to six eggs are laid twice during the summer in moist sand. Provide the sand in one corner of the terrarium as soon as the female begins to fill out.

Handling

This lizard hops for short distances, even using just its hind legs. Place one hand in front of the lizard and grasp it gently with the other under its belly.

IGUANA IGUANA, THE GREEN IGUANA

Legal status: both *Iguana* species are CITES B.

A widely kept large lizard, renowned for being easy to care for, yet unfortunately too many mistakes are still made (see 'Sickness' earlier in the Lizards section). The main mistake people make is in buying a baby iguana without any idea how big they become.

Appearance

The green iguana grows to 150-200cm (59-78³/₄in) overall with a body of about 50cm (20in) with males and 40cm (16in) with females. It is a diurnal, tree-dwelling lizard. The grey-green animals often have dark banding on their bodies and tails and dorsal combs and on the base of the tail. A large yellow throat pouch hangs beneath the blunt head. There is a very large rounded scale beneath the bottom jaw.

The subspecies *I. i. rhinolopha,* originating to the north of Costa Rica, has two or three soft horns on its nose unlike *I. i. iguana,* which originates to the south of Costa Rica.

Distribution

Central and South America and certain Caribbean islands. This iguana inhabits a range of different biotopes, but chiefly rain forest, especially alongside water.

Accommodation

Bear in mind before buying one that an adult green iguana needs a terrarium of at least 200 x 100 x 200cm (78³/₄ x 40 x 78³/₄in). This is sufficient for one male and two females, with iguanas being group animals. More can be kept together in a larger terrarium. Dominate males are intolerant of other dominant males.

Young green iguanas can be reared in a smaller terrarium. Provide a tall terrarium with plenty of branches to climb. Green iguanas like to rest on a

Pair of Crotaphytus collaris.

Green iguanas have a large throat pouch.

Black iguanas are also green when young.

This looks like a male but is a female.

horizontal branch in the top of the terrarium, close to a spotlight.

Make sufficient hiding places, so that the animals do not continuously see each other. Thick PVC pipes with a plank or some floor covering inside them, or duck shelters are ideal.

The tropical rain forest terrarium must be at least 25-30°C (77-86°F) with localised hot spots of 35-40°C (95-104°F) under pressed-glass spot lamps (at least one per iguana) and night-time temperature of 20-25°C (68-77°F).

This green iguana terrarium takes up a quarter of the hobby room. It is 2 x 1.5 x 2.5 metres (5ft 6in x 5ft x 8ft 2in) and is mainly lit by halogen lamps.

Spray the terrarium and the animals each day throughout the year but not so that conditions remain wet (60-80% humidity by day and 80-100% at night). Create a dry and cooler period from December to April of 30-35°C (86-95°F) by day and 15-20°C (59-68°F) at night.

Provide a large water bowl and clean this out every day, and even better to use a good filter. Heat the water with under-floor heating or a heater in the filter to about 25°C (77°F). Iguanas prefer to defecate above water so bear this in mind when equipping the terrarium! The floor needs to be kept clean, covered with linoleum, tiles, peat, leaf mould, or wood chips. Materials that can be swallowed such as gravel and water-retention granules must on no account be used.

Excessive salts are often sneezed out by iguanas, frequently requiring the glass walls to be cleaned.

Green iguanas can be happily combined with red-footed tortoises, and box turtles *(Terrapene)* from warmer climates. Combining them with double crested basilisks and water dragons can cause stress because of the similar size, colour, and shape.

These animals can be allowed in a heated outdoor terrarium on warm days from May to September. Provided the temperature can be prevented from dropping below 20°C (68°F) they can remain out at night too.

Feeding

Provide as varied a diet as possible, particularly green vegetable matter (60% in the wild), flowers (30%) and fruit (10%). See the main section on Feeding. Strangely enough almost no-one feeds these tree dwellers leaves from trees yet they happily eat willow and other leaves.

Pregnant females have an enormous appetite for the first five weeks of their pregnancy but then eat little or nothing. Feed young iguanas up to two years old and pregnant women with about 15% animal foodstuffs (insects, soaked dried cat food, eggs). Give a maximum of 5% animal foodstuffs to other adults, which prefer a herbivorous diet. Too much animal foodstuff causes kidney problems between the ages of three to seven years.

Sex determination

This is often difficult. Generally the males have a throat pouch that is a third bigger from the age of one to two year, a dorsal comb, femoral pores of 1-4mm ($^1/_{32}$-$^5/_{32}$in) compared with 1mm ($^1/_{32}$in) for females, a thicker base to the tail, broader head, and slightly more dominant behaviour. During the mating season the male is often more intensively red, orange, and golden coloured, especially with *I. i. rhinolopha*. Males are generally bigger.
Subordinate males often resemble females for some time.

Mating

Wild iguanas court and mate with each other at the start of the dry season, often from November to January. They often deviate from this in captivity. If a pair accept each other, mating follows often extensive display with head bobbing. Separation of the male and female can sometimes stimulate mating. Females also attempt from time to time to mate with each other.

Egg laying

Iguanas in the wild lay their eggs in the dry season, from February to April, two to two and a half months after mating. The 20-40 (to a maximum of 80) eggs are laid in a moist sandy soil. In the wild this may often be a river bank or island in a river. Provide a 40cm (16in) deep laying box in the terrarium that is sufficiently large for the female to get into it to bury her eggs. The opening should be narrow (e.g. a pipe) and the box should be heated with an infrared lamp from above or bottom heating to about 30°C (86°F). Fill the laying box with a moist mixture of peat and sand.
Dig the eggs out as quickly as possible. The absence of a good laying box can lead to the females not laying their eggs and serious consequences, including need for an operation, often leading to the female becoming barren, or loss of life.
The eggs can sometimes also be laid in an open container filled with soil and on occasion the female will even drop her eggs from a branch.
Fertilized eggs are about 38 x 27mm ($1^1/_2$ x $1^1/_{16}$in), while infertile ones are sometimes smaller. Eggs placed in water soaked vermiculite (1:1) and incubated at 28-30°C (82.4-86°F) hatch in 65-90 days (can be up to 115 days). A higher temperature produces a larger proportion of males. Hatching in the wild coincides with the rainy season in May and June.

Rearing

Allow young bright green iguanas (about 60mm/ $2^3/_8$in long with 170mm/$6^3/_4$in tail) grow up together in a fairly small terrarium (e.g. 50 x 50 x 100cm/20 x 20 x 40in at first then 100 x 60 x 100cm.40 x 24 x 40). This way they are less shy and are stimulated to eat by seeing others do so. Create resistance to disease by mixing stools from healthy adults or a little garden soil with the food. Wood shavings can lead to intestinal blockages. Try to prevent them growing too quickly. The head and body should be about 150mm (6in) after one year. These iguanas are sexually mature after three to four years but the battle for supremacy starts when they are one year old. Once this is established, the fighting usually ceases. The same is true of new additions.

Defence and handling

Green iguanas that are not used to being handled can slam out with their tails, scratch with their claws, and bite.
Such iguanas need to be handled with leather gloves. It is therefore better to get them used when

Young green iguana.

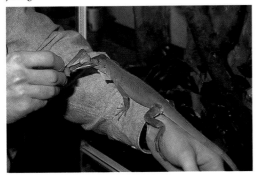

young to human contact. Therefore feed by hand as much as possible.

An untamed semi-mature or adult iguana can only be tames with a great deal of patience and a lot of scratches. When handling an iguana, place it on an arm and hold it at eye level, talking to the animal and gradually loosen your grip. Only return the iguana when it is calm.

PHRYNOSOMA SPECIES, HORNED LIZARD

Legal status: *P. coronatum* CITES B.

The 15 species of *Phrynosoma* (horned lizard) look like a smaller version of the popular bearded dragon *Pogona vitticeps*. Almost all *Phrynosoma* species die within six months. They are listed here because their amusing appearance tempts many beginners into buying them.

Distribution

Horned lizards comes from Central and North America where they inhabit semi-desert, prairie, and open forests.

Feeding

The principal diet of most horned lizards consists of ants and termites. Formic acid appears to play an important role for them in digesting their food.

Recently imported specimens will survive for a few months on a diet of crickets and other insects but will then die, so never buy or sell one.

Phrynosoma platyrhinos, *horned lizard.*

Other care

Since they die other care notes are of no importance.

The Lacertidae family, 'true' lizards

Legal status: many species are CITES A.

This family consists of more than 200 species in 20-25 genera. These are small to medium-sized lizards with typical lizard form.

Appearance

The slim body is almost always shorter than the tail. The body is covered with ridged, flat, or knobbly scales; the head with large bony plates. Lacertidae never possess a dorsal comb or throat pouch. These are diurnal creatures that love to bask in the sun, and they are excellent climbers.

The best known genera are *Lacerta* (Europe, North Africa, and western Asia), *Podarcis* (Europe), and *Takydromus* (South-East Asia).

Distribution

Lacertidae inhabit a wide range of dry biotopes in moderate and subtropical regions of Europe, Africa, and Asia. Certain species are found to within the arctic circle. Both the more aggressive males and the females form relatively small territories which they fanatically defend.

Female Lacerta agilis *of sandy habitats.*

An artificial burrow in a terrarium for Lacerta lepida. The female has laid her eggs under the slate.

Accommodation

A 'steppes'-type terrarium with quarry sand or sandy soil covering the bottom needs to be at least ten times longer than the head and trunk length of the lizards. Create ample hiding places with stones. Daytime temperature should be 23-28°C (73.4-82.4°F) and up to 35°C (95°F) under the spot lamps, dropping to 15-20°C (59-68°F) at night. Let the spot lamps shine for the same length of day as the sun.

Males are extremely intolerant of each other. Larger species are difficult to combine with other terrarium animals. The European and North African species can remain throughout the year in an outdoors terrarium provided a 1m (40in) deep barrel is buried in the ground filled with lava and leaves. The barrel protects the lizards during hibernation against the cold and rain.

Feeding

Provide mainly arthropods (wild collected insects), with larger species also eating small rodents. Many species eat a little fruit from time to time. Provide a water tray and spray water once each week.

Sex determination

Males clearly have larger femoral and pre-anal pores than females, and often have larger heads and sturdier bodies, with a thickening of the base of the tail. They also sometimes have more attractive colourings.

Mating

Mating follows hibernation of two months at 10-15°C (50-59°F) for North African species and 4-10°C (39.2-50°F) for European ones.

Egg laying

Most small species lay two to ten eggs in moist soil once or twice each year. *Lacerta lepida* lays up to twenty eggs. These hatch after two to four months at 25-30°C (77-86°F). *Lacerta vivipara* and certain *Eremias* species carry the eggs in the body and give birth to live young.

Rearing

These lizards can be brought up in groups without any major problems.

Defence

True lizards are all able to shed their tails in danger (autotomy). The tail is regenerated but seldom grows back to the original length.

Handling

Many Lacertidae are renowned for their aggression and powerful bite. Some species. such as the wall lizard *Podarcis sicula* can become quite tame.

LACERTA LEPIDA, OCELLATED LIZARD

The largest European lizard (not yet included in CITES).

Appearance

The head and trunk of the males is up to 200mm (8in) with an overall length of 600-800mm (24-31¹/₂in). Ocellated lizards are mainly olive green with black, marked with two or three rows of round blue flecks.

The closely related *Lacerta pater* grows to 450-550mm (17³/₄-21⁵/₈in), with the females up to 500mm (19³/₄in). They are green-yellow with less distinct blue flecks on their sides. The tail and hind legs are often brown. This species was previously considered a subspecies and they regularly cross breed.

Distribution

Lacerta lepida is active from April to October in the dense undergrowth of the dry hilly regions of the South of France, Spain, and Portugal. *L. pater* originates from Tunisia, Morocco, and Algeria, and is active from February to November.

Mating

Mating follows hibernation. The male often bites the female's hind legs and holds her with his leg over her tail. The female lays eggs up to three times each year.

Rearing

The five to twenty eggs hatch after two-and-a-half months at 27°C (80.6°F). The hatchlings are 50mm (2in) long. Males are sexually mature at two years but the females not until three to four years.

LACERTA VIRIDIS, GREEN LIZARD

Legal status: CITES A.
This slender green lizard grows to 400mm (15³/₄in) of which 250mm (9³/4in) is tail.

Young pair of Lacerta lepida.

The femoral and pre-anal pores of the male are especially large during the mating season.

Lacerta lepida *mating: the male's head is twice as big.*

Distribution
Dense undergrowth in central and southern Europe and Asia.

Sex determination
Males have an enlarged base to their tail. They have blue throats during the mating season but so do the females on occasion.

Egg laying
After hibernation 6–15 eggs are laid several times in spring and summer. These hatch after 45 days at 32°C (89.6°F) and 65 days at 27°C (80.6°F).

Rearing
The young are brown, perhaps with lighter lateral stripes. They are sexually mature after one-and-a-half to two years.

Male Lacerta viridis.

TAKYDROMUS SEXLINEATUS, SIX-LINED GRASS LIZARD

A long and slender lizard that is often kept in conditions that are too damp.

Appearance
These extremely slender lizards have tails of about 300mm (12in) with bodies of 60mm (2³/₈in). The upper side of the body is dark brown or olive green with beige lateral stripes below.

They run rapidly amidst vegetation (grass) and actively hunt. The jaws are regularly licked clean with their long tongue.

Distribution
South-East Asia (Southern China to Java) in hot sunny grassland and open woodlands.

Accommodation
Give these lizards a fairly dry terrarium of at least 100 x 40 x 40cm (40 x 16 x 16in) for a small group of four to six. The general temperature should be 22-28°C (71.6-82.4°F) and several hot dry placed beneath spots of 35-40°C (95-104°F). Cover the bottom with dry quarry sand, sandy soil, or leaf mould and place plenty of plants and grasses for climbing, such as dry clumps of reed or living plants.

These lizards are often kept in marsh terrariums where it is moist and cool. They pine away in such an environment.

A marsh terrarium which has hot dry places higher up i.e. beneath halogen spots is fine. Males are reasonably tolerant of one another.

Feeding
These lizards eat plenty of insects, especially flies and grasshoppers. Fairly large prey are first bitten by the neck before the limbs are torn off and then thoroughly chewed.

Sex determination
A male has a thickened base to his tail, several larger femoral pores, and a slightly broader head.

Egg laying
Females lay a maximum of ten eggs up to six times each year in a moist place.

Rearing
Feed fruit flies and small crickets to the young.

Takydromus sexlineatus.

Young and semi-mature specimens have a greener haze over their bodies.

The Scincidae family, skinks

This family consists of 750 species from about 50 genera, some of which have well-developed legs, others of which have rudimentary legs. The rarely seen skink is often kept in company with another type of lizard.

The best known species are in the subfamilies Scincinae which includes the genera *Chalcides*, *Eumeces*, and *Mabuya)*, and Tiliquinae (giant skinks) including *Tiliqua*.

Appearance
Skinks have a noticeably cylindrical, smooth and shiny body with a pointed nose and tail. The tongue is slightly forked at the front. Many skinks are shy and often crawl covered by sand. There are often scales like a comb covering the ears, to prevent sand entering.

Distribution
They inhabit all manner of biotopes in Africa, Australia, Asia, America, and Europe. They are chiefly ground-dwellers.

Accommodation
Provide a 'steppes' terrarium that is at least five times as long as the head and trunk of the lizards, with a thick covering of sand on the bottom. Keep one side of the bottom slightly moist. The males of certain species are less tolerant towards each other, especially in the mating season.

Reproduction
Skinks do not have femoral pores. Males have a slightly broader head and sometimes have stronger colours. If in doubt the hemipenis can be popped out. About a third of the species carry their eggs and give birth to live young. Rearing skinks holds no special problems.

EUMECES SCHNEIDERI AND EUMECES ALGERIENSIS

Schneider's skink *(E. schneideri)* and the Berber's skink *(E. algeriensis)* are popular large skinks. Until recently the Berber's skink was considered a subspecies of *E. schneideri (E. s. algeriensis)*.

Appearance
These species grow to 400mm (15³⁄₄in) long, of which more than half is tail.

Mabuya *species from Chad.*

Eumeces schneideri.

Eumeces schneideri: *the missing tail was bitten off by a bearded dragon.*

There are orange, yellow, and small black markings across the body on the grey-brown upper side of the body. The underside is plain pale yellow.

E. schneideri has a yellow stripe on each side, from cheek to tail. With *E. algeriensis* the stripe is missing. This latter species also has black scales with white flecks in them, whereas *E. schneideri* does not have these markings.

Distribution
Eumeces schneideri has seven subspecies found from north-west India to eastern North Africa. *Eumeces algeriensis* originates from Morocco and Algeria. These species inhabit hot, dry, sandy areas, with and without rocks.

The other *Eumeces* species are found in semi-arid areas of Southern Asia, North Africa, plus Central and North America.

Accommodation
Provide a desert terrarium of at least 100 x 40 (40 x 16in) on the bottom, with 50-100mm (2-4in) sand covering, for a pair. These species often lay beneath the sand but are often to be seen. The temperature should range from 25-45°C (77-113°F), with 17-23°C (62.6-73.4°F) at night. In addition to a spotlight, place gentle under-floor heating to recreate the heat of the desert sand as it warms up in the sun.

Males compete unbearably strongly with each other for females during the mating season so only put one male in each terrarium.

Feeding

All manner of insects, baby mice, canned pet food, and occasional sweet soft fruit, such as banana or mango.

Sex determination

Females are somewhat less brightly coloured while males are more heavily built, with sturdier heads.

Mating

Mating follows two or three months hibernation at 10-20°C (50-68°F) during the day and 10-15°C (50-59°F) at night, with six to eight hours lighting. Males fight to mate and females can be seriously wounded in the neck as a result of heated males. These skinks mate a number of times each day over a few weeks. Remove the male once a number of successful matings have occurred.

Egg laying

After carrying them for six to seven weeks, the female lays five to twenty eggs in a hole and remains with them for a time to guard them. She also moistens them by urinating on them. Remove the eggs quickly because they can be eaten by skinks. The eggs hatch after seven to ten weeks following incubation at 28-30°C (82.4-86°F).

Rearing

The 130mm (5¹/₈in) long hatchlings eat a smaller version of their parents' food. These skinks are rarely bred in captivity and therefore little is known about rearing them.

Defence and handling

These skinks can give a hard bite during handling of them. Do not pull away but wait for the skink to release its grip.

It is quite possible to get these skinks used to people by letting them eat out of the hand and to run along one's arm.

MAYBUYA SPECIES

A widely kept genus but one about which little is known.

Appearance

Mabuya species are variable in colour, 200-300mm (8-12in) long, and typical skinks. These are ground-dwellers that are often good climbers, but generally shy creatures.

Eumeces schneideri *mating.*

Distribution

Eighty species inhabit every manner of mainly dry biotope, except desert and thick forest, in South-East Asia, Africa, and tropical parts of the America continent. *Mabuya perodetti* originates from Tanzania where it often lives in proximity with humans.

Accommodation

Provide a fairly dry terrarium of at least 100 x 40 x 40cm (40 x 16 x 16in), with ample hiding places and things to climb. Cover the bottom with quarry sand or dandy soil and ensure the rear wall has a texture or construction that they can climb. Temperature should be 25-40°C (77-104°F) and 20°C (68°F) at night. Spray two to three times each week.

Feeding

Insects including spiders, and sweet soft fruit such as bananas.

Sex determination

Males are more colourful than females, although some females can resemble males in colour. If doubtful pop the hemipenises.

Reproduction

Egg laying species bury 15-30 eggs in moist ground but some species carry their eggs until birth. The hatchlings are 80-100mm (3¹/₈-4in) long and very colourful.

Male Mabuya perodetti.

Female Mabuya perodetti.

Female blue-tongued skink, Tiliqua gigas.

Young Tiliqua scincoides.

TILIQUA SCINCOIDES AND T. GIGAS, BLUE-TONGUED SKINKS

Legal status: CITES D for both species.
Popular large skinks that are often tamed.

Appearance
Blue-tongues are heavily built, with short, stout limbs and a large head. *Tiliqua scincoides* has same colour legs and back, but *T. gigas* is slightly larger (max. 500mm/20in) with black legs and golden or silver backs. Both are cross-bred. *T. scincoides intermedia* has clearer brown stripes on light brown. Difficult to differentiate these species.

Distribution
T. scincoides from semi-desert in Australia, *T. gigas* from Irian Jaya.

Accommodation
Provide a dry 'steppes' type terrarium of at least 150 x 50 x 50cm (59 x 20 x 20in) with a moister corner for a pair or trio. Cover the bottom with sand, which can be mixed with bark, or moss. Ensure ample hiding places for this fairly shy animals. Temperature about 30°C (86°F) to 40°C (104°F) under pressed-glass spot lamps, reducing to about 20°C (68°F) at night. These skinks need to have a large water tray to bathe in.

Feeding
All types of fruit, insects, small mice, baby rats, and slugs or snails. Fruit and vegetables can be mixed with tinned cat food. Those that stop eating will often eat custard!

Female Tiliqua scincoides intermedia.

Sex determination
This is difficult. The male has a slightly thicker base to his tail and marginally broader head.

Reproduction
These skinks carry their eggs to give birth to six to twenty young, following hibernation at 15-20°C (59-68°F). Provide the young skinks with the same food as their parents but in smaller form.

The Varanidae family, monitors

Legal status: four species including *V. komodoensis* and *V. griseus* are CITES A, the remainder are CITES B.
This family comprises just the one genus: *Varanus.* The 30 species are all protected for both the animals and their eggs are eaten and their skin and limbs are used for medicines and amulets. Although their care is fairly straightforward, only specialist should take on the keeping of these animals. The family and species name is derived from El Quaran, the Arabic for lizard.
The best known is the Komodo dragon, *V. komodoensis*, that grows to 3 metres (10ft) long, and weighs 150kg (330lb).

Appearance
Monitors are imposing creatures of 150mm-4m (6in-13ft) long, with *V. salvator* being the largest. These lizards have long, almost entirely rounded

The Komodo dragon, Varanus komodoensis, *can be seen at some zoos.*

tailed. This is flattened at the side with species that spend much of their time in water to help them swim. The strong limbs have sharp claws. Characteristic features are a long neck with large pointed head that has visible openings for the ears. Monitor lizards taste the air with their forked tongues in the same way that snakes do. In common with snake, the monitors have no bladder. Some lizards of the Teiidae family from America resemble small monitors.

Distribution
These lizards are found in various biotopes in Australia, Africa, and southern Asia.
- *V. giganteus*, *V. griseus*, and *V. gouldi* inhabit deserts and arid plains
- *V. niloticus*, *V. salvator* and *V. indicus* are semi-aquatic
- *V. exanthematicus* and *V. komodoensis* inhabit dry plains and open woodland
- *V. prasinis* lives in trees.

Accommodation
Create a terrarium that is appropriate for the biotope that is at least six times the head and trunk length long and three times as wide of the species to be housed. Keep temperature in the range 25-35°C (77-95°F) with 45°C (113°F) under the spot lamps but reduce to 20-25°C (68-77°F) at night. Use quarry sand or sandy soil and keep humidity at 60-70% for dry biotopes and a bark/peat mixture and humidity of 70-90% for moister biotopes,

Varanus gouldi.

Varanus indicus.

Savannah monitor just before mating. The male has the raised head.

A bare vinyl or linoleum covered floor is easier to keep clean. Provide at least one hideaway per animal and as large a water area as possible because monitors bathe, swim, and often flee into water. Keep the water clean and hygienic by regularly replenishing it and filtration. Do not put sand at the bottom of an aquarium area.

The territorial males cause each other stress. Watch the animals closely for many days to make sure occupants get along with each other.

Feeding
Monitors are carnivores with huge appetites (rodents, insects, tinned pet food, meat, eggs, poultry) but take care not to overfeed. They will eat all manner of prey, whether it will fit their mouths or not. Semi-aquatic species also eat crustaceans, fish, and other aquatic creatures.

Prey are gobbled in large chunks or whole with the backward facing teeth.

Sex determination
This is difficult, with males sometimes being recognizable by their slightly broader head and thickening of the base of the tail. When handled, males often eject their hemipenises. Monitors are sometimes sexually determined by popping their hemipenises.

Mating
The presence of a second male and/or ritual fight between them will sometimes stimulate mating. Take care though that the males do not kill each other and never leave them alone together. The female is not always bitten in the neck during mating. The female seeks somewhere to lay her eggs one to two months (sometimes longer) after mating. The pregnant female eats little or nothing for the final month before laying her eggs.

Egg laying
Monitors lay 5-65 eggs in a warm burrow (under a lamp) which they cover with plant material. The eggs are naturally incubated by the heat of rotting vegetation. The eggs are sometimes laid in a (hot) termite mound. They hatch in the rainy season, when the soil is soft. Sometimes the mother comes to give help them. Incubated at 28-32°C (82.4-

Young Komodo dragon.

Pair of Varanus exanthematicus.

Young savannah monitor, Varanus exanthematicus.

89.6°F) with humidity of 80–90%, the eggs usually hatch in 130-220 days, though they can take just 70 days. Eggs that over-winter in the wild only hatch after 220-330 days. At 28°C (82.4°F) the brood mainly comprises males, while at 32°C (89.6°F) there are more females than males.

Rearing
Young monitors grow rapidly. Provide them with sufficient hiding places to prevent stress. It is preferable to rear them separately. Monitors are sexually mature after two to five years.

Defence
The larger monitors in particular have powerful jaws and can cause severe wounds with their long teeth and their long, sharp claws can rip through any type of skin. When they fight they strike out with their tail which cannot be ejected, as there is no mechanism to do so. They use defecating and vomiting as defence and threaten by blowing through their wide open mouths.

Handling
Many monitors can be readily tamed if they become accustomed to people when they are young. Do not trust them though. Every monitor can suddenly attack without warning, even when it has been 'tame' for years.

VARANUS EXANTHEMATICUS, THE SAVANNAH MONITOR

Legal status: CITES B.
Savannah monitors are often offered for sale and fairly inexpensive.
The subspecies *Varanus exanthematicus exanthematicus, V. e. angolensis,* and *V. e. microstictus* are differentiated by the number of scales on the back, throat, and belly, and the manner in which they lay. *V. (e.) albigularis* (with white throat) is now regarded as a species in its own right.

Appearance
This species readily grows to 1.5m (5ft) long and is grey-brown with rows of flecks, with large, rounded scales on the neck. The nostrils are immediately in front of the eyes.

Distribution
This inhabitant of dry steppe and savannah inhabits much of Africa south of the Sahara, but not the West African rain forests.

Egg laying
Offer the female an egg box 1m (5ft) deep, filled with loose and moist quarry sand or sandy soil. Savannah monitors lay 15-45 eggs in a chamber about 50cm (20in) deep. If there is nowhere for the female to bury her eggs she will scatter them throughout the terrarium so that they may well be eaten.
Incubate the eggs in vermiculite mixed with the same volume of water at 27-32°C (80.6-89.6°F). They hatch in 180 days at the lower temperature to 140 days at the higher end.

Rearing
The hatchling are 150-200mm (6-8in) long and they start to eat about one week after hatching. They become sexually mature after three to four years.

VARANUS NILOTICUS, NILE MONITOR

Legal status: CITES B.
The Nile monitor becomes a large, self-assured animal so that it can readily become aggressive. Think carefully therefore before deciding to acquire these cute, spotted animals as young specimens.

Appearance
This approx. 2m (6ft 6in) long species is dark in colouring (green, grey, black, or brown) with light diagonal banding. The nostrils are midway be-

Young Varanus niloticus.

Young Varanus niloticus.

Two-year old Nile monitor threatening.

tween the tip of the nose and the eyes. Young specimens are black with rounded pale yellow spots over their entire body. The head is slender, particularly with males, but more stout when fully-grown. The tail is about 60% of the body length.
The subspecies *V. n. niloticus* generally has seven pale diagonal markings on the back and a black tongue, while *V. n. ornatus* has five bands and a pink tongue. Both subspecies share certain characteristics.

Distribution
Nile monitors inhabit virtually the whole of Africa except the north-west. This fairly aquatic species can remain under water for an hour. *V.n. ornatus* from the West African coastal region generally inhabits forests and prefers higher humidity and cooler temperatures than *V. n. niloticus* of more open habitats. They are good climbers.

Mating
Nile monitors are very aggressive towards one another. It is often not possible to keep a male and female together. Only put them together for mating. Specimens from close to the equator mate throughout the year but those from southern Africa mate chiefly in June and July.

Rearing
The hatchlings are 200-300mm (8-12in) long and they emerge after 130-220 days. They become sexually mature after about three years when they are about 1m (40in) long. Young Nile monitors easily become distressed and need to be separated quickly from each other.

The suborder Serpentes, snakes

Snakes are elongated reptiles without limbs. Certain primitive snakes (e.g. some of the giant constrictors) still have remains of a pelvic ring and 'spurs' that appear as remnant claws to the side of the cloaca.
Thanks to their 160-435 vertebrae, snakes are extremely flexible in their movements. Snakes crawl along with their belly scales of by pushing bends in their body against the surface over which they are moving. The tail is usually quite short, with heads being either indistinctly or clearly delineated from the rest of the body. Snakes are often classified according to the type of teeth they possess.

Eating prey
Most snakes kill their prey either by suffocation or with venom. The constrictors squeeze tighter as their victim breathes out and then cannot breathe in again so that it suffocates. Venomous snakes bite their prey in a rapid movement and then follow the prey by scent until it dies, if it runs away. Smooth prey such as new-born mice, fish, amphibians, and earthworms are often swallowed while still alive. Snakes can dislocate their bottom jaw from the top because of a bone linking the two

A Burmese python eats a rat.

jaws. The combination of this bone, independently moveable left and right-hand halves of the lower jaw, bulging windpipe, and 'floating' ribs which move aside, make it possible for a snake to ingest large prey.

Senses

The eyelids have grown to a static transparent membrane (or spectacle). A few days before the skin is shed, a discharge of fluid separates the old spectacle from the new membrane, giving the eye a blue-white appearance. Try not to disturb the snake with its poor sight at this time, do not feed it, and keep the terrarium sufficiently humid. Snakes do not have ear openings and have no ear drum, so that they are deaf. They can sense vibrations, particularly those through the ground. They taste the air with their forked tongue and specialized scenting Jacobson's organ in the roof of their mouth.

Some large constrictors have heat sensitive lip 'grooves' and blood vessels with extremely heat sensitive sensors between nostrils and eyes which enable them to detect tiny temperature changes in their vicinity, so that they can sense a prey in the dark.

Except with certain large constrictors, there is only one lung, with the right-hand lung having more

or less atrophied. Snakes can remain under water for around half an hour, thanks to an air supply in the rear, bag-like half of the lung. The right-hand half of all other paired organs are also reduced in size.

Distribution

The 2,700 species of snake are found throughout the moderate and tropical climate zones throughout the world in all manner of biotopes.

Accommodation

There are a number of basic requirements for a snake terrarium or vivarium.
- Ground-dwelling and climbing snakes need either a bottom surface at least three quarters to one times their length or a similar dimension for the diagonal height.
- Ultra hygienic conditions! Clean the water tray every day and remove excreta as quickly as possible. Snakes drink a lot. If their resistance is lowered for some reason, snakes can quickly suffer from mouth decay (a bacterial infection) in a dirty terrarium. Clean out the entire terrarium several times each year.
- A water area preferably at least large enough for the snake in its entirety to bathe in. Many snakes bathe before they shed their skins or if the terrarium is too hot. The water container must be heavy enough to prevent the snake from turning it over.

The bone linking the jaws helps snakes to dislocate their jaws to swallow large prey.

Terrarium with Burmese pythons.

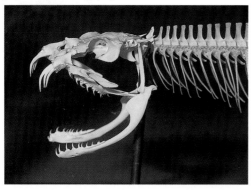

Blue-white eyes and dull colouring indicate a snake is about to shed its skin.

238

- An easily cleaned or replaced bottom substrate such as wood shavings, wood chips, leaf mould, peat, tree bark, or newspaper.
- Sufficient hiding places such as wooden boxes, upturned flowerpots, or a drawer in the base of the terrarium (accessible through a hole in the bottom).
- Snakes generally prefer a moderately humid climate with a dry place under an inaccessible spotlight above or under-floor heating. If the temperature is too hot, snakes will spend much of their time in the water tray.
- Good ventilation through grilles at the top of the terrarium, prevent draughts which are often caused by having one ventilation grill in the front of the terrarium and a second in the top.
- Provide several branches for the snakes to climb, even for those that rarely do. These need to be horizontal for tree-dwelling snakes. Climbing branches and other decorative material help snakes to shed their skin by being able to rub against them.
- Perfect seal of the terrarium since snakes can escape by the smallest of apertures and sliding doors that are not wholly closed. Escaped snakes create a degree of panic and ideal fodder for the tabloid press ('Baby-eating boa escapes'), which is not the image the hobby needs. Sliding doors are the best to use with snakes however because they create less stress for them than a top opening access.

Most species of snakes are not aggressive towards other snakes of a similar size but it is best to keep them apart during feeding. Snakes are sometimes kept on their own and only introduced to a potential mate a few days or weeks before the mating time.

Feeding

Feed one to two prey each week, although large constrictors may eat just one large prey every three to four weeks. Feed fish-eating snakes two or three times each week. Do not feed just before the skin

A Burmese python strangles a rat.

Provide a water tray large enough for the snake to get in.

is shed or during a resting period. Increase feeding to females during the mating season and after they have laid their eggs. Pregnant females sometimes eat little or nothing.

Do not feed prey that are thicker than the thickest part of the snake. If smaller prey are fed then the frequency of feeding can be increased. This can be beneficial with snakes that present difficulties in getting them to eat. A snake may not eat for a long time after swallowing a large or too big a prey.

Feed live, thawed, or newly-killed prey (e.g. rodents). The last of these methods eliminates any risk of injury for the snake and retains the maximum nutritional value. Freezing of prey is useful for times when no other source is available.

Feed snakes by preference apart from each other. Prevent two snakes from both starting to eat the same prey. Control feeding by keeping the snakes apart. Do not remove the hand if a snake bites for this pulls the teeth through one's skin, making the bite worse for yourself and probably injuring the snake too. Snakes that do not let go can be forced to do so by holding them under water or by pressing a wad of cotton wool soaked in medicinal alcohol against their nose.

Snakes sometimes refuse to eat other food than they are accustomed to (live or dead, the type of food, quality, or even colour of a prey). They can sometimes be introduced to new food by gradually increasing its content with their customary food, by placing them with another snake that is eating, or offering the dead prey with its brains or belly split open.

Snakes can refuse to eat because they are stressed (insufficient hiding places, or wrong humidity), ill (e.g. vitamin deficiency), are too cold, or being fed at the wrong time of day.

Snakes excrete between seven to fourteen days after eating. Indigestible remains such as hair and claws are ejected but bones are digested. Concentrated urine is discharged as a firm- pale yellow substance.

Sex determination

- Fully-grown females are often larger than fully-grown males and have a shorter tail but this is an unreliable characteristic.
- In common with lizards, male snakes have a thickening at the base of the tail whereas the tail immediately narrows with females. This is often only apparent by direct comparison from beneath. With some species such as the ball python this cannot be wholly relied upon.

Take care to prevent two snakes starting to eat the same prey. Here young yellow and red ratsnakes have one baby rat between them.

Probing a ball python.

- The hemipenises are located with male snakes at the base of the tail. These are elongated narrow organs which can be pushed outwards by the swelling immediately behind. This turns them inside out so that the barbs on the hemipenis come to sit on the outside.

Female snakes have a shallow, wide cloaca in which a matching musk gland is housed. Sex can be determined on this basis by probing. While a second person subdues the snake, a blunt probing needle can be introduced carefully to the left of right of the cloaca, in the direction of the tail. The probe must first be sterilized with 70% proof alcohol and coated with a medical lubricant. Udder ointment and other wound salves are suitable. The needle probe can be pushed further (into the hemipenis) with males. Depth of insertion is measured against the number of scales below the cloaca. Males sometimes squeeze their hemipenises closed which prevents probing or makes it appear to be female. There may also be other matter in the penis duct that gives the same result.

Males have thickening o the base of the tail. This is Elaphe obsoleta quadrivittata.

Counting the scales after probing. Two scales make this a female.

Probing is a reliable but risky method of determining sex. If the snake twists or is pushed too hard it can be seriously injured internally. An infection of the cloaca is also very difficult to heal. **Learn to probe under expert guidance (or have it done by an expert).** Only probe with a special probing needle and never with a paper clip or such like.

– Young snakes must not be probed for safety reason but can be 'popped' at two months old. Lay the snake on its back over a finger with the cloaca in line with the finger. Try to push a possible hemipenis out by pressing carefully from the rear towards the front. This requires caution to prevent injury to the spinal column. If a hemipenis pops out the snake is definitely male. If not it is probably (but not certainly) female. Learn this too from an experienced person.
– With large constrictors the spurs (remnants of legs) are clearly longer with males than females.
– If a thumb presses from the cloaca towards the tip of the tail, the hemipenises can sometimes be felt plopping back. This method is more difficult and less reliable.

Mating

Snakes mate with and without stimuli such as hibernation or the rainy season. Males may stop eating once they are ready to mate. Females usually eat more than usual. In the mating season snakes become restless and often react jerkily towards each other. Many snakes mate after the female has shed her skin.

Mating snakes lay alongside each other and entwine their bodies, with the male sometimes rubs the front of his body over her back. He twists her to left or right to access her tail, find her cloaca, and penetrate her with one half of his hemipenis.

Egg laying

Several weeks or months after mating the eggs are usually laid in a hole or crack. Provide an egg-laying tray in ample time, filled with crumbled peat, sphagnum moss, or leaf mould. The lack of a suitable place to lay her eggs results in a clutch of dried up eggs.

Yellow ratsnake mating.

Several weeks before the eggs are laid, the female often stops eating, sheds her skin, seeks out a warm spot, or adopts different body positions. She then crawls away to some moist ground. After laying the eggs, the female often stays close by for a few days. Watch out each day very carefully whether there are eggs and lay them, without turning them, in an incubator. Leave any eggs that are stuck together as they are but empty any dead or unfertilized eggs with a syringe.

Elaphe guttata *laying her eggs.*

It can take some time after the first hole is cut with the egg tooth before the young hatch. Do not disturb them.

Hatchlings of Elaphe guttata.

Eggs and a single rearing container in an incubator.

Incubation
See 'Incubation of reptile eggs'. Make sure the incubator is entirely escape-proof.

Rearing
Hatching snakes first make a hole in the egg with their 'egg tooth'. Do not disturb them too much or they may not hatch. It can take two weeks with some species before the hatchlings emerge from the egg.

Place the newly-hatched snakes in a plastic container ($^1/_2$-5 litres) with some kitchen roll, a small water tray, somewhere to hide, and a few pieces of lava for them to rub their skins against. Put the containers at about 30°C (86°F) and a high humidity (for better skin shedding, less risk of drying out), and replace the water and paper every day. By housing each young (nervous and quick to bite) snake individually, it is easier to keep an eye on each of them, although it is more time consuming. The young snakes usually shed their skins after one week and up to this point they eat virtually nothing. From then on they can be offered day old mice, earthworms, pieces of fish, or other small prey. Some snakes eat immediately the day after they shed their skins, others not for one month. The water tray is removed during feeding because baby mice etc. quickly drown. Write the date on the container and ring this around if the prey is eaten or cross it through if not. Once they have eaten three times, the young snakes can be sold after their sex has been determined by 'popping' or

Ticks are found first in the water bowl.

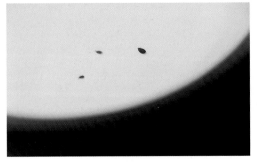

added to others of the same sex in a larger terrarium (30 x 40 x 50cm/12 x 16 x 20in) with hiding places, water tray large enough to bathe in.

Those that refuse to eat can sometimes be helped with dead prey that has the brain exposed or by placing them in a very small container with their prey. Many *Lampropeltis* species among others eat lizards. Their offspring will sometimes only eat baby mice if they have first been scented by rubbing them against a lizard.

Forced feeding
In extreme cases if the snakes will not eat after the first skin shedding or they are visibly wasting away, they can be force fed. Take a dead prey that has been made smooth with plastic forceps holding the snake behind the head and very patiently work the food into the upper and larger opening in the mouth (the smaller opening at the bottom of the mouth is the windpipe). Massage the prey along the snake, while keeping its mouth held shut, until it reaches about one third of its length. Sometimes the snake starts to eat after being force fed, sometimes it takes ten times to do so, and sometimes it never eats.

Illness
Read pages 193-197 about sickness.

A healthy snake
– Feels powerful rather than limp (especially the

Support a snake in sufficient places and hold it firmly behind the head if it bites.

Handling with a snake hook.

Handling with a snake hook.

constrictors), and does not have a swollen appearance
- Has a rounded back running along the ridge
- Tastes the air frequently and rapidly with its tongue, especially if something is held in front of it
- Has a mouth that closes properly
- Has undamaged and smooth skin without remnants of an old skin or open scales
- Has a clean cloaca
- Sheds its skin in one piece and within one hour
- Has clear eyes without indentations
- Rests coiled up not stretched out.

Fish eating snakes can suffer from vitamin B1 deficiency.
A snake with blue-white eyes is about to shed its skin. It does not eat and does not want to be disturbed. Shedding can give problems in a terrarium that is too dry and vitamin A deficiency can also lead to problems with shedding. Bathe snakes that are shedding poorly in luke-warm water, moisten the terrarium, and provide if required vitamin A (consult a vet).
Drying out can be spotted by a recessed eye membrane. Snakes can easily burn themselves on heat rocks or lamps that they can reach in the terrarium. Burnt scales turn black. The paramyxo virus can sometimes be detected through signs of cramps and the snake not holding its head straight. In this case the snake tastes the air slowly with its tongue and without aim. This can lead to the scales standing up and the snake drying out. The big snakes are particularly susceptible for this, ratsnakes less so, and garter snakes probably not at all. Remove the snake immediately from a group and try to keep the others in good condition by giving vitamin B complex, force feeding if necessary, and getting the vet to inject fluids. There is no medicine for this virus, it depends entirely on the snake's own immune system.

Handling
- Hold non aggressive and non venomous snakes loosely with both hands, with its weight distributed between both hands.

- Hold aggressive or unknown non venomous snakes quickly as close to the head as possible without pressing too hard, if necessary placing the thumb and third finger behind the jaws, with the index finger on the head. Indecisive movements attract defensive actions. Use a towel or snake hook if a quick decisive action does not succeed.
Then hold the snake by its middle and only then to pick it up. The connection between the first neck vertebrae and the head are easily injured if the head is picked up too quickly by its head. Handle really large snakes with one person per metre (40in) of snake.
- The neck of small snakes can be broken if the are picked up by the head. They must be held by several fingers in the middle.
- Snakes can bite when being fed. If this occurs do not pull the hand away. A bite is rarely painful, hardly bleeds, and except for venomous snakes does not cause poisoning. Many snakes form an S-shape with their head and neck when they feel threatened and just before they strike, often with vibrations from their tail.
- Escaped snakes can be enticed into a box filled with moist leaf mould, especially if a dead prey is placed inside on a heat mat. Check each morning if the snake is in the box.
- If the snake's mouth has to be opened, push a pencil or lollipop stick in the tongue opening and then push the stick at a slant into the back of the mouth as soon as the snake opens its mouth. The prominent windpipe can be clearly seen. This enables the snake's health to be checked and medicine can be administered with a long lubricated silicon probe. Real refusal to eat (some snakes naturally eat nothing for a couple of months) can be overcome by forced feeding in this manner with small prey. Smear the prey with low viscosity petroleum jelly or water. Put everything needed for treatment to hand before carrying out this action.

Transport
Larger snakes are best placed in a linen sack or pillow slip which is then immediately tied with rope

Venomous Mexican mocassin snake.

while the snake is in the bottom of the sack. Carry small snakes in plastic containers packed with absorbent paper.

Venomous snakes

Only 10% of all snakes are venomous, making 250-300 species. About 1,500,000 people are bitten by venomous snakes each year of which between 30,000 and 40,000 die.

Venomous snakes strike with lightning speed, biting their prey which dies later with the digestive process already under way.

Not all venomous snakes are equally deadly.

Because of my limited experience in this area I cannot assume responsibility for comprehensive advice and restrict myself to some general tips.

– Handle every unknown snake as a venomous snake. In other words do not handle it at all and call the police. Venomous snakes can bite through gloves and linen sacks. Some even bite through their own lower jaw.

An expert will use a snake hook and keep his hands well away from the snake. If necessary he will carefully press the snakes head against the ground with a special snake hook and then firmly grasp the head at the side and top.

– Do not put your faith in the species name given to a snake for e.g. a shipment from overseas.

– Some venomous snakes (e.g. rattlesnakes) bear their eggs and give birth to live young. Enthusiasts have been surprised by a bite by an undis-

covered offspring.

– Some venomous snakes are extremely inexpensive. Do not give in to an impulse to buy. Holding a venomous snake puts others in danger as well as yourself.

There are of course people who very responsibly care for, breed, and distribute venomous snakes.

– Laws vary throughout Europe but a licence and approval is required from your local authority in Britain to keep a dangerous animal.

– Make sure that the snakes can be shut away in e.g. their hiding place, separated from the main part of the terrarium, so that it can be safely cleaned out.

– Lock the doors and make sure the family knows what to do in an emergency.

The Boidae family, large constrictors

Legal status: a few species are CITES A, with the rest being CITES B.

Large constrictors are mainly nocturnal snakes which strangle their prey. These snakes have a pair of lungs and often have spurs (residual limbs) next to the cloaca.

The best known subfamilies are the Boinae (boas and anacondas), and the Pythoninae (pythons). These snakes are often camouflaged with various shades of brown, black, and pale yellow. Pythons have two rows of subcaudal scales below the cloaca, boas just one. Snakes of both families have large teeth.

Distribution

Boas and anacondas originate from the New World (South and Central America) and pythons from the old world (Africa, Asia, and Australia).

Accommodation

Large constrictors clearly need a large terrarium (see general information on snakes) with a water area big enough for the snake to get into.

Keep the bottom bare or cover with bark or leaf mould. Do not use aquarium gravel or sawdust which can cause mouth infections.

Rattlesnake.

Boa constrictor and Python molurus.

Feeding

Mice, rats, hamsters, gerbils, rabbits, doves, and chickens. Guinea pigs are fat and have a thick and often indigestible skeleton. They can be fed exceptionally to very large snakes because of their big large and small intestines that contain a lot of pre-digested nutrition, rich in vitamin B complex. Some snakes will not touch guinea pigs though because they 'smell'. Feed large constrictors separated from each other, certainly with the bigger specimens. It is troublesome to have to separate two 3 metre (10ft) long snakes from each other that are both gobbling the same rat.

Many large constrictors can hunt down warm-blooded prey by their heat sensing ability that comes from a row of deeply recessed sensors on the upper and or lower jaw.

Sex determination

Probing results of 4-6 scales indicates a female and 10-15 scales a male. The male often has longer spurs and sometimes also has a thickened base to the tail.

Mating

Certain species (chiefly South American ones) only mate following a fight between several males.

Egg laying

Boas carry their eggs and give birth to their young while pythons lay eggs. Almost all the species guard and incubate their eggs by laying around them and regularly pulling them against their bodies. The warmth, created by muscle contractions, can raise the temperature of the eggs by 10°C. Remove the eggs if possible without damaging them by placing a towel under the female, lifting her out of the way, and then taking the eggs away. Brooding females can be very aggressive.

Rearing

Large constrictors grow rapidly in the first three to four years and more slowly thereafter.

Handling

Large constrictors can become very tame but always remain on your guard. Pick them up with one person per metre (40in). Pythons in particular can be very aggressive. Handle dangerous snakes

Boa constrictor.

when they are inactive, such as early in the morning.

A large constrictor of 2.5m (8ft 2in) is stronger than most adults. Strangulation can occur in the following manner: a snake wrapped around the neck tightens its hold to prevent itself from falling. The person carrying the snake tries to get the snake loose but the snake thinks it will fall so squeezes harder and so on. Grab a strangling snake by the tail and unwrap it to get yourself free, supporting its body as you do so.

BOA CONSTRICTOR, BOA CONSTRICTOR

Legal status: CITES B.

The genus *Boa* has only one species but numerous subspecies. *Boa constrictor* has about 25 dark bands or saddles on the ground colour of light brown. The final saddles are often a very attractive reddish brown, especially with young specimens. Subspecies from South America are often known as red-tailed boas.

These snakes grow to between 2-4m (6ft 6in-13ft) long, 120-170mm (4³/₄-6³/₄in) in diameter, and up to 50kg (110lb) in weight. They have a broad head and mainly active at twilight and in the night.

Distribution

Boa constrictor mainly inhabits well vegetated areas close to water in the pampas and woods of northern Mexico to southern South America. Adult specimens are mainly ground dwellers but

Clearly visible spurs with a male Burmese python.

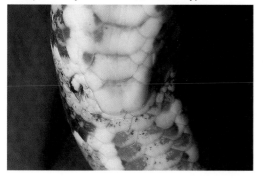

Boa constrictor.

younger ones live in bushes. There are many subspecies. *Boa constrictor constrictor* comes from northern and central areas of South America. The darker coloured *Boa c. imperator* is rarely larger than 1.5m (5ft) and it originates from Mexico through to north-western parts of South America.

Accommodation

Provide a terrarium of at least 120 x 70 x 100cm (47$^1/_4$ x 27$^1/_2$ x 40in) for a pair. Temperatures should be 27-32°C (80.6-89.6°F) with 35-40°C (95-104°F) under the spot lamps and 22-25°C (68-77°F) at night. Use both spot lamps and bottom heating. Spray each day but do not disturb boas, especially if you want them to breed.

Sex determination

With a probe, 10 scales clearly indicates a male, 2-4 a female.

Mating

Allow the partners two to three months rest from October to December at about 20°C (68°F) in a dry terrarium (humidity about 70%), with hiding places, and water tray, that is lit for four to six hours per day. After this return to normal temperatures and humidity.

Feed the snakes well for several weeks before placing ideally three males with one female. The males stimulate each other to mate, sometimes within a few hours but mainly three to five weeks of courtship are required first.

Ovulation takes place one to two weeks after copulation, apparent by clearly distended female body about two-thirds of the way back from her head, immediately behind the place where a prey remains. Put the female on her own and feed her well. During the final six to eight weeks of the pregnancy she will eat little. Feed small, newly killed prey. The female becomes slimmer and lays in unusual positions.

Giving birth

About 16-23 days after ovulation the female starts a slow shedding of her skin. Then 96-114 days later she starts to give birth, usually between March and the end of June. Boinae species snakes carry their eggs and give birth to their young.

Boa constrictor.

The female starts to become restless from one day to a week before she gives birth to from 15 up to a maximum of 70 offspring. The young quickly break out of the membrane surrounding them at birth.

Rearing

The new born are 200-300mm (8-12in) long, shed their skin after one to three weeks and already eat semi-mature mice. During the first two years of their lives they grow rapidly and become sexually mature after three years when they are 1.75-2m (5ft 9in-6ft 7in) long.

CHONDROPYTHON VIRIDIS, GREEN TREE PYTHON

Legal status: CITES B.

Chondropython viridis, the green tree python, previously formed part of the genus *Morelia* and is even sometimes known as *Python viridis*. The species is renowned as both aggressive and difficult to keep in captivity.

Appearance

These are 1.8m (5ft 11in) long, normally green, more rarely blue snakes with white/yellow/brown flecks. The body's cross-section is triangular. The tree python has small scales on the head and those where the nostrils are located are visibly bulbous.

Adult green tree python, Python viridis.

The emerald tree boa, Corallus caninus.

There are heat sensors on the lips but these are absent from the back of the top lip. The tree python looks very much like the emerald tree boa *(Corallus caninus)* from the tropical rain forests of northern South America. With the tree boa though the head scales are larger, the nostrils are at the side of the head, and there are heat sensors along the entire bottom and top lips. The tree boa requires the same care as the tree python but is much more difficult to keep alive.

Distribution
Rain forests in Irian Jaya (Indonesian New Guinea), and northern Australia.

Accommodation
Provide a high terrarium with horizontal branches at least 50mm (2in) thick. Bear in mind that a python laying on an upper branch can defecate on another if the branches are in line with each other. Hang up hiding places to recreate hollows in trees, filled with moist sphagnum moss. Spray ideally twice each day with luke-warm water to achieve humidity of 70-80%. Temperature should be 25-35°C (77-95°F), with 35-40°C (95-104°F) beneath the spot lamps, and 20-25°C (68-77°F) at night.
Males can fight fiercely with each other during the mating season so it is best to have one male per terrarium.

Feeding
Feed birds and rodents. Tree pythons can be hard to coax to eat but less so than tree boas.

Sex determination
Males have larger spurs. Probing results in about 10 scales giving a clear indication of a male and 2 scales for a female.

Mating
Reduce the temperature from October for eight weeks to 20-22°C (68-71.6°F). Reduce the period of lighting and reduce the humidity slightly. Afterwards return to 28-30°C (82.4-86°F). These snakes mate hanging from a branch.

Egg laying
A female lays 5-30 eggs in a hiding place filled with sphagnum moss, where she incubates them.

Rearing
The eggs hatch after six to eight weeks. It is best to remove them from the mother and incubate them

Young Chondropython viridis.

Python molurus bivittatus *showing the windpipe ejected during eating.*

Python molurus bivittatus *has a spear-head marking.*

at 30°C (86°F). Make sure humidity is high without the eggs actually becoming wet. When they emerge, the hatchlings are yellow with brown markings or reddish brown, but never green. The young change colour within a year and are sexually mature after two years.

PYTHON MOLURUS, INDIAN PYTHON

The Indian python, *Python molurus,* is a massive 6m (19ft 8in) long constrictor. *P. molurus bivittatus* (CITES B), the darker Burmese python originates in China, Burma, and the Far East to Indonesia. The darker spear-head marking on its head runs to the tip of the nose. It is usually this sub species of (Burmese) pythons that are kept in terrariums. Albino, 'green', and several other colour varieties are frequently offered for sale but some of these colours are not inherited by the offspring.
P. molurus molurus (CITES A), the lighter coloured Ceylon or Sri Lanka python from southern India and Sri Lanka is closely protected and rarely seen in hobby circles. With this subspecies the spear-head softens in the region of the eyes. There are no black edges to the darker and more rounded markings.

Distribution
Grassland and open woodland but also moister biotopes of South-East Asia but not the Philippines.

Accommodation
A very large terrarium, in reality an entire room, with large, sturdy, and easy to clean pool of water. These generally inactive snakes like to bathe. En-

sure 27-30°C (80.6-86°F), with 35-40°C (95-104°F) under the spot lamps and 22-25°C (68-77°F) at night. Spray with water each day.

Sex determination

The male has larger spurs. With a probe, results of 10-15 scales clearly indicate a male, 3-5 suggest a female.

Mating

This species is not difficult to breed. Reduce the temperature gradually in October-December to about 23°C (73.4°F) and leave it like this for six weeks. Feed and spray less (humidity 70%) and light for four hours each day. During the cool period separate the pythons. At the end of this period, feed them well before reintroducing them to each other. Mating follows and four weeks later the female stops eating. Two to three months after mating, the eggs are laid.

Egg laying

Provide an egg-laying box filled with moist sphagnum moss or crumbled peat. The eggs are sometimes laid in the water tray, so empty this just before the eggs are due to be laid.

With the eggs in an incubator at 30-32°C (86-89.6°F) between 15 and 100 hatchlings emerge after 60-75 days. If the decision is made to leave the eggs with the mother to incubate them the chance of something going wrong are much greater.

Rearing

The 450-600mm (17³/₄-23⁵/₈in) long hatchlings will eat a fully-grown mouse after their first skin shedding. The can grow to 2.5-3m (8ft 2in-10ft) within two years when they become sexually mature and weigh 20kg (44lb).

Handling

In contrast with the reticulated python *(P. reticulatus*, up to 9m/29ft 6in) and rock python *(P. sebae*, up to 7m/23ft), *P. molurus* is mainly not aggressive but such a large constrictor is always dangerous.

PYTHON REGIUS, BALL PYTHON

Legal status: CITES B.

Because of their friendly nature, smaller size, attractive colouring, and low prices, specimens captured in the wild are extremely popular. A beginner should never ever buy a wild captured specimen of these snakes that are renowned for refusing to eat, being parasite carriers, and easily stressed.

Appearance

Ball pythons are usually no longer than 1.2-1.5m (4-5ft). In danger the head is hidden with the body coils to form a perfect ball from which the name is derived. This behaviour quickly disappears in terrariums.

Distribution

This species inhabits tropical rain forests and drier savannah in West and central Africa. They lay in wait for prey on the ground or in trees.

Accommodation

Provide a terrarium at least 120 x 60 x 60cm (4 x 2 x 2ft) with thick branched climbing boughs. Ensure 27°C (80.6°F) to 35°C (95°F) beneath the spot lamps and 20-25°C (68-77°F) at night with the help of bottom heating. Heat the water area to 25°C (77°F).

Create a fairly humid atmosphere of 75-85% but make sure there is at least one dry place (beneath the spot lamps). Spray every 2-3 days.

Ball pythons prefer hiding places that have their opening at the top.

Feeding

Wild captured examples often refuse food. Ball pythons often have a preference for one type of food, e.g. desert rats. These snakes are largely ac-

The openings of the heat sensors can clearly be seen on the upper lip of this Python regius.

tive at twilight but will catch prey during the day. Well accustomed ball pythons eat virtually nothing from October to April.

Keep the snake cooler at night during this period with daytime temperature of 28-32°C (82.4-89.6°F) and somewhat drier, with a smaller water container.

Sex determination
Both sexes have small spurs. A probe will insert up to 10 scales with a male and 3 scales with females.

Mating
Breeding is possible following a period of cooler nights if healthy adults are used. Ball pythons mate during this cooler period. Raise both the temperature and humidity about one month after mating.

Egg laying
Make a laying box and fill it with boiled (sterilized) moist peat and a layer of filter wads. Six to ten eggs are laid about four months after mating. These hatch after two to three months at 30°C (86°F).

Rearing
When they hatch, the young are 400-450mm (15³/₄-17³/₄in) long. They become sexually mature after three years, when they are about 1m (40in) long.

Handling
Ball pythons generally do not bite and are very calm. Despite this, handle them as little as possible, specially at first to prevent regurgitation of the prey.

The Colubridae family, colubrids

This is the largest and most varied family of snakes in terms of numbers of species with 185 genera in about 14 subfamilies and two-thirds of all species. Colubrids are found throughout the world except in the extreme north and south.

Colubridae have short teeth and the minority that are venomous are largely not a danger for humans with a bite likely not even to be noticed. The subfamily Colubrinae contains some well-known genera of snakes: *Coluber, Elaphe, Lampropeltis, Opheodrys, Pituophis,* and *Lamprophis.* The genera *Natrix, Nerodia, Thamnophis* are part of the sub family of Natricinae or water snakes.

The grass snake, Natrix natrix, *is legally protected.*

Elaphe taeniura *(CITES D) from South-East Asia.*

ELAPHE SPECIES, RATSNAKES

The genus *Elaphe* consists of about 60 species of robust snakes that are found in a variety of biotopes (including forests) in North America, Asia, and Europe. Many of the North American species are ideally suitable for beginners.

The American species of *Elaphe* referred to have now been moved to the genus *Pantherophis.*

Appearance and distribution
Ratsnakes are quite slender and long snakes that are extremely variable in colour. They have a clearly defined head, divided anal shield, and small teeth. The species described here are rarely aggressive and not generally prone to stress.

Elaphe guttata guttata is the red ratsnake, generally known in its native US as corn snake, or plains ratsnake. This 1.5-1.8m (5-6ft) long snake is red, orange, brown, or black and can have grey colouring. The sides of the belly have chequered markings. This snake originates from the south and west of the USA and northern Mexico, especially in pine woods.

There are numerous colour variations being bred, such as the 'missing black', albino, red albino, and Miami face.

Elaphe obsoleta quadrivittata, the yellow ratsnake, from woods in north-eastern parts of North America grows to 1.7-2m (5ft 7in-6ft 7in) long. With for brown and yellow stripes on a yellow ground, this looks much like *E. quatuorlineata,*

The red ratsnake, Elaphe guttata guttata.

Elaphe guttata guttata *'missing black'*.

the four-stripe ratsnake from southern parts of Europe.

Elaphe obsoleta spiloides, the grey ratsnake, inhabits sparsely wooded eastern parts of the USA and is grey with grey-brown flecks, 2-2.5m (6ft 7in-8ft 2in) and climbs well.

Elaphe schrencki schrencki, the Russian ratsnake or amor, inhabits forests in north-east China, Korea, and eastern parts of the former Soviet Union. This dark black (sometimes dark brown) snake, with irregular yellow, grey, or white bands, grows to a maximum of 1.8m (6ft). This latter species resembles *Lampropeltis getulus getulus*.

Accommodation

Provide a fairly dry terrarium at least 100 x 40 x 40cm (40 x 16 x 16in) for a trio, with a sufficiently large water tray. Daytime temperature is 25-30°C (77-86°F) with 35-40°C (95-104°F) beneath pressed-glass spot lamps. Keep *E. schrenki* at 20-25 °C (68-77°F). Things to climb may be little used but they are still appreciated.

Feeding

Feed rodents with an occasional bird. In the wild they also eat eggs, lizards, and amphibians.

Sex determination

The male has a thickening of the base of the tail. A probe gives a result of 4-6 scales for males but 1-2 for females.

Elaphe obsoleta quadrivittata, *the yellow ratsnake.*

Mating

Stop feeding in mid October and allow the snakes to hibernate for two to three months at 10°C (50°F). These snakes mate in March through to June, during which time they should be fed well.

Egg laying

Five to thirty eggs of about 50mm (2in) long are laid four to nine weeks following mating so place an egg-laying box filled with moderately moistened peat, leaf mould, or sphagnum moss in early April. Look for eggs regularly from April through to June. Do this each day shortly after a skin shedding. There may also be a second clutch of eggs.

Incubation

At 25°C (77°F) the eggs hatch in about 70 days and at 30°C (86°F) this is reduced to 55. Humidity should be 70-90%. *E. schrenki* often retains the eggs for a month insider herself before laying them. This species is not ovoviviparous but this does reduce incubation time.

Rearing

The 200-400mm (8-16in) long young of these species mainly eat day-old mice as their first food. Strips of chicken, pigeon, or chicken hearts should be supplemented with vitamins and calcium.

The colour of the offspring differs from that of the parents. Young yellow ratsnakes look more like young grey ratsnakes. They are sexually mature in two to three years.

The grey ratsnake, Elaphe obsoleta spiloides.

This Elaphe schrenki schrenki *is just changing from its grey-brown colouring of youth to the darker markings of adulthood.*

LAMPROPELTIS SPECIES, KINGSNAKES AND MILKSNAKES

The seven species and many subspecies of kingsnake need to be kept on their own because their diet includes other snakes. With the exception of *L. getulus* and *L. calligaster* all the other *Lampropeltis* species will soon to moved to the genus *Oseola*.

Appearance

Lampropeltis species are quite robust, rounded snakes with a moderately delineated head and undivided anal plate. The variation in colouring and many subspecies have led to a lack of clarity in the

Lampropeltis getulus holbrooki.

Lampropeltis getulus californiae.

Lampropeltis getulus nigritus.

taxonomy of these snakes. Many species have diagonal banded markings.

Lampropeltis getulus grow to 1.5-2m (5ft-6ft 6in) long and are renowned for eating rattlesnakes, even though they rarely do. The at least seven subspecies of this species *(L. g. californiae, floridana, getulus, holbrooki, nigritus, niger,* and *splendida)* are black or brown with white or yellow stripes or spots. *L. g. californiae* in particular can have widely differing markings, even with the same brood: yellow or white lateral or diagonal stripes on a black or brown ground. Some people call them chain snakes because of the type of markings of certain subspecies.

Lampropeltis mexicana has variable colour markings but mainly has red-orange banding with alternate black and white margins on a grey ground. This species remains hidden from view more than the other species of this genus. There are about four subspecies, including *L. m. alternata,* which some regard as a separate species.

The false coral snakes *L. pyromelana, L. triangulum,* and *L. zonata* mimic the yellow-black-yellow-red bands of the venomous coral snakes *(Micrurus* sp. and *Micruroides* sp.). Folk wisdom in North America says: 'Red on yellow, kills a fellow.' This rule does not hold good for Central and South America.

It used to be believed that the many subspecies of *Lampropeltis triangulum,* known as the milk-

Young Lampropeltis mexicana alterna.

251

snake, drank milk from cows udders but this is anatomically impossible. These snakes are 1.5-1.8m (5-6ft) long.

Distribution
This ground-dwelling genus is found from southern Canada to northern parts of South America, particularly in the USA and Mexico. These snakes are active during both twilight and daylight but change to nocturnal living during the hot summer.

Accommodation
House kingsnakes and milksnakes on their own in view of their cannibalistic behaviour. It is possible to keep them in groups provided they are constantly well fed. Keep the terrariums fairly dry and at 25-30°C (77-86°F) but 40°C (104°F) beneath the spot lamps. Make plenty of hiding places and provide a water tray large enough for the snake to bathe in.

Feeding
These snakes have a diverse diet: mammals, earthworms, eggs, birds, lizards, and other snakes. Make sure the snakes are so well fed during the mating season that they have no appetite.

Sex determination
Males have a clear thickening of the base of the tail. Probing results for males are 7-10 scales and 1-2 scales for females.

Mating
Place the male with the female during the final

Lampropeltis triangulum sinaloae.

These young Lampropeltis getulus californiae *emerging from their eggs all have different markings.*

week of a four to six week winter rest. Mating between March and June follows an increase in temperature and lasts for 48 hours.

Egg laying
Lampropeltis species lay 5-25 elongated eggs twice each year between May and August. It can happen that a snake will eat the eggs that another has just laid. Place the females in separate terrariums ahead of time to prevent this happening. The eggs hatch in 75 days at 26°C (78.8°F) and 60 days at 30°C (86°F).

Rearing
Rear the 200-300mm (8-12in) long hatchlings in the same way as ratsnakes.

Defence
Lampropeltis species often continue to chew if they bite. Some of them defecate when handled.

OPHEODRYAS AESTIVUS, THE ROUGH GREEN SNAKE

Opheodryas aestivus is an 800-1,115mm (31$^{1}/_{2}$-45$^{1}/_{4}$in) long, slim, bright grass green, diurnal snake. The lips are white, it has a long tail, and divided anal plate. This species has ridged scales so that it feels rough to the touch. The other American green snake *O. vernalis*, from south-east Canada and north-east USA, has smooth scales and is known as the smooth green snake. It is smaller at 650mm (25$^{1}/_{2}$in).

Distribution
This snake lives in bushes and grass in lush semi-moist biotopes in the south-east of the USA and north-eastern Mexico.

Accommodation
For a trio, provide a well-planted terrarium of at least 40 x 40 x 80cm (16 x 16 x 31$^{1}/_{2}$in) with a fairly large water area. Daytime temperature should be 25-30°C (77-86°F), 20°C (68°F) at night, and humidity of 70-80%. Spray lightly twice each day and make sure there is a dry area. Provide a tray with moderately moist crumbled peat covered with a layer of moss.

Feeding
Feed all types of insects and their larvae but not too many spiders. If the snake refuses one insect,

Opheodryas aestivus.

Opheodryas aestivus.

Thamnophis proximus *eats a salamander.*

One month old Opheodryas *eggs.*

try a different type. Grass snakes eat the occasional lizard and amphibian.

Reproduction

There is only rarely success in breeding this snake. Let them have a winter rest of two to four months at 10-15°C (50-59°F). These snakes mainly mate in spring. Between 3-19 eggs of about 30mm (1³/₁₆in) are laid in moist peat and they hatch in 55-75 days. The 120-150mm (4³/₄-6in) long hatchlings are grey-green and they achieve sexual maturity after one to two years.

Life expectancy in captivity

These snakes are reputed to be difficult to keep successfully in captivity. In the past these snakes were kept by all manner of traders and middlemen, which caused stress and poor health. This often resulted in the death of the snake within a few weeks of a hobbyist acquiring it. Now that these snakes are passed on quickly, their life expectancy has improved and they will probably also be successfully bred.

THAMNOPHIS SPECIES, GARTER AND RIBBON SNAKES

This genus has about 20 species. These are popular snakes with beginners because they eat fish, earthworms (and amphibians).

Appearance and distribution

Garter and ribbon snakes are found in extremely diverse biotopes, in the proximity of water, and often in proximity with humans. They are found from as far north as Alaska and Canada to the northern parts of South America.

These black or green snakes usually have three light-coloured lateral stripes (the garters or ribbons), and certain species are flecked. The anal plate is not divided in contrast with *Natrix* species, the true water snake.

The western ribbon snake, *T. proximus*, has six subspecies originating from the central zone of the USA through to Costa Rica. These snakes are 800mm-1.2m (31¹/₂-47¹/₄in) long. The tail comprises up to a third of the total body length. There are eight lip plates along the upper jaw. The three light-coloured lateral stripes contrast strongly with the much darker colour that surrounds them. Counting from the belly scales upwards, the side stripe is at the level of the third or fourth scale. There are two oval spots that run into one another on the head. *T. proximus* was formerly regarded as a subspecies of the eastern ribbon snake, *T. sauritus*, which is closely resembles. This latter snake though has a brown stripe on the edge of the belly scales and does not have the two spots on the head.

The common garter snake, *T. sirtalis*, has 12 subspecies in southern Canada, the USA, and Mexico. These are not found in desert areas. This snake grows no longer than 1.3m (51¹/₄in) and it is extremely variable in colour. The lateral stripes contrast fairly clearly with the rest of the back. The

Thamnophis sirtalis sirtalis.

side stripe is located at the second or third scale. There are often red spots or black flecks between the stripes. This species has seven lip plates along the upper jaw.

T. sirtalis infernalis, from the Californian coast, had a series of red flecks on its sides. The side stripe is difficult to discern, and the top of the head is reddish.

T. sirtalis parietalis, from southern Canada has red and black chequers between the back and side stripes, and the top of its head is olive green.

T. sirtalis similis from northern Florida has a yellow or ochre back stripe and bluish side stripes. The back is greenish with a double row of darker flecks.

T. sirtalis sirtalis mainly has yellow stripes on olive green sides with a double row of black markings. The colour varies, but can be red on the back. This subspecies is found in eastern parts of the USA through to Iowa and Missouri.

Accommodation

These active, semi-aquatic snakes demand a well-ventilated terrarium of at least 100 x 40 x 40cm (40 x 16 x 16in). Beware of possible draughts. Aim for a temperature of 20-27°C (68-80.6°F) and as high as 35°C (95°F) beneath the spot lamps. The temperature can climb so high on sunny days that the lamps need to be switched off. Make sure there is somewhere dry, such as above a bottom heater.

If the terrarium is humid use an hygienic substrate such as linoleum. Compost encourages ticks which garter and ribbon snakes are prone to. Skin scarring results from the entire bottom of the terrarium being moist. In a dry terrarium a mixture of leaf mould and sharp sand makes a good covering. The water tray needs to be large but it is not necessary to heat it separately. The rim of the water tray needs to be at least 50mm (2in) above the surface level of the bottom substrate to prevent this becoming wet and to reduce fouling of the water by snakes crawling in and out.

Provide plenty of branches for the snakes to climb and ample hiding places. *Thamnophis* species prefer peace and quiet and like to hide away.

Feeding

Feed live fish, coley fillet, and earthworms twice

Thamnophis sirtalis sirtalis.

each week. These snakes will also sometimes eat baby mice and strips of beef. Garter and ribbon snakes are easily overfed. In the wild they may also eat amphibians, skinks, other lizards, and crustaceans. Heat most dead fish up to 80°C (176°F) to get rid of a substance that breaks down vitamin B1. A deficiency in this vitamin causes nervous disorders, including strange bending behaviour (the snakes fall over backwards). Sprinkle fish with a vitamin B1 containing preparation. The destructive compound is not present in trout, herring, cod, mackerel, haddock, pike, and whiting.

Snakes catch fish by a rapid strike as they hang above the water, or by swimming through water with their mouths open. The prey are often not killed.

Sex determination

Males have a thickening of the base of the tail, longer tail, smaller but less flattened head, and they are both thinner and shorter.

With a probe a result of 4-6 scales indicates a male and 1-2 suggests a female.

Mating

Get the snakes to hibernate for eight weeks by reducing the temperature to 10-15°C (50-59°F). Put the snakes back together immediately after hibernation. Snakes are stimulated to mating by living in small groups. Mating lasts for several hours. The females can store sperm for a considerable time.

Thamnophis sirtalis parietalis.

Thamnophis proximus.

Egg laying

All *Thamnophis* species are ovoviviparous. Depending on the species, the female usually gives birth to between five and thirty young *(T. proximus)* or up to eighty *(T. sirtalis)* new born after a pregnancy of two to three months. The female stops eating about a week before she gives birth.

Rearing

Remove the young to prevent accidents during feeding. The new born are about 200mm (8in) long and the thickness of a matchstick. Within a couple of days they can already eat earthworms, fish of 20-30mm (³/₄-1³/₁₆in) long, tadpoles, and finely sliced fillet of whiting. After a few weeks they can be introduced to cat food by adding the smell of fish to it. Watch the group of young snakes for half an hour after feeding to make sure they do not eat each other. *Thamnophis* species grow rapidly and become sexually mature after one-and-a-half to two years.

Handling

Handle these shy snakes that like a quiet life as little as possible. If they are held they are likely to wriggle and bite but their bites are barely noticeable.

Nerodia species

Snakes of the genus *Nerodia* (from North America) are water snakes with a similar lifestyle to *Thamnophis* species. They too eat fish, carry their eggs and give birth, are easy to keep, and are a bit thicker than garter and ribbon snakes. The fairly popular *Nerodia fasciata* grows to between 90mm-1.5m (35¹/₂in-5ft). Provide a fairly dry terrarium with a large water tray for them at a temperature of 20-25°C (68-77°F), with a slightly higher temperature beneath a spot lamp.

The order Testudinata (Chelonia), turtles and tortoises

This order of reptiles protect themselves with a

Young terrapins such as these Graptemys kohni *are among the most widely sold reptiles.*

Male turtles and tortoises have a broader and longer tail than females. With Cuora amboinensis *illustrated, the base of the tail is thicker.*

shell covering their back (carapace) and another covering the belly (plastron).

Both shells consist of a layer of horny material over bone. The entire shell forms part of the animal's skeleton, with the carapace being connected to the vertebrae and the ribs. Soft-shelled turtles have no horn layer but these are difficult to keep. All the protruding parts of the body can be more or less withdrawn within the shell. Tortoises are the only vertebrate animals with shoulder blades inside their rib cage. A tortoise mouth is a sort of beak with sharp bony edges.

Tortoise jaws consist of horny material and can be very sharp (principally for carnivores) or sawtooth (mainly herbivores).

The most widely kept tortoises are of the suborder Cryptodira (hidden-necked turtles) of which there are ten families. These withdraw their head at sign of danger. The most important families are the land tortoises (Testudinidae), fresh water turtles/terrapins (Emydidae), and the snapping turtles (Chelydridae).

Tortoises of the Pleurodira family, which is split into two subfamilies, bend their heads to one side in danger. The genera *Emydura*, *Pelusios*, and *Pelomedusa* are occasionally kept in captivity.

Distribution

The approx. 220 species of about 75 genera are found in all manner of biotopes throughout tropical, subtropical, and moderate climate zones.

Accommodation

The appropriate type of terrarium differs for each type of turtle and tortoise and is dealt with per species or group. Every tortoise and turtle is susceptible for draught though. Although many species from moderate climate zones such as North America can be kept in an outdoor terrarium, they must not be placed there too early. An outdoor terrarium must also incorporate a warm and draught-free shelter.

Turtles and tortoises from the USA, Europe, and North Africa can be kept throughout the year in a conservatory or greenhouse. Tortoises and turtles captured in the wild are renowned for carrying extensive internal parasites. Such a tortoise may look well but be passing on harmful amoeba (*Entamoeba invadens*). Lizards die in a matter of weeks from this amoeba. For this reason keep such specimens in quarantine for six months, have the tortoise checked for this infection, and treat it if necessary before placing it with others. Treat preventively with metronidazole (50-75mg/kg given orally for 10 days).

Sex determination

It is possible to visually determine the sex of adult turtles and tortoises, and sometimes half-grown examples.

– Most male tortoises have a thicker and longer tail than females and the cloaca is closer to the tip.
– Many male terrapins such as the red-eared slider, have one or more longer claws on the front legs that are used during mating.
– The carapace of many tortoises and terrapins is more domed and less angular with females while the plastron is often slightly more indented at the rear with males and without indentations with females. This provides better grip during mating.
– With many species the adult females are larger and heavier. Males can have larger heads.
– The carapaces of the two sexes vary in colouring and texture.

Mating

Tortoises from regions that have a true winter benefit from hibernation, even though this is not strictly necessary for breeding. Tropical species are accustomed to dry and wet seasons and are stimulated to mate by imitating the passing of the seasons. There is often a long courtship between tortoises before they mate.

Egg laying

The females become restless and show a tendency to dig just before they lay their eggs. Eggs can sometimes be felt in the groin but this can damage

Regular weighing will indicate if eggs are shortly to be laid.

the oviduct. A sudden gain in weight is a sign of pregnancy so weigh the female regularly.
All tortoises lay their eggs in moderately moist soil. The eggs usually harden off.

Rearing

Incubation temperature often determines the sex of offspring with many reptiles. With tortoises, mainly males are produced at lower temperatures and chiefly females at the higher ones. Temperature range for species from moderate climate zones is 22-32°C (71.6-89.6°F).
Feed young tortoises with a varied diet and do not forget they need a vitamin and mineral supplement rich in calcium.
Small species become sexually mature after about five years and larger ones after ten.

Sickness

Read pages 193-197 first.

– With a healthy tortoise, its shell is hard, without damage or deformities. A lack of calcium, or ultra-violet light and vitamin D₃ causes shell weaknesses and deformities. The exception to this are the soft-shelled turtles (Trionychidae family).
– When a tortoise walks it should lift its plastron from the ground. If not then it is an indication of weak or crooked legs.

Red-footed tortoises mating.

Place sick and injured terrapins apart.

256

- Is the animal alert? Most tortoises withdraw their head and legs inside their shell if disturbed. The legs should offer resistance to efforts (not too literal) to pull them out of the shell. Freshwater turtles often try to escape and are very agile while being handled. A tortoise laying on its back that is not trying to right itself is not healthy.
- Check the folds of skin, especially with animals caught in the wild, for external parasites (ticks and mites) and have the stools checked for worms and flagella etc.
- Put tortoises with fungal infections (light- and differently-coloured patches covered with slime or wounds) in a solution of 1 gram potassium permanganate to 100ml water for an hour, after cleaning the affected area. Alternatively bathe with 10g cooking salt per litre of water.
- Land tortoises should not have loose stools.
- Give hard food such as a carrot to tortoises with a 'parrot beak' and clip or file the horny 'beak' into shape.
- Dry and loosely hanging skin on the legs and neck of land tortoises indicate a surfeit of vitamin A. This can even lead to open sores. Put these animals as quickly as possible on a diet that is low in vitamin A for many months and have any sores treated.

Set ill or wounded terrapins apart from others to prevent them from being bitten.

Handling

Holding a terrapin by its sides can present no problems for some time until the animal unexpectedly bites, using its long neck, or scratches with sharp claws on its powerful legs to fight free and is then dropped on the ground. Hold terrapins firmly by the back of their shell.

A large snapping turtle *(Chelydra serpentina)* or alligator snapping turtle *(Macroclemys temminckii)* can easy bite fingers off. Lift them by their back legs (of by the tail) and turn them over with the plastron facing the person holding them.

The top tortoise has a vitamin D or calcium deficiency so that its shell is bobbled.

A snapping turtle.

Land tortoises are usually much more peaceful and these can be picked up by holding both sides of the shell.

It is difficult to grasp hold of the head if a medicine has to be administered. Let someone with experience do this. This person will wait until the tortoise sticks its head out and then grasp it with lightning speed. If the back legs are pushed into the shell the head will usually appear after a little wait. The head of a snapping turtle can be pulled out if they bite into a cloth. The front legs can also be pulled sideways and the head can then be grasped, if necessary with an L-shaped hook under the lower jaw. Much patience and then speed is required to grasp the head of a box turtle. Opening the shell with a fork causes considerable stress.

To open the mouth press a flat object such as a lollipop stick between the jaws and press upwards. While the mouth is held open a second person inserts a lubricated probe into the intestine as far as possible until light resistance is felt. Do not insert the probe into the windpipe which is behind the base of the tongue. Hold a tortoise upright for a while after administering a liquid.

Pack tortoises in sturdy, draught-free boxes and keep them warm.

The Testudinidae family, land tortoises

Legal status: **T. graeca, T. hermanni, T. kleinmanni,** and *T. marginata* are CITES A. All other land tortoises are CITES B.

Appearance

Land tortoises have a strongly boned, high arched shell of horny plates with few if any joints. The toes are on rounded, column-like legs and have grown together to form a clump foot. Only the nails or claws stick out.

Indoor terrarium with Russian tortoises.

Hermann's tortoise.

Many land tortoises can live to be 50 to 100 years old.

Distribution

Land tortoises are found above all in Africa, but also in Europe, Asia, and America, but not in Australia.

Accommodation

Provide as big a ground area as possible and provide hiding places with stones, bricks, and timber. Plants will be eaten or destroyed. Provide heating during the day with spot lamps and perhaps with under-floor heating. Make sure that the air temperature is higher than the ground because it is harmful to breathe in cold air with a warm belly. Certain tortoises such as the *Testudo* species can be kept in an outdoor terrarium in the summer (see *Testudo hermanni*.)

Provided it does not stress the tortoise, they can be bathed for 30 minutes each week in tepid water but do not do this with *Agrionemys horsfieldii*, and do not use soap!

Feeding

Feed two to three times each week, mainly with vegetables and fruit (see main section on feeding). Do not feed more than 15% animal derived food such as soaked dry cat food (without colouring), earthworms, slugs, and snails, to adults but young ones can have slightly more (max. 30%). Young tortoises in particular have a major need for calcium and vitamin D₃. These should be fed ideally each day. A varied diet is very important.

Mating

Males display with head bobbing and make a noise as part of the mating process. Females can store sperm and have been known to fertilize eggs with it up to four years later.

Rearing

Create a rearing terrarium with similar conditions as the parent's enclosure but keep young of European species slightly cooler than their parents. Make about half of the ground fairly moist to prevent deformations of the shell. Provide a shallow water tray large enough for them to get into but not deep enough for them to drown in. Spray each morning.

A few days after hatching the young start to eat finely shredded leaves and soft fruit. Feed between 15-30% animal derived protein.

Miss out the first hibernation but not subsequent ones (because of deformed shells). Do not let young tortoises grow too rapidly or their shell will not take on an attractive domed shape. Tortoises are sexually mature in five to ten years.

Handling

Land tortoises rarely bite and are mainly peaceful. They can be picked up firmly by the sides but make sure they do not scramble free with their powerful legs and do not drop them.

AGRIONEMYS HORSFIELDI, *RUSSIAN TORTOISE*

Synonym: *Testudo horsfieldii*.
Legal status: CITES B.
Fairly small, widely kept land tortoise.

Appearance

Females grow to 200mm (8in) long and males to 160mm (6¹⁄₄in). The sandy-coloured carapace with its dark patches has a quite rounded outline with reasonable flattening at the top of the carapace. There is a claw on the tip of the tail. Russian tortoises dig deep burrows.

Distribution

This species inhabits plains in south-western parts of Asia (Afghanistan, Iran, Pakistan, the former Soviet Union) where they are active from April to September. In extremely arid regions they take a summer rest.

Accommodation

Cover the bottom of a 'steppes' terrarium of at least 2 sq m (21¹⁄₂ sq ft) with sand, quarry sand, or sandy soil. Summertime temperature is 25-35°C (77-95°F) with 40-45°C (104-113°F) under the heat lamps. Provide under-floor heating as well.

Males are aggressive towards other male tortoises, even if these are three times their size.

Feeding

They are mainly herbivorous.

Sex determination
Males have a thicker and longer tail but do not have the hollow plastron of most of land tortoises.

Mating
See *Testudo hermanni* regarding hibernation. In nature these tortoises mate in August and September, laying their eggs in May and June. In terrariums the couples often mate in the spring and lay their eggs two-and-a-half months later.

After head bobbing, circling around the female, and biting, mating occurs the moment the female stops 'running' away.

Egg laying
The female digs a hole in loose sandy soil where she lays two to eight oval eggs. These hatch after 65-70 days at 30-32°C (86-89.6°F) or 80-100 days at a slightly lower incubating temperature.

CHELONOIDIS CARBONARIA, RED-FOOTED TORTOISE

Legal status: CITES B.
This species is sometimes incorporated with the genus *Geochelone*.

Appearance
These tortoises have shells of 300-500mm (12-20in) long with a dark carapace that has light yellow patches on each horn plate. The northern

The darker male Agrionemys horsfieldii *bobs his head in display before 'running' around the female as a prelude to mating.*

Russian tortoises at an egg-laying box.

Chelonoidis carbonaria.

form has yellow to orange scales on the limbs and head, while the southern form only has red patches.

Distribution
Red-footed tortoises originate from South America, inhabiting diverse biotopes ranging from savannah to forest margins in the region from Venezuela to northern Argentina. Attempt to find out the origins of the tortoise in order to provide the right conditions for it. If the skin shedding does not go smoothly the terrarium is too dry.

Accommodation
Keep these tortoises as pairs in a terrarium with a ground area of at least 4 sq m (43 sq ft). Cover the ground with beech chips or peat, which must be fairly dry. Provide a box or other shelter for them to hide in.

Daytime temperature is 25-30°C (77-86°F) with 45°C (113°F) under the spot lamps. A small central heating radiator or fan heater can be used but radiated heat is important. The minimum night-time temperature is 20°C (68°F). The northern form appreciates a high humidity (80% by day and 100% at night), with a waterfall or misting apparatus, with the 150mm (6in) deep water tray being heated to 25°C (77°F). The northern forms avoid bright light. Red-footed tortoises make a hollow in which to lay their eggs. Provide an egg-laying box of 100 x 50 x 50cm (40 x 20 x 20in) with leaf mould. Fix a pressed-glass spot lamp above the box.

Red-footed tortoises can be kept in the same terrarium as green iguanas.

Feeding
See Land tortoises.

Sex determination
Males have a hollow plastron together with a thicker and longer tail.

Mating
The northern form mates in August and October in the wild but this depends on how the seasons are imitated in captivity. The males make a striking sound during mating.

Egg laying
Forthcoming egg laying is not signalled by any stop in eating by the female. They mainly lay their

Chelonoidis carbonaria.

eggs between September and April in three clutches, each of two to fifteen eggs. If there is nowhere for the female to dig a hollow for her eggs she will fail to lay and can die.

Place the eggs in one part sand to two parts garden soil, or in vermiculite. This should only be moderately moist. The eggs hatch in four to six months at 28-30°C (82.4-86°F).

Rearing

Depending on the amount of yolk remaining in the egg, the young start to eat several days after hatching. Feed them with food that is not too high in protein. The sex can be determined of young tortoises after six years and they are sexually mature in seven to eight years.

TESTUDO HERMANNI, HERMANN'S TORTOISE

Legal status: CITES A.

Testudo hermanni is the most widely kept tortoise and they are widely bred. They are protected because up to 1977, millions of this species were imported as pets.

Appearance

T. h. boettgeri is the most-widely kept and bred subspecies. The females grow to 250mm (9³/₄in) and have black patches on the plastron. The fairly rounded carapace is noticeably broader towards the rear.

T. h. hermanni grows to 180mm (7in), has a more oval shell with more clearly defined colour areas. There are two continuous black bands from front to back on the plastron. The central seam between the third pair of belly plates is smaller than those between the fifth pair (this is the other way around with *T. h. boettgeri).*

T. hermanni has a divided tail plate and claw on the tip of the tail.

T. graeca, the spur-thighed tortoise (3 subspecies), usually has an undivided tail plate, no claw on the tip of the tail, but has two spurs to left and right of the tail on the legs. These spurs are the only truly determining factor. This species is sensitive for sickness and stress and is therefore not suitable for beginners.

T. marginata, the up to 350mm (13³/₄in) long marginated tortoise is almost entirely black with broad marginal plates (up to 80mm/3¹/₈in at the back), and large scales on the front legs.

Distribution

These tortoises inhabit 'steppes'-like habitats and dry woodland. They are all threatened with extinction in the wild. Fortunately there are many captively-bred specimens available.

T. hermanni boettgeri originates from eastern Italy through to Turkey, and northwards to Bulgaria and Rumania.

T. hermanni hermanni comes from north-eastern Spain through to western Italy, including the larger Mediterranean islands.

T. graeca is found in virtually all the countries surrounding the Mediterranean and in the Middle-

The tail shield is generally divided with T. hermanni *but not with the spur-thighed tortoise.*

East.

T. marginata is chiefly found in southern Greece and in Sardinia, where it was introduced.

Accommodation

Provide a terrarium with as big a ground area as is possible, with a minimum of 3 sq m (32¹/₄ sq ft) for a pair. Temperatures are 25-30°C (77-86°F) generally, 35-40°C (95-104°F) beneath spot lamps, and 15-20°C (59-68°F) at night. Ensure there are several cool, sheltered places with a box and plants. The drinking tray must be shallow but at least the size of the tortoise to permit bathing.

Provide a variety of ground types: sand, grass, stones, and wood, and keep parts of these fairly moist. Adults need an egg-laying box with a moist substrate.

An outdoor terrarium is the ideal summer home but allow the tortoises to adjust to the temperature. Ensure there is plenty of sun, protection from the wind, and shady, cool places. Create a warm area with for instance an acrylic cloche or heated shelter, with loose soil. Cover this with a loose layer of hay and have the entrance facing south-east for the morning sun.

Beware of possible escape. Make sure the outer material of the cage is buried at least 50cm (20in) into the soil and there is a smooth partition above ground that is at least twice as high as the tortoises are long; this should also cantilever inwards.

Outdoor terrarium for Testudo *species.*

Only males have an indentation in the plastron.

Young spur-thighed tortoise and egg.

Even then tortoises sometimes climb on top of each other to escape.

Vertical partitioning prevent the tortoises constantly seeing each other. This is equally important for indoor terrariums.

Feeding

See land tortoises.

Sex determination

Males remain smaller and have thicker and longer tails, plus a clear indentation in the plastron.

Mating

Let the tortoises hibernate for three to four months at 5-10°C (41-50°F) dug into a mixture of loose soil/leaves/sand 30cm (12in) deep. This can be indoors, in a box, a greenhouse, or in the shelter in an outdoor terrarium, except in this case the tortoises need to bury themselves in a 1m (40in) layer of the loose mixture. Cover the ground above with leaf mould or hay and keep rodents at bay with wire netting. Moisten the soil from time to time.

These tortoises mate in the wild in September and October but do so in a terrarium throughout the year. This can lead to fights between males.

Egg laying

From one to twelve eggs are laid up to three times each year from April to late July in loose, sandy soil. Incubation at 28°C (82.4°F) causes mainly males to hatch in 60-65 days and at 32°C (89.6°F) mostly females emerge in 55-60 days.

Young *Testudo* species tortoises should not weigh more than 40 grams (less than 1¹/₂oz) at one year old and not more than 70 grams (less than 2¹/₂oz) at two years old.

The Emydidae family, freshwater turtles and terrapins

Most freshwater turtles and terrapins originate from North America and Asia. Principally aquatic genera such as *Trachemys, Chrysemys, Pseudemys, Graptemys,* and *Cuora* require housing in the manner described in the following text. The exception to this if the genus *Terrapene.* Box turtles

(*Cuora* and *Terrapene)* can close up their shell in danger.

Appearance

Freshwater turtles often live semi-aquatic lives. With the exception of box turtles, these creatures have streamlined, fairly flattened shells and are equipped with legs flattened at the side to act as flippers, and possess large or small membranes between the toes for webbed feet. The carapace and plastron are directly joined.

Maximum life-span is estimated at 25-50 years or longer.

Accommodation

Provide a large water area that is at least as deep as the largest turtle is wide, so that a capsized turtle can right itself without risk of drowning. Cover the glass bottom either with sand or nothing. A rough bottom will wear away the plastron too much. Heat the water to 18-25°C (64.4-77°F) with the heating securely and safely fixed e.g. with the filter. Freshwater turtles eat little or nothing below 17°C (62.6°F). Prevent draughts because of the strong risk of them catching colds.

Make sure there is a dry spot on land with a powerful spot lamp above it so that the turtles can dry themselves at 35-40°C (95-104°F), or they run the risk of fungal infections. Fix the 'sun-lamp' close to the water's edge so that the turtles can immediately escape into the water.

Eggs can be laid in a land area filled with equal parts of sand, aquarium gravel, and bark/peat/leaf mould. Offer this only during the laying season or the water area will be fouled constantly.

An area of land on stilts increases the living area and offers them somewhere they can swim under to hide. A good biological filter or large external filter is essential because terrapins and freshwater turtles make the water extremely dirty. Making sure the filter inlet is safe and that a turtle will not drown because it is stuck against the intake. Clean the filter at least once each month and replenish at least one third of the water each week. Tap water needs to be brought to the correct temperature before adding it to the terrarium.

Many terrapins/freshwater turtles can be kept with each other. Slow fish will be quickly eaten but quicker ones stand a chance of survival, although they will be chased for the first few days.

Clipping of the claws is not only unnecessary, it can be harmful. Decorate the terrarium with stones which will help to wear the claws down.

Salmonella

Young freshwater turtles and terrapins carry many bacteria with them that cause illnesses equivalent to food poisoning *(Salmonella)*, leading to vomiting, high temperature, sever stomach ache, and diarrhoea. Take particular care of children who tend to play with these animals a great deal. Always wash hands after handling these animals and rinse siphon tubes before and after refreshing the water. There are good disinfectants available specially for terrariums.

Feeding

These gluttonous omnivores eat 50% animal protein and young ones even more. Freshwater fish, meat (dead rodents, tinned cat food, lean beef), earthworms, soft animals, vegetables, and fruit are all eaten. Feed them two or three times per week.

Mississippi map turtle, Graptemys kohni.

Cuora aboinensis in a terrarium with a 'floating' area of land.

It is not difficult to feed terrapins a varied diet. This one is eating cat food.

Cuora aboinensis.

Terrapene carolina *closed up.*

Those that mainly eat lean meat and/or a commercial 'complete' terrapin food will suffer from vitamin A deficiency which will cause eye inflammations. A deficiency of vitamin D3/ultra-violet light causes weak shells. Supplement the diet with sufficient vitamins and minerals. Calcium can also be given in the form of eggshell.

Reproduction
A number of North American turtles/terrapins over-winter underwater by breathing through their skin.

Many turtles/terrapins mate in water and bury their eggs ashore on land. Some *Cuora* and all *Terrapene* species mate on land.

CUORA AMBOINENSIS, MALAYAN BOX TURTLE

This widely sold box turtle protects itself by slamming its plastron shut when threatened.

Appearance
These are turtles with an oval to round carapace that is dark brown. The shell is 150-200mm (6-8in) long. The single plastron hinge hardly works with *C. a. amboinensis.* There is a raised ridge from front to back of the carapace that becomes less apparent with older animals. The edges of the shell are curled up. Both the head and neck are brown with yellow lateral stripes on the top and yellow with brown stripes below.

All three of the subspecies are offered for sale. *C. a. amboinensis* has the lowest carapace, *C. a. kamaroma* the highest, while *C. a. couri* is in between them. There are also some differences in the markings on the plastron.

Distribution
These box turtles inhabit marshes and other watery areas in South-East Asia (The Philippines, Moluccas, and Sulawesi). They are usually found in the water.

Accommodation
An aquarium terrarium of 100 x 40 x 40cm (40 x 16 x 16in) is sufficient for a trio of Malayan box turtles. Make the land area at least 40 x 20cm (16 x 8in) and 10cm (4in) deep. For other details see Freshwater turtles and terrapins but do not let the

temperature drop below 25°C (77°F) and the water should be 22-26°C (71.6°F).

Feeding
These box turtles are omnivores: see Freshwater turtles and terrapins.

Sex determination
Females are more bulbous, rounded, slightly larger, and often have bite scars on the neck (from during mating). Adult males have a hollow plastron, and thicker base to the tail, which is longer. The head behind the eyes is slightly broader.

Mating
Allow these turtles eight weeks hibernation at 15-20°C (59-68°F) in a dark box with layers of successively drier soil. Mating follows hibernation, after the male bites the female. Remove overeager males from the females.

Egg laying
Two or three eggs each time (approx. 50 x 30mm/2-1^3/$_{16}$in) are laid regularly. Fertilized eggs show a light banding around the middle within a week. The eggs hatch in about 60 days at 32°C (89.6°F) and 85 days at 25°C (77°F). Eggs that are infertile look yellowish.

Rearing
See rearing of 'red-eared slider' in Freshwater turtles and terrapins. Young box turtles show a ridge on the carapace.

TERRAPENE CAROLINA AND T. ORNATA, EASTERN AND ORNATE BOX TURTLES

Legal status: all *Terrapene* species are CITES B.
When danger threatens, these box turtles can clap their shell shut due to two hinges in the plastron. These box turtles are part of a different subfamily though than *Cuora* (the Asian box turtles, which have a single hinge) and originate in North America.

Appearance
The high shell resembles that of a land tortoise. The fairly stumpy legs do not have large webs for swimming. These box turtles can close themselves up perfectly with the front and rear hinges. This species is usually dark brown with yellow-orange

markings but there are variations, hybrids, and exceptions, making precise species determination often difficult.

With *T. carolina*, of which there are six subspecies, the front plate of the carapace is at an angle of 50 degrees or more, with the hinge located opposite the fifth edge plate. The height divided by the length of the carapace is at least 0,42.

T. c. carolina usually has four toes on the back legs and grows to 120-140mm (4³/₄-5¹/₂in).

T. c. triunguis normally has three toes on each back leg and grows to 110-130mm (4¹/₄-5¹/₈in).

T. ornata, which has two subspecies, has a front shell that lifts up at least 45 degrees. The hinge is opposite the fifth edge plate. *T. o. ornata* (100-120mm/4-4³/₄in) has few yellow lines on the carapace and the hinge is opposite the seam between the fifth and sixth edge plate. *T. o. luteola* (120-130mm/4³/₄-5¹/₈in) has lots of lines and its hinge is opposite the sixth edge plate.

Distribution

Box turtles are not so dependent on water and live more like land tortoises but they can swim.

T. carolina inhabits open woodland in southern Canada and the USA. *T. ornata* is found in drier areas from the middle of the USA to Mexico.

These box turtles are chiefly active in the morning and evening, particularly after a shower of rain.

Accommodation

Provide a fairly dry terrarium with a base area of at least 2 sq m (21¹/₂ sq ft) with a wetter corner. A water tray with 50mm (2in) deep water that is large enough to bathe in is sufficient for the water area. The land area should be covered with quarry sand or other sand mixed with peat, leaf mould, and bark to a depth of at least 20cm (8in). These box turtles burrow a great deal as they are fairly shy. Provide places to hide. The temperature should be 25°C (77 °F) to 35°C (95°F) under the spots. Provide local bottom heating as well.

T. carolina can be placed in a sheltered outdoor terrarium. Males are intolerant of each other.

Terrapene ornata.

Terrapene carolina triunguis *mating.*

Feeding

Provide animal foodstuff (earthworms) and fruit (see Freshwater turtles and terrapins). Clean the water daily.

Sex determination

Males have longer and thicker tails. Males of *T. c. carolina* have an obviously hollow plastron, but this is less pronounced with *T. c. triunguis* males. The claws are longer, heavier, and more crooked with males.

Mating

Let both species hibernate from November to March in fairly loose soil at about 15°C (59°F). Mating follows the courtship ritual with its panting and biting. The male, who rears up, and often falls over, clings on during mating and is sometimes hauled around the terrarium for hours still copulating. Females can store sperm for several years.

Egg laying

Two to eight eggs each time are laid in moist soil around about June. These hatch in about 50 days at 30°C (86°F) or 120 days at 22°C (71.6°F).

Rearing

Feed the 30mm (1³/₁₆in) long young with a smaller version of the adult's food but with a higher content of animal protein. Make about half the terrarium fairly moist.

Terrapene carolina triunguis. *The male usually falls over backwards during mating.*

Red-eared slider sunning itself in a big outdoor terrarium with large pond.

TRACHEMYS SCRIPTA ELEGANS, RED-EARED SLIDER

Legal status: CITES B.

The red-cheeked slider previously formed part of the *Pseudemys* and *Chrysemys* genera. This was clearly the most widely sold terrarium animal until the trade was stopped in 1998. Females captured in the wild in the USA were collected to lay their eggs and the young hatchlings were exported soon after they hatched with a empty stomach and often got nothing to eat for three months. Animals with a full stomach pass stools which have to be cleaned up.

These tiny creatures were sold cheaply in a container with a little palm tree to people with no knowledge. The containers could not be equipped with heating or filtration and provided far too little room for these active little animals. Most of them died within a few months and the survivors were either taken to an animal rescue centre or dumped in the local pond or ditch. There they become a threat to the natural fauna or perish through the cold. In countries where the European terrapin is still indigenous, the red-eared introduction is a formidable opponent.

Appearance

Females grow to 300mm (12in) long, the males to 200mm (8in). The base colouring is green with black patches and stripes and bright red patches

Trachemys scripta elegans.

on the ears. The plastron is yellow with black patches.

Distribution

Red-eared sliders inhabit quiet ponds and rivers that are rich in plant growth in the east and south east of the USA (subtropical climate).

Accommodation

Provide an aqua-terrarium of at least 120 x 50 x 50cm (4ft x 20 x 20in). See also the paragraphs 'Accommodation' and 'Salmonella' at the beginning of this section on Freshwater turtles and terrapins. Keep the water temperature at 18-22°C (64.4-71.6°F).

Do not combine the red-eared slider with many smaller or less active freshwater turtles or terrapins. *Graptemys* species such as the widely sold *G. kohni*, the Mississippi map turtle (150-300mm/6-12in) and *Cuora* species are possible joint residents

The red-cheeked slider can certainly spend May to September in a garden pond sited in a sunny position, provided it also offers shade and is not exposed to winds. The banks must not be too steep. Lay a thick branch from a tree in the water as a sun basking spot. With smaller ponds use a pond filter. Terrapins are good climbers so make sure there is a smooth partition with an overhanging top that is at least twice as high as the terrapin's length. Red-eared sliders lay their eggs in a sandy beach covered by glass. Make sure the difference in temperature is not too great when they are put out of doors. They can normally over-winter in a pond that is at least 1m (40in) deep.

Feeding

They are omnivores: see Freshwater turtles and terrapins.

Sex determination

Males have long claws on their front legs, a larger tail, and very shallow dishing of the plastron.

Mating

Let them hibernate from December to February at 3-5°C (37.4-41°F) or have a winter rest at 10-15°C (50-59°F) with lighting for six hours each day. In the wild this species often rests in loose substrate

An egg-laying box with moist sand.

at the bottom of a pond or water course. These animals mate soon after winter but also often after their water has been replaced. The male bites the female's neck during mating, which can lead to wounds.

Egg laying

Eggs are laid from March to May, in one to three sessions with intervals of a month. About ten eggs (four to twenty) are laid and this sometimes occurs only after the substrate in a laying box has been changed (generally moist sand). The eggs hatch after about 65-105 days at 28-30°C (82.4-86°F).

Rearing

Rear the young in a small aquarium in which an area of land has been created with e.g. heaps of flagstone or slate. A spot lamp is needed above the land area so that the terrapins can warm themselves up and dry off. The water should be 25°C (77°F).

The young terrapins have a shell of about 20mm (³/₄in) but grow quickly. Feed them the same as the parents but they can also have water fleas, tubifex, and other aquatic life. Young terrapins have a major need for calcium and vitamins (D), but this is less so in adults. Place the young terrapins outside in the sun if possible but make sure there is also shade available.

The order Crocodilia, crocodiles, alligators, and caimans

Legal status: Virtually all species are CITES A (including *caiman crocodilus apaporiensis* and *Osteolaemus tetraspis*).

The remainder (including the other *Caiman crocodilus* subspecies, *Alligator mississippiensis*, and *Paleosuchus* species are CITES B.

Young crocodilians of fairly small species such as *Caiman crocodilus*, the spectacled caiman, look fascinating and are often purchased on impulse. If crocodiles, alligators, and caimans are not properly cared for they will quickly die, and if they

are properly cared for they grow too big and much too dangerous. It is very difficult to find suitable accommodation for animals of three years old. Zoos rarely want cast off crocodilians because newcomers will not be readily accepted in a group and will cause stress and major problems. Therefore think carefully before you begin and don't do it!

These animals are not suitable terrarium creatures for virtually any hobbyist. In order to recognize this go and look at some fully grown examples at a zoo.

This paragraph is written to warn everyone, and for those who have bought one on impulse.

The order consists of following three families with their genera: Crocodylidae *(Crocodylus, Osteolaemus, Tomistoma)*, Alligatoridae *(Alligator, Caiman, Melansochus,* and *Paleosuchus)*, and Gavialidae *(Gavialis)*.

Appearance

Crocodilians are massively built animals with strong, flattened tails for swimming. There are four toes on the fairly short legs. The eyes (with protected 'third eyelid'), ears (with external mechanism to close the ears), and nostrils (with encircling folds of skin to close them) are mounted high on the flattened head. When hunting, these are the only parts of the body visible above water. The teeth are large. There is also a fold of skin in the throat to close off the throat.

The large angular scales are borne on strong plates of bone which makes them look armoured. There are ridges of 'teeth' on either side of the back which only come together at the tail. There are two separate chambers to the heart and two atria with one valve between them. The valve closes when a crocodilian dives so that oxygen rich blood goes first to head and not straight to the internal organs. Because of this system and their enormous lungs,

The eyes, ears, and nostrils are often the only bits above water (crocodile farm in Thailand).

Alligator mississippiensis.

Terrarium with young spectacle caiman.

Adult spectacle caiman.

crocodilians can remain under water for more than one hour.

Young spectacled caimans (Caiman crocodilus) are light brown with black flecks. This species becomes 2.5m (8ft 2in) long and dark green. There is a raised ledge between the eyes like the bridge between two spectacle lenses. There are four subspecies.

Mississippi alligators (Alligator mississippiensis) that are sometimes offered for sale grow from 3m to a maximum of 6m (10ft to almost 20ft). Alligators have an extremely large mouth.

Paleosuchus species and Osteolaemus tetraspis 'only' grow to be 1.5m (6ft) long. The latter of these species is extremely rare.

Distribution
The various subspecies of spectacle caiman inhabit southern parts of North America through to subtropical South America. The Mississippi alligator originates from the southern states of the USA.

Accommodation
An aqua-terrarium, with a large water area, needs to be at least three times as long and one-and-a-half times as wide as the overall length of the specimen. The water temperature should be 25-28°C (77-82.4°F). The water area needs to be filtered and replenished at frequent intervals. Anyone who thinks a crocodilian can be 'put in the bath' should think long and hard before buying one.

Many crocodilians live in the tropics and subtropics so create a place with a row of pressed-glass spot lamps, large halogen or metal halide lamps with localised temperature of 40°C (104°F). The general air temperature should be 20-25°C (68-77°F) in winter and 25-30°C (77-86°F) in summer. Plant large and sturdy plants such as *Marantha* and *Philodendron* species if there is sufficient room.

Design and build the terrarium so that it is not necessary to go in with the animals in order to clean their enclosure, instead been able to do so from outside with a high-pressure spray from outside. Make sure the animal's hiding place can be shut with the animal inside while these works are carried out.

Feeding

Crocodilians are carnivores. They eat fish, mammals, beef, heart, chicken, and other poultry. Try to get the crocodilian used to dead prey. Feed once or twice per week but not too much for they quickly become fat. They snatch their prey (or the hands of a careless keeper) with a lightning quick strike and then tear it to pieces by one means or another. Crocodilians that are reluctant to eat dead food can sometimes be encouraged with fish offered in still water, where they can see the 'prey' better.

If fish or meat is fed without bones then it will be necessary to supplement the diet with calcium. Problems with the alignment of the teeth are the first signs of calcium deficiency. Supplement also with about 500IU vitamin D₃ per kilogram body weight or provide ultra-violet light.

Sex determination

Externally sexing crocodilians is not possible by observation and endoscopic means are risky because of the dangers of anaesthetic. With crocodiles and caiman from 800mm (31¹/₂in) upwards, the cloaca can be probed with one or two fingers, while another person holds the animal with both hands (see photo). The jaws must be held closed and the head blindfolded. With a lubricated finger

Sexing a spectacle caiman of 900mm (35¹/₂in).

A young spectacle caiman gets a mouse as food.

inserted towards the head, a single bulging crooked penis can be found with males while there is solely the walls of the cloaca with females. Larger crocodilians can be first placed by remote control in a transport or capturing box that securely fastens and then sexed via a sliding panel on the underside. Entering via a ladder to determine sex causes far greater stress.

The (generally larger) males defend their territory and attract females by roaring. The females of many species can also make a noise. Slamming the head against water forms part of the courtship ritual. Young crocodilians of up to 750mm (29¹/₂in) thud, snort, whistle, or growl.

Mating

Mating takes place side-by-side in the water. Because of the unusual position and shape of the elongated penis, mating can last from several minutes to hours. For the spectacle caiman the water needs to be at least 1m (40in) deep.

Spectacle caimans mate in the wild in December and lay their eggs in January. The hatchlings emerge in March-April to coincide with the rainy season.

Egg laying

Crocodilians are the only reptiles that build complex nests from plant material and earth in which to lay their eggs. A breeder must give them this opportunity. A land area of a good many square metres is required for spectacle caimans. Provide ample plant material in addition to a container filled with mixed sand and peat.

The female sometimes becomes restless as much as one and a half months before laying her eggs and shows a tendency to dig. The clutch of 20-100 eggs are guarded by the female from the water. Eggs of spectacle caimans that are removed for incubation hatch in 73-75 days at 30-32°C (86-89.6°F) if placed in one part vermiculite to two parts water.

Rearing

Newly hatched caimans first digest the egg yolk. They then eat swordtails, guppies, all manner of insects, soft animals, crustaceans, and mammals. Freshen the water at regular intervals.

Raise the young in groups of similar size since larger specimens will eat smaller ones of their own kind. A spectacle caiman grows about 100-200mm (4-8in) each year for the first few years and is sexually mature when 1.5m (6ft).

It is fun to breed these creatures but finding responsible homes for them is a problem.

Sicknesses

Newly acquired or ill crocodilians are best observed in a smaller pool of water with no running water. These animals are often full of amoebae which does not generally present a problem but after a period of stress from being caught and transported their resistance can be severely reduced.

Prevent rachitis (rickets) caused by a lack of calcium by feeding a varied diet supplemented with adequate calcium and vitamin D_3. Crocodilians can suffer from failure to lay their eggs.

Defence and handling

Crocodilians can be very snappy from an early age. Only if crocodilians become accustomed to a calm and reasonable relationship with humans from an early age can there be any chance of being able to have some trust in dealing with them later. Handling should be avoided as far as possible. Hold small crocodilians (up to 1m/40in) under the head and grasp the back legs and base of the tail with the other hand. With larger specimens first cover

the eyes with a cloth. Pull the mouth with is ample teeth shut using a strap on the end of a pole. One of the front legs should also be held by the same strap to prevent the animal from running around and strangling itself. Bind the mouth shut with bandage or cloth but never with difficult to remove adhesive tape or plaster.

In addition to large teeth, crocodilians also have a very powerful body and tail. These animals can be truly dangerous from 1.5m (6ft) upwards.

Spectacle caiman in its egg.

This 900mm (35¹/₂in) specimen can still be handled unlike the baby above.

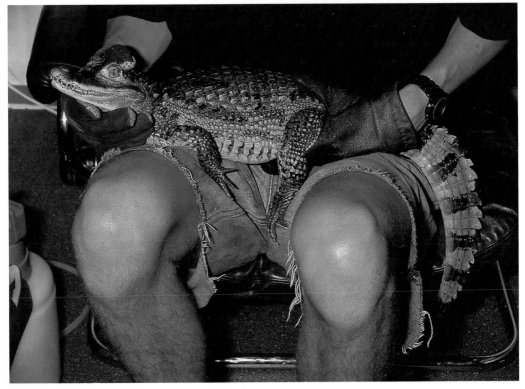

White's tree frog, Litoria caerulea.

The class Amphibia, amphibians

Amphibians are vertebrate animals which are reliant on water for their reproduction. While certain species live both in and out of water, others live almost exclusively aquatically.

There are three orders of amphibians: the Anura or Salientia (approx. 4,600 frogs and toads), the Urodela or Caudata (450 species of newts and salamanders), and the Apoda or Gymnophiona (consisting of more than 160 species of worm-like creatures that are rarely kept in captivity.

The skin

The skin of amphibians is not scaly but thin, often moist and slippery, and with many species covered with poison glands (or warts). Adult amphibians breathe through lungs (lungless salamanders solely breathe through their skin). The larvae of amphibians (such as tadpoles) breath through their skin and for several days or weeks, also through external gills.

Few amphibians survive in arid areas because of their thin skins. They cannot allow themselves to

A worm-like Ichthyophis kohtaoensis *from South-East Asia.*

Amphibians also shed their skins: the old skin of a giant toad.

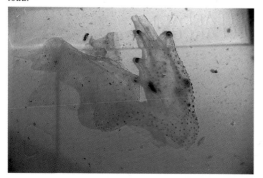

become hot in the full sun as reptiles do in order to reach their body temperature. Regulation of temperature with amphibians is done through change in colour of the skin. Excessive radiation from the sun can be reflected back by a lighter colour. Because of their ability to breathe through their skin, amphibians can remain under water for a long time. Other gases and fluids can also pass through the skin in addition to oxygen. Amphibians shed their skins mainly at night, very quickly, and then eat the old skin.

Almost all amphibians secrete substances from their skins. These substances smell awful and are often toxic, frightening predators, and aiding the healing of wounds. Always wash the hands after handling amphibians. The skin discharges can cause eye irritations among other things.

Accommodation

Amphibians prefer a fairly to very moist terrarium or aquarium. Raise the humidity with regular spraying or a waterfall but never by reducing ventilation. Many species such as Dendrobatidae ideally need a misting system operating for half an hour early in the morning and each evening. Create sufficient hiding places but do not use any sharp materials.

Do not make the terrarium too warm: 15-20°C (59-68°F) for those from moderate climate zones, 20-28°C (68-82.4°F) for those from tropical areas. Any plants will need plenty of light so use tubular fluorescent lamps which give plenty of light with little heat. A small (7 watts) ultra-violet emitting lamp can also be used. Sufficient ventilation and

This frog (possibly Leptopelis bufonoides) *in the African Sahara region is having a summer sleep. They reflect the sun's rays with a light colour to prevent becoming too hot and drying out.*

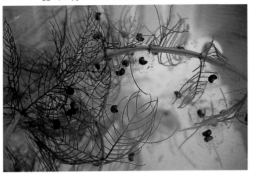

Axolotl eggs (a type of salamander).

A Triturus larva.

good hygiene help to prevent fungal and bacterial infections. Acid soil (peat, leaf mould, fern root) also help prevent infections. Clean the ground, decor material, and panes of glass regularly. Rinse thoroughly after using any cleaning materials. Remove food remnants quickly, especially from aquaria. Filter large water areas and replace one third of the water each week.

Feeding

All adult amphibians are carnivores. They grab all manner of living and moving prey in nature. Sprinkle multi-vitamin and mineral supplements on their food or give them as injections, especially for young animals.

Feed small amphibians every one to two days, and larger ones once or twice each week.

Sex determination

The difference between the sexes can often only be seen with amphibians during mating. Adult females are often fatter. Other sexual differences are dealt with by the species themselves. Buy a minimum of six examples if the genders cannot be ascertained.

Hibernation

Amphibians from areas where there are cold winters hibernate. The principles are the same as with reptiles. Allow the temperature to drop over a number of weeks and gradually reduce the period of lighting. Place the animals in a perforated plastic box, filled with crumbled peat and sphagnum moss and put this in a dark place at 5-10°C (41-50°F). Spray every other day with a little water. Coming out of hibernation can be done slightly more quickly. Do not hibernate young or sick amphibians.

Egg laying

Many amphibians lay eggs. These are not encased within a shell but gathered together in a gelatinous mass. The eggs are often laid in water. With species that lay their eggs somewhere moist out of water, the embryonic and larval stages (and with certain species also a metamorphosis) partially occur within the egg.

The larvae that hatch from most amphibian eggs are fish-like aquatic creatures.

Metamorphosis

Amphibian larvae frequently go ashore in adult form following metamorphosis. During this change in form, gills make way for simple lungs, legs appear, the tail disappears (with frogs and toads) and the stomach and intestines adapt to a carnivorous diet. The heart with one chamber and one atrium changes following metamorphosis into two chambers and two atria.

Amphibian larvae are capable of substantial regeneration with damaged body parts growing back quickly.

Rearing

For the rearing of amphibian larvae assume neutral to slightly acidic water. If water is too alkaline, dissolved calcium salts settle and are no longer available for development of the skeleton. Less calcium becomes available too if the temperature is high.

Work hygienically (see Accommodation). Filter pumps will quickly suck up eggs and larvae. An air filter or bottom filter does not have this risk and provides clear, moving water. Carefully replace one third of the water at regular intervals. Use either rainwater or water that has been aerated for at least 24 hours, of 18-24°C (64.4-75.2°F). The weaker larvae generally do not survive.

Sicknesses

With healthy amphibians:
- the skin is in good condition. Injuries, white patches, and ulcers indicate infections;
- skeleton and mouths are not visible. If they are then it suggests malnourishment or worm infestation;
- the eyes are clear and open.

Amphibians often spend the day motionless, hidden away. When disturbed the animal most want to escape or use a warning and defensive discharge (toads). However many entirely healthy amphibians take little action when disturbed.

Infections spread very easily in moist terrariums or aquaria in which amphibians are housed. Isolate these sick animals at once and ensure good hygiene. Boil or disinfect materials used. Make sure that nothing that has been in contact with the infected animal or terrarium can come into contact with another terrarium.

Amphibians that give a bloated impression are not healthy. It is difficult to be certain of the cause but they often become infected with single cell parasites. Get a vet to check out both the animals and its droppings. The puffing up or other increase in size of the body during reaction to threat is not a matter for concern of course.

A worm infection is not uncommon in specimens captured in the wild and with stressed animals. In some cases the flanks become concave and the underlying skeleton is visible. Stress is caused by too much handling, too many (male) animals housed together, or the wrong type of accommodation. Treat affected animals with 10-30mg fenbendazol per kilogram of body weight, given orally for three days or dilute one part levamisol with two to three parts water. It is also possible to mix 1 gram of a powder preparation for treating flagella with each 100ml of the previous treatments. Filter the murky suspension with a coffee filter and give one drop per 3–5 grams of body weight once a day for three days onto the animal's moist back (which must first be sprayed with water). The solution can be kept for one month in a refrigerator.

Amphibian larvae are difficult to worm and following metamorphosis remain at risk from worming treatments for the first three months after the change of form.

Flagella cause loss of weight resulting from not eating and diarrhoea. The protozoa can also be found by examination of the droppings. Treat these as described above or place infected animals for five days in water with 400mg Dimetridazol per litre of water. Fungal infections appear as downy white patches (surrounding an infected area) on the skin. These are initially caused by injuries, stress, or wrong living conditions (too hot/unhygienic). Spray the animals or place them in 10mg Trypaflavine per litre of water and ensure careful hygiene or place them for five minutes each day in malachite green, until the infection has vanished.

Fungal patches on a fire-bellied newt.

With 'red-leg disease' blood poisoning causes subcutaneous bleeding (red undersides of the limbs and belly), refusal to eat, and death. The illness is caused by too many animals in too small a space, too high a temperature, and/or stress. The primary infections is caused by *Aeromonas* bacteria with secondary fungal infections often following. Isolate affected animals and put them at 18°C (64.4 °F). Add 6 grams of salt per litre of water and treat with antibiotics from a vet.

Salamanders and newts that refused to eat, move strangely, do not shed their skin properly or eat it, and in extreme cases have open wounds right through to the bone are suffering a disease that is quickly fatal that results from water that is too warm, poor diet, or bad hygiene. If caught early enough, the disease can be treated by a vet with antibiotics. Work with a strict regime of hygiene and disinfect the terrariums.

Animals that suffer epileptic fits have a deficiency of calcium or vitamin D_3. Calcium is important for nerve impulses. A small ultra-violet light in the lighting box above the terrarium helps to enable vitamin D_3 to be synthesised. Calcium can then be absorbed. Sprinkle the food with calcium lactate.

Animals in the same terrarium as a sick or dead amphibian are probably also sick or infected.

Take care to avoid animals getting too fat, especially with fairly inactive amphibians. Give animals that are too fat only a little, small, and active live prey.

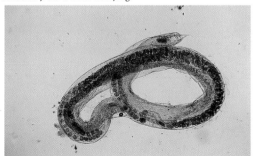
A worm from a dead tree frog.

The order Anura or Salienta, frogs and toads

Appearance

Frogs and toads lose their tails during metamorphosis. There are two pairs of legs attached to the compact body with the rear pair of legs being generally powerfully developed.

Anura have four fingers and five toes. The eardrum is often readily visible. Sounds made by them is amplified by one or two vocal sacs beneath the throat and behind the corner of the mouth.

Distribution

They inhabit various biotopes throughout the world but not in the Arctic or Antarctic regions.

Accommodation

A tree frogs and other climbers require a tall terrarium. Ground-dwellers demand one with a large surface area. The terrarium should not be too cold but certainly not too warm. For most species aim for 18-26°C (64.4-78.8°F) in summer with nights about 13-21°C (55.4-69.8°F). Many frogs die in captivity during long hot summer periods. Prevent this by locating the terrarium in a cool place or by cooling it adequately. Frogs and toads like to hide away so ensure there are plenty of places for them to do so.

Males are often territorial and plague each other to the point of stress. Frogs and toads are a danger for all fellow inhabitants that will fit in the large and wide mouth, including others of their own kind. Some are unable to cope with the skin toxins produced by another frog.

Animals captured in the wild are often stressed so set these in a fairly darkened terrarium to allow them to calm down.

Feeding

Frogs and toads are carnivorous and can grab prey fairly quickly with their long unrolling tongues or by making a leap forward in combination with a shorter tongue. Provide them with varied food consisting of all manner of prey that easily fit their mouths e.g. insects, rodents, or earthworms. Sprinkle these with vitamin and mineral supplements.

Sex determination

It can be very difficult to determine the sexes with many species, particularly with immature specimens.

– An adult male is usually smaller then a similar female and sometimes has brighter colouring.
– Only the males make the mating call. Their vocal sac can some times be seen as a result of ripples and wear of the thin skin. Males sometimes have larger ear drums. Females can often also make a sound as a defensive action (when handled).

Front legs of male and female bullfrogs. The mating pads can be seen on the male's legs.

Hyla septentrionalis, *Cuban tree frog.*

Common frog, Rana temporaria, *amid the eggs.*

The left-hand giant toad is being held uncomfortably but safely. It has puffed itself up.

Many nocturnal frogs and toads are captured through the sound they make. The chance is therefore high that only males are sold.
- With many species the males grasp the female during mating (amplexus) and the males have mating cushions on their fingers and legs to grip better.
- For the same reason males of certain species have longer and stronger front legs than the females.
- Male poison frogs often have broader gripping discs on the tips of their fingers than females.

Mating
Fertilization occurs externally with virtually all frogs and toads. The males clasp on to the female from above, usually just behind the front legs or just in front of the back ones. During this embrace (amplexus) the eggs and sperm are simultaneously ejected, usually into water.

Egg laying
Frogs and toads lay their eggs in clumps, strands, clusters, or individually. Certain species care for the eggs, larvae, and sometimes even the young frogs and toads. One genus is ovoviviparous, retaining its eggs inside the body and giving birth to them.
Many frogs lays eggs after water has been refreshed with cold water.

Rearing
Adult frogs and toads often eat either the larvae or the young frogs and toads. For this reason place the eggs in a separate breeding container with water at 18-22°C (64.4-71.6°F). Hygiene is extra specially important in rearing terrariums (see 'Rearing' earlier about Amphibians).
Tadpoles are usually omnivorous. They begin eating after three to four days, consuming mainly plant material (algae, powdered dry stinging nettle, bruised lettuce, cooked spinach), but also chopped midge larvae, or earthworms, dead tadpoles, flaked aquarium fish food, and yeast. For additional calcium add a little sepia to the water, although the tadpoles only need lots of calcium after metamorphosis. Tadpoles from different species can be raised together except those of poison frogs.

The external gills are subsumed within internal respiratory sacs after a few days. Most tadpoles have an airway tube on the left-hand side of the head linking to these sacs but this is missing with newts and salamander larvae. Anura larvae get bag legs before front ones in contrast to newt and salamander larvae. The front legs often develop very quickly, through a gap in the respiratory sac. Do not worry that the larvae is ill. Provide a cover for the terrarium in plenty of time as the larvae often come ashore as soon as the front legs have developed, while they still have complete tails. Make sure the larvae can come ashore easily, using sloping banks and floating plants *(Pistis stratiotes* or *Eichhornia crassipes).* Many tiny frogs and toads can drown during the first few weeks in water deeper than 10mm (^{3}/₈in).
Start to feed the young amphibians springtails or fruit flies once their tails disappear and remember to add vitamin and mineral supplements.

Defence and handling
Frogs and toads often attempt to escape or take on a threatening demeanour (e.g. puffed up body). Most frogs and toads together with certain newts and salamanders secrete chemicals from the skin. These substances are to a lesser or greater extent toxic, causing irritation, as does the urine from some amphibians.
Frogs and toads are often slippery and inclined to leap. To prevent injuries they need to be handled safely.
Touch amphibians as little as possible in view of their delicate skin. Handle them by getting them to walk or jump into a container without touching them. If they must be handled, hold them with one or two closed, wet hands. Larger species can be held with two fingers around their waists. Always wash the hands after handling them.
For moving them, pack amphibians in a plastic bag with moist paper or some moss. Some amphibians have to be packed on their own because others cannot cope with the secretions they make

when stressed. Aquatic amphibians can be transported in a tight bag with a little water and plenty of air.

Escaped amphibians can be recaptured as quickly as possible after discovering they have gone by laying wet cloths on the floor beneath the terrariums.

The Bufonidae family, toads

The best known toads are from the genus *Bufo*, such as the common toad, *Bufo bufo*, and the giant toad *Bufo marinus*.

The fire-bellied toad is not a true toad and forms part of the disc-like tongued toads or Discoglossidae.

Appearance

Toads have a heavy and compact body, usually covered with poison glands or warts. The limbs are short and strong with almost no webbing between the toes. The jaws are toothless. Males always have rudimentary ovaries or Bidder's organ.

Toads are generally nocturnal animals.

BUFO MARINUS, GIANT, MARINE, OR CANE TOAD

Appearance

Bufo marinus is a 250mm (9³/₄in) long 2kg (4lb 6oz) black, dark brown, or grey brown toad. There are several ridges on the head. There is a very large ear gland, a poison gland behind the ear. A milky coloured toxin is exuded by this gland which is very harmful and renowned for its LSD-like working. *B. marinus* is one of the two most poisonous toads, with the toxin being very dangerous and capable of stopping the heart.

This giant toad exudes a harmful toxin.

The ear gland is clearly visible with this Bufo marinus.

Distribution

Toads occur, except for certain islands, throughout the world.

The giant toad inhabits moderate to tropical forests and fields from southern Texas to Argentina and is found in various places scattered throughout the world to get rid of sugar beet beetle, especially in Australia where it is known as a cane toad.

Accommodation

Toads are fairly slow-moving creatures, not jumping much or very far. They are largely burrowing animals that live at ground level but there are aquatic species.

Provide the giant toad with a ground area of at least 50 x 50cm (20 x 20in) covered with about 100mm (4in) of moderately moist soil (leaf mould, peat/sand mixture, or foam rubber mats). Toads bathe and often excrete in a large water dish which they make very dirty. The soil or bottom needs to be cleaned before it starts to reek of ammonia. The temperature should be 23-28°C (73.4-82.4°F).

Feeding

These toads eat large insects, earthworms, rodents, slugs and snails, smaller toads, and moving bits of meat.

Sex determination

Males are smaller and thinner and have 'nuptial pads' on their fingers. The vocal sac is sometimes visible.

Pair of giant toads. The male's vocal sac on the throat is darker coloured.

Bufo marinus: *only the male has brown 'nuptial pads' on the fingers.*

Ceratophrys ornata.

Mating and egg laying

Amplexus (locking together to mate) usually starts on land after which the animals seek water. The males make a low vibrating sound rather like a machine-gun.

Bufo marinus needs no hibernation and lays strands of up to 20,000 eggs twice each year in slowly moving or still water.

Rearing

The tadpoles hatch within a few days and take between one to three months to metamorphose. They become sexually mature after one to two years.

Defence

When first threatened, toads tend to turn their backs towards the threat and puff themselves up. The toxin is then possibly discharged and they will also urinate in your hands. Wear gloves if required to handle them.

The Ceratophrydae family: (Leptodactylidae)

CERATOPHRYS ORNATA, ARGENTINE HORNED FROG AND C. CORNUTA, SURINAM HORNED FROG

The *Ceratophrys* genus comprises about 10 species and some authorities continue to list it as part of the Leptodactylidae. *C. ornata* is the species most frequently offered for sale.

Appearance

These large frogs have a stumpy head on a rounded body with short legs. *C. cornuta* grows up to a maximum diameter of 200mm (8in) while *C. ornata* achieves 150mm (6in). There are bony plates below the skin. The mouth is half the width of the body. There are flaps of skin or horns above the eyes. These are small bobbles with *C. ornata* and large pointed flaps with *C. cornuta*. The colours vary widely but are usually green with brown, red, or black patches and stripes. The skin is covered with warts.

Distribution

C. ornata originates from the pampas (marshy grasslands) of Argentina through to southern Brazil.

Ceratophrys cornuta.

C. cornuta inhabits pools in the rain forests of north-western Brazil to Guyana, and western Ecuador.

Accommodation

Horned frogs sit in wait of a prey the whole day long, half buried in moist soil (crumbled peat, sphagnum moss, leaf mould). Replace the soil covering regularly because horned frogs make a great deal of mess. Provide a deep layer of soil, a dish of water and daytime temperature of 25-28°C (77-82.4°F). Spray twice each week. If the terrarium becomes too dry the frogs will dig themselves in covered in mucous. Place only one frog in each terrarium.

Feeding

This mouth on legs eats lots of large insects, rodents, earthworms, and fish. Do not overfeed and ensure a varied diet.

Mating and egg laying

Breeding these frogs is difficult. Recreate the dry season by reducing humidity and raising the temperature. The frogs dig themselves in to the ground and surround themselves with mucous. Reverse the process after eight weeks and spray regularly. The frogs mate and lay hundreds of eggs in the water during the 'rainy season'. Hormones are also used to stimulate these frogs to breed.

Rearing

Care for the young in the same way as the parents. They are extremely cannibalistic both before and after metamorphosis, eating anything they can get in their mouth.

Defence and handling

Horn frogs bite their handler's fingers. Because of horny teeth-like projections on the jaws this can be very painful.

The Dendrobatidae family, poison frogs

DENDROBATES, PHYLLOBATES, AND OTHER SPECIES

Legal status: all *Dendrobates, Phyllobates, Allobates, Epipedobates, Minyobates,* and *Phobobates* species are CITES B.

The family consists of eight genera with more than 160 species of diurnal frogs. The small *Dendrobates* and *Phyllobates* species with their bright warning colourings are very popular and often found in terrariums.

The native people of South America (Amerindians) coated the tips of their arrows and darts for their blow pipes by rubbing them across the skin of *P. terribilis* and *P. aurotaenia.* As a result of this these frogs are known as poison arrow or poison dart frogs. The neurotoxin secreted from the skin will kill a large ape in a short time. The poison is only dangerous if is enters the bloodstream so take care of any cuts or abrasions.

Appearance

Poison frogs are generally 10-60mm ($^3/_8$-$2^3/_8$in) long, slimly built and very colourful. The colouring and markings can vary widely within one species (certainly within the *Dendrobates* genus. The eight genera differentiate themselves among other characteristics by the skin toxin, relative length of fingers, the presence or absence of teeth, and reproductive behaviour. Most species have no webbing between the toes of their feet. Poison frogs have little pads of glandular and muscular cells on the uppers side of the finger tips: the gripping discs. The *Dendrobates* species have very enlarged fingertips with the first finger being shorter than the second. With *Epipedobates* and *Phyllobates* species these fingers are of equal length and the finger tips are only moderately enlarged. This latter genus produces young that have orange or yellow stripes from eye to thigh. The thighs have bluish 'metallic' fleck markings. *Colostethus* species are mainly brown in colour. These animals

Dendrobates ventrimaculatus.

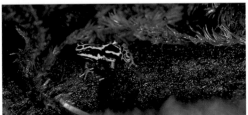

Dendrobates tinctorius.

are not at all shy and are often fascinating to watch, and they whistle a great deal.

Most poison frogs live on the floor of the rain forests in Central and South America, or a few metres above ground. Certain species only live in the tops of trees. Many species existence is threatened by the destruction of the rain forests.

Some 'beginner's species':

Dendrobates auratus is generally a green and black or green and brown frog, in which the green parts are diagonal stripes, flecks, spots, or marbling on the body and legs. The Taboga population produces many specimens with a golden sheen from which the species name is derived. Certain of the Panamanian population have black and blue diagonal stripes. These frogs are 30-40mm ($1^3/_{16}$-$1^1/_2$in) long.

The yellow and black *D. leucomelas* is fairly territorial. This approx. 40mm ($1^1/_2$in) long species is not shy and will cross-breed with both *D. tinctorius* and *D. auratus* so is best not kept with them. The frogs of the *D. quinquevittatus* group grow to 25mm (1in) long. Depending on the particular species and population, these have yellow, green, or orange lateral stripes, sometimes with diagonal links, against a black ground. The legs are flecked or marbled with black on red, or green on blue. A few species have an orange or yellow head *(D. fantasticus),* or back *(D. reticulatus). D. arboreus* lives solely in the tree tops of the forests. - *D. ventrimaculatus-* is the most widely kept of this group in captivity. These are 15-22mm ($^9/_{16}$-$^7/_8$in) and they have yellow lateral stripes on a black ground. A pair will often inhabit and defend a *Bromelia* species plant, making these more difficult to care for.

The normally yellow-black-blue *D. tinctorius* has wide variation in colouring. The females grow to a maximum of 60mm ($2^3/_8$in).

The up to 25mm (1in) long *Epipedobates tricolor* is reddish brown with yellow, green, or white stripes. This species makes an ideal poison frog for beginners.

Phyllobates vittatus is black with two orange lateral stripes and blue-black marbling of the legs. These frogs are a maximum of 30mm ($1^3/_{16}$in) long.

Dendrobates tinctorius *has wide variety of colourings. This one is from French Guyana.*

Distribution

Dendrobates auratus lives in Nicaragua to Panama.

D. leucomelas originates from Venezuela.

Frogs of the *D. quinquevittatus* group originate in Peru, Ecuador, Colombia, Brazil, and French Guyana.

Epipedobates tricolor lives in south-west Ecuador through to Peru.

Phyllobates vittatus inhabits the Pacific coastal lowlands in the south of Costa Rica.

Accommodation

Males defend their territories that are sometimes several metres in size. Females have smaller territories and often eat the eggs of neighbouring females. For this reason place a pair of one male and one female in a marsh terrarium of 50 x 40 x 40cm (20 x 16 x 16in) or a small group in a larger terrarium. The ground (moss, peat, fern roots) should not be soaking wet. Provide sufficient *Bromelia* species plants, film canisters (one third filled with water) or half a coconut with a hole in it on a Petri dish as both hiding place and egg laying container. These must all be possible to check for any eggs being laid.

Vary the humidity from 80–100% by spraying with luke-warm water (25-30°C (77-86°F), a waterfall, and or a misting system. Aerate tap water for 24 hours before use to dechlorinate it.

Most species thrive at a constant low temperature (22-24°C (71.6-75.2°F) by day and 18-22°C

Film canisters and coconuts on Petri dishes used as hiding and egg-laying places.

(64.4-71.6°F) at night), although wider temperature ranges (20-28°C (68-82.4°F by day) will be tolerated for a short time. Keep the water temperature at about 23°C (73.4°F). Mountain dwelling species such as *E. tricolor* need to be kept cooler (20-22°C (68-71.6°F) by day and 18-20°C (64.4-68°F) at night).

with the exception of *Colostethus* and *Arombates* species, all poison frogs have strong toxins they exude through their skin to defend themselves. The constituency of these toxins depends on the food available and extent of any stress. A small amount is sufficient however to kill large animals if the blood is able to enter their bloodstream.

279

In addition to this, poison frogs are very territorial. They will wrestle and fight from time to time, even with frogs of different species. Frogs absorb the poison readily through their thin skin.

A stressed out, dead or very poisonous frog in a terrarium is therefore a source of danger for other occupants, including its own kind. For this reason one terrarium for one species seems the better solution. Those who want to combine species in spite of this, can keep one ground-dweller (e.g. *D. tinctorius, D. auratus,* or *P. vittatus)* with one or more climbing types *(D. quinquevittatus* group).

Combinations of ground-dwelling species of poison frogs can be combined with small tree frogs, toads, and lizards (anoles and geckos such as small *Phelsuma* species), provided these are from a moist biotope or have a dry warm place higher up in the terrarium.

Feeding

Feed fruit flies, spring tails, mites, house flies, collected wild insects, small young crickets, small wax moths, and their larvae. Although these frogs eat lots of ants in the wild, European ants are not suitable food for them. Some Dendrobatidae *(D. tinctorius)* are very sensitive to a period with a poor diet.

Pair of Dendrobates leucomelas.

Dendrobates azureus.

A less common problem of older specimens is a lack of vitamins and minerals but this is probably the main cause of 'matchstick' legs with small frogs just after metamorphosis. Inbreeding and breeding with weaker specimens needs to be avoided completely. If the frogs bring their larvae to the water (natural brooding behaviour) so that the eggs are not removed, the incidence of 'matchstick' legs is reduced.

Sex determination

Females are 2-5mm ($^2/_{64}$-$^3/_{16}$in) longer than the males and they are more rounded. Males sometimes have larger gripping discs on their toes, as though they had two discs rather than one per toe or possessed 'thumbs'. The single vocal sac of the male can sometimes be seen to have damage through use. The males of *D. tinctorius* and *D. azureus* have thicker second and third toes than their female counterparts.

Mating and egg laying

Males defend their territory and attract females by buzzing, vibrating, chirruping, or whistling, other remarkable behaviour, and ritualised wrestling matches. When humidity is high (the rainy season) the male leads the female to a dark, moist, smooth place to lay her eggs. This might be a leaf, a film canister, or a dish under a coconut of flowerpot. After a ritual dance between two or three to as many as 25 eggs, depending on the species, are laid and the male ejects his sperm directly on the eggs without amplexus taking place.

The males and females guard and moisten the eggs and then after one to one-and-a-half weeks the male carries the tadpoles on his back to still water or a tube filled with water or axil of a *Bromelia* plant. The carrying of the entire brood can take a week but the larvae can survive this because of a large store of protein in the egg. It is possible that they also ingest nutrients from the adult's skin. There are a number of variations of this reproductive behaviour. With *D. quinquevittatus* group species the fertilization and egg laying occurs in a water-filled leaf axil of a *Bromelia* plant.

Epipedobates tricolor *male with eggs.*

Try to ensure that the natural brood behaviour can place in the terrarium. If this is not possible the eggs can be removed a few hours or days after they are laid to prevent them being eaten by other frogs or being infected with mould. Lay them with the dark side uppermost on a dish with 1mm (¹/₆₄in) water at 22-23°C (71.6-73.4°F) in a dark place. Raise the water level to 10-20mm (³/₈-³/₄in) when the larvae become slim and active within the egg. Fertilised eggs are clear and hatch after seven to eighteen days.

Epipedobates tricolor lays 15-25 eggs every ten to fourteen days, preferring a *Bromelia* leaf or film canister. The eggs can be left in the terrarium. If kept at 22°C (71.6°F) by day they will hatch after fifteen days and are taken to the water by the male. Metamorphosis follows in about two months.

Rearing

Because of both cannibalism and secretions that restrict growth *Dendrobates* young should be reared separately in plastic or glass jars at 22-24°C (71.6-75.2°F). The omnivorous or herbivorous larvae of *Phyllobates*, *Colostethus*, and *E. tricolor* can be reared in groups in a small aquarium.

The larvae eat nothing for the first three to four days. After this feed them with finely shredded aquarium fish flakes, chopped earthworms or tubifex, water fleas, algae, or vegetable matter. Refresh the water every one to two days, using soft water that is almost neutral in pH and that has been aerated for 24 hours. Do not clean single cellular organisms and algae from the glass of the aquaria or jars. Larger systems using a number of containers with perforated bottoms in a dish or water can also be used. This saves time but produced smaller frogs. A biological filter purifies the water that streams beneath the containers. If the water streamed through perforated sides to the containers from first to last container the fouling on the bottom would not be removed. Use active charcoal filters and replace them about every six weeks. The perforated containers can also float in an aquarium with filtered water, hanging from a raft of polystyrene foam. Fungal or bacterial infec-

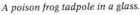
A poison frog tadpole in a glass.

Dendrobates lehmanni.

Male Epipedobates tricolor.

tions can be held at bay with a very small amount of methylated spirits or malachite green.

The larvae first get their legs and colouring. When the front legs appear after about 8-20 weeks, place the larvae in a small well covered terrarium with good opportunities for the larvae to come ashore. The tiny frogs drown very easily. Lay moist moss, peat, or cork on the ground and use film canisters as hiding places. Feed the very small frogs with abundant springtails, aphids, fruit flies, and tiny crickets once their tails disappear. They are sexually mature after six moths to two years and live for 3-15 years depending on the species.

Defence

The strongly alkaline skin toxins remain active for a long time with specimens captured in the wild but captively bred ones contain virtually no skin toxin because of the absence of required substances in their diet (these frogs mainly eat ants, termites, and mites in the wild).

The toxin is dangerous if it enters the bloodstream. The poison smells awful and causes irritation, swellings, and pain in mucous membranes. The toxin keeps parasites, infections (fungal and bacterial), and predators at bay.

Only the poison of *Phyllobates terribilis*, *P. bicolor*, and *P. aurotaenia* can kill mammals (humans are probably too big). All three species originate in Colombia.

Colostethus species have no alkaline skin toxins.

Handling

Read page 275 first. Have respect for and take care with every species. Irritation of the mucous membranes is extremely unpleasant. Wash the hands after handling. Poison frogs are sensitive for stress and can sometimes drop down dead of shock (although sometimes they are not really dead).

The Discoglossidae family, disc-tongued toads

BOMBINA ORIENTALIS, ORIENTAL FIRE-BELLIED TOAD

This interesting, active, and attractive beginner's toad is simple to care for and easy to breed.

Appearance

These are 40-60mm ($1^9/_{16}$-$2^3/_8$in) long toads with green and either brown or black backs with black and red bellies (although this is usually diminished to yellow-orange in captively bred specimens). These toads have large webbing for swimming between their toes. The eardrum is hardly apparent.

Distribution

These toads inhabit cool still water and slowly flowing streams in China, Korea, and eastern parts of Russia.

Accommodation

These animals are not very demanding and can be happily kept in an aqua-terrarium, riparium, or marsh terrarium. The water needs to be filtered or frequently replaced to keep it clear. Too powerful a filter pump can suck in the toads and their eggs. The toads move in and out of the water and land areas frequently so floor covering with compost or peat will quickly soil the water. A land area of flagstone surrounded by urethane foam is easy to clean and therefore more hygienic. Fire-bellied toads do not like temperatures above 30°C (86°F) but can happily survive down to 5°C (41°F). The fire-bellied toad can live in a garden pond during summer.

Sex determination

Males are smaller than females and have small 'nuptial pads' on their thumbs. When they are ready to mate they can be heard softly calling 'hoo-hoo'. By the time they are one-and-a-half years old they have longer and more sturdy front legs than the females.

Mating and egg laying

Let these toads hibernate at 5-15°C (41-59°F) by giving them somewhere to crawl away to in leaves or moss. When they emerge after hibernation the males leap on anything approximately their own size and can be in danger of drowning some tree frogs.

Healthy specimens usually lay their eggs after the water is replaced with cold water. The around 100 eggs are towed one by one all over the place and laid on the bottom.

Rearing

There are no special problems in rearing the young of this species. Adults will readily eat their own offspring.

Defence

When disturbed the toads dive to the bottom of the aquarium; on land they lay on their back.

The family Hylidae, tree frogs

This family consists of about 600 species of mainly nocturnal tree frogs. The best-known genera are *Hyla*, *Phyllomedusa*, *Agalychnis*, and *Litoria*.

The fire-bellied toad, Bombina orientalis.

Fire-bellied toad.

A tree frog holds on to glass with its suction pads.

Males often have a clearly apparent vocal sac. With this
Hyla gratiosa *this is yellow.*

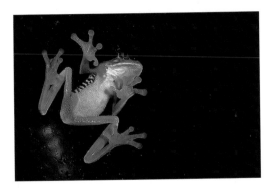

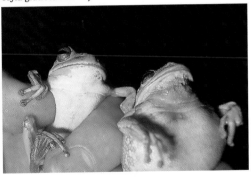

Appearance

Tree frogs have broadened disc-like fingertips that act as suction pads. The eardrum is clearly apparent and they have a wide mouth and large eyes.
During the day these frogs mainly remain firmly stuck to a leaf or the terrarium glass. Their green colouring on the upper part of the body provides ideal camouflage. Those species that spend their time mainly on branches and bark are generally brown. Most species will also be active in the daytime if they are fed.

Distribution

Tree frogs live in most parts of the world except Antarctica but also not south of the Sahara in Africa and not in India through to South-East Asia.

Accommodation

Tree frogs live mainly in trees and therefore need a tall terrarium. The size depends on the amount of activity and territorial behaviour of the frogs. Plant large leafed foliage plants from the genera *Croton, Cyperus, Dracaena, Marantha, Philodendron,* and *Vriesea*. A number of large leaves need to hang immediately above a fairly large water area. Depending on the species, the water may need to be heated.

Feeding

All manner of insects, with nocturnal wax moths being ideal.

Sex determination

Males are small and often have a clearly visible single vocal sac beneath the throat *(Hyla)*. With

An alert Agalychnis callidryas.

certain *Hyla* species, the males also have a spike on one finger.

Mating and egg laying
Many tree frogs lay their eggs during the rainy season and following a dry period. This wet season can be recreated by spraying or with a sprinkler system.

AGALYCHNIS CALLIDRYAS, RED-EYED TREE FROG

This attractive and well-known frog is not for beginners.

Appearance
The genera *Agalychnis* and *Phyllomedusa* form part of the subfamily Phyllomedusinae which has slim bodies and legs, small webbing between the toes, moderately sized gripping pads, and opposable fingers and toes with which they climb more than leap (especially *Phyllomedusa*).

Agalychnis can vary greatly in colouring, depending on its geographic origins. The ground colour is green and when opened the eyes are fiery red. There are yellow and blue stripes on the flanks which are brighter in wild captured specimens than those bred in captivity. This frog is nocturnal and wakes up with a series of exciting shrieks and rubbing of its eyes.

Distribution
Moist and hot forests of southern Mexico through to Panama. Several isolated populations live along the coast on low-lying land.

Accommodation
The red-eyed tree frog requires a large terrarium because of its territorial behaviour and in order to breed, preferably a conservatory. Males need to be at least 50cm (20in) apart from each other. Good breeding results can be achieved with a terrarium of 100 x 50 x 100cm (40 x 20 x 40in) for a pair.
Mexican animals live at temperatures of 22-28°C (71.6-82.4°F) and those from further south at 20-25°C (68-77°F). Try to recreate a rainy season. The water in the water area must be slightly acidic.

Feeding
Feed plenty of large wax moths, crickets, blow-flies, and other collected wild insects.

Sex determination
The males are no bigger than 55mm (2⁵/₃₂in), the females 70mm (2³/₄in). Females are also slightly fatter and when seen in profile have a blunter nose. Both the male and females mark their territories by croaking but only the male has a mating cry.

Mating and egg laying
These frogs mate during the rainy season, which is from March to September in Mexico. A pair or even a trio enter the water locked together in amplexus. The female takes in water, climbs on top, lays the eggs on a leaf, and moistens the eggs with the water she has taken in.
A female can lay five clutches of 250 eggs in total during a night of mating. These eggs are 2-3mm (²/₆₄-²/₁₆in) long and blue-green. Do not spray the eggs with water but keep the terrarium moist.

Rearing
The larvae hatch from the eggs after about one week and are approx. 12mm (¹/₂in) long. Rear them in small groups in water about 100-150mm (4-6in) deep. The larvae eat micro-organisms on the surface of the water, flaked fish food, powdered dried stinging nettle, and plankton collected from ponds and ditches. The metamorphosis occurs after 40-45 days when the larvae are 45-50mm (1³/₄-2in) long. The little frogs of 25mm (1in) only acquire their colouring after several months.

PHYLLOMEDUSA HYPOCHONDRIALIS

Appearance
This up to 40mm (1⁹/₁₆in) long frog normally has a green back during the day but generally turns brown at night. The legs are decoratively striped with orange and black on their insides. The first two fingers and toes are opposed to the others to form gripping hands with which these frogs can grasp branches and stems. They climb with wide steps. The subspecies *P. h. azurea* has tadpoles with a blue tail.

This resting Phyllomedusa hypochondrialis *is brown at the moment but can become green very quickly.*

An adult Agalychnis callidryas.

Phyllomedusa hypochondrialis.

Litoria caerulea.

Litoria caerulea.

Distribution
This tree dweller inhabits forests and savannah areas with clearly defined wet and dry season in northern and central parts of South America, east of the Andes.

Accommodation
Provide a well-planted tropical rain forest terrarium. Males require a territory of at least 50cm (20in) diameter. Temperature should be 23-28°C (73.4-82.4°F) with adequate ventilation but no draughts and humidity not too high.

Sex determination
The males are smaller, thinner, and less rounded than the females.

Mating and egg laying
Breeding this species is not straightforward. Mating is stimulated by a wet, cool period following a hot, dry period. Between 40 and 80 fertilized eggs – plus several hundred more to retain water to prevent the eggs from drying out – are laid on a large leaf above water after several days of amplexus. The leaf is then folded up. If it is opened up all the eggs will be killed.
Put the frogs somewhere dry following mating to prevent fungal and bacterial infections.

Rearing
The eggs hatch after about eight days. The larvae eat flaked aquarium food, blanched vegetables, and algae. The metamorphosis happens after about 50 days.

LITTORIA CAERULEA, WHITE'S TREE FROG

An easy to keep and popular species that has a big appetite.

Appearance
This 100mm (4in) long, plump and powerful frog is green, turquoise, or brown. The skin is waxy rather than slimy and there is a fold of skin from the eye to the front legs.

Distribution
Near ponds and in forests in northern and eastern parts of Australia, New Guinea, and New Zealand. In their natural habitat there is a dry season from April to November and a wet season for the rest of the year.

Accommodation
Provide a large terrarium of 80 x 40 x 60cm (31$^{1}/_{2}$ x 16 x 24in) for a small group of six. Furnish the terrarium with stout branches and sturdy plants and cover the bottom with leaf mould or beech chips. Ensure good ventilation but prevent draughts. These frogs like 26-32°C (78.8-89.6°F) during the day and about 20-24°C (68-75.2°F) at night (which is very hot for an amphibian). Make sure that these frogs cannot leap against a hot lamp which would burn them. Provide a water tray big enough for them to bathe in. Keep the humidity fairly dry (50-60%) by spraying briefly each day.

Feeding
This frog can be fed by hand day and night with insects, earthworms, and dead but moving mice. Take care they do not become fat.

Sex determination
Males are slightly smaller, sometimes have a visible vocal sac , and emit a loud mating cry.

Mating and egg laying
Raise the humidity to 70-85% following a dry season at 50-60% by spraying more often. Put a couple together in a moist terrarium with sprinkler system if an attempt at amplexus is made. The water needs to be about 50mm (2in) deep. Several hundred eggs will be laid within a matter of days and these hatch after one to three days. The larvae are omnivorous. Metamorphosis occurs after five to ten weeks and the little frogs grow rapidly.

285

Handling

L. caerulea is a calm frog that does not rapidly leap to escape. Despite this handle as little as possible.

The Pipidae family, tongueless toads

This family consists of four genera: *Pipa* (with seven species of Surinam toads from South America), *Xenopus* (fifteen species of clawed frogs or toads from central and southern Africa), *Hymenochirus* and *Pseudhymenochirus* (four species and one species of dwarf clawed frogs or toads from central and southern Africa).

Appearance

These somewhat squat grey to brown toads never leave the water. They have webbed rear feet and eyes with eyelids (except for *Pseudhymenochirus*). They have no tongue.

Accommodation

Aquariums with water at 10-32°C (50-89.6°F). The inhabitants have to be about the same size to prevent cannibalism.

Feeding

Chopped tubifex worms, earthworms, water fleas, and other small aquatic creatures, minced meat, strips of meat, small fish but not for the dwarf claw toads, and all manner of amphibian eggs. Feed as

Dwarf clawed toad (also called frog), Hymenochirus boettgeri.

Xenopus laevis: the female's cloaca lips can be clearly seen as a tube between the hind legs.

much as these toads can eat in five to ten minutes and remove left over food.

Sex determination

The larger females can be recognized by the prominent lips to the cloaca. With *Xenopus* in particular these can be seen as a small tube between the hind legs.

Mating and egg laying

Pipidae males do not grasp the female behind the front legs but immediately above the back ones. Provide a mesh grill on the bottom which the eggs can pass through but not the parents. This prevents the eggs from being eaten.

Handling

Handle Pipidae with a fishing net and transport them in a bag with a little water and plenty of air.

HYMENOCHIRUS BOETTGERI, DWARF CLAWED TOAD OR FROG

The dwarf clawed toad (also known as a frog) is often sold for use in aquaria with fish. There are three subspecies: *H. boettgeri boettgeri, H. b. feae,* and *H. b. camerunensis.*

Appearance

This brown toad (or frog) with its dark brown spots and warts on the back has a dirty white belly. The males grow to 30-35mm (1³/₁₆in-1³/₈in), the females 35-40mm (1³/₈-1⁹/₁₆in). This species has webbing between the toes to swim with, claws on three toes, and a small, pointed head.

Distribution

Tropical ponds, pools, and small lakes in West Africa with ample vegetation and slightly acidic to neutral water.

Accommodation

Place them in an aquarium with at least 5 litres of water per animal, with sand or gravel on the bottom. Make hiding places with stones and plants but leave sufficient space for swimming. Provide a small area of shore. Cover the aquarium even though these animals rarely escape up a short length of vertical glass.

Put the aquarium in a sunny position or light it well or the animals will not breed. They like to

Close off the top of the aquarium to prevent escape.

Hymenochirus boettgeri, *the dwarf clawed toad (or frog).*

Pipa pipa, *the Surinam toad.*

bask in the sun, semi-submerged, resting on a plant or other decor, and close to a lamp. Take care to prevent overheating by the midday sun. The water temperature should be 23-30°C (73.4-86°F). Dwarf clawed toads (or frogs) adapt themselves to almost every type of water.

Sex determination
Adult females are large and fatter than males. The males have a clearly visible gland behind the front legs.

Mating and egg laying
Mating is stimulated by cool fresh water and also by bringing the pair of animals back together again after separation. During attempts at mating, the male makes a soft clicking or buzzing sound. After the courtship dance by the male the eggs and semen are distributed over the surface while the pair are locked together as they move about (in amplexus). After an hour some 100 to 200 brown eggs are discharged. The parents will eat the eggs and so must be removed.

The female is unable to discharge more eggs for a few days. Make sure she does not become exhausted.

Rearing
The type of water is not an important factor in rearing. The eggs hatch after two days at about 26°C (78.8 °F). The 4mm (^{5}/$_{32}$in) long brown larvae swim about on the surface for the first few days. They seek out single celled organisms with their large eyes and suck them in (these can be cultivated in jars of ditch water with a small dice of swede or turnip). Metamorphosis begins when the tadpoles are about 15mm (^{5}/$_8$in) long and is completed after five to eight weeks. The little toads (or frogs) are sexually mature after 12-18 months.

Defence
In danger dwarf clawed toads sometimes lay on their backs as if dead, like fire-bellied toads.

PIPA PIPA, SURINAM TOAD

Appearance
These up to 200mm (8in) long grey-brown flat toad has an angular body and triangular head. *Pipa* species have strongly developed sensing organs

on the tips of the fingers in contrast with other tongueless toads. These nocturnal toads have webbing between the toes and no claws.

Distribution
These toads inhabit streams and still water in northern parts of South America, including the Amazon including cultivated areas.

Accommodation
Provide two or three specimens with at least an 80 x 40 x 60cm (31^1/$_2$ x 16 x 24in) aquarium that is not too strongly lit and that has plenty of hiding places. The height is needed for the mating dance ritual. The temperature should be 25-30°C (77-86°F). A good filter is needed for these gluttons. Do not allow them to become too fat.

Sex determination
Males have a visible vocal sac and 20mm (^{3}/$_4$in) long 'nuptial pads' on the back legs.

Mating and egg laying
The female lays 100-300 eggs during a series of underwater somersaults. The eggs stream between her back and the belly of the male, who is clamped onto her. After fertilization the eggs are pushed into the pores of her back. Within 24 to 36 hours the eggs have grown through the skin. The larvae develop in little brood chambers in the female's back over three to five months into 20mm (^{3}/$_4$in) long toads. The female is quite shattered after the infants are finally released and requires good feeding. The young are sexually mature in one to on-and-a-half years, when they are 120-150mm (4^3/$_4$-6in).

XENOPUS LAEVIS, CLAWED FROG OR TOAD

This frog (some call it toad) looks like, requires the same care, and reproduces like *Hymenochirus boettgeri.*

Appearance
This up to 100mm (4in) long grey-brown frog with dark brown web markings has a fairly smooth skin and claws on the inner three toes. Webbing of the feet is restricted to between the toes. Albino specimens are often available for sale. There are five subspecies.

Distribution
This frog inhabits tropical moderate water areas in

Xenopus laevis, *the clawed frog.*

Xenopus laevis, *the clawed frog.*

the east and south of Africa. They are often found in murky water but never in fast flowing streams or rivers.

Accommodation

Use an aquarium of 80 x 40 x 40xm (31¹/₂ x 16 x 16in) for six clawed frogs. These frogs can survive water temperatures of 15-35°C (59-95°F)' but the optimum is 22-25°C (71.6-77°F). Place the aquarium where it will catch the morning sun but not where there is a danger of it overheating from the midday sun.

Sex determination

The cloaca lips are visible with females as a tube between the back legs. Males often stand up on

their toes and have darker 'nuptial pads' on fingers one to three during the mating season.

Mating and egg laying

These frogs mate during the wet months in Africa. Mating is best stimulated in aquaria by replenishing the water with warm water after several cooler weeks at 12-15°C (53.6-59°F). There is no ritual dance with *Xenopus* species, which mate swimming around on the bottom. These frogs spread 500-2,000 eggs throughout the aquarium and then start to eat them at once. The eggs hatch after two to three days.

Rearing

The tadpoles have two long, threadlike gills. Rear them at 20-25°C (68-77°F). During the first few weeks larger food such as algae, powdered nettle, yeast, and crumbed fish food can cause blockages. Sieve the food first through a cloth. Metamorphosis occurs in five to seven weeks, with females growing more rapidly. These frogs are sexually mature at one year old.

Special remarks

This frog is widely used in laboratories. It was used for instance to develop a pregnancy test.

The Ranidae family, 'true' frogs

RANA SPECIES

There are about 220 species of the genus *Rana*, including the green or edible frog *(Rana esculenta)*, the marsh frog *(Rana ridibunda)*, and the brown or European common frog *(Rana temporaria)*. The bullfrog and certain other large species are sometimes caught and bred for human consumption.

Appearance

The 'true' frogs have characteristic frog form with pointed outward facing toes and fingers. There is a broad mouth with teeth Those that live primarily aquatically are mainly green, have large webbing between the toes, and they often over-winter under water (such as the bullfrog). Those that are brown mainly return to the water to reproduce.

The green frog.

The bullfrog.

Bullfrogs eat everything that will fit into their mouths, including mice.

Large, dark-coloured, and plump frogs covered with warts often live in mountain streams.

Distribution

Frogs of *Rana* species are found throughout the world except in Australia and large parts of South America.

Accommodation

Most species are unsuitable for terrariums because of the way they jump. They injure themselves a great deal. Caring for species from moderate climate zones in a garden pond can be considered but the escape of non indigenous species can be harmful for the ecology. For the other Ranidae a terrarium with an area of land covered with peat or urethane foam and a shallow water area can suffice. Spray with water daily.

Feeding

Feed the larger species with crickets and grasshoppers. Bullfrogs can even be fed mice and young rats. The smaller species eat fruit flies and similar small insects.

RANA CATESBEIANA, BULLFROG

Legal status: CITES B.

Some years ago large quantities of bullfrog tadpoles were sold for garden ponds. These frogs escaped and disturbed the native ecological balance. Fortunately these frogs find it difficult to survive

Because bullfrogs naturally do not leap much they can be kept in relatively small water's edge ripariums. This 100 x 50 x 50 (40 x 20 x 20in) unit has a urethane rear wall.

and breed in the northern European changeable climate, especially in late winter. Imports into the European Community are now being controlled.

Appearance

The body of this usually green or brown frog grows up to 200mm (8in) long.

Distribution

These frogs originated from the east and central parts of the USA where they mainly lead an aquatic life.

Accommodation

Create a riparium (water's edge terrarium) of at least 100 x 50 x 50cm (40 x 20 x 20in) for a pair but much better one and a half times bigger than this. Provide a large water area. Males fight to defend their territory.

Feeding

All manner of living prey, including adult mice. In the wild they also eat crustaceans, snakes, turtles, and terrapins.

Sex determination

The slightly more colourful and smaller males have large black 'nuptial pads' on their thumbs which are usually visible during the mating season. They also have slightly larger eardrums.

The mating cry of the males is just like a bull bellowing, even in terms of volume, which is how the frog gets its name. There is a single sound bladder. Both males and females repeatedly make a much softer 'bweh' when they are handled.

Mating and egg laying

Mating and egg laying follows hibernation at about 15°C (59°F). Several thousand eggs are laid between water plants in spring.

Rearing

It is natural for the development of the bullfrog to take several years.

The Rhacophoridae family, nest-building tree frogs

This large African and Asian family are the counterparts of the Hylidae tree frogs. Some taxonomists consider the subfamily Hyperoliinae as a

family in its own right and place the Mantelinae and Rhacophorinae with the Ranidae ('true frogs'). Important genera are *Afrixalus, Hyperolius, Kassina, Mantella,* and *Rhacophorus.*

HYPEROLIUS SPECIES, REED FROGS

There are more than 100 species of *Hyperolius* that are difficult to determine, with many sub-species. The best known is *H. marmoratus.*

Appearance
These very colourful, slimly-built frogs usually have a dark green or brown back with red, yellow, white, or blue markings. The side of the belly is white or yellowish and there are red or yellow suction discs on the fingers and toes. The inside of the limbs are mainly reddish. These frogs grow to 25-40mm (1-1⁹/₁₆in) long and they have large eyes. The eardrums are barely visible. The webbed membranes between the fingers are minimal and come about half way up the toes. These nocturnal frogs regularly bask in the sun.

Distribution
Africa, south of the Sahara, in open savannah, wooded areas, gardens, and other grassland. Often found close to water but not in deserts or rain forests.

Accommodation
The males defend their territory by stamping their

Female Hyperolius fusciventris.

feet. The terrarium must not be smaller than 100 x 50 x 50cm (40 x 20 x 20in) for six specimens and at least a quarter of the ground area should consist of about 100mm (4in) deep pool of rainwater. Plant floating plants such as Pistia stratiotes, reed stems, and other plants. Keep the temperature throughout the year at 28-32°C (82.4-89.6°F).

Feeding
Feed small insects. Spray every day with a little water to which vitamins and minerals have been added.

Sex determination
The male's throat is a brighter yellow and is more grainy, with the vocal sac often being wrinkled. Males call with an enormous single croak. There can be a difference in colour between the sexes during the mating period.

Mating and egg laying
When the days lengthen or if it rains, the males start to sound off and to fight with other males. During mating the female lays from tens to hundreds of eggs on the surface of the water, often on floating plants, and sometimes just above the water.

Rearing
The eggs hatch after four to ten days at 22-24°C (71.6-75.2°F). Feed the fussy tadpoles with flaked aquarium food, algae, other green fodder, and chopped earthworms after three days. The little frogs are usually green after their metamorphosis which occurs after four to six weeks. They are sexually mature in six to eighteen months. Take care to avoid inbreeding (colour weakening, mutations).

Purchase
Reed frogs are captured by their sound in Africa, which produces almost only males. Buy at least ten specimens because it is so difficult to get females of the same subspecies from another source.

MANTELLA AURANTIACA, MADAGASCAR GOLDEN FROG

Legal status: all *Mantella* species are CITES B.
The *Mantella* genus consists of about eleven species of which *M. aurantiaca, M. madagascariensis* (previously *M. cowani*), and *M. viridis* are the best known. *Mantella* species frogs do not belong, as is often thought, to the poison frogs.

Hyperolius *species.*

Hyperolius *species.*

Mantella aurantiaca.

The pale urethras are more apparent on the lighter belly of M. aurantiaca *males.*

Appearance
Mantella aurantiaca is a plain yellow to reddish orange frog of 10-25mm ($^3/_4$-1in).

Distribution
M. aurantiaca inhabits dense scrub on Madagascar. Their biotope is very humid from April to October with the daytime temperature varying between 20-28°C (68-82.4°F) and 16-22°C (60.8-71.6°F) at night. For the rest of the year it is 15-20°C (59-68°F) during the day and about 10°C (50°F) at night. The biotope is dry from July to September when the frogs are usually deep in burrows in the ground. The deep layer of soil insulates them against drought and cold and also serves as somewhere to lay their eggs. During the time that fruit falls from the trees many of these frogs take the opportunity to hunt fruit flies.

Accommodation
House six to eight of these frogs in a well ventilated terrarium of 80 x 40 x 50cm (31$^1/_2$ x 16 x 20in). Place at least two males with each female.

Lay broken peat, leaf mould, or a well-washed and fairly moist piece of artificial matting on the bottom. Decorate with pieces of timber, stone on top of moss. Provide a shallow 100mm (4in) diameter water dish in a cool position and clean it twice per week. Light for 12-14 hours per day in the summer and ten hours in winter, ideally with some supplementary ultra-violet source as well. These frogs escape easily through the smallest of apertures.

Feeding
Feed fruit flies, finely prepared wild captured insect life, house flies, aphids, and tiny crickets.

Sex determination
Males remain smaller, are slimmer, often have a darker throat, have larger femoral glands (pairs of elongated pads around the cloaca) and make a whistling sound. With the males of *M. aurantiaca* their pale urethras are also more visible on the lighter-coloured belly.

Mating and egg laying
The territorial males stimulate each other to reproduction/fertilization, sometimes with aggression. Hibernation can be also considered if required. It is rare to actual witness mating taking place.

In the wild these frogs mate from November to January but clutches of eggs can be expected at any time of the year in a terrarium. The 20-100 eggs of 1.5mm (¹/₁₆in) long eggs are laid in moist hollows (beneath moss or kitchen paper in a double bottom above water that is sprayed daily). The eggs must not be exposed to light! Leave the eggs for two to five days until the young have almost emerged. Moisten then with rainwater that has been boiled and then cooled to 20-25°C (68-77°F). Place the eggs half submerged so that the young can reach water of about 22°C (71.6°F).

Rearing
The 8mm (⁵/₁₆in) long white tadpoles are omnivorous (vegetable matter, fish food). They turn brown after a few days. House them in a 30 x 15cm (12 x 6in) container with 30-50mm (1³/₁₆-2in) lightly acidic water and a few plants. Keep the temperature at 20-23°C (68-73.4°F) and aerate the water gently for the first three weeks and keep it clean (freshen it and remove dead tadpoles).

The back legs appear after about one month and the front ones after two months. Make sure then that they can easily crawl out onto land. Place the 5-7mm (³/₁₆-⁴/₁₆in) long little brown frogs in rearing containers and feed them springtails, aphids, and later with fruit flies. They turn orange by the time they are 15mm (⁵/₈in) long.

Males are smaller and thinner.

Mantella madagascariensis.

Defence and handling
Both *M. aurantiaca* and *M. madagascariensis* are known to exude alkaline toxins from their skin that is similar to that of poison frogs. Adult frogs often act dead, laying on their back, when confronted with danger. The young in particular can drop down dead instantly if they are stressed by humans.

The order Urodela or Caudata, newts and salamanders

The 450 species of newts and salamanders can be divided into two groups by their lifestyles. There are those that live on land, rarely if ever returning to water and those that spend at least several months of the year in water. The land group has a round tail while the water newts and salamanders have flattened tails for swimming.

Appearance
Most newts and salamanders are between 50-300mm (2-12in) long.

The front and back legs are more or less of equal size and fairly weakly developed. Newts and salamanders are generally slow moving. Their tails are longer than the bodies. Eyes are small and there are no ears. The lungs are primitive or absent. Those species without lungs breathe through their

Aqua-terrarium with salamanders and air filter.

292

skin and the mouth. The terrestrial species are often more brightly coloured, signalling that they are poisonous or want to give the impression they are.

Distribution
Except for the genus *Bolitoglossa,* all the species originate in the northern hemisphere.

Accommodation
Provide a moist and humid terrarium that is not too warm. There should ideally be a large water area (this is a must during the mating period). This needs to be easy to clean so choose a substrate which dirt cannot get hidden behind (2-3mm gravel or sand). Ensure there are a few water plants for the laying of eggs. Replace one third of the water each week with new cold water that often stimulates breeding behaviour within a few day. Salamanders and newts like to hide away by day under stones, timber or bark. There must not be any sharp objects on the land part of the terrarium (use leaf mould, peat, and sphagnum moss). Make sure that half of the terrarium is kept moist while the other half remains drier. The animals can then regulate their own moisture levels. Those that are kept too wet tend to suffer from fungal and bacterial infections.

Position the terrarium where it can catch the morning sun but not the heat of the midday sun. Close the terrarium off properly because even the aquatic species are good climbers.

Newts and salamanders do not like it too hot.

Aqua-terrarium with fire salamander.

Earthworms are excellent food for all salamanders.

The thickened cloaca of a male axolotl.

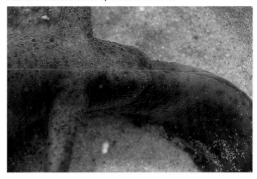

Swings between a maximum of 22°C (71.6°F) in summer to 10°C (50°F) in winter are fine for most species. If it is too warm the life expectancy is reduced and egg laying stops. Many of the tropical species have a summer sleep in a cool place if conditions become too hot.

Newts and salamanders over-winter in a layer of leaf mould or in a loose bottom layer underwater. Species from moderate climate zones over-winter at 5-10°C (41-50°F). Do not combine salamanders and newts with large or very active animals because they prefer peace and quiet.

Feeding
Earthworms, tubifex, Enchytraeidae worms, slugs, water fleas, all manner of slow moving and soft insects and their larvae, small fish, mice, and baby rats. Water living species can be fed a little minced beef, beef heart, fish, and frozen fish food from time to time. Do not feed too much and remove uneaten remnants quickly. Prey are caught underwater by rapidly opening the mouth, causing suction, by suddenly rushing at it, or by means of a sticky tongue.

Sex determination
The males of water living types acquire skin extensions such as a dorsal comb, normally only during the mating period, but also brighter colours. The male is often smaller but with a longer tail. Land-living species males are slightly larger than the female.

The female's cloaca with many species is elongated during the mating period and slightly dilated. The male's cloacal lips are even more pronounced during the mating time to make room for the glands that produce the jelly for the spermatophores.

Sometimes the males have rough thickening of the front legs to form copulation bristles or 'nuptial pads' to enable him to grip during mating.

Mating
Healthy newts and salamanders usually mate following hibernation.

The males attract a female with their fine colours and fins, and by displays of strength (swimming circles while holding the female tight) or they entice her with scent from the cloacal glands, spread by waving the tail about.

After the courtship the female follows the male, sometimes turning somersaults. The male ejects a series of spermatophores to the bottom of the aquarium. The female needs to take in at least one. The fertilization occurs internally and some species develop the eggs ovoviviparously (carry and develop the eggs internally until birth). Females store the sperm in the spermatheca next to the cloaca.

Egg laying
The female fertilizes the eggs as she lays them, usually several days after mating. Eggs are usually placed one at a time under water on plants, wood, or stones. Certain species guard their eggs. Many of those without lungs (Plethodontidae family) develop wholly out of water in moist places.

Rearing
Remove the eggs quickly to prevent the parents eating either the eggs or their tadpoles. The tadpoles lay motionless on the bottom for the first few days. Feed the carnivorous larvae with very finely sieved ditch water plankton and later with tiny brine shrimp nauplii *(Artemia)*, water fleas, midge larvae, chopped tubifex, and a little egg yolk. The tadpoles have to be placed in the food and hygiene is extremely important. The temperature should be 18-25°C (64.4-77°F). Sort

A lungless salamander.

An axolotl egg and tadpole.

Tritus species tadpole. The front legs develop first with newts and salamanders.

The 'adult' form of an axolotl. If the correct hormone is provided and the water level reduced, axolotls (and other creatures to which neoteny applies) will metamorphose.

the tadpoles by size frequently to prevent cannibalism.

The tadpoles have a vertically flattened swimming tail.

Prior to their three pairs of external gills the tadpoles have wispy tendrils that disappear once the front legs develop. Most species undergo a metamorphosis in which the external gills disappear. A few species such as the axolotl have no metamorphosis and live and reproduce in the larval form (neoteny).

Defence
Newts and salamanders lead secretive lives, hidden away and being active only at night. Many species have skin toxins like frogs. Certain species have bright warning colours and some have tails that will drop off.

Handling
Handle water-dwelling newts and salamanders with a fishing net and carry them in a plastic bag with plenty of air and a little water. Wash salts off the hand before touching land species and do not dry the hands, leaving them wet. Carry them in a plastic box with damp paper or moss in it.

The Ambystomatidae family, mole salamanders and axolotls

AMBYSTOMA MEXICANUM, AXOLOTL

Legal status: CITES B.

The axolotl, *Ambystoma mexicanum*, is the best known mole salamander. In the wild, metamorphosis never happens. Adult animals continue to possess three pairs of external gills and tail fin (neoteny). Metamorphosis can, however, be induced.

Appearance

Axolotls are up to 300mm (12in) long with dark gills, a compact body with broad, squat head and small eyes. The tail fin is shorter than the rest of the body. The fairly common albino form has red gills. Axolotls hardly move in water. They can breathe via their gills and through both their skin and lungs, coming regularly to the surface of water to breathe. Because of strong regeneration capabilities, gills and limbs that are bitten off will be replaced in a matter of weeks. The gills have the appearance of tubifex. These animals can live for 25 years.

Distribution

These creatures are found in the Xochimilco and Chalco lakes in Mexico.

Accommodation

Keep two to four axolotls in an aquarium of at least 80 x 40 x 40cm (31$^1/_2$ x 16 x 16in) and the water at 15-20°C (59-68°F) in summer and 5-10°C (41-50°F) in winter. Grow plants in the 30cm (12in) deep water but never combine axolotls with fish.

Sex determination

Males have a swollen cloaca, are slightly larger, and have longer tail fins than the sturdier females.

Mating and egg laying

Reducing the water temperature to 5-10°C (41-50°F) by adding ice or cold water recreates the coming winter in the autumn or melting snow in the spring. When this is followed by a increase in temperature it will rapidly stimulate well nourished specimens to mate and lay eggs. The male deposits spermatophores as he swims in circles and waves his tail fin. Remove the eggs complete

The natural colour and albino forms of axolotls.

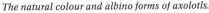

with the plant on which they are placed and rear the young in 50mm (2in) deep water. Between 200 and 1,000 eggs are laid and 7mm ($^4/_{16}$in) long larvae hatch after 15-20 days with the water at 15-20°C (59-68°F). The larvae are sexually mature in one to two years.

The Salamandridae family, newts and 'true' salamanders

A large family from the northern hemisphere with many genera, species, and subspecies.

Appearance
The appearance is often typical of newts and 'true' salamanders with a rounded tail for land-dwelling species such as *Salamandra* species or sideways flattened tail fin for water-dwelling ones such as *Triturus* species. The skin is either rough or smooth but not slimy. True salamanders have lungs.

Accommodation
See Caudata, although certain *Cynops* and *Pleurodeles* species are adapted to slightly higher temperatures.

CYNOPS SPECIES, FIRE-BELLIED NEWTS

Widely sold species.

Appearance
Cynops eniscauda grows to 110-140mm (4$^5/_{16}$-

Cynops eniscauda.

Cynops orientalis.

Cynops pyrrhogaster.

5$^1/_2$in) long and are dark with a yellow or orange belly. There are grey flecks on the back.
Cynops orientalis, the Chinese fire-bellied newt, grows to 70-90mm (2$^3/_4$-3$^1/_2$in), is dark with a red-orange belly and has a rounded tail.
Cynops pyrrhogaster, Japanese fire-bellied newt, grows to 90-120mm (3$^1/_2$-4$^3/_4$in) with similar colours as *C. orientalis* but with a thin, pointed tail.

Distribution
Southern Japan, and China.

Accommodation
Provide ten newts with an aqua-terrarium of at least 80 x 40 x 40cm (31$^1/_2$ x 16 x 16in) that has a large water area. Keep the temperature at 14-18°C (57.2-64.4°F), although *C. ensicauda* can withstand about 25°C (77°F). Provide plants in the aquarium area for the newts to lay their eggs on. The newts like to hang from the roots of floating plants such as water lettuce *(Pistia striatiotes)* and water hyacinth *(Eichornia crassipes)*.

Sex determination
The female becomes thicker following hibernation and the male acquires a purple fin on his tail.

Mating
Let the newts hibernate for three months at 4-7°C (39.2-44.6°F) by placing in a refrigerator of outside shed. A pair have to accept each other in order to mate. Place six to ten newts together. They mate without physical contact just as *Triturus* species.

Egg laying
The around 200 eggs are attached to floating and other plants and hatch at 15-17°C (59-62.6°F) in two weeks. Metamorphosis follows in three to four months.

NOTOPHTHALMUS VIRIDESCENS

Interesting newts (sometimes known as the red eft) with three development stages.

Appearance
These olive green to brown newts with about five red to yellow flashes on their sides grow to 120mm

Notophthalmus viridescens.

Notophthalmus viridescens.

(4³/₄in) long. The back legs are longer than the front ones.

Distribution
Small shaded waters in moderate eastern parts of North America.

Accommodation
Keep them in an aquarium of at least 50 x 30 x 30cm (20 x 12 x 12in) for a group, with 100mm (4in) of water and several islands, such as floating cork. Temperature about 20°C (68°F). Light for eight to ten hours each day with a fluorescent tube.

Sex determination
Males have 'nuptial pads' in the mating season and a semi-circular cloaca compared with the female's conical form. The males also have a higher fin or comb.

Mating
Place the breeding animals for six to eight weeks at 10-12°C (50-53.6°F) in a darkened container with water 50mm (2in) deep and islands. Then put them in an aquarium with water plants at 20°C (68°F). Spermatophores will quickly be passed to the female by means of an aggressive embrace.

Egg laying and rearing
The 200-300 eggs laid in spring on water plants hatch after three to five weeks. Keep the larvae in water 100mm (4in) deep with islands of stones and moss. The larvae can develop further in a few months in one of two ways.

– If the water level drops the larvae go ashore and turn into superb reddish-orange land-dwelling newts in one to three years, living between moist leaf mould, peat, and moss, and hiding away under all manner of materials. Spray them daily. Increase the water level after three years so that they achieve their adult green aquatic form and start to breed.
– If there is sufficient water, the larvae remain aquatic and shortly acquire their adult colouring.

PLEURODELES WALTL, RIBBED NEWT

At 200-300mm (8-12in) this is Europe's longest amphibian.

Appearance
This greyish or dark green newt with black patches has a yellow-orange lateral stripe. The underside is yellowish. There are countless 'warts' on the skin, which are orange to yellow on the flanks. The body is rounded with a flattened tail. The squat head has a broad mouth.

Distribution
This nocturnal newt inhabits quiet waters and sluggish streams on the Iberian peninsula and Morocco.

Accommodation
This species remains in water most of the time but can cope ashore. An aquarium that is three-quarters full or a swamp terrarium is ideal. Provide islands of cork or make land areas of timber or stones. Cover the bottom of the water with aquarium gravel, provide plants to act as hiding places and somewhere to lay eggs.
Ribbed newts are entirely non-aggressive towards other animals of their own size. An aquarium of 1 sq m (10.76 sq ft) can hold six specimens.
These newts thrive well at 15-20°C (59-68°F). The temperature should not be allowed to climb to 30°C (86°F) for very long in summer. Ensure there is a good filter. Siphon off uneaten remnants of food the same day.

Feeding
These newts eat earthworms, tubifex, water insects, small fish, amphibian larvae (tadpoles), filleted fish, and minced beef. They eat little if it becomes too warm or during their winter rest.

Female Pleurodeles waltl.

Male Pleurodeles waltl.

Males have widely set apart front legs with dark 'mating bristles'.

Sex determination

Males are smaller, slimmer, have a longer tail, and more widely set apart front legs, which has a practical function during mating. During the mating period the males acquire darker 'mating bristles' or 'nuptial pads' on the undersides of the front legs and the cloaca becomes swollen. The females are more sturdily built.

Mating

A winter rest in colder water at 5-10°C (41-50°F) and shorter length of day stimulates mating. It is also possible for these newts to over-winter in moist peat or moss. During mating, usually from September to May, the male works himself under the female and grasps her with his front legs (as do *Salamandra* species). With the female on top the two newts swim around together for a while. The male and female then encircle each other. This ensures that the spermatophores are released and received.

Egg laying

Several days after mating, the female lays tens to many hundreds of white eggs. These are stuck in clusters to plants and other decorative material in the aquarium, including the glass. Depending on the temperature (17-22°C (62.6-71.6°F), the eggs hatch in one to three weeks. The larvae when they emerge are 5-10mm ($^3/_{16}$-$^3/_8$in).

Rearing

For the first five days the larvae lie on the bottom of the aquarium while they form the external gills. Once this has happened feed them with sieved ditch plankton and newly hatched brine shrimp nauplii *(Artemia)*. Increase the size of the food later. If the water is replenished frequently (every day) the larvae grow rapidly. Front legs appear in about twenty days and the back ones after thirty-five days. The external gills subsequently disappear and the larvae start to assume a different form. The metamorphosis can take up to 100-150 days by which time the newts are 45-50mm (1$^3/_4$-2in) long. Sort the young by size as they grow to prevent cannibalism. Sexually maturity is achieved after nine months to two years.

Defence

The upward facing ribs feel hard to the touch which is unpleasant for predators.

The order Apoda or Gymnophiona, caecilians

Most of the 160 species of caecilians live underground (photo page 271), so that little is known about them. Only the Typhlonectidae family leads an exclusively aquatic life. The best known species, *Typhlonectes compressicauda*, is part of that family.

Appearance

T. compressicauda grows to 520mm (20$^1/_2$in) long. They are blue-grey with thin and darker rings around the body. These creatures have a smooth, slimy skin and small but broad head. The lower jaw is short. The back of the animal is triangular with a white patch surrounding the cloaca. These animals are sometimes wrongly called 'eels'. These are not fish and there are no fins. Caecilians breathe both by means of lungs and through their skin.

Distribution

Caecilians originate from tropical climates. *T. compressicauda* inhabits slow-running streams of lightly acidic water in French Guyana and Guyana

Typhlonectes compressicauda.

through to the Amazon region of Brazil and Peru. They live in the water or in hollows in the muddy banks.

Accommodation
Care for a maximum of semi-aquatic caecilians in an 80 x 40 x 40cm (31¹/₂ x 16 x 16in) aquarium that is securely closed at its top to prevent both escape and lung problems. Ensure very clean water that is very soft and acidic (pH 5-6.5), kept at 24-30°C (75.2-86°F). Make sure the water is well filtered and replace it regularly. Caecilians are very intolerant for calcium and iron in water which causes them skin shedding problems, white patches on their skin, and ultimately death.

Light the aquarium for these twilight and night active animals with one fluorescent tube. They like to remain hidden under a shelter of stone or wood. Make sure the vegetation is firmly anchored because of the way caecilians thrash about or use floating plants.

Feeding
Feed twice each week with a variety of earthworms, tubifex, water fleas, midge larvae, Enchytraeidae worms, minced beef, beef heart, fish, and frozen fish food. Keep the water clean. Do not feed them too much and quickly remove any uneaten remnants.

Aquarium fish will not be harmed.

Sex determination
The white patch around the cloaca is much larger with males.

Mating
These animals are stimulated to mate by replenishing their water with soft, clean water. They hold their rear ends against each other for more than an hour during mating so that sperm can be directly transferred. The male has a reproductive organ for the coupling that can still be visible after mating has concluded. The sperm is surrounded by a mucous secretion.

Birth
Aquatic caecilians in contrast with the mole sala-

Typhlonectes compressicauda.

manders are ovoviviparous (carry their eggs full term). The female gives birth seven to seven-and-a-half months after mating to a maximum of seven 100-140mm (4-5¹/₂in) long offspring. These have two transparent white gill sacs with red veins on their heads but these fall off after two days.

Rearing
Separate the offspring to ensure they get sufficient food. Care for them as the parents and refresh their water regularly. Males are about 260mm (10¹/₄in) when sexually mature and females 450mm (17³/₄in).

Handling
Handle caecilians with a fishing net and carry them in a plastic bag with plenty of air and a little water.

Sicknesses
Caecilians with white patches on their skin are living in water that is either too hard or impure, or they have a fungal infection. Use soft water (rainwater, reverse osmosis or demineralised water) and keep it clean.

Use an anti-fungal treatment that is suitable for use in aquaria. A caecilian that is having difficulty shedding its skin can be helped to do so by wrapping it in a wet cloth. *T. compressicauda* can live for about four years.

The white patch around the cloaca is much larger in males than females.

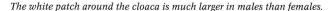

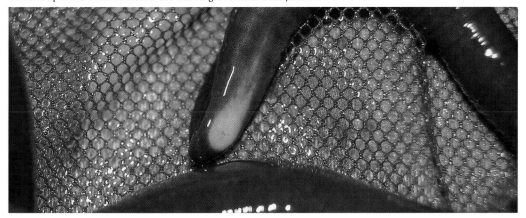

Glossary

Antenna(e)	feelers
Biotope	natural living environment
Carapace	upper (back shell)
Carnivore/carnivorous	meat eater/ meat eating
Cephalothorax	head and thorax
Chelicerae	jaws
Chitin	hardened material of external skeleton of an invertebrate
Cloaca	common opening for reproduction and excreta with reptiles, amphibians (and birds)
Coxa(e)	hip(s), first leg segment
Diurnal	active during the day
Epigyne	female sexual organ in spiders
Exoskeleton	external skeleton of an invertebrate
Femur	thigh, third leg segment
Genus/genera	group(s) of species
Gonopods	male sexual organs in arthropods
Gynandromorph(ism)	female with (external) characteristics of a male, genetic deviation
Hemimetabolous metamorphosis	change of form without pupation
Hemipenis	reproductive organ in male lizards and snakes consisting of two hemi (or half) penises
Herbivore/herbivorous	Plant eater/ plant eating
IU	international unit
Labium	bottom lip
Larva(e)	young immature stage before metamorphosis, caterpillar in insects, tadpole in amphibians
Luke warm/hand hot	30-40°C (86-104°F)
Mandibles	upper jaws
Maxilla(e)	bottom jaw(s)
Metamorphosis	change of form from larvae to adult
Metatarsus/metatarsi	middle foot/feet, sixth leg segment with spiders
Necrosis	tissue death
Nocturnal	active during the night
Nymph	young immature arthropod prior to complete metamorphosis
Omnivore/ omnivorous	eater of anything, eats anything
Opisthosoma	abdomen or rear body section
Oral	by mouth
Ovipary	eggs laid with embryo developing outside the mother's body
Ovovivipary	eggs retained in mother's body but separated by a membrane with embryo developing before birth
Parthenogenic	of parthenogenisis (q.v.)
Parthenogenisis	asexual reproduction without fertilization

300

Patella(e)	knee(s) fourth leg segment in spiders
Pedipalps	sensing and tasting legs
Plastron	belly shield
Pronotum	neck shield
Prosoma	head and thorax
Rachitis	rickets, bone illness caused by deficiency of vitamin D_3 or calcium
Reverse osmosis water	water that has had minerals removed
Sclerotized	skin hardening
Spermatheca	female receptacle to store sperm
Spermatophore	receptacle containing male sperm
Spp.	abbreviation for species
Sternite	belly shield of the rear body segment
Sternum	breast plate
Stigma	respiratory opening
Stridulate	make a rasping sound
Tarantula	name commonly but incorrectly used in North America and throughout English speaking world for large 'bird-eating' spiders
Tarsus, tarsi	foot, feet
Tergite	dorsal plate of the rear body segment
Thorax	body, chest
Tibia	shin, fourth leg segment in insects, fifth in spiders
Toxic	poisonous
Toxin	poison
Trachea	windpipe
Trochanter	thigh joint, second leg segment
Venom	poison
Vivipary	the embryo develops inside the mother's body and is nourished by it before birth

Photography

Almost all the photographs in this book were taken by myself. Those in which I am to be seen were taken by my friend Anne-Marie Koster.

For most of the macro photographs I used a macro converter between the reflex body and a 35-200mm zoom lens. A flash with a guide number of 45 was set for use with an aperture of f11. The lens works at two stops less (f5.6) because of the converter. In dark situations or when it is necessary to photograph through glass the aperture is f4.

For the higher quality photograph of *Romalea microptera* a second slave cell flash was used with the main flash set at full power to the left of the subject and the slave unit to the right. The lens was set to f16. This provided a greater depth of field and a less obvious 'flash' photograph. To aid quality for this photograph a 50 ASA film was used instead of the usual 100 ASA film to achieve smaller grain size.

For the super-macro photographs, such as those of the whip scorpion's spermatophore and spermatophore of a praying mantis, the lens was mounted in reverse on the converter using either an adapter ring or adhesive tape. In this mode the lens enlarges rather than reduces. In order to achieve some depth of focus a card with a pin hole was placed between the lens and the converter to act as an aperture and the exposure was 10 seconds.

Wherever possible an attractive background was created for the photographs of the animals. The specimens were placed on a plant in front of a black or brown background. Some animals, such as what I prefer to call bird-eating spiders (tarantulas) were not disturbed in order to photograph them, which explains the visible pane of glass and rather dull background.

Flying insects, such as praying mantises with pointed eyes, were photographed in the tropics under a mosquito net which was hung up in a sunny place.

No single animal was made to suffer, except for a certain amount of handling, for the purposes of photography.

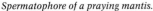
Spermatophore of a praying mantis.

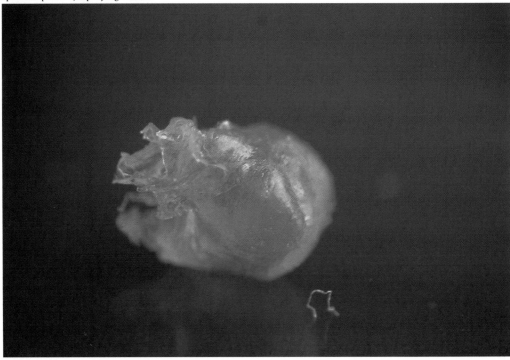

Bibliography

Bauer, l. et al, *Een paludarium of riparium als hobby*,
Studievereniging Het Paludarium, NL, 1997.

Brock, P., *Rearing and Studying Stick and Leaf-Insects*,
The Amateur Entomologists' Society, Middlesex, GB, 1992.

Denardo, D., Reproductive Biology, in Mader, D.R., *Reptile Medicine and Surgery*,
WB, Saunders Company, Pennsylvania, USA, 1996.

Gordon D.G., *The complete cockroach*,
Ten Speed Press, Berkeley, California, USA, 1996.

Heath G.L. & G. Cowgill, *Rearing and Studying the Praying Mantis*,
The Amateur Entomologists' Society, Middlesex, UK, 1989.

Henkel, F.W. & S. Heinecke, *Chamäleons im terrarium*,
Landbuch-Verlag, Hanover, D, 1993.

Henkel, F.W. & W.S. Schmidt, *Terrarien*,
Verlag Eugen Ulmer, Stuttgart, D, 1997.

Herrmann, H.J., *Amphibien im Aquarium*,
Verlag Eugen Ulmer, Stuttgart, D, 1994.

Hevers, J. & E. Liske, *Lauerende Gefahr, das Leben der Gottesanbeterinnen*,
Voigt Druck, Gifhorn, D, 1991.

Hopkin, S.P. & H.J. Read, *The biology of millipedes*,
Oxford University Press, Oxford, GB, 1992.

Klaas, P., *Vogelspinnen im Terrarium*,
Verlag Eugen Ulmer, Stuttgart, D, 1989.

Köhler, G., *De Groene Leguaan*,
Verlag Gunther Köhler, Offenbach, 1994.

Löser, S., *Exotische insekten, Tausendfüsser und Spinnentiere*,
Verlag Eugen Ulmer, Stuttgart, D, 1991.

Manthey, U. & N. Schuster, *Agamen*,
Herpetologischer Fachverlag, Munster, D, 1992.

Obst, F.J., k. Richter & U. Jacob.,
The completely illustrated atlas of reptiles and amphibians for the terrarium,
T.F.H. Publications, Neptune City, USA, 1988

Schmidt, G., *Vogelspinnen*,
Blüchel & Philler Verlag, Minden, D, 1989.

Vosjoli, P. & T. Maillous, *Bearded Dragons*,
Advanced Vivarium Systems, California, USA, 1993.

Wilms, T., *Dornschwanzagamen*,
Herpeton-Verlag, Offenbach, 1995.

Barnes, R.S.K., P. Calow, P. J. W. Olive & D.W. Golding,
The Invertebrates: a new synthesis,
Blackwell Science Ltd, Oxford, GB, 1988.

Ruppert E.E. & R.D. Barnes, *Invertebrate Zoology,*
Sixth Edition, Saunders College Publishing, Orlando, USA, 1994.

Publications

Iguana Varia, Target Group Green Iguanas

De Schilpad (The tortoise), Dutch Tortoise Association

Reptile Hobbyist, TFH Publications,, USA

Het Aquarium (The Aquarium), Dutch Aqua Terra Union

Werkgroep Vogelspinnen (Study group tarantulas), Tarantula study group

Phasma, Dutch stick insect enthusiasts group

Newsletter, Mantis Study Group

Newsletter, Phasmid Study Group

Beginnersboeje, (Beginner's book), Target Group Chameleons

Tillandsia *sp.*

Index

A

D

E

M

Young praying mantises.

T

Acknowledgements

I am indebted to the following specialists and 'lay-persons' for their helpful comments on the manuscript of this book. Thanks are also due to the many experts for the information they provided and/or their help with the photography.

Ann-Marije Koster, Erwin Blezer, Ronny Dobbelsteijn, Coen Elemans (reptiles),
Sandy van Felius (tarantulas),
Kim D'Hulster (insects),
Marja Kik (disease and nutrition), Mirjam de Koning, Leo Koopman (prey animals),
Hans Rotteveel (ERATO, Holland, insects and spiders),
G.J.Tolido (CITES bureau, legisation), J.P. de Vries (lighting),
Hans Waardenburg (chameleons),
Tonnie Woeltjes (amphibians),
Prof. Dr. P. Zwart (reptiles)
and Henk Zwartepoorte (reptiles).

My thanks are also due to those people who helped me to take my photographs and who provided valuable information, including IPC DIER Barneveld, The Netherlands,
Johan van Gorkom (stick insects),
Tim bij 't Vuur (tarantulas),
Arendo Flipse, Mr. Jeekel (arthropods),
Arie van der Meijden, Maurice Starren, and Gerrit Vergonet.